Elegy & Paradox

Elegy & Paradox

Testing the Conventions

W. David Shaw

The Johns Hopkins University Press ❧ Baltimore and London

©1994 The Johns Hopkins University Press
All rights reserved
Printed in the United States of America on acid-free paper
03 02 01 00 99 98 97 96 95 94   5 4 3 2 1

The Johns Hopkins University Press
2715 North Charles Street
Baltimore, Maryland 21218-4319
The Johns Hopkins Press Ltd., London

ISBN 0-8018-4836-9

In memory of Douglas Bush, the humblest of great men,
and of Northrop Frye, who "was not of an age but for all time"

Contents

Acknowledgments

This book could not have been written without the generous aid of the Killam Foundation of Canada, which awarded me a Senior Research Fellowship for the years 1991–93. I am equally indebted to the frank and discerning reactions of my wife, Carol; to the example and encouragement of my colleague, Eleanor Cook; and to the friendly but critical responses of the three audiences to whom parts of the book were first presented as public lectures.

A short version of chapter 4 was originally delivered in April 1992, at the University of Lethbridge, Alberta, as the sixth annual lecture in the F.E.L. Priestley Lecture Series. Entitled "Elegy and Silence: The Romantic Legacy," the address was subsequently published by the University of Lethbridge. An early version of the seventh chapter, later published in the journal *Victorian Poetry*, was originally given as the keynote address at the centenary conference entitled "Tennyson 92: Retrospect and Prospect," held at West Virginia University during the weekend of November 13–15, 1992. Finally, an abbreviated version of chapter 5 was delivered as a paper, "Breakdown and Breakthrough in Modern Elegy," at the 1993 MLA convention's special session on "The Modern Elegy: Poetic Mourning from Hardy to Heaney."

I am also indebted to the sharp and expert evaluations of readers for the *New England Quarterly*, which published a part of chapter 6 as "The Poetics of Pragmatism: Robert Frost and William James" (vol. 59, no. 2 [1986]:159–88). I am grateful, too, to Kim Blank and Margot Louis, editors of *Influence and Resistance in Nineteenth-Century English Poetry* (Macmillan, 1993), for the opportunity to contribute to their collection of essays a paper entitled "Shelley's *Adonais* and Arnold's *Thyrsis*: Words of Power in Pastoral Elegy" (pp. 39–59), which is now incorporated into the book's first chapter.

I thank the Houghton Library of Harvard University for permission to quote from manuscript material by Wallace Stevens, fMS, Am 1333.5 (1); Emily Dickinson, Autograph file, TL to Louisa Norcross; Robert Lowell, bMs Am 1905 (2812); and three letters of Robert Frost to Amy Lowell, bMS Lowell 19 (459). Permission to quote excerpts from the following sources is also gratefully acknowledged: A. R. Ammons, "Easter Morning," in *A Coast of Trees* (New York: Norton, 1981); *The Complete Poems of Thomas Hardy* (Oxford: Clarendon Press, 1937); Allen Tate, "Ode to the Confederate Dead," in *Allen Tate: The Collected Poems 1919–1976* (New York: Charles Scribner's Sons, 1977), reprinted with permission of Mrs. Helen Tate; W. B. Yeats, "In Memory of Major Robert Gregory," "The Folly of Being Comforted," and "Two Songs from a Play," reprinted with permission of Macmillan Publishing Company from *The Poems of W. B. Yeats: A New Edition,* edited by Richard J. Finneran (New York: Macmillan Publishing Company, 1983); Robert Lowell, "For the Union Dead," in *For the Union Dead* (1956), reprinted with permission of Farrar, Strauss and Giroux, Inc.; W. H. Auden, *Collected Poems* (New York: Random House, 1976), Wallace Stevens, *The Collected Poems* (New York: Alfred A. Knopf, 1954), and three elegies of Amy Clampitt, reprinted with permission of Random House, Inc., and of its subsidiary, Alfred A. Knopf, Inc.; Geoffrey Hill, *The Mystery of the Charity of Charles Péguy,* in *The Collected Poems* (London: Penguin Books, 1985), reprinted with permission of Penguin Books Ltd.; and Philip Larkin, *Collected Poems,* edited by Anthony Thwaite (London and New York, 1989), reprinted with permission of Farrar, Strauss and Giroux, Inc. and of Faber and Faber Limited.

I owe a more particular debt to four scholars who devoted time to reading my work and sharing with me their learning and sharp accuracy of judgment. I am grateful, first of all, to Professor Marshall Brown of the University of Washington for his comments on the book's final chapter, which were as trenchant as they were courteous. I must also thank Professor John Woolford of King's College, University of London, for taking time to exchange ideas about Browning's elegy, *La Saisiaz.* For his appreciative comments on my discussion of the divisions, breakages, fractures, and stammerings of modern elegy I am grateful to Professor Jahan Ramazani of the University of Virginia, himself the author of a fine book on elegies. My greatest debt is to Professor Timothy Peltason of Wellesley College. His critical attentiveness to everything I try to say in this book has been learned and painstaking. It has also been an act of exceptional generosity.

I realize that a layman of the first century would have thought two or three times before dedicating a book of homilies to St. Paul. Douglas Bush and Northrop Frye, however, two leading humanists of our age, were always tolerant of wayward disciples. They would, I think, have understood and forgiven the small vanity of my dedicating this book to them. When I was a student and young teacher, Douglas Bush was a second father to me. Among the humblest of men, he counseled me well into middle age. Later, at Victoria College, over a period of more than twenty years, I came to know Bush's friend, Northrop Frye, not merely as a seer—as an aloof and formidable Coleridge of our times—but also as a humanist of great wit and feeling, and, finally, as a friend.

A master of paradox, Frye turned my mind to elegies, musing that the world beyond death is like the medium of air, the means by which the visible world is seen. If Bush could translate my dullest questions into searching ones, Frye had a way in conversation of making even my platitudes seem profound. Unlike my frail memorial to them, their legacy is a "monument without a tomb." Like a few rare elegies, that legacy will survive as long as the humanities survive, and "we have wits to read and praise to give."

Elegy & Paradox

Introduction

In Donne's confessional elegy on Christ's death, "Goodfriday, 1613. Riding Westward," the paradoxes push to an extreme doctrines of incarnation and atonement that are already full of paradox and contradiction. The paradoxes are not mere "empty signs of the inexpressible." Nor are they rhetorical ornaments, "giving pith and force to a paraphrasable claim" (T. R. Wright, 1988, 153). Instead, Donne finds that, as his language approaches the limits of logic, he can express what he has to say in no other terms. Seeing God face to face is a death sentence: "And Manoah said to his wife, 'We shall surely die, for we have seen God'" (Judges 13.22) How much greater a death we must die to see, not merely the living God, but His very death. The elegist stammers over the unutterable thought, before he can bring himself to voice it.

> Who sees Gods face, that is selfe life, must dye;
> What a death were it then to see God dye?
> ("Riding Westward," ll. 17–18)

The ominous "dye" and "death" ring out three times in the only couplet that repeats without variation the weighted end word. Donne hopes God will be merciful by forgetting him, by allowing him to be a Judas, a traitor who turns his back on the perfect chiasmus of the Cross, which is even mirrored in the rhetorical turn upon "set" and "setting": "There I should see a Sunne, by rising set, / And by that setting endlesse day beget" (ll. 11–12). To be merciful God should desert the poet. But that is too outrageous a paradox, even for Donne. And so the concluding prayer is for God to disregard everything Donne has asked for. Though he looks eastward in spirit, he is too ashamed to turn his face until some measure of health is restored. But since health depends upon his turning, it is difficult to see how healing can ever begin. Dying is intimately connected with the disease of the whole body—not only with Donne's body but with Christ's body and the body of a cracked and shrunken nature, whose sun grows dark and winks. The larger pain is something Donne feels about the heart; it dilates, as one's lungs fill and strain with breath drawn in labor. Because Donne thinks with his body, his blood, and the marrow of his bones, he allows us to experience the pain of a homeopathic cure that adds fire to fire, acid to acid, to burn off Donne's rusts and purge his fever. It is the most physical and unmediated, and also the most paradoxical, experience an elegy can offer.

Paradox is seldom under such pressure in English elegies, and when it is, as in Tennyson's oxymoron of a "silent-speaking" word or a "lucid veil," it tends to break down into a verbal form with which paradox is sometimes confused: into an antinomy or a contradiction. T. R. Wright believes that many modern writers "feel the need to say with Simone Weil that there both is and is not a God" (1988, 152). Unlike Donne or Hopkins, however, they lack the tolerance for paradox that the deeply contradictory nature of faith seems to require. Walter Redfern points out that the word "paradox" is "in itself paradoxical, self-contradicting, for it can mean a statement which seems false but is true, or which seems true but is false" (1984, 44). I use "paradox" in the first sense, but not the second. And to preserve important distinctions, I call words that house opposite meanings, like Shelley's use of "stain" in "Adonais," which can mean either "color" or "discolor," antinomies rather than paradoxes. Unlike Rosalie Colie, who asserts that "the paradoxical form denies commitment" (1966, 38), I also dissociate paradoxes from puns and uses of two-way syntax that cultivate modes of wind-hovering or ambivalence.

Though it may defeat the intelligence almost successfully, I define a paradox as a contradiction that, even in defying resolution, is characteristically resolvable. Like a puzzle or a riddle, a paradox may balance on a knife edge between the perfunctory and the profound. But like a good joke, which is capped by the unexpected, a paradox invites a solution. William Poundstone argues that "in a puzzle just one of the many conceivable hypotheses avoids creating a contradiction. That single hypothesis is the puzzle's solution." He goes on to say that "in a paradox, no hypothesis at all is tenable" (1988, 93). It seems to me, however, that a skillful practitioner of paradox, like a Socratic ironist or Zen master, sends us in search of some latent solution. We try to resolve a paradox the way we try to "get" or understand a joke. All humor rests on paradox, though not all paradoxes are funny. The Zen master who understands the tie between verbal play and paradox does not force hypotheses into his disciple's mind. Instead, he uses paradox in the spirit of the Zen koan, to crack the shell of linguistic habit and tease truth out of us. The fact that something not immediately apparent is the reason for the paradox invites the thinker to remove the contradiction to a plane of consciousness where nothing is banished, everything included. Because a paradox both *demands* and *resists* translation, it escapes the grasp of categories. Tennyson's assertion that Hallam is "deeplier loved" as he is "darklier understood" offers paradoxical escape of this kind, for it causes the mind to expand, moving beyond closed fortresses of skepticism and belief.

More often, however, Tennyson substitutes for the "both-and" of a genuine paradox the "either-or" of a paralogism or antinomy, which is the kind of contradiction logic cannot digest. To compass the divine nature, Tennyson finds himself forging chains of harsh and glaring antinomies, which read like footnotes to H. L. Mansel's riddling definitions in *The Limits of Religious Thought*. Both a "He" and a "They," a "One" and an "All," God is simultaneously personal and impersonal, singular and plural, both "Within" and "without" the human mind (*In Memoriam*, 124.3). As a "Power in darkness whom we [can merely] guess" (*In Memoriam*, 124.4), God possesses attributes that are inexpressible because not strictly conceivable. Tennyson is constrained to circumscribe his subject, to draw a circle of antinomies around it, because like Kant, Sir William Hamilton, and Mansel, he finds he cannot properly describe a subject that has no content in sense experience.

By contrast, Tennyson's invocation to Hallam—"Strange friend, past, present, and to be; / Loved deeplier, darklier understood" (*In Memoriam*, 129.9–10)—is beautifully paradoxical rather than boldly contradictory. The best comment on the lines comes from Christopher Ricks: "The suggestion of paradox in 'Strange friend' (the dead friend cannot but be almost a stranger) is . . . taken up in 'Loved deeplier, darklier understood'—when you love someone deeply, you do indeed understand them more and yet the understanding is not a simple illumination—love makes you more aware of the mysteriousness of another, makes you understand 'darklier' the person you understandingly love" (1972, 223). One might add that there are earlier passages in the elegy, paradoxes about lucid veils and about truths that "darkly join, / Deep-seated in our mystic frame" (36.1–2), which help readers resolve the apparent contradiction. But in section 124 there can be little comparable understanding of a "Power in darkness," because God, unlike Hallam, has never had any content in Tennyson's sense experience. There can be no *Aufhebung*, no transcendence of the antinomies, which would allow one term to preserve its identity in a wider context, like a butterfly that outgrows its chrysalis. And since there can be no reduction of one term to the other, nothing can be done to make the contradictions disappear.

I think Timothy Peltason is right when he says that *In Memoriam* "never tires of confessing that its faith in God is provisional and ultimately groundless" (1985, 170). But I am less convinced when he says that "it is no more the poem's skepticism than its faith that finally secures its value." T. S. Eliot seems closer to the truth when he says the "elegy is not religious because of the quality of its faith, but because of the quality of its doubt" (1932, 336). The deconstruction of faith need not bring in its wake "a new and mild orthodoxy," "agnosticism as dogma" (Peltason, 1985, 170). On the contrary, the vulnerability of any affirmation usually brings a quite different sense that, precisely because neither skepticism nor faith can be "proved," there is nothing to prevent Tennyson's affirming the conventional validity of any religious belief he chooses to entertain, as long as he entertains it self-critically and provisionally. Like his Ancient Sage, Tennyson is under no illusion that his beliefs can be made to coincide with any grounds he has for holding them. Yet for Eastern thinkers who invite us, like Tennyson's sage, to ponder "This double-seeming of the single world" ("The Ancient Sage," l. 105), no proposition is beyond possibility. Like T. S. Eliot and Arnold, Tennyson seems to have learned from his study of Indian philosophy that "skepticism implies not simply the incredibility of all beliefs, but also," as Jeffrey Perl has said, "their equivalent conventional validity" (1989, 92).

As a meditation on elegy, this book shows how poetic forms and paradoxes may be called upon to help us in our human extremities. Today the love of abstraction is the major vice of the critical intellect, which tends to assume that, like the pursuit of virtue, the pursuit of theory is its own reward. To understand paradox it is not enough to define the term or even theorize about it. Because paradoxes often serve elegists during moments of crisis, we have to use the idea of an elusive truth, an apparent contradiction that invites resolution, to explain the power of many elegies we read.

I associate pastoral elegy with the paradox of verbal power. Though the elegist's words seem grounded in a world of imitative magic, where chanting the right name, like finding the right number to dial on the phone, can channel a beneficent force or deflect a malign one, how can the efficacy of the speech act, its passage from ignorance to knowledge, be guaranteed in advance? If Milton's words of power in "Lycidas"— "Hence forth thou art the Genius of the shore, / In thy large recompense, and shalt be good / To all that wander in that perilous flood" (ll. 183–85)—are a mere description of fact, then they lack the authority of prophecy or decree. And if they are a mere audacious boast, they lack the stamp of truth. How can a word of power be empirically grounded and still bring into being the state of affairs it purports to describe?

And how can a word of power create a world by verbal fiat, like God's creative act in Genesis, and still claim to be empirically grounded? If an act of faith is authentic, it is not subject to empirical verification. And if it can be empirically verified, it is not an act of faith.

Many confessional elegies grapple with a second paradox: the paradox of ends. Because the beginning of an elegy like *Pearl*, Donne's *Anniversaries*, or Tennyson's *In Memoriam* presupposes a turning point or conversion, Donne and Tennyson can organize only what their transformed selves discover. But how can they discover anything until they have transformed and organized it? Until conversion or discovery takes place, it is difficult to imagine how a confessional elegy can ever begin. One unsettling corollary of this paradox lurks in the pun on "end": the aim of life and the end of life may be one. Even when a paradox of ends introduces a form of circular reasoning that seems to constitute a mere parody of proof, an elegist may still be able to explain the possibility of things he can never hope to prove logically. As Browning shows in *La Saisiaz*, an elegist's explanations may be more valuable than proofs, because they substitute for the logical coercion of a proof a form of free assent.

Any Socratic ironist will be familiar with a third paradox I explore: the paradox of the unspeakable. Because one's own death is always at issue in elegy, I assume that elegists deploy the ineffability topos for two main purposes: to declare the unspeakability of their sorrow, and to intimate that one's own death is inconceivable. Epicurus explains the second paradox this way: "when death comes, we no longer are" (cited by Wollheim, 1984, 265). Since death is not an experience inside life, but an event that takes place on its boundary, every elegy sooner or later reaches the limits of language. J. F. Ferrier, Tennyson's acquaintance, develops a slightly different version of Epicurus's paradox, based on the axiom that it is impossible to divorce death from a perceiving subject. We can never actually conceive of our own death; we merely *think* that we think it. The need to speak of the unspeakable is especially acute in Romantic and post-Romantic elegies, where the inexpressible depth of a mourner's sorrow or the inconceivability of another's death—as in Wordsworth's "We Are Seven"—generates a pathos of its own.

In many modern elegies the uneasy peace of a paradox breaks down into an open war of opposites: an insurrection of the self, a civil strife. Though T. S. Eliot declares that factions can be united "in the strife which divided them" ("Little Gidding," 3.25), how exactly are we to interpret his paradox? Are we *united* in the strife, and somehow made one? Is the apparent breakdown really a breakthrough? Or are we touched only by the genius of warfare, united only by our fighting? Because the holocaust and other atrocities of modern war extinguish any lodestar of value, they seem to demolish or rob of meaning the elegists' claim to dignity, their claim to create something out of life that withstands the destructiveness of time. If there is no God and if death is the end, then, to adapt Dostoyevsky's disturbing inference, everything seems permissible.

Reading Elegies: Life-and-Death Issues

To commemorate death rightly is also to magnify the life and love that make death terrible. Since there is "an image of death," as George Eliot says, in every "entrance on the new and strange" (1973, 114), the satisfaction of reading elegies is often inseparable from the satisfaction of being open to adventure and risk, including the fear of dissolution that any enlargement of consciousness may bring in its wake. In *In Memoriam*, for example, it is difficult to understand but easy to love the momentary uncertainties of tone and syntax that leave all the blur of being on some of Tennyson's most beautiful and nuanced lines: "Sad Hesper o'er the buried sun," or "He is not here; but far away / The noise of life begins again" (*In Memoriam*, 121.1, 7.9–10). Conferring on his poems a striking indeterminacy, Tennyson reminds us that the real temptation in reading elegies is to make them less tremulous and hovering than they are. Tonal indecisions, puns, and the imaginative touch of two-way meanings allow the elegist to speak with a reticent ambiguity and a deeply divided mind. As Eric Griffiths shows, it is sometimes difficult to speak aloud a poem's written words without violating their strangeness (1989, 71). How can one vocalize the capitalized "T" in the phrase "When That within the coffin fell" in Tennyson's verse epistle to Dufferin (l. 43)? Or how can one preserve the odd two-way flow of Milton's line: "For *Lycidas* your sorrow is not dead" (Lycidas," l. 166)? Is the sorrow forever alive, or is it Lycidas who lives, in which case the sorrow may be thought to abate? If the elegist resembles Tennyson's Tithonus, there may even be an unsettling disparity between the durability of his verse and his yearning to die. When we try to remove one of the contradictory elements—the consolation from the inconsolability; the remembering from the forgetting; the certainty from the uncertainty—we are in danger of making death noncontradictory or devoid of strangeness, which is the one thing it never really is. In the epistles to Dufferin and Fitzgerald, as we watch Tennyson's life wear away at the edges and blur into the death he at last half welcomes, we are hard pressed to say whether so much strange ordinariness—or ordinary strangeness—is heartbreaking or consoling. In addition to sketching the outlines of a critical history of elegy, I have tried to conduct a tolerant and humane testing of individual poems. I have tried to explain how their adventurous encounters with the new and the strange magnify life and enlarge its meaning.

Values that seem at first to be firmly mortared together tend to fall apart under the pressure of a crisis. This is nowhere truer than in elegies and in cultural and psychological theories designed to explain them. In saying that nothing we say about the noumenal world is true, is Kant saying something true? If he succeeds, then, of course, he fails, for if it is true that nothing we say about death or a world after life is true, something is true after all. If it is false, then something again is true. In marking the limits of any attempt to expel the deep falsehoods and unexpendable fictions that surround the subject, theorists as diverse as Kant, Foucault, and Kristeva, all show why no study of death, the noumenal world, or even the complex mechanisms of depression and melancholia, can aspire to the conditions of an exact science.

Miguel de Unamuno says that "the absolute certainty that death is a complete and definitive and irrevocable annihilation of personal consciousness, a certainty of the same order as our certainty that the three angles of a triangle are equal to two right angles, or, contrariwise, the absolute certainty that our personal consciousness continues beyond death in whatever condition . . . —either of these certainties would make our life equally impossible" (1972, 131). As opposed to that absurd faith that consists in not thinking at all about faith, but in handing ourselves over in blind confidence to a power whose secrets are inscrutable, only a faith based upon uncertainty can become a form of saving faith. A poetry of loss that fosters the distinctively aesthetic qualities Keats associates with negative capability makes it easier to remain in mysteries and doubts, "without any irritable reaching" after logical demonstrations that coerce rather than free each inquirer by pretending that matters are less puzzling or uncertain than they really are.

Reading elegies, like writing them, is more than an academic exercise; it is also a life-and-death issue. Long before we die our most cherished projects may fail or sink into oblivion: it is like watching our children precede us to the grave. When the world we love "seriously, sadly runs away / To fill the abyss's void with emptiness" ("West-Running Brook," ll. 48–49), I want to know how far the consolations of a life-and-death art, of a poetry of loss, can be made to seem reasonable, even compelling, to readers living now, in our own time and place. How far can the elegiac rhetoric of a Milton or an Arnold, whose evangelism is often hortatory or denunciatory, assertive and homiletic, succeed in seducing even disbelieving readers?

Readers today, I think, are most likely to be moved by the casual sophistication of elegists like Tennyson and Yeats, whose fine nuances of tone impose a practice of discrimination on their critics, too. Despite the slight constraints of their decorum, it is easy to be charmed by the relaxed manner of Tennyson's impromptu, diary-like entries in *In Memoriam*, or by the casual unfolding of Yeats's elegy, "In Memory of Major Robert Gregory." We may be so absorbed by intimacies of pathos and disarming confidences in these poems that we seem to be reading letters from a friend. Yet their impish play, criticizing what they love and giving voice to what they fear, often makes it difficult to predict outcomes or to read the poems complacently. Only a criticism that is attentive to the unpredictable conduct of these poems, to their play with two-way meanings and changing norms, can show how the elegists' volatile puns and sinuous allusions, doubling back on themselves, put everything at risk, often in service of truths we had not anticipated at the start.

To commemorate the dead is to affirm that their lives do not fall totally into nothingness. Gathering up, pondering, and justifying the meaning of these lives, elegies bring into play values that did not exist before. Death has no privileged import we can know in advance: to prevail over superannuated beliefs, its meaning must be tested and posited afresh in each new elegy. When death inflicts wounds on our consciousness, elegists often turn descriptions of these wounds into performances that are self-therapeutic and cathartic. Like the kind of speech acts Austin calls performative, an elegy's life-and-death acts are authentically inaugural. To the extent that death itself shares in the excitement of these acts, which is often the excitement of starting the world over, death may *not* be the opposite of life after all, but only the last of our new beginnings.

Though it may be currently unfashionable, I have written this book out of an urgent and timely sense of a humane, experience-based testing of elegy's rhetoric and conventions. In appealing from the conventions to our sense of what death means to us, here and now, I am simply doing what the elegists themselves have always done when modifying tradition and relating what is new in their poems to conventional elements. A functional history of elegy tries to explain why certain conventions that appear suitable to Milton are later modified by Wordsworth and Arnold. What happens to Romantic elegy, for example, when Wordsworth's testing of the dead Lycidas's entry into a glorious paradise of groves and streams discloses in its counteryearning for a lost paradise of childhood, for a vanished "visionary gleam," a radically different impulse, more akin to Milton's "Paradise within thee, happier far"? Again, when Arnold, no longer believing in a resurrection beyond the grave, turns God from a noun into an intransitive verb, into a form of pure disinterested questing, what are the consequences for a pastoral elegy like "Thyrsis"?

Often the most moving moments in an elegy occur when a poet juxtaposes the mourner's address to the dead person with a sympathetic but skeptical testing of that convention: If the dead are forever deaf and inert, how can they hear what we say? When all conversations with the dead become one-sided monologues, Tennyson in his verse epistle to Dufferin has to turn aside from the real but mute subject of his elegy to address a sympathetic letter reader instead. And in his elegy, "When Lilacs Last in the Dooryard Bloom'd," Whitman reluctantly abandons altogether the convention of intimately addressing his dead subject. In a humane but critical testing of existing pieties and formulas, Hopkins and Geoffrey Hill even have to honor the silent dead by composing a poetry of silence. Cutting into their lavish appositional style with surgical slashes of ellipsis and deletion, both elegists learn to economize and be frugal.

Testing the conventions helps us rediscover the difference between beliefs and desires. "Personal immortality would not be very personal," F. H. Bradley concedes, "if it implied mutilation of our affections." But aware that a belief in the afterlife is not true simply because we want to believe it, Bradley immediately turns on himself: "This general appeal to the affections—the only appeal as to future life which to me individually is not hollow—can hardly be turned into a proof" (1893, 451). "Each desire offers us," as Richard Wollheim says, "a view through a keyhole," a view through the unopened door into Eliot's rose garden. "But there is no reason," he concludes, in a chilling valediction to the subject, "that there should emerge from these views a coherent picture of what lies on the far side of the gate or that, should it be thrown open, there would be revealed a garden there that we could conceivably enter" (1984, 53). If death is the last of our new beginnings, I want to see how far the paradoxes of elegy can satisfy our desires. I also want to see how far our minds may incline toward skepticism when we test the genre's conventions against a sadder, more somber sense that desires cannot make consoling fictions true, and beliefs grounded in logical arguments may not be consoling to people who want to build a portal to meaning over the apparent nothingness of death. Caught between alternatives that are deeply desired and deeply feared, few of us can avoid the imbalance of Donne's rider in "Goodfriday, 1613" who hurtles westward when he should be moving east.

1 ❧ The Paradox of Power: Doing-by-Saying in Classical Elegy

Critics of elegy face the same dilemma as interpreters of the holy book of a living religion who want perennially to renew its meaning. Either a religion of the book risks irrelevance when we no longer believe what Moses, Christ, or Mohammed believed, or else it loses any institutional and cultural ground for its identity. The safest middle way between an antiquarian pedantry and iconoclasm seems to be a cultivation of what C. S. Lewis calls "a taste in universes." By recovering the Renaissance and late medieval models that delighted Milton and later English imitators of classical elegy, we may educate ourselves to see that "no model is a catalogue of ultimate realities, and none is a mere fantasy" (Lewis, 1964, 222). In English criticism a typical exponent of the structures of knowledge and belief informing classical elegy is Philip Sidney: the "zodiac" of the poet's wit, to borrow Sidney's phrase, is a hierarchical world of resemblances under the sway of prophecy and divination. According to Sidney, wit combines the powers of sympathy and antipathy, identity and difference, which later critics like Pope and Dr. Johnson would distinguish as the rival provinces of judgment and wit. Only with the poet's expulsion from the golden world of the pastoral and the fall into a brazen world, will judgment come to discriminate differences amid similitude and wit come to discern the most occult resemblances among things apparently dissimilar.

To the modern reader Milton's learning in "Lycidas" seems to consist in an unstable mixture of biblical knowledge, classical erudition, and imitative magic. The many vocatives, prophecies, and ritual namings in the elegy suggest a vestigial belief in the magical power of words, in their capacity to make something happen. To divine the semimagical properties in the humble "Ivy never-sere" ("Lycidas," l. 2), a sign of enduring life like the sacred amaranthus, is not, as in a later scientific age, an obscure or occult branch of learning; in early Renaissance culture it is a principal body of knowledge itself. By mastering the archaic categories of metaphor and identity, the poet, like Orpheus, charms trees and tames serpents, performing what Pico della Mirandola calls the chief function of magic: a marriage to the world (*maritare mundum*). For those who know how to read its conventions, the magical power of signs, whether inscribed in ivy leaves and flowers or in the lines of ancient elegies by Theocritus and Virgil, is everywhere the same, and is coeval with the death and resurrection of the Son of God, a kind of Christian Orpheus.

As imitations of classical elegy, Shelley's "Adonais" and Arnold's "Thyrsis" try to emulate "Lycidas" by re-creating quasi-imperative words capable of expressing through verbal magic, as Orpheus expressed through lyre music, an energy common to art and nature. In Shelley, as in Milton, such an energy or force is best expressed as a metaphoric identity of subject and object. Lycidas is the risen sun; Adonais is the beaconing star; and Arnold would like to say that Thyrsis is the "single elm-tree," "Bare on its lonely ridge" (ll. 26, 160). Unfortunately, Arnold, like many Victorians, is skeptical: he does not believe in the seer's metaphoric identities. He cannot substitute a tree or even a landscape for the presence of his friend, nor does he share Shelley's faith in the almost physical energy released by words and their power to tame a hostile or uncaring world.

Like "the dear might of him that walked the waves" in "Lycidas" (l. 173), the never-wearied love of Adonais, folding the universe in upon itself, supporting it from beneath and kindling it from above, sustains a powerful identification of A and B. Just as Lycidas is the sun, sunk at one moment on the "ocean bed" but flaming the next moment "in the forehead of the morning sky," so Adonais can be seen "beaconing" to Shelley from his immortal star. In "Thyrsis," by contrast, the classical elegist's marriage of the dead man to nature shows severe signs of strain; even the genre's survival seems at stake. For the metaphoric identity of A and B, Arnold substitutes an analogy: A is to B as C is to D. The Oxford of the past, the landscape in the mind, is to the present scene, the landscape before the eye, what a transcendent reality is to the world of the senses. The metaphoric identity between dead people and nature spirits or geniuses of the shore is further eroded by Arnold's minute floral descriptions, not of a pastoral paradise, but of an actual English meadow.

As the mythological time of classical elegy and its fable of the resurrected Daphnis ("Thyrsis," ll. 188–89) become separated from the one-directional time of nineteenth-century evolutionary science, the question of what is real and what is illusion becomes central. In Shelley's essay, "A Defense of Poetry," the power that Milton or Sidney would have ascribed to God's revelation is identified with an imperial "Power

. . . seated on the throne of [the poet's] own soul" (Woodring, 1961, 513). Instead of enslaving himself to what he creates, like Frankenstein, Shelley's elegist must celebrate, in Northrop Frye's phrase, "the recovery by the imagination of what it has projected" (1971, 96). And for Arnold such words as immortality and God, though metaphorically efficient, become mere symbols of the dominance "over man's ordinary or passing self" of a "higher or enduring self" (1972, 8:154). So far as these symbols are descriptive, what they describe—a divine force outside the mind—becomes increasingly illusory. In internalizing "the natural truth" of Christianity, then renouncing personal wisdom for himself, Arnold's elegist in "Thyrsis" shares the fate of his critic in "The Function of Criticism at the Present Time": like Moses, each can glimpse the Promised Land only from afar (1962, 3:285).

To realize the illusion of abiding life is to abolish its future and turn it into a living presence, like the God of Browning's St. John, who "Is, here and now: I apprehend naught else" ("A Death in the Desert," l. 210). But the elusive elm that might make Clough's future a present reality for Arnold is difficult to track. When Arnold, crossing a field, glimpses the elm only from a distance, then fails to pursue it farther, the transitive verbs of a pilgrimage turn into the intransitive verbs of a failed pilgrimage—a mere ramble or excursion. Phrases like "Roam on" or "wandered till I died" ("Thyrsis," ll. 237–38) lack the teleologically directed future of a pilgrimage, whose traditionally transitive verbs carry a believer like Dr. Arnold from the rocks of the wilderness to the City of God in "Rugby Chapel." Lacking Shelley's faith in the power of a god-like mind to cross boundaries, Arnold believes intransitively. He is faced with the challenge of manifesting the light's existence, not merely gazing at it from afar. Whereas Keats's creative energy has already made the illusion of immortal life a reality for Shelley, Arnold, like many Victorians, must make Romantic illusion real through his own creative energy. Unlike Shelley's trumpeting proclamations, Arnold's discoveries must be communicated only in silence, in the caesural pauses and breaks between lines. With Arnold's help Clough's whisper may restore everything the mourner has lost, but only at the last moment, and only after it seems to disappear forever.

Classical elegy breaks down when its practitioners find it increasingly difficult to sustain its paradox of power. The classical elegist's power to do things with words is grounded in archaic categories of identity and metaphor. But a grounded performative is not genuinely performative, and an ungrounded performative generates a skepticism that is quite subversive of the classical elegist's faith in the archaic categories, which is ultimately the ancient Greek faith in knowledge as divination.

Doing-by-Saying: The Performative Paradox

The ritualized language of all classical elegy retains strong traces of verbal magic. As a species of liturgy that releases emotion even while controlling it, the ancient language and traditional symbols of classical elegy promote the form of utterance that J. L. Austin calls "performative" (1962, 25). Like the ritualized words of the marriage service, which is Austin's own example, performative language brings into being the state of affairs it purports to describe. No marriage exists, for example, until the words "I do" are spoken. To say something is to perform an act, if you will—the act of saying something. It is important to distinguish, however, between a mere act of saying that Lycidas is dead and the elegist's performance of a ritual act of naming, a kind of baptism, in which Lycidas is pronounced "the genius of the shore" (l. 183). By functioning as an imperative in disguise, exhorting Lycidas to live up to his new name, to "be good . . . / To all that wander in that perilous flood" (ll. 184–85), such a baptism, if felicitous, may even release quasi-physical power. Moreover, as a summons to activity, the mourner's resolution to return to "fresh Woods, and Pastures new" (l. 193) is a self-commissioning or "doing-by-saying," to borrow Geoffrey Hill's phrase (1984, 119). Without such verbal action, or "doing-by-saying," an elegy may remain a self-isolating meditation, not a socially responsible or moral act.

The classical elegist must be faithful to both sides of a paradox. If belief in apotheosis is willed into being by the radical faith of each elegist, then "the dear might of him that walk'd the waves" ("Lycidas," l. 173) is a power the elegist has helped create. But an invented power is a fiction, even though it may be a supreme fiction, and so not a ground at all. Conversely, if God is the unalterably given, the antecedent ground, and Edward King's death is not a distressing accident but the result of God's will, then the mourner's energetic rebuke of the nymphs for neglecting Lycidas seems unwarranted. We feel the shock of "the blind Fury's" slitting "the thin-spun life" with her "abhorred shears" ("Lycidas," ll. 75–76). As Douglas Bush says, "Atropos, the third Fate, is not enough; God's providence seems to act with more malign irresponsibility" (1963, 282).

The paradox of power might be put another way. If the elegist's words of power are grounded, they annihilate the conditions of religious faith. If they are ungrounded, they destroy the specifically religious character of the elegist's appeal in "all judging *Jove*" to the ground of a "perfect witness" he can only partly apprehend ("Lycidas," l. 82). Strictly speaking, there is no such thing as a grounded performative. Only God's performatives are grounded. And that is not because God is a master electrician who has wired His universe in advance of decreeing "Let there be light," but because God is God. The classical elegist speaks as if the benign power of Lycidas, who "shalt be good" to future voyagers, both *is* and *is not* fully real until a pastoral elegist like Milton's "uncouth Swain" works at the height of his powers to bring that gift into focus and receive it.

The performative paradox is under pressure not just in later pastoral elegists like Arnold and Shelley. Milton is troubled by it, and we can see the paradox breaking down even in Spenser. In *The Shepheardes Calender* Spenser's Colin is said to be "uncouthe," not because his speech is rustic and uncultivated, but because his habits of thought are still quasi-magical and primitive. Like Milton's swain, Colin seems at first to have a firmer grasp than more refined poets of the archaic categories of analogy and metaphor, which (as the categories of magic) remain closer than more logical operations of induction and comparison to the original sources of poetic power. The amputation of the proper name in Colin's heartfelt appeal to Lobbin—"O Lobb! thy losse no longer lament" ("November Eclogue," l. 168)—is affecting, "grave for the straungenesse," as the epistle to Harvey says, and it goes quite deep. As a half-comic counterpart to the sad moment in "Lycidas" when the drowned shepherd is addressed for the only time in the elegy as Lycid, not Lycidas, the onomastic humor also marks a moment of ritual naming and renewal. But in other plaintive eclogues there still lurks a black king on the chessboard, a figure more sinister than any character, like the faithless Rosalind or Menalcas, whom we actually meet in Spenser's poetry.

This dark force is a variant of the great boar Time in the Garden of Adonis: it has killed Chaucer and eroded faith in the archaic poet's magic and his quasi-physical words of power. Colin's expulsion from Eden in the December eclogue seems to be a direct result of his subversively entertaining Hobbinol's heresy that only frivolous nymphs still worship Pan. In a blasphemous parenthesis, Colin even queries whether Pan is a god at all (l. 50). To lose faith in Pan is to lose faith in the performative paradox, in Colin's power to turn wasted hills into Eden while still claiming to speak as Pan's oracle, the magician through whom the god works. Colin, in a word, is no longer "uncouth." His loss of faith in Pan is part of an antipoetic myth of progress. He has discovered the incongruities between a logical and a poetic outlook. But is his intolerance of paradox, his inability to entertain both outlooks simultaneously, a loss or a gain? We may prefer the "uncouthness" that asserts the cogency of magical words of power and the crudity of more logical operations. Having surrendered to the more analytic and discursive powers, which are often aggressive and used as intellectual weapons in polemic and debate, he no longer has any taste or talent for paradox. It is time for Colin to write *finis* to his eclogue and his "calendar."

The performative power of words, which tends to erode the believer's knowledge of a gift God has already bestowed, appears to be one of the paradoxes of religion. If Lycidas is already a "Genius of the shore," if that office has been graciously bestowed on him before elegists and mourners dare grasp or even name it, how can they then exercise faith by finding the right names for him? Spenser's Colin Clout no longer has any interest in sustaining faith in such a paradox: in saying farewell to the conceptual model informing late medieval and early Renaissance habits of mind, he is also saying farewell to pastoral elegy. But Milton cultivates the tolerance for paradox that the elegist's words of power seem to require. Though Lycidas has already "mounted high" through "the dear might" of a much greater power, he does not ascend until the poet says so in the soaring ritual decrees of the apotheosis, which tower majestically above everything else in the poem. The performative power of line 166—"For *Lycidas* your sorrow is not dead" —reverses the flat descriptive force of line 8—"For *Lycidas* is dead, dead ere his prime." The grammar of the culminating decree is still active; its syntax can be arranged to read "your sorrow for Lycidas is not dead." But no sooner is that dark possibility entertained, in fleeting memory of line 8, than it is fenced off by the reassuring alternative: "For Lycidas, the object of your sorrow, is not dead." At the elegy's climax classical and biblical typologies of resurrection come together in the apotheosis of Lycidas, who is said to hear "the unexpressive nuptiall Song" (l. 176) of Revelation. As J. L. Austin recognizes, performative speech is always trying to approximate the condition of such ritual language. But that condition is achieved only when Lycidas, like Orpheus and Christ, is shown to be too good for the world and goes in the only way he can: out of it.

The classical elegist is always trying to break through the barrier of mere descriptive naming in quest of the vocative of direct address. To speak to the dead is already to have made a breach in the wall, to have battered down a boundary or divide. Lycidas is named nine times in the elegy. But only on the fourth and final occasion is he directly invoked. The first vocative use of the proper name, "Such, Lycidas, thy loss to Shepherds ear" (l. 49), stands as a shoal between two low points: the mourning by the woods and caves and the swain's arraignment of the nymphs. Like the chiasmus "Together both" and "both together" (ll. 25, 27), which dramatizes intimacy and rapport, the vocative momentarily summons up the drowned man as a silent but responsive auditor.

At the culminating point in the elegy, when the vocative of direct address is used for the second and final time, the alternating current between descriptive and performative speech reverses its flow once more, as the admonitory "Weep no more, woful Shepherds weep no more" (l. 165) is echoed by a merely descriptive use of the same verb: "Now *Lycidas* the Shepherds weep no more" (l. 182). Though "weep" is indicative, "Lycidas" is a vocative that keeps intact the power of words to summon up and address the dead.

It is often said the "Lycidas" is asymmetrically framed: it has a frame at the end but not at the beginning. But there are actually two frames, one introductory and one terminal. The main asymmetry is that different people step out of them. Instead of framing the swain's story himself, as he does at the end of the elegy, Milton allows the swain at the beginning to step outside the frame of his own life by reflecting that a gentle muse may some day compose "lucky words" (l. 20) for his own funeral urn. This appeal to a compassionate poet to commemorate him is also an oblique appeal to each reader. If daffodils can fill their cups with tears, and mere echoes offer the gift of melodious grief, why should a responsive reader, capable of his own ritual performance, be allowed to do less? It takes both the reader and the swain a long time getting launched, however: each still seems uncertain of his ability to turn factual chronicle into ritual act. "Begin then, . . . / Begin" (ll. 15, 17), the swain keeps exhorting in an injunction that uses as well as mentions the idea of beginning by appearing at the head of the second verse paragraph and also at the beginning of neighboring lines.

Though the elegy's one diminutive use of the dead man's proper name is partly endearing, the lopping off of the final syllable cannot repress totally the alarming thought that Lycidas's amputated remains, like his contracted name, have been laid low by a darkness too sinister to identify: "The Laureat Herse where *Lycid* lies" (l. 151). Is the last power to be trusted? What if God is a void or an absence rather than a friend? Does a malign force stand behind the corrupt clergy and the blind Fury with her abhorred shears, like some unnamed black king on the chessboard? Nothing has quite prepared us for the subversive questions Milton seems to be asking under his breath. Yet is it not odd that at the precise moment Lycidas is acknowledged to be gone, "never" to "return" (l. 38), he should be addressed four times in three lines by the intimate pronouns "thou" and "thee"?

> But O the heavy change, now thou art gon,
> Now thou art gon, and never must return!
> Thee Shepherd, thee the Woods, and desert Caves,

> With wilde Thyme and gadding Vine o'regrown,
> And all their echoes mourn. ("Lycidas," ll. 37–41)

A crisis in utterance discloses that absences can be more potent than presences, and things invisible and unheard more vivid than objects the eye and ear directly apprehend. Even the grammar wavers unsteadily between an inventory of stark impressions and the reassuring vocative of intimate address that resurrects the "Shepherd" from the tomb of dead descriptive words in which the striking shifts from the nominative "thou"s to the accusative "thee"s threaten for an instant to bury him.

Everything fluctuates on a knife edge. No sooner has the swain denounced the nymphs than his hope winds down and the possibilities of renovation seem to die. The mourner is heartsick. We hear the scurry and strain of a mind under stress, whose ritual naming of the Muse can do nothing to annul the Maenads' savage counter-rites. The dismal vowel music sounds as thin and sinister as the shearer, who is said to slit "the thin-spun life" in a succession of cramped, flat monosyllables (ll. 75–76). Fear and trembling are allayed only when Phoebus, in a ritual exercise of verbal power, decrees what fame, properly understood, must be. One definition is nested in another: the swain's limited descriptive understanding of fame, as the achievement of earthly reward, is contained and reversed by Phoebus's decree that "*Fame* is no plant that grows on mortal soil" (l. 78). But to tell us what Fame *is*, Phoebus has to defer to the perfect but silent witness "of all judging Jove" (l. 82), whose words of power, if audible, would swallow up everything else in the poem.

Like creation by verbal fiat in Genesis, a mere utterance by God will establish "lastly" (l. 83)—both in the sense of at the *end* of time and *for* all time—the precise fate of each soul. Because the swain's ultimate postulate of faith is that God can be trusted, he is able to execute toward the end of the elegy a massive grammatical turn upon the hinge verb "Look."

> Where the great vision of the guarded Mount
> Looks toward *Namancos* and *Bayona's* hold;
> Look homeward Angel now, and melt with ruth.
> ("Lycidas," ll. 161–63)

Though the second use of "Look" deceptively resembles its first use, it is difficult to exaggerate the difference between these imperative and indicative moods. When "Look" replaces "Looks," a descriptive chronicle of maritime geography turns into heartfelt invocation, potently compressing two commands in a single line: "Look homeward

Angel now, and melt with ruth." So potent is the swain's "doing-by-saying" that his final address to Lycidas is a commissioning, like the benediction and instruction at the end of a liturgy. It hovers in grammatical force between a prophecy and a baptism, in which Lycidas receives a felicitous new epithet: "Hence forth thou art the genius of the shore, / In thy large recompense, and shalt be good / To all that wander in that perilous flood" (ll. 183–85). The concluding frame allows Milton the elegist, in stepping out of the mourner's story, to commission the uncouth swain himself and ultimately each reader. The final self-commissioning through the swain—"To morrow to fresh Woods, and Pastures new" (l. 193)—lacks a verb. It has the force of a resolution, a decree that each reader is invited to issue to himself. The absence of a verb makes it timeless, as if the swain were eliding a tenseless infinitive: every tomorrow will offer a fresh wood and new pasture. So the temporal specificity of "To morrow" is balanced by the quasi-magical energy of words, neither immortal nor invulnerable like Jove's words, but still able to order the mourner's chaos and serve as a light by which Milton and his readers live.

Milton assumes that creation by verbal fiat is the prerogative of God; prophets and poets exercise verbal power only as God or the Holy Spirit inspires them. For Shelley, however, man makes his own world, and at the center of that creation is the "doing-by-saying" of the poet. Both descriptive and performative, the halting opening stanzas of "Adonais" look two ways at once. Adonais seems swallowed up in the first line's dash and by its late-breaking seventh-syllable caesura: "I weep for Adonais—he is dead!" But the next line initiates a sudden and striking shift: "I weep" becomes the deceptively similar but potently different, "O weep." A mere "saying" becomes a "doing-by-saying," a resolve by the poet to mourn properly by commemorating Keats in an elegy.

By framing a word of power, a decree, inside a second decree, the first stanza makes its performative language self-embedding and reflexive.

> I weep for Adonais—he is dead!
> O, weep for Adonais! though our tears
> Thaw not the frost which binds so dear a head!
> And thou, sad Hour, selected from all years
> To mourn our loss, rouse thy obscure compeers,
> And teach them thine own sorrow, say: "With me
> Died Adonais; till the Future dares
> Forget the Past, his fate and fame shall be
> An echo and a light unto eternity!" ("Adonais," ll. 1–9)

The echoing that the "sad Hour" decrees is itself an echo of the elegist's threefold decree to the hour: "Rouse thy obscure compeers," he exhorts, "And teach them," then "say." One might think that such pervasive echoing would attenuate the force of the decrees. But in the acoustic chamber of the long concluding alexandrine, the echoing of the poet's undying fame, sounding "unto eternity," amplifies rather than attenuates the words' performative power. Trembling at the brink of each indefinite caesura, like the mourner's mind, the stanza advances by coiling back on itself in self-impeding loops. As if replicating Coleridge's picture of the mind's innate resilience and energy, the interlocking quatrains, which keep doubling back on the same rhyme word, move like a serpent, "which the Egyptians made the emblem of intellectual power." At each step the poet of power "pauses and half recedes, and from the retrogressive movement" of his Spenserian stanza "collects the force which again carries him onward" (Coleridge, 1906, 173).

Whenever "Thyrsis" tries to emulate "Adonais" by making the landscape before the eye match the landscape in the mind, Arnold finds he has lost Shelley's adventurous confidence in the power of words to make something happen. Before baptizing Oxford as the loveliest of cities, Arnold uses language that is already half-performative, capable of invoking absent seasons like spring and the heightened beauty of Oxford in June as midwinter blessings. But there is still a sense that such consecration has to be achieved, that it is a triumph of making belief and not just descriptive. The boundary between stanzas 2 and 3, visible to the eye but inaudible to the ear when the lines are read aloud, fortifies the challenge of having to cross the divide between descriptive and performative speech.

> Humid the air! leafless, yet soft as spring,
>   The tender purple spray on copse and briers!
>   And that sweet city with her dreaming spires,
> She needs not June for beauty's heightening,
>
> Lovely all times she lies, lovely to-night! —
>   Only, methinks, some loss of habit's power
>   Befalls me wandering through this upland dim.
> ("Thyrsis," ll. 17–23)

The white space of the break also stands for the silent powers of change, for the ravages of time that the elegist must try to exorcise through a magic, ritualized use of words. That power is clearly latent in Arnold's benedictory phrase, "Humid the air!," which recalls Keats's "tender is the night" ("Ode to a Nightingale, l. 35). Though leafless on this warm winter evening, the tender purple spray on copse and brier is also "soft as spring," partly because the poet provides the felicitous simile. But the pause we expect at the end of stanza 2, after "beauty's heightening," is less emphatic than the pause that occurs at the end of the next line, when the aspiring celebrant, the would-be user of ritual words, laments "some loss of habit's power." In the triply enforced break after the phrase "lovely to-night," which is created by the exclamation point, the dash, and the ending of the line, the celebrant's consecration and elation subside into sudden disenchantment and fear. In the loss of a rooted expectation, Arnold seems to experience once again the loss of his friend Clough, which is like the loss of a habit or a skill.

Though at first surprised, a reader is also half prepared for what takes place after the dash in line 21. Is there not, after all, something sinister about Oxford's "lovely" lying? Is she not trying to seduce Arnold into a delusive picture of her, as Peele Castle seduces Wordsworth? As the fond haven of an unreal paradise, Oxford may lie in the sense of deceive, and she may also lie or repose in the attitude of one who wants to seduce Arnold. The sinister possibilities resurface three lines later in his admission that he once passed here "blindfold." That could mean either that he knew every cranny of Oxford intimately, or that he was blind to the delusiveness of her charm. The second more disturbing possibility seems confirmed a moment later when the words that complete the ritual, making the landscape in the mind match the landscape before the eye, are used to concede defeat: "I miss it! is it gone?" (l. 27). All words of power are now consigned to the past: while the elm "*stood*," "we *said*, / Our friend, the Scholar-Gipsy, *was* not dead" (ll. 28–29; my emphasis). The shift to a past-tense sequence in Arnold's allusion to the culminating words of power in "The Scholar-Gipsy"—"No, no, thou hast not felt the lapse of hours!" (l. 141)— places any triumph of "doing-by-saying" over descriptive matching in a world that now seems as remote from Arnold's Oxford as Moschus's "Lament for Bion," Virgil's seventh Eclogue, or Shelley's almost Pelagian faith in the natural goodness of a god-like soul like Keats.

Austin on Felicity: Milton's Rhymes and Shelley's Breathing

J. L. Austin argues that one characteristic of both poetic and performative speech is that neither can be said to advance a strictly "true-or-false" proposition. As Austin whimsically insists, when propounding his "doctrine of the *Infelicities*" (1962, 14), the poet is not judged by true-or-false criteria. What he says will be evaluated as more or less happy or apt. The efficacy of any ritual act of "doing-by-saying" in "Lycidas" or "Adonais" may depend on an auspicious use of the most minimal elements of prosody and grammar. Just as it is infelicitous to baptize a monkey, so Milton's apotheosis of Lycidas or Shelley's apotheosis of Adonais will be inauspicious unless a suitable use of rhymes in Milton's elegy or of pauses for breath in Shelley's provides a propitious preparation or setting for the poem's culminating act. Austin's "doctrine of the *Infelicities*" is really a doctrine of contextual meaning. If the context is felicitous, then the ritual may succeed. And if "truth" is a matter of poetic aptness, "correctness" may be a matter of critical fertility. What do the most elusive or minimal poetic patterns allow the critic to discover in each elegy?

F. T. Prince has shown how Milton's "rhetoric of rhyme" controls the pace of scanning blocks of short and long lines in "Lycidas" (1954, 86–88). Widely separated rhymes also help Milton's mourner distance death in the lens of a moving recollection, which places the traumatic event far enough away to re-present and reevaluate it. The recollection at a distance of an earlier rhyme gives the lie to the cynic's jibe that out of sight is out of mind. Rhymes that hark back impart a deep, backward-reaching intimacy to Milton's verse. And since an object that has been once recollected is always longing for a future recollection, rhymes that look back also look ahead. Using the graceful spans of his rhymes to throw an arch forward, the mourner can face his future with hope.

When Milton introduces a chain of rhymes, often the second or third rhyme is imperfect: it may either reverse some deathward decline or produce momentary distraction. The chiming of "long" and "song," for example (ll. 35–36), is followed by the imperfect rhyme of "gone," which continues to sound like a funeral gong that would have supplied in the word "gong" itself the perfect rhyme: "But O the heavy change, now thou art gon, / Now thou art gon, and never must return!" (ll. 37–38). The "heavy change" can be heard in the mindless, gong-like use of "gon," which refuses to rhyme with anything, even though it struggles to echo the lost chiming sounds of "long" and "song." "Return" in line 38 harks back wistfully to the rhetorical "turn" of "lucky words" upon the rhymes "Urn" and "turn" (ll. 20–21). But separated from its rhyme words by seventeen lines of verse, the word "return" cannot literally return: it is too far removed to register more than a subliminal echo now.

The only end word in the closing lines of "Lycidas" that is denied a rhyme is the towering "Mount" (l. 161). It is too sacred, too lofty, like Sinai in its custodial authority, to rhyme with anything. By contrast, successive couplets dramatize as powerfully as any poetry can the moment of turning and reversal, where the rhymes' massive simple clinching locks the statements into place. As the mourner turns on the hinge of the spacious phrase, "And yet anon," the relentless sinking of both the drowned Lycidas and the daystar is spectacularly reversed. The pivot upon that phrase is made more expansive by the chiasmus of sound, which repeats the rhymes in reverse order: "floar," "bed," "head," "Ore" (ll. 167–70). "Floar" and "bed" are literally "repaired" in the second pair of end words. And with the repairing of rhymes comes the great reparation of Lycidas, mounted high like the sun, made golden now and lucid. Though the reparation of the sun, flaming in the forehead of the morning sky, is logically the end of one unit of thought, the solemn break after "sky," made emphatic by the colon, is partly bridged by the deft use of a couplet: "sky" and "high."

> Flames in the forehead of the morning sky:
> So *Lycidas* sunk low, but mounted high . . . ("Lycidas," ll. 171–72)

The break is not as great as we might first think. The chiasmus of sound and sense in the daystar's reparation can also be appropriated by Lycidas, who is now assimilated by the bridging rhyme to the same pattern of reversal.

As Milton moves toward apotheosis, the clear march of rhyming units, without chiasmus now—"waves," "along," "laves," "song" (ll. 173–76)—establishes a perfect parallelism between the streams of the paradise where Lycidas dwells and Christ's taming of the waves, already prefigured in the valleys' taming of the wanton winds to mild whisperings. The symmetry of the rhymes helps afford a perfectly natural and untroubled transition from the waves of the Galilean lake to the streams and groves of paradise. George Steiner says that words at their limit open on light, silence, or music (1967, 39). Having exhausted the resources of light in the splendid ascent of the daystar from his ocean bed, the elegist now turns to nuptial song, and ultimately to silence, for he concedes that his song is inexpressible. At the end of the elegy, even while the alternating rhymes are dispersing the sounds, the return of the same rhyme—"gray," "lay," "bay"—three times in five lines (ll. 187–91) has the same terminal effect as the dominant's persistence in music. The return to heroic couplets in the final two lines, like the knell-like use of anaphora in the two preceding lines—"And now," "And now"—clearly signals closure.

The most daring and exalting conjunctions of rhyme are reserved for the apotheosis, where Milton's mourner speaks his culminating words of power. "So *Lycidas* sunk low" traces out a very gradual decline, brought to a full stop by the half-smothered "O"s and by the coincidence of stressed syllables with long vowels. The alliterating sibilants link up "low" to form "slow." No hemistich unfolds more slowly, and the breaking of the midline caesura is also a braking that allows the mourner to reverse direction with ease: "So *Lycidas* sunk low, but mounted high" (l. 172). Even as the clinching of the simple rhymes locks the moment of slow turning and majestic reversal into a lucid affirmation, the mounted corpse begins to tower magisterially, looking far beyond the auspices of its chiming couplet (ll. 171–72).

> For *Lycidas* your sorrow is not dead,
> Sunk though he be beneath the watry floar,
> So sinks the day-star in the Ocean bed,
> And yet anon repairs his drooping head,
> And tricks his beams, and with new spangled Ore,
> Flames in the forehead of the morning sky:
> So *Lycidas* sunk low, but mounted high,
> Through the dear might of him that walk'd the waves
> Where other groves, and other streams along,
> With *Nectar* pure his oozy *Lock's* he laves,
> And hears the unexpressive nuptiall Song . . . ("Lycidas," ll. 166–76)

If rhyme binds the corpse to the spangled ore of the sun, flaming in the forehead of the morning sky, syntax and logic also unite Lycidas to the dear might of a greater Sun, Christ, and to the inexpressible nuptial song of Revelation. Though the reflections of the sun's glory and the greater glory of the Son have power to enlighten, their might, like the ruth that melts the angel (l. 163), can be invoked and petitioned only by the mourner's own words of power.

Linked to the adjuration, "Weep no more, woful Shepherds" (l. 165), the heart-melting ruth evokes the moisture of tears. But unlike the "whelming tide" (l. 157), this water is benign. For it links "ruth" to the wafted "youth" (l. 164), as if the arch of a great causeway had been thrown across the ocean that closes over Lycidas. Such linkages of the murderous element of water with life-restoring tears reverse the dark association of rivers and oceans. Like the mourner's own words of power, the dominion of ruth can be felt repairing the sun and exalting Lycidas. While many of Milton's dispersed rhymes and images reach back in memory like the heart-melting ruth, which recalls the "moist vows" that were earlier "deny'd" (l. 159), the elegy's culminating words of power also reach forward: they "look homeward" like the angel. Milton's use of both converging and dispersing rhymes helps make the language performative, a "doing-by-saying." Conclusive couplets anchor the causeways on secure pillars of sound. More adventurously, dispersed rhymes can be used to throw an arch of sound *forward*, building a bridge of prophecy and hope into an uncertain future.

Whereas Milton makes the apotheosis of Lycidas "felicitous" in Austin's sense by using dispersing and converging rhyme words to reach back in memory and forward into the future, Shelley associates the power of Adonais with a spirit animating nature and breathing through the poet's words. Many stanzas in "Adonais" are exercises in controlled pausing and breathing; occasionally they even use the word "breath." Stanza 50, for example, makes the last exhaling of breath in an ideal reading coincide with the phrase "scarce extinguished breath" (l. 450); the stanza and the breath expire together. In stanzas 38 and 43 the breath that labors to meet and surmount obstacles seems to compact pain in the reader's lungs with strain "in the pure spirit" (l. 338) and an almost physical sensation of its "plastic stress" (l. 381). "Spirit" means "breath," and Keats's own "poignant sense of breathing and the heart," as Christopher Ricks calls it (1987, 64), informs both the great concluding stanza of Shelley's elegy and the stanza in which Adonais receives a felicitous new epithet as "a portion of the loveliness / Which once he made more lovely" ("Adonais," ll. 379–80).

In this latter stanza of rededication and renewal both the reader's breath and "the one Spirit's plastic stress" (l. 381) are checked at first by a perilous thickening of alliterative sounds and stresses. The harshly compacted triad, "dull dense world" (l. 382), is spoken as laboriously as Hamlet's words: "And in this harsh world draw thy breath in pain / To tell my story" (*Hamlet.* v.2.359–60). The breath is drawn in pain because it has to voice three successive stresses. Momentarily thwarted by harsh accentual blows, the final release of the spirit depends on replacing two transitive participles ("compelling" and "Torturing," ll. 382, 384) with a participle ("bursting," l. 386), which is defiantly intransitive, liberated at last from any need to shape or inform matter.

> He is a portion of the loveliness
> Which once he made more lovely: he doth bear
> His part, while the one Spirit's plastic stress
> Sweeps through the dull dense world, compelling there
> All new successions to the forms they wear;
> Torturing th' unwilling dross that checks its flight
> To its own likeness, as each mass may bear;
> And bursting in its beauty and its might
> From trees and beasts and men into the Heaven's light.
> ("Adonais," ll. 379–87)

In "Lycidas," even when the felt pressure of despair and pain is at its most intense, Milton manages to exclude us from any immediate experience of it. Though the reverberating wail of the Muse's grief for Orpheus seems to touch off all chords of lament in a mighty diapason, appropriate to the death of her own "inchanting son," we are too enchanted by the intoning of sounds and the tremor of open vowels to melt with grief for Orpheus. In "Adonais," by contrast, the constriction of pain and the intimacies of loss are as immediate as the reader's own labored breathing. At the end of the quoted stanza, after clearing the triple hurdle of Aristotle's vegetable, animal, and rational souls—"trees and beasts and men" (l. 387)—which are spaced out by polysyndeton and made more obstructive by the coincidence of harsh stresses and long quantities, the lungs of each reader seem as ready to "burst" as the Spirit. Only in the lighter stresses of the stanza's concluding adverbial phrase, "into the Heaven's light," is the reader's own breathing made lighter. Having used up their breath to experience the triumph of spirit over nature, readers may now feel content to fade out like the air they exhale. A perfect finish, as Yeats understood, makes it easier to accept death as a consummation, as an expenditure of life without remainder.

Like Urania's descent into the inspired elegist in the final stanza, the descent of breath into a reader's lungs allows the voice to drive the lines forward, even as the spirit's bark is driven.

> The breath whose might I have invoked in song
> Descends on me; my spirit's bark is driven,
> Far from the shore, far from the trembling throng
> Whose sails were never to the tempest given;
> The massy earth and sphered skies are riven!
> I am borne darkly, fearfully, afar;
> Whilst, burning through the inmost veil of Heaven,
> The soul of Adonais, like a star,
> Beacons from the abode where the Eternal are.
> ("Adonais," ll. 487–95)

The bare final copula has a blankness on the page that only a reader's voice can quicken into life. But no reading aloud of the final hemistich can hope to achieve what the written words achieve, for we can imagine several contradictory ways of reading them. If we read the final six syllables as two dactyls, we ponder the mystery of existing eternally. If we read them as a trochee followed by two iambs, we subordinate the mysteries of eternal existence to the mystery of bare being. To speak the final copula inconclusively may even imply that the elegy remains unfinished: "where the Eternal are [what?]" Inhabitors of the ancient earth, perhaps? "Inheritors of unfulfilled renown" (l. 397)? Just as the late-breaking caesuras after "fearfully" and "Adonais" (ll. 492, 494) hover sorrowfully over death, even as they exult in the adventure of moving on, so the sublime blankness of the copula verb, its withholding of any indication of what "white radiance" (l. 463) might be like, induces numbness as well as awe.

Like the awkward grace of ending on a copula, the word "breath" looks two ways at once. Even in asserting its softness, Shelley uses the phrase "soft enamoured breath" (l. 15) to rhyme ominously with "Death" (l. 18). Though the terminal rhyme marks a terminal event, the cessation of all breathing, the many caesural pauses that make the "coming bulk of Death" (l. 18) suspenseful and alarming also have an opposite effect of rocking the mourner gently back to sleep.

> The leprous corpse, touched by this spirit tender,
> Exhales itself in flowers of gentle breath; ("Adonais," ll. 172–73)

If the "flowers of gentle breath" are a metaphor for the breath exhaled by the corpse when touched by another breath, "the spirit tender" of line 172, then we confront the spectacle of a corpse exhaling not merely breath but also itself, as if everything corporeal were already touched to spirit. Contrary to what is asserted about death's feeding on the breath that was once used to speak, we experience a compact sense of breathing in the heart with a sensation of the breath informing a gently animated world. Shelley's pauses for breath help make the apotheosis a felicitous rite. For the "vital air" (l. 26) is not only the life-giving atmosphere from which the dead Keats is removed by the disease in his lungs. A driving forward that is also a slow descent into death also describes the reader's experience of inhaling breath that is gradually expended in the act of propelling the poem forward to its last fearful word, the most withholding but also the most promising of all, which opens on the unknown.

The Poetics of Caution: Arnold's Run-Ons

Shelley's simultaneous mention and use of the word "breath" display an adventurous confidence in the power of language to convince the nerves and make something happen. Arnold's far more modest confidence expresses itself in his initially cautious but gradually bolder crossing of the boundary spaces between stanzas. The weakest crossings, like the one between the second and third stanzas, depend wholly on punctuation. If Arnold had used a period instead of a comma after the phrase "beauty's heightening," no crossing would have occurred. The second spanning of a break between stanzas, the crossing that takes place between stanzas 11 and 12, is more confident than the first crossing. Part of the new verbal potency depends on Arnold's use of anaphora—"I know the wood," "I know the . . . tree"—to straddle both sides of the boundary.

> I know the wood which hides the daffodil,
>   I know the Fyfield tree,

> I know what white, what purple fritillaries
>> The grassy harvest of the river-fields,
>> Above by Ensham, down by Sandford, yields,
>> And what sedged brooks are Thames's tributaries;
>
> I know these slopes; who knows them if not I?
> ("Thyrsis," ll. 105–11)

When Arnold asserts for the third or fourth time, not merely *that* he knows but also *what* he knows, his assertions become a "doing-by-saying." The insistent anaphora builds up rhetorical momentum; and in the absence of any period, there is no obstacle to prevent the elegist's crossing the boundary between stanzas.

The reversing flow of the verse is charged with as much averted fear as hope. Its alternating current makes us conscious of a significant space, a vacancy, which will increasingly claim attention in the rest of stanza 12. The space between stanzas stands for an unseen undertow more potent than any current in an Oxfordshire tributary of the Thames. Across the slow effacements of time, the abyss in things, the elegist must now make his steady advance. Though Arnold speaks of the "sedged brooks" of the river's "tributaries" (l. 110), he also makes us subliminally aware of that other brook, that unseen "cataract of death," as Frost calls it, "That spends to nothingness" ("West-Running Brook," ll. 56–57). More has gone "Down each green bank" than "the ploughboy's team" (l. 118). By the end of stanza 12 the elegist's hopes have also died.

Once Arnold has subsided from high confidence into self-distrust and doubt, the pulse of his verse all but ceases and the metrical beat can barely carry him to the end of a line. In stanza 14 we pause fearfully at the brink of each successive line break, afraid to discover what loss or affliction will follow next. In the stanza's third and last run-on, we hear a stress after each word: "finger light / Laid pausefully" (ll. 136–37). With so many pauses, the heart itself seems to stop beating. But the pattern of failing powers, once established, seems impossible to cut off. There can be no stopping short of the final stopping place of death itself.

The crossing of the boundary between stanzas 11 and 12 proves to be no permanent crossing, then, but a quick reversion to old fears and doubts. By contrast, the crossing of the breaks between stanzas 17, 18, and 19 is grammatical as well as typographical: it marks a sustained transition from descriptive to performative speech. In stanza 16 a prayerful optative and injunction usher in the climactic vision: "But hush! the upland hath a sudden loss / Of quiet!" (ll. 151–52). The imperative force of "hush" prepares for the hortatory verbs "let me fly, and cross" (l. 156), and for the final prayerful injunction, "see," whose direct object is suspensefully delayed for three full lines.

> Quick! let me fly, and cross
> Into yon farther field!—'Tis done; and see,
>   Backed by the sunset, which doth glorify
>   The orange and pale violet evening-sky,
> Bare on its lonely ridge, the Tree! the Tree! (ll. 156–60)

The exhortation to "see" (l. 157) points back to the verb's earlier use in lines 77–78, "shall see; / See him come back," which wavers ambiguously between a simple future tense and an auxiliary verb of decree. But now the injunction "see" seems unambiguous and fully justified. Instead of being half lost in a tangle of prepositional phrases at the center of a stanza, as in lines 11–14, the vision of the elm is now placed climactically in the foreground at the *end* of a stanza. In crossing the field Arnold crosses the divide between life and death. His crossing of a boundary is enforced by a run-on at the end of line 156. To "cross / Into yon farther field" is also to cross a line and to break through a boundary created by the enclosure of lines 151–56 by the widely separated rhyming of "loss" and "cross." The crossing itself inaugurates the climactic event in the elegy, which takes place when we least expect it, when favoring circumstances seem marred by the intrusion of boisterous hunters. The imperative "hear"s that follow—"Hear it from thy broad lucent Arno-vale," "Hear it, O Thyrsis, still our tree is there!" (ll. 167, 171)—can be heard calling across the boundary that divides one stanza from another. No longer an idle apostrophe to a tree (l. 166), the self-referring "Hear" of line 171, which invites us to hear the other uses of "hear," is now a poetic happening, a way of doing something unexpected with words.

No sooner has Arnold crossed the space between stanzas 17 and 18 than he wakes up on the far side in a state of disintoxication and despair: "Ah, vain!" (l. 172), he concedes. Though there is a sense in which the ritualized apostrophe, "Hear it, O Thyrsis" (l. 171), has actually brought Clough back to life, Arnold can reenact only the transport and then the shock in Wordsworth's elegy, "Surprised by Joy." When he sees the tree, he turns to share his transport of joy with his old comrade, Clough, half forgetting that Clough is dead. His words to Clough are dismissed as doubly "vain." Buried in the Protestant cemetery at Florence, Clough is no longer in England; more to the point, he is no longer alive. Is Arnold too despairing, or is he just trying to recognize, like Clough, that ambivalence and uncertainty are central rather than peripheral features of a fully examined life?

Unlike the space at the end of line 170, the space between stanzas 18 and 19 acts, not as an absence, but as the divide between art and life, where the imaginary can be felt trembling for a moment on the brink of the real. In stanzas 18 and 19 Arnold makes his utterance performative, a "doing-by-saying," by folding the parenthesis in lines 178–79 within the appositional units modifying the long delayed principal subject "Thou" (l. 181), which makes its appearance only after we cross the boundary between stanzas.

> Hear it, O Thyrsis, still our tree is there! . . .
>   And now in happier air,
>   Wandering with the great Mother's train divine
>   (And purer or more subtle soul than thee,
>   I trow, the mighty Mother doth not see)
>   Within a folding of the Apennine,
>
> Thou hearest the immortal chants of old! ("Thyrsis," ll. 171–81)

As Clough wanders within a folding of the Apennine, so the mighty Mother seems to wander casually into Arnold's poem. But not even the grammatical "wandering" of the protracted participle "Wandering" (l. 177) from the pronoun it modifies can impede the march across lines, brackets, and stanzas of the reiterated verb: "Hear it, O Thyrsis," "Thou hearest."

Whenever lineation and verse units fail to coincide with the units of syntax and sense, we are ready for something extraordinary to happen. The syntactic units beginning at lines 167 and 176 are not completed within the boundaries of the stanzaic units. In each case the doubt as to what that unit will be is resolved only as we round the corner into the next stanza. As we enter stanza 19, we find ourselves in a cornfield that, though mythical, is as immediate to the senses as Arnold's Oxford.

> Putting his sickle to the perilous grain
>   In the hot cornfield of the Phrygian king,
> For thee the Lityerses-song again
>   Young Daphnis with his silver voice doth sing:
>   Sings his Sicilian fold,
>   His sheep, his hapless love, his blinded eyes—
>   And how a call celestial round him rang,
>   And heavenward from the fountain-brink he sprang,
>   And all the marvel of the golden skies. ("Thyrsis," ll. 182–90)

The ellipsis in line 186, "Sings (of or about) his Sicilian fold," creates a flicker of hesitation. Is "Sicilian fold" the subject or object of the verb? Since one does not literally sing a fold, perhaps Arnold is using hyperbaton to reverse the normal order of verb and subject. In classical myth singing Daphnis and the subjects of his song are bound together in potent unity, which the momentarily uncertain grammar, its possible two-way flow, helps restore. Though the fabulous possibility of singing sheep is raised only to be fenced off or rescinded, it prepares for the greater marvel of Daphnis's mounting to heaven and of a fountain's being made to spring from the place of his ascent.

At the end of "Thyrsis" pastoral and urban worlds still seem far apart. Items that share an affinity of space are severed rather than joined by the grammatical sense.

> Too rare, too rare, grow now my visits here!
>   'Mid city-noise, not, as with thee of yore,
>   Thyrsis! in reach of sheep-bells is my home.
>   —Then through the great town's harsh, heart-wearying roar,
>   Let in thy voice a whisper often come,
>   To chase fatigue and fear:
> *Why faintest thou? I wandered till I died.*
>   *Roam on! The light we sought is shining still.*
>   *Dost thou ask proof? Our tree yet crowns the hill,*
> *Our Scholar travels yet the loved hill-side.* ("Thyrsis," ll. 231–40)

On the printed page the phrase "my home" (l. 233) is indeed within physical "reach of sheep-bells." But the adverbial phrase does not attach itself grammatically to the words in its immediate neighborhood; instead, it reaches back to the "city-noise" at the head of the preceding line. Invisible links are still being forged, however. Two of the links that move Clough's pastoral world into the vicinity of Arnold and his city noise are the white space off the end of line 233, which brings the reader to a full pause, and the blank created by the dash at the beginning of the next line. Deafened by the city's "roar," Arnold invites us to experience the heavy pauses at the end of lines 233 to 236 as moments of fearful suspension, hanging between linguistic life and linguistic death: the possibility of Clough's speaking to him in a whisper, and mere emptiness and silence. The prospect of communing with a mere whisper in a setting so harsh and uncongenial comes as a providential surprise. After the comma at the end of line 234, the roar dies for a moment, and in the silence of that empty space, which threatens to impose another form of verbal death, like the roar itself, the silent communing takes place. Clough comes to life in the hyphens and dashes of "the great town's harsh, heart-wearying roar" (l. 234), in the poetry that lies between the lines, in the strange half-silences, fraught with suspense, where the voice most worth listening to can finally be heard, not as a trumpet call of ascent, as in the triumphal apotheosis of Adonais or Lycidas, but as a barely audible whisper.

So far I have been concentrating on Arnold's use of enjambment to cross the breaks between stanzas. Equally resourceful is his employment of "run-on" lines inside a stanza. Though "unbreachable" in itself, the power of "the fort" to breach the line ending and pass with barely a pause to the sturdy amplitude of "the long-battered world" shows that its strength is a triumph of "doing-by-saying."

> Unbreachable the fort
> Of the long-battered world uplifts its wall; ("Thyrsis," ll. 146–47)

"Unbreachable" also acts out its meaning by crowding to one side everything in its short three-word line. Repeated three times in as many lines, the "tops" of the mountains establish their primacy, not by crossing lines like the "unbreachable fort," but by moving from sixth-syllable position in line 143, to fourth-syllable position in the next line, to first-syllable position at the "top" or head of line 145.

> And high the mountain-tops, in cloudy air,
> The mountain-tops where is the throne of Truth,
> Tops in life's morning-sun so bright and bare!
> ("Thyrsis," ll. 143–45)

Like his use of enjambment to break through stanzaic boundaries, Arnold's employment of run-ons within stanzas tends to be performative and self-referring, a form of "doing-by-saying." Even the resurrection of Proserpine is made to depend on a line break and run-on. The slight pause at the end of line 86 is like the interval of death, which the run-on at the end of the next line is able to cross effortlessly.

> Some good survivor with his flute would go, . . .
> And relax Pluto's brow,
> And make leap up with joy the beauteous head
> Of Proserpine, ("Thyrsis," ll. 83–88)

Heads and brows, the circumscribing or bounding elements, must be relaxed or breached. At first "head" (l. 87) seems to run counter to its meaning by being placed at the foot, not the head, of its line. But, buried at the foot of line 87, Proserpine's "beauteous head" "leap[s] up with joy" at the head of the next one. Brought to life in the classical myth, she is resurrected in the verse by Arnold's graceful run-on.

Coming in terminal position, and crossing the boundary between lines 114 and 115, the straddling phrase "far descried / High towered the spikes of purple orchises" helps Arnold both contract and open up his stanza. While the triple stresses are contracting the sound, the crossing of the line break expands the field of vision. As the voice slows down, the braking motion is enforced by the thinly odd assonance in "descried" and "High." A repeating vowel sound survives, even after its consonantal body has died.

Even the wake, or tiny swell of waves, left by the boat finds its counterpart in the "tiny swell" of Arnold's run-on.

> Where are the mowers, who, as the tiny swell
>   Of our boat passing heaved the river-grass,
>   Stood with suspended scythe to see us pass?
> ("Thyrsis," ll. 127–29)

Like their suspended scythe, left hanging in midline by heavy stresses and alliteration, the noun "mowers" and its relative pronoun "who" are left grammatically suspended, separated from the principal verb "Stood" by a line and a half of adverbial qualification.

At the end of line 156 Arnold uses a run-on to cross the last remaining boundary between himself and the tree.

> Quick! let me fly, and cross
> Into yon farther field!—'Tis done; and see, . . .
> Bare on its lonely ridge, the Tree, the Tree! ("Thyrsis," ll. 156–60)

Merely to say that he crosses into the farther field lacks a dimension of enactment, of "doing-by-saying," which operates in the placement of the verb "cross" at the very place where the eye must pass across the space between lines. The rite of passage involves a crossing of boundaries that is validated by the placing of "cross" at the end of one poetic line and the entry into the longed-for field at the head of the next one. "'Tis done," Arnold says, partly because his "crossing" has actually crossed the line break and partly because his seeing ahead is literally a peering forth across the dash and the grammatical space separating the rhyme word "see" from its completion three lines later in the long deferred "Tree."

Even when lines are strongly end-stopped or bound by punctuation, Arnold may make his sound an echo of the sense by other means. The heavenward ascent of Daphnis, for example, is made more miraculous, not by a run-on, but by an odd backing away motion of the word "brink" from the brink or edge of the poetic line:

> And heavenward from the fountain-brink he sprang,
>   And all the marvel of the golden skies. ("Thyrsis," ll. 189–90)

The phrase "fountain-brink" pivots on the hinge of its hyphen, looking two ways at once. Instead of falling off the edge of the line into an abyss, we find ourselves on the edge of heaven and "all the marvel of the golden skies." Similarly, by appearing as a boundary word, in strongly punctuated terminal position, the verb "bound" is able to dramatize opposite meanings simultaneously: "Thou too, O Thyrsis, on like quest wast bound" (l. 211). The emphasis on "bound" suggests adventure, voyage on the high seas. But the strong end-stopping also tolls like a knell: Arnold and his friend are time-bound as well as quest-bound. Thyrsis is destined to wander with Arnold only "for a little hour" (l. 212).

A Genre under Siege: Romantic Seer and Victorian Skeptic

Is Victorian pastoral elegy merely a foreseeable development of its Romantic counterpart? Or are its transformations so radical that the genre itself seems under siege? Answers may depend on how "Romantic" and "Victorian" are defined. If a Romantic, like a Marxist, is a latter-day Pelagian, an optimist who does not believe in the Fall of man, then Shelley's Romantic gesture of bringing the "one Spirit's plastic stress" down to earth, allowing it to sweep freely "through this dull dense world," is clearly at odds with Arnold's Victorian attempt to revive, even in the legend of the scholar-gipsy, a traditional center of moral and spiritual authority. Being "driven / Far from shore" in response to a beaconing star may be all very well for visionary geniuses like Shelley or Tennyson's Galahad in "The Holy Grail." But salvation for most Victorians will depend on work in their allotted field and service to humanity. At the heart of Arnold's attempt to revive traditional centers of authority, however, lies a negative agnostic moment of self-questioning and doubt, corresponding to the rise of Victorian agnostic theology. Doctrines of utility and self-making encourage Victorians to conduct what J. S. Mill in his essay *On Liberty* calls "experiments in living." No concept of utility is identified straight off, but only after a process of trial and error. In theory, utilitarian thought should serve such experiments well, for what happens in a process of trial and error is appealed to as a definition of what is; a preconception of what ought to be is not appealed to for an understanding of what actually occurs. As Mill's "experiments in living" allow his contemporaries to evolve their idea of the world from their experience of the world rather than the other way round, Victorian culture leaves behind its earliest authoritarian, and its later agnostic, phases, to enter a third and final phase of experiments in self-making.

Allied to the moral theology of the evangelicals and the legacy of the post-Kantian idealists, the teaching that we forge an identity for ourselves through moral vocation and work is reflected in Arnold's resolve in "Thyrsis" to become the architect, like Clough, of his own humanity and values. In substituting performative for descriptive speech, Arnold might simply seem to be reviving the Viconian, Romantic doctrine that each individual self is, by birth and by nature, an artist and creator, a lesser god, capable of fashioning new and better worlds. But the ease with which Shelley collapses the distinction between nature and grace, allowing Adonais to ascend to his star by appealing to the goodness of his god-like soul in protest against the dogma of original sin, suggests that in Romantic elegy nature is still largely responsive to human control. In Victorian elegy, by contrast, the external pageant of *mens* in nature, which God alone can understand because He is its author, seems to end in the terrifying absurdity of a world that slides suddenly away into a void, as in section 123 of *In Memoriam*. The more faithful a Victorian elegist like Arnold or Tennyson is to Vico's revolutionary idea that literature and history provide the privileged forms of knowing, *verum/factum*, the greater the gulf he creates between *mens* in nature and *mens* in human affairs.

Our brief comparison of "Adonais" and "Thyrsis" discloses five more specific differences between Romantic and Victorian elegy. Whereas Shelley's more consistent Platonism unifies his sensibility, conflicting philosophical impulses pull Arnold in opposite directions. Shelley, moreover, never doubts the intrinsic worth of Keats's "godlike mind" ("Adonais," l. 258) or his ability to celebrate it. Arnold, by contrast, is deeply critical of Clough: tortured at the center of his faith, he spends most of his elegy preparing for a ritual exercise of verbal power that Shelley blithely takes for granted. A third difference is the Romantic elegist's preference for the view from inside. He draws us into his elegy, making our breath conspire with the Spirit's "plastic stress" and the breathings of Urania. Arnold, on the other hand, excludes us from intimacy. He marks the limits of sympathetic trespass. A marginal figure and observer, looking on from outside, Arnold seldom allows his empathy with Thyrsis to deepen into sympathy. This last contrast brings us to a fourth difference. Though the stanzaic form of both elegists tries to adjudicate the rival claims of parts and wholes, Shelley is a monist, consistently subordinating the many to the One, whereas Arnold, like Tennyson in *In Memoriam* 47.6–7 ("Eternal form shall still divide / The eternal soul from all beside"), dreads absorption of the individual soul in a general soul. He has no desire to be part of the universal glue. However threatened Arnold may feel by the "world's multitudinousness," he is compelled to honor pluralism. Finally, as a descriptive poet, Arnold finds himself entombed in a grave of dead words, the legacy of a correspondence theory of truth. Though responsive to "the immortal chants of old" ("Thyrsis," l. 181), the Victorian elegist is a skeptic who fears that pastoral convention may also shackle him to a mummified mythology. Shelley, by contrast, believes that forces can be released by the pastoral elegist's words of power. He forges metaphorical identities that retain strong traces of a magical view of language. There is still alive in Shelley, as in Tennyson, "something of" what Dwight Culler calls "the older conception of language as a magical instrument, a means of incantation or ritual, which gave one power over reality or revealed its true nature. By this view words were proper names, containing the ontological secret of a thing" (1977, 4).

Both Arnold's wavering allegiance to the values of Cambridge Platonism and Shelley's more consistent Platonism can be studied in their verse forms. In Shelley's hands the Spenserian stanza becomes a war zone in which the Platonic One wages battle against the constraints of matter and celebrates in the concluding alexandrine its anticipated victory. The final release of the *c* rhyme (*ababbcbcc*) is celebrated in the hypermetric alexandrine, where it seems to boast of its victory over the *a* and *b* rhymes, just as "the white radiance of Eternity" boasts of its victory over the shattered "many-coloured glass" ("Adonais," ll. 462–63). In stanza 52 the One at first occupies a mere four-syllable unit, and six syllables are allotted to the changing many. But in the contest between Heaven and Earth, Heaven has begun to crowd out its adversary. Seven syllables—or six if we take "Heaven's" as monosyllabic—are devoted to the One's domain, while the remaining shadows of earth are given a mere four syllables: "The One remains, the many change and pass; / Heaven's light forever shines, Earth's shadows fly" ("Adonais," ll. 460–61). As spirit wages its Platonic war against matter, and the One combats the many, victory is predictable but never final. Because of Shelley's metrical dexterity, the sense of fulfilled expectation also seems the opposite of obvious.

Unlike the Romantic elegist, whose Platonic allegiances are seldom in doubt, Arnold veers in "Thyrsis" between the realism of a Cambridge Platonist like Joseph Glanvill, the scholar-gipsy's seventeenth-century chronicler, and the nominalism of Vico and Herder. Even Arnold's verse form becomes a playing field on which the ambitions of the Cambridge Platonist, in quest of some authoritative ground, the equivalent of a Platonic Idea or universal, is continually being challenged by the skepticism of a Viconian nominalist, who would locate the truth nearer home. In Arnold's stanza the hallmark of the Petrarchan sonnet—the quatrains' *abba* rhyme scheme—does not appear until the last four lines, where only half the octave is given. Arnold not only reverses the order of octave and sestet in a Petrarchan sonnet; he also reverses the pattern Keats uses in "Ode to a Nightingale." In Keats the Petrarchan sestet comes second, and the quatrain—in Keats's case Shakespearean rather than Petrarchan—comes first. Arnold recalls Romantic convention, but self-consciously inverts it. In seeming to stabilize the wayward, oracular impulse that is sanctioned in Keats by the irregularity of the Pindaric ode, Arnold's elegy accommodates two conflicting impulses. He shares the oracular poet's desire for some authoritative ground, and to that end he uses ancient pastoral convention and the ode's irregular line lengths to revive the mysteries of Cambridge Platonism. At the same time, he believes that to be accessible Victorian values must be fashioned through some version of Clough's religion of work; it is not enough to lose oneself, like Tennyson's Galahad, in pursuit of some elusive grail or Unknowable God. To this second end Arnold transplants the mysteries. Creating an authentic English form of pastoral out of homely, but possible more enduring materials, he writes of Platonism on very familiar Oxford soil. Though Glanvill is a Cambridge—not an Oxford—Platonist, whose scholar-gipsy will act only after he has something to teach, Arnold, like Clough, is committed to the Viconian doctrine that he will know only after he acts. Truth becomes a property of what the elegist himself can create out of common words and familiar themes.

A second difference between the Romantic and Victorian elegist is the reluctance of the latter to use ritualized words of praise. In "Adonais" Shelley does all he can to distance his own adverse view of Keats's early poetry from the criticism of the hostile reviewer who hastened Keats's death. Like the dream looking at the tear awakened in Keats by the dream itself ("Adonais," ll. 85–87), Keats is both a dead fellow poet and an introjected power, a region of Shelley's mind. Though Clough was Arnold's closest friend, no comparable appropriation of the dead man takes place in "Thyrsis." It is true that Arnold's refusal to force his praise of Clough early in the elegy makes his tribute at the end all the more moving. The appeal of a "fugitive and gracious light" not to be "bought and sold" on the markets of this world (ll. 201, 205) comes in no small part from Arnold's recognizing elsewhere the limits of an imperfect sympathy. But Arnold is far more diffident than Shelley. He is skeptical about his capacity to address his dead friend, and far more critical of Clough than Shelley is of Keats. The Victorian elegist spends most of his poem preparing for what his Romantic predecessor confidently assumes at the start: the mourner's power to praise the dead poet and address him as a living presence.

Implicit in the distinction I have just drawn is a third difference: Shelley gives the interior view, and Arnold the view from outside. As an alienated Victorian, Arnold gives an unforgettable sense of what it is to be an outsider, on the boundaries or margin. Whereas Arnold wants to exclude us from intimacies of feeling he once shared with Clough, Shelley can experience events from the perspective of even a Judas or Cain. Even in loading vituperative abuse upon Keats's destroyer, for example, Shelley finds it hard not to empathize. Sundered syntax conveys, not just the mourner's anguish, but also the desperate swoops and rush of the murderer's own feelings, as words are shredded to pieces in an agony of frustration:

> It felt, yet could escape, the magic tone
> Whose prelude held all envy, hate, and wrong,
> But what was howling in one breast alone,
> Silent with expectation of the song,
> Whose master's hand is cold, whose silver lyre unstrung.
> ("Adonais," ll. 320–24)

Until the grammatical sense is completed, it sounds as if Keats's music embraces, rather than suspends, "all envy, hate, and wrong," and that, as an exception to that disorder, only the "howling" in the murderer's "breast" is able to express the accents of genuine grief. Because "Silent" is sundered by an intervening line and a half from "held," the verb whose sense it reaches back to complete, the grammar, like the viper, is made to sound for a moment quite as "unstrung" as the dead poet's lyre.

Arnold has little of Shelley's "negative capability," except perhaps for domestic animals and pets. The Victorian elegist hopes that posterity will remember him as the owner of a pathetic, soul-fed little creature, with long "liquid, melancholy" eyes ("Geist's Grave," l. 13), who walked on all fours and who lived only four short years, one for each leg. Arnold is a poet who could love animals if not people. Even when he allows us to empathize with Clough's premature migrations, he refuses to soften toward Clough's impetuous impulses. Any sliding from empathy into sympathy is gently resisted. Dogs have one advantage over people: they will not argue back, the way Clough did with Arnold. And so the Victorian elegist can be closer in some ways to Geist and Kaiser than he can be to Clough or Wordsworth, or even his own father in "Rugby Chapel." Perhaps this is why the elegies on dogs are far warmer poems than the austere "Rugby Chapel" or even the reflectively solemn "Thyrsis," which are seldom so full of solicitude and good temper.

Arnold wants to be remembered, not as the elegist of Wordsworth, Clough, or Dr. Arnold, but as someone who built a grave for a dog. The concluding stanza of "Geist's Grave" is as close as Arnold comes to writing his own epitaph.

And stop before the stone, and say:

People who lived here long ago
Did by this stone, it seems, intend
To name for future times to know
The dachs-hound, Geist, their little friend.
("Geist's Grave," ll. 76–80)

The deaths of Arnold and his family are made more manageable by approaching them obliquely through the closing reflections of some future passer-by, in a recollection of the epitaph in Gray's *Elegy*. We remember, however, that three of Arnold's sons died early. Of the loss of his third son at the age of eighteen, an old friend, J. D. Coleridge, writes to his father: "I enclose you dear Matt's letter. . . . It is a most bitter and heavy blow. Forster told me he was terribly cut up by it, but that his behaviour was admirable. He had to be at an examination of pupil-teachers, and Mr. Forster found him there with his poor eyes full of tears, yet keeping order and doing his duty till he could be relieved" (quoted in Bush, 1971, 19). In the elegy for Geist nothing can quite mute the trauma of assimilating the dog's "grave upon the grass" to the graves of the Arnold family, "When [they] too," like their little dog, will be "mere clay" (ll. 74–75). Arnold can talk with less deception about his own impending death and the death of his sons by seeming to talk about something else. "There are those," as F. H. Bradley says, "who would not sit down among the angels, till they had recovered their dog" (1893, 451). But "Geist's Grave" is not just about a dog. When pathos starts to build and Geist becomes an almost epic figure, we are reminded by his broad brown paws, his scuffling on the stair, and the flapping of his ears, that, like Arnold and the lost Marguerite, or like Arnold and his dead sons, the dog and his master move in different spheres. In its pathos, waggish affection, and blend of both high seriousness and humor, "Geist's Grave" is one of Arnold's most charming, yet deeply felt, elegies.

A fourth difference between Romantic and Victorian elegy concerns the way each elegist tries to honor what is individual without allowing the whole to fall apart into fragmentation and separateness. Like his beloved Geist, Arnold is a Shelley on all fours, more in danger of being overwhelmed by the world's multitudinousness. More eager than Arnold to bring the parts of his elegy into ampler connection with the "One," Shelley allows no runovers between stanzas. The One controls the many, and the boundaries proclaiming the One's authority are strictly observed. "Thyrsis," by contrast, uses a longer ten-line stanza, whose boundaries Arnold feels free to cross (as we have seen earlier in this chapter), even while he respects the limits imposed by his ingenious adaptation of ode and sonnet forms.

It is not easy for a monist like Shelley to adjust the claims of the many and the One. There is always a danger that the Romantic elegist will retreat into a Platonic mist that God Himself would think twice before penetrating. "The burning fountain" in "Adonais," for example (l. 339), is a kind of nuclear furnace or volcano. If this furnace does not truly absorb the spirit, then the spirit changes but is not truly a portion of the eternal. If, on the other hand, the spirit is truly absorbed by the fountain, it becomes "unquenchably the same" (l. 341). But then in annihilating all sustaining difference, it also annihilates Keats. Though logic cannot quite resolve the dilemma, Shelley, like Tennyson, believes that "the very obscurity which veils revelation is itself a revelation" (Culler, 1977, 154). Moreover, Shelley provides at least a formal demonstration of how the parts and the whole might harmoniously relate. He grants each Spenserian stanza its own autonomy, but without allowing it to devour its parts too greedily by collapsing a chain of intricately linked sounds and rhymes.

In "Thyrsis," by contrast, Arnold sometimes dawdles with the painted shell of the universe, lingering fondly over the "blond meadow-sweet," the "darting swallows," and "light water-gnats" (ll. 124–25), even while deploying them in his *ubi sunt* formula. Unlike Shelley, he is even prepared to honor a wayward sound or half-forgotten impression, which he is likely to restore just when it seems to have dropped from mind. In stanza 13, for example, "shore" echoes "door," but at a distance of six lines. Like a dying echo of "door," "shore" falls off into silence at the end of its short, three-stress line (l. 126). Because Arnold's stanzas read like Petrarchan sonnets from which the octave is removed, we have the uneasy feeling that the rhymes and thoughts we hear should echo something that has gone before, something much more fleeting or subliminal than anything we hear in Shelley. The Romantic elegist is a self-confident visionary. His Victorian counterpart gives a much more tentative experience of déjà vu, of vision that eludes the memory and defies precise recall.

A final difference between Arnold and Shelley is the former's sense that classical elegy is not just a genre in transition; it is a genre under siege, whose very survival is at stake. How can its traditional language and ancient symbols hope to live again if the biblical beliefs and classical legends that nourished them have now become mere superannuated myths? Traditionally, a pastoral elegy expresses corporate grief, like a liturgy. But because Oxford has changed and Clough died abroad, there is really only one mourner in "Thyrsis": the solitary elegist himself. Mourners like Byron and Moore, who attend Keats's funeral in "Adonais," are displaced by an inventory of absent people who might, under different circumstances, have mourned Clough. Where is Sibylla, late keeper of the local inn (l. 4)? Where is the girl who unmoored their skiff (l. 121)? Where are the mowers (l. 127)? Just as the cyclical liturgical form of Keble's poem, *The Christian Year*, can be faintly intuited behind the aphoristic fragments of *In Memoriam*, which has more in common with Coleridge's *Aids to Reflection* or Julius Hare's *Guesses at Truth* than with "Lycidas" or "Adonais," so pastoral conventions survive in "Thyrsis," but in disguised forms. Arnold replaces the traditional floral tributes in "Lycidas" with native English flowers, with the bounty of musk carnations, "gold-dusted snapdragon," and "Sweet-William with his homely cottage-smell" (ll. 63–65). And these flowers in no sense adorn the dead friend's hearse, since Clough has died in Florence and has been buried abroad.

Shelley's agnostic essay "On a Future State" and Arnold's skeptical essays on religion identify an area of overlap between them. For Shelley God is beyond being and language, as Plato says, and "the deep truth is imageless" (*Prometheus Unbound*, II.iv.116). Arnold's agnosticism may have originated in the doctrine of learned ignorance advocated by his seventeenth-century hero, Joseph Glanvill. But Arnold is agnostic in a further sense than Shelley. In one of the reading lists found in his early diaries, Arnold makes mention of Victor Cousin's lectures on modern philosophy. As I have argued elsewhere, Victorian agnosticism can be said to begin with Sir William Hamilton's seminal review essay of Cousin's course of philosophy, published in the *Edinburgh Review* in October 1829. The sublime transcendence of the Hindu God apparently appealed to Arnold, who was already familiar with the grandeur of that concept from his study of Victor Cousin, from his knowledge of the theology of the *Bhagavad Gita*, and from an awareness of the affinities between the Vedantic apology for art and his own idea of disinterested objectivity. But the "incognisable" God of Kantian, agnostic thinkers like Hamilton and Mansel is also criticized by Arnold for being too Asiatic, too indistinguishable from the Brahm of Indian theology. Arnold tries to retain the venerable emotive meaning of mystery words like "God" and "immortality" while giving them a new descriptive meaning with some specific content in sense experience. In his prose writings Arnold keeps proclaiming the futility of metaphysics, and concludes that all transcendent religious speculation, as opposed to concrete moral and cultural inquiry, is meaningless.

In Romantic elegy essence precedes existence; in Victorian elegy the reverse is true. The change in models from Shelley to Arnold involves a change from a devolutionary to an evolutionary scheme. Theories of evolution and self-making prompt Victorian elegists as diverse as Arnold, Tennyson, and Swinburne to quicken truth in pursuit of the wider premise, the more inclusive synthesis. A value like utility is no longer impersonally conceived. It is reached through the evidence of one's own life—in a process of trial and error that is part of what Mill, in a well-known phrase to be taken quite literally, calls "experiments in living." Such experiments set the stage for the experiments in confessional elegy to be undertaken by Browning in *La Saisiaz* and Tennyson in *In Memoriam*, as I hope to show in the next chapter.

By contrast, Shelley's cosmos in "Adonais" is as hierarchical as Milton's. Despite its yearning for a developing world, in harmony with the Romantic poet's revolutionary temper, "Adonais" has a strangely medieval feel. The soul's Platonic essence, "the white radiance" of its "Eternity" ("Adonais," l. 463), *precedes* existence. Like Shelley's "dome of many-colored glass" (l. 462), life on earth "stains" the mind's transcendent consciousness, restricting it to Kant's two forms of space and time. According to William James, "Adonais" illustrates a "transmission" or "filtration" theory of immortality. Because Keats's brain keeps transmitting his experience to a "godlike mind" that exists before he is born and presumably outlasts his earthly life, there is no need for God to re-create Keats when he dies. His earthly consciousness is an interval of darkness between two eternities of light.

In striking contrast, Arnold is convinced that Clough creates his own immortality. If Clough possesses life after death, it is because of the inexhaustible energy of the new life he originates on this side of the grave. The key to Arnold's theory of immortality is the remarkable passage in *Culture and Anarchy* where he attacks Puritanism's merely mechanical use of the word "resurrection." "In nine cases out of ten where St. Paul thinks and speaks of resurrection," Arnold claims, he is referring "to a new life before the physical death of the body, and not after it" (5:183). Since we are all architects of our humanity and values, nobody's immortality can be guaranteed in advance. Moreover, the dead Clough is powerless to speak to Arnold until Arnold, in his search for Clough, has come, "within the limits of his present life, to a new life" himself. In emulating Clough's own self-making, Arnold substitutes for essentialist theology's "mechanical and remote conception of a resurrection hereafter" (5:183) St. Paul's own notion that life in the resurrection is already here, waiting to be recognized.

Like Nietzsche's God, Arnold's Thyrsis is not really dead; he is merely buried in a dead language. Until Arnold can substitute a new model, a new "taste in universes," as C. S. Lewis says (1964, 222), Clough is merely the casualty of the Puritan use of the word "resurrection" in a single mechanical sense that seems wholly to miss or change the "grand

Pauline idea" of a "living and near conception of a resurrection now" (5:183). Shelley's Romantic cosmology assumes, in Lewis's phrase, "that all perfect things precede all imperfect things." In Arnold's new Viconian world, however, "it is axiomatic that the starting point (*Entwicklungsgrund*) is always lower than what is developed" (Lewis, 1964, 222). Readers may have to play Orpheus to Eurydice: from a grave of dead words, they may be asked to raise up spirits, as the voice itself resurrects from marks on the printed page the ghosts of departed poets. Even in "Adonais," for example, the conservative Platonic model of Keats's frightened "angel soul" (l. 153), the mere "earthly guest" of its body, introduces a Gnostic split that is quite at odds with the radical, incarnational model of a Neoplatonic world-soul sweeping through nature. Just as Shelley, in the strangest, most beautiful stanzas of "Adonais," has to turn Keats from a noun into a verb, into an energy streaming through the verses like a comet's hair, so Arnold discovers that Clough, like the Dorian shepherds and vanished ploughboys, can be reclaimed from the grave of a discarded classical mythology only by the elegist's own ritual exercise of power. For a moment in stanza 12, after the poetry of the classical myths has become "the reality," as Arnold says in his Preface to Wordsworth, and skeptical "philosophy the illusion," the revival of a lost glory carries the elegist across the divide between sestet and quatrain. The strong run-ons extend to the penultimate line, where "gleam" and its rhyme word "team" seem to come from different planets. Though a ploughshare may gleam, this is Wordsworth's visionary gleam. And "team" reaches out to rhyme with a different part of speech, a verb, which is still awaiting grammatical completion in a direct object, the "orphans of the flowery prime" (l. 120). Though such feats of resurrection could be performed only by Arnold, we seem to hear behind them the voice of classical elegy itself. This we feel, even in an age of growing skepticism and doubt like the Victorian, is the kind of faith in the magical properties of words, and in an energy common to man and nature, which pastoral poetry exists to commemorate and preserve.

Such created realities as Clough's hortatory whisper, which is physically absent but spiritually present, preserve an openness of attitude that is foreign to the strong sense of closure in Shelley's elegy. When the "plastic stress" in "Adonais" empties into the world, in a Neoplatonic version of Paul's conception of *kenosis*, what dies for Shelley is the antithesis between a human subject and divine object. But so remote has God become for the agnostic Arnold that when he starts to search for an abstract formula that will give peace to his soul without insulting his intelligence, he finds God has become as fugitive and elusive as the notorious elm tree. Even the final whisper amid the heart-wearying roar is not a sound Arnold actually hears. Because the whisper is an illusion made real by a fiat of the poet's inner ear, his culminating hope must be inscribed in a tentative optative mood: "Let in thy voice a whisper often come," he prays diffidently ("Thyrsis," l. 135). Both Shelley and Arnold seem to understand God as a verb. But when the god-like soul of Adonais ascends with ease to its star, Shelley is using God as a "verb of simple asserted existence," whereas Arnold understands God as "a verb implying a process of accomplishing itself" (Frye, 1982, 17). Instead of closing anything off dogmatically, Arnold, in the spirit of many post-Romantic poets who pursue a goal that is always eluding them, is ready to believe and quest intransitively. Like Clough and the scholar-gipsy, the Victorian elegist "travels yet the loved hill-side" ("Thyrsis," l. 240), not in pursuit of something objective like Adonais's star, the elm tree, or even God conceived as a noun, but in an act of disinterested searching as such. "Thyrsis" is more than just an elegy for Clough. By introducing such extraneous deaths as the death of God and the death of the pastoral elegist's traditional exercise of verbal power, Arnold has also composed an elegy for elegy.

Models of Creation in Classical Elegy

Whereas "Lycidas" assumes that models of creation are established by God, "Adonais" locates these models in man's own imagination. Unless the imagination can recover what it has already projected, it becomes another Frankenstein, a slave to its own creations. In "Thyrsis," by contrast, Arnold's elegist must engender truth about a world, like Vico and Herder. He must project into the future a new model of creation, a mythology of concern that can take the place of a discarded classical or biblical mythology, what in "Stanzas from the Grande Chartreuse" he calls "a dead time's exploded dream" (l. 98).

These models of creation determine the form of elegiac contest each poet presents. Just as Milton's uncouth swain is trying to win his laurels by composing an elegy worthy of Lycidas, so we know that Milton himself was contributing his elegy to a volume of verse on the same subject: he is in contest with other elegists, including John Cleveland. Though Milton wants his life to be an *imitatio Christi*, he is also carrying on a contest with a corrupt clergy and with an apparently indifferent deity, who allows poets to die prematurely without fulfilling their promise. Presumably the two-handed engine will take the corrupt contestants out of play at the very moment they seem to be awarded the prize ("Lycidas," ll. 130–31). But because no one has satisfactorily explained the meaning of the two-handed engine, each reader has an acute sense of what it is to be outside or excluded, just as the sinners must have a terrible sense of being excluded from God. Mysteries of exclusion remind us that no one is ever permanently protected against the future, and that King's luck in finding the appropriate elegist in Milton is no guarantee that the uncouth swain will also be so lucky. The real subject of the elegy is the ever-present contest of faith, hope, and love, as they open, not just on the boundaries of death, but also on a larger horizon, toward surprise, where nothing is prescripted.

To receive a title like "The pilot of the Galilean Lake" (l. 109) is generally to be removed from the contest. A title is a sign that the contest is over, and that the titled person, in this case St. Peter, has won and should now command respect. But Christ's title in *Paradise Lost*, "By Merit more than Birthright Son of God" (3.309), subverts the logic of entitlement. If one is entitled by merit, one has continually to prove one's claim to the title by reentering the field of play. The power of a magician, of a greater Orpheus, whose "dear might" can tame the waves, is outward and dramaturgical, like any miracle or feat of magic. By contrast, the inner strength of the mourners—of Milton, the reader, and the uncouth swain—cannot be measured, because it opens on the future: it is expressed in an initiatory, not a closing act. The power of a miracle worker seeks to resolve all issues, bringing the past to an outcome. Strength, by contrast, is willing to remain in uncertainties. To the degree that King's own life, death, and afterlife have become a true *imitatio Christi*, he must be strong enough to relinquish immortality even after achieving it. He must become once more a merely finite guardian who may not be able to save all future voyagers from a watery grave, and who may not be as good to "all that wander in that perilous flood" as he would like. A strong mourner knows that if there were nothing beyond the grave, his motivation for living would disappear. He also knows that, if something were to survive death and he knew what it was, there would be no difference between this life and the next one. So Milton's swain, realizing that the mystery of death guarantees the liveliness of life, knows that none of the great puzzles is capable of decisive resolution.

Apotheosis never writes *finis* to a mourner's contest with death. Because such confidence in closure would be radically at odds with Keats's own adventurous pursuit of negative capability, Shelley does everything in his power to combat it. To keep the contest open he even appears to foresee his own death by drowning. In allowing his bark to be driven far from shore ("Adonais," ll. 488–89), Shelley continues to expose himself to risk. He is preparing *for* surprise and not *against* it.

Shelley ascribes to Adonais's "godlike mind" the same power that Milton reserves for Christ alone. But what exactly does a "godlike mind" confer on Adonais? Is it a continuing existence or a continuing recognition and recovery of the imaginative world he has projected?

Does he get an afterlife or an afterworld? Presumably he gets both in the end. And yet he gets the former *because of* the latter. Shelley keeps implying that what we call life is the mere "dream of life" (l. 344), and what we take to be solid is phantasmal; our so-called opponents are "Invulnerable nothings" (l. 348). But if "Death is the veil which those who live call life" (*Prometheus Unbound*, l. 113), it is not because each soul is antecedently and in essence imperishable. Shelley finds that death has lost its sting for him because, like Adonais, he is the fashioner of a humanized world in which each creative self is the true sovereign.

Arnold's task in "Thyrsis" is not to recover a model of creation established by God or other "godlike minds" but to project forward, moving toward the open, toward the horizon, toward surprise. By contrast, Daphnis's defeat in the reaping contest is an outcome Lityerses has plotted in advance. He does not foresee, however, that Hercules will move into his theater to set up a counterplay, inflicting death on Lityerses himself. When we play to win, like Lityerses in his contest with Daphnis, we try to terminate the play. The countertruth is that a contestant like Glanvill's scholar-gipsy may play best when he stops playing himself, allowing disciples like Arnold and Clough to carry on the quest in his name.

As a true apostle of culture, Arnold, like his Tyrian trader in "The Scholar-Gipsy," can subvert the power plays of the sciolists and "merry Grecian coaster" ("The Scholar-Gipsy," l. 237) by playing fast and loose with their boundaries. Committed, not to power politics, but to a free play of the mind for its own sake, Arnold is always moving toward the horizon where the tree-crowned hill can be glimpsed. But since the elm tree, like the gracious light, encloses no field, he can never reach the tree. Nor can he and Clough ever finish their quest. Like other mysteries, the elm tree eludes Arnold because it is not an ordinary object of knowledge. Until a quest for the tree and what it stands for has liberated Arnold, the tree itself cannot be seen.

Unlike a boundary, a horizon is not a finite line. Like the untraveled world glimpsed through the arch of Tennyson's Ulysses, whose margin fades for ever and for ever as we move, a horizon always shifts with the observer's changing point of view. Because Arnold wants to find a vision that promises still more vision, he prefers to wander in the wilderness like the children of Israel rather than arrive at the Promised Land itself. Living with horizons rather than boundaries, Arnold is content to be homeless.

To look is a territorial activity. Only when driven out of one territory by the Oxford hunters can the elegist begin to see inclusively instead of viewing one thing after another inside a bounded space or field of consciousness. Territorial viewing assumes that if one looks inclusively enough within a bounded space, in time everything can be seen. But to pass from mere looking to seeing, it may be necessary to substitute horizons for boundaries, and to give up territorial viewing altogether. The quantum leap required is like moving from two to three dimensions.

The only words to truly touch anyone in "Thyrsis" are the italicized words in the coda. We are touched when, like a spark from heaven or a providential surprise, the whisper that is heard amid all the "heart-wearying roar" catches us offguard. As a true storyteller like Glanvill, Arnold does not really know the outcome of Clough's or the gipsy's story. All he can accurately say of Clough is that he went forth and sought the light, then died. That is all Arnold or any storyteller can say. The exegesis or commentary belongs to a different genre. So, too, does the unspoken thought that, if Arnold can complete their abandoned quest, the dead will have something to learn from the living as well as the other way round. But until Arnold writes the elegy he cannot even say what "the fugitive and gracious light" (l. 201) means. For the "light" is not an emblem but a sign, and a sign depends for its meaning on the discoveries of questers who spend their lives in its pursuit.

The greater the story a poet has to tell the greater the desire to make the poet's own life a retelling of it. Arnold does not seem to have gone out searching for the story of the gipsy, the way the gipsy goes out in quest of some elusive truth. The story seems to have found Arnold, just as the stories of Christ and Orpheus seem to have found Milton in "Lycidas." Arnold and Milton do not understand the stories and myths in terms of their own experience; they understand their own experience in terms of the story.

At stake in "Thyrsis" is, not just the future of religion or society, but of literature itself. Milton and Shelley speak words of great creative power. But these words are also grounded in a world that is already full of responsive signs. When we come to Arnold, the performative paradox of a word that is simultaneously grounded and ungrounded has ceased to apply. Arnold must create his own signs and words of power. No ground exists until he wills it into being. Arnold's real task in the elegy is not to find the elm tree but to transform it and other objects into signs that will validate his master texts. These include elegies by Theocritus and Moschus, his own poem "The Scholar-Gipsy," and especially Glanvill's book, *The Vanity of Dogmatizing*, which Arnold seems eager to propagate, as if he were a one-man Gideon Society dispensing bibles to the unconverted. Unfortunately, the light that fades from the sky in "Thyrsis" is no longer a sign of that "intellectual fire and spiritual enthusiasm" that, in the words of one historian, "brought the Platonic light to Britain" (Turner, 1981, 321). Nor is it a mark of the Hellenic light, the light of reason, which Arnold extols in *Culture and Anarchy*. The fugitive and gracious light, shy to illumine, must be consigned to the same category as a chimera, lodged in the yellow pages of Glanvill's fiction.

The status of literary fictions is a continuing puzzle, extending well beyond the boundaries of the elegy itself. Arnold would like to believe that, in their lonely quest for the light, he and Thyrsis have both become signs: like Don Quixote and the scholar-gipsy, they are books in flesh and blood. But if they are characters who have stepped out of literature, they are characters wandering through a world that ceases to recognize them. The great circle of similitude is broken, and Arnold seems banished to a world where pastoral elegy is increasingly difficult to write, because the postulates of knowing are different. The words in "Thyrsis" no longer represent a world outside the poem. They represent instead the words inside an earlier poem, "The Scholar-Gipsy." Because the scholar owes his reality to Arnold's and Glanvill's language, he resides entirely in the power of words to represent, not a world outside literature, but only a relation between themselves and other words.

Dominating the classical elegist's highly formalized drama of mourning are four figures of similitude. Foucault identifies these figures as adjacencies of convenience (proximities of space and time), echoes of emulation, linkages of analogy, and the sustaining power of sympathy. He calls the similitudes *convenientia, aemulatio, analogy*, and *sympathy*, respectively (Foucault, 1973, 25). Though eroded by skepticism, the four similitudes of classical elegy survive in Arnold's "Thyrsis." *Convenientia* is still sought in the proximity of objects: carefully positioned prepositions ("*Past* the high wood," "The hill *behind* whose ridge"—ll. 12–13, my emphasis) connect the track by the farm with the hill, ridge, and tree. But the "lone, sky-pointing tree" (l. 174) is now no longer part of the web of correspondences that allows blushing roses to communicate with the goddess Proserpine (l. 96), and plants with people, as in classical mythology. *Aemulatio*, Foucault's second figure of similitude, functions as a form of resemblance freed from time and place. The hero whom Arnold and Thyrsis both try to emulate is Glanvill's scholar-gipsy. Keble's Tractarian typology is to his godson, Arnold, what Cambridge Platonism was to Glanvill. Though both know that figural readings can draw distant worlds together, the forces of attraction are weaker and more volatile in Arnold's world, where types and antitypes are likely to reverse polarity at any moment. Is Clough a Victorian scholar-gipsy, or the gipsy a seventeenth-century Clough? Is Arnold Clough's mentor, or Clough Arnold's? Standing at the center of such analogies, which form the third similitude in

"Thyrsis," is the elegist himself, the new mythmaker, upon whom there begin to converge unstable resemblances between his own loneliness and the solitude of the elm, between the scholar-gipsy's shyness and the shyness of a light that is slow to illumine.

The power of sympathy, classical elegy's fourth similitude, is greatly curtailed in "Thyrsis." If sympathy had freer play, it might completely assimilate Clough to Arnold, who is always in danger of making Clough over in his own image. So the power of sympathy is counter-balanced—indeed, some might say overbalanced—by antipathy. The more closely Arnold approaches the tree and its light, the more Clough retreats from them, as if the two friends were negative electrical charges, each repelled by the other. This drama of attraction and repulsion is even acted out in Arnold's verse form: the enclosing *a* rhymes seem to hold the included *bcbc* rhymes together, while driving each other apart. At its center, each stanza seems to collapse, to fall in upon itself, in the truncated trimeter of the sixth line. But then it opens out again, held together at the center of its last four lines by the included couplet. All the proximities of wood, tree, and ridge in "Thyrsis," all the echoes of emulation between the scholar-gipsy and his Victorian disciples, all the linkages of analogy between Daphnis and Thyrsis, between Glanvill's hero and Arnold, presuppose, like the stanzas themselves, an interplay of sympathy and antipathy, attraction and repulsion, which is endlessly drawing things together and driving them apart.

Whereas Milton's centers of authority are created by God, and Shelley's are projected from god-like human minds, the center of authority that Arnold seeks is still to be created. Its light is invisible and unperceived. Its emblem, the single elm tree, waits in silence for an observer initiated in its mysteries. Though the object of Arnold's divination is itself divine, most of his contemporaries, inheriting a descriptive theory of knowledge based on truth by correspondence, disavow his quest, because they believe that a sign can be constituted only by an act of sense perception: if the light cannot be seen, it does not exist. They have no tolerance for the performative paradox that the fugitive and gracious light is both a light Arnold kindles and a light that antecedently exists as an ultimate goal or ground.

Classical elegy assumes that, even in moving from ignorance to knowledge, a speech act that is grounded in imitative magic can be both performative and descriptive. The pastoral elegist has power to "invent" in both senses of that verb: he creates and discovers truth simultaneously. As a Cambridge Platonist, Joseph Glanvill still grounds his words for God in an unknowable goal or end that continues to function as an object of disinterested inquiry. Arnold's problem is that,

when his words are grounded, like Glanvill's, they become thin and attenuated. When they become concrete and metaphorical, like Vico's or
Herder's, they cease to be grounded. An authoritative, grounded language is too impoverished to appeal. And an ungrounded language,
fully performative and Viconian, lacks the authority of Augustine's
City of God, which Arnold envisages at the end of "Rugby Chapel" as
a disinterested alternative to any merely partisan consensus about what
qualifies as a useful fiction. Unlike the reductive knowledge of the sciolists, the light of Hellenism in *Culture and Anarchy* does not dispel a
mystery but reveals it. When that light eludes the elegist's grasp in
"Thyrsis," we reach the end of a poetic tradition. Classical elegy is
under siege in Arnold. Later it becomes impossible to write, because
knowledge has lost its ancient Greek affinity with divination.

2 ❧ The Paradox of Ends: The Circuitous Return in Confessional Elegy

In testaments of grief like Donne's *Anniversaries* and *In Memoriam*, where mourning takes the shape of an Augustinian confession, the elegist lives his life backwards. In an anomalous but real sense, the end of each elegy precedes its beginning. Hegel puts the paradox of ends this way: the journey is "a circle that returns into itself, that presupposes its beginning, and reaches its beginning only in its end. . . . The road [*Weg*] to *Wissenschaft* is itself already *Wissenschaft*" (Hegel, 1967, 144, 801; Abrams, 1971, 235). In evoking his life explicitly as the present recollection of the past, the mourner as he was is co-present with the elegist as he is. The logic of such elegies is the logic of confessional narrative: "I am I, but I was not always so." Though Tennyson has ceased to believe it, he says at the beginning of *In Memoriam* that he once "held it truth . . . That men may rise on stepping stones / Of their dead selves to higher things: (1. 1, 3–4). Expressing grief allays it; but before the elegy begins, the grieving "I" must first be converted from a mourner into the poet whose story we are about to hear. Even in *In Memoriam*, where the protracted and piecemeal composition means that the author of section 1, of section 50, and many others is not yet the person he will become, the very act of writing such lyrics has already converted the mourner into an elegist. We are waiting to see how that elegist will develop into the author of the Prologue, who is clearly the person the mourner has become.

All elegists are mourners, but not all mourners are elegists. The making of an elegist requires a mourner to perform "the work of mourning." It invites a critic to explore "how an elegist's language emerges from, and reacts upon, an originating sense of loss." As Peter Sacks has argued, "each elegy is to be regarded, therefore, as a *work*, both in the commonly accepted meaning of a product and in the more dynamic sense of the working through of an impulse or experience— the sense that underlies Freud's phrase 'the work of mourning' " (1985,

1). Sacks's theory of "the work of mourning" produces powerfully conceptual readings of many elegies. But I have two objections to it. An elegy may be a good work of art but a flawed work of mourning, and vice versa. Because the two meanings of "work," the psychological and the aesthetic, are sometimes at odds, I shall argue in chapter 5 that grief therapy is a dangerous basis for a theory of elegy. I have a second, more qualified objection. In a classical elegy like "Lycidas" the work of mourning may be so concentrated and prescripted that we have little leisure to observe it. The procession of mourners, the questioning of nature, the floral tributes, the movement toward apotheosis, the return to the world with fears allayed and faith renewed, all allow the classical elegist to orchestrate a rich repertoire of dramatic personae and actions. But the elegist may be in such secure control of his repertoire that the work of mourning is empty and pro forma. Only in a longer confessional elegy, where lyric anxiety threatens to delay consolation and even thwart catharsis altogether, and where the outcome seems more at risk, is it possible to study in slow motion that gradual "working through of an impulse or experience" that converts a mourner into an elegist.

In Memoriam's Prologue is an unmistakable sign that, like Dante's pilgrim in *The Divine Comedy*, the mourner has returned from his elegiac ordeal to tell his story. Even the first words of T. S. Eliot's "East Coker"—"In my beginning is my end"—let us know that the speaker's story will have a reassuring end. He has *made* it to the end, and that allows events "which in real or imagined History move in a *strait* Line" to "assume to [his] Understanding a *circular* motion—the snake with its Tail in its Mouth" (Coleridge, quoted in Abrams, 1971, 141). The paradox of ends raises three difficulties, however. Unless the mourner has already reached his goal, it is difficult to see how he can ever get started. Moreover, if the elegist's journey is necessarily circuitous, it may be a mere detour around a roadblock, a tmesis or separating out of two points that ought to coincide. Finally, the paradox of an end implicit in its beginning threatens to reduce the elegist's discovery to a form of circular reasoning or tautology. Only by internalizing truth and appropriating ideologies as part of his own experience, can the confessional elegist use his circuitous returns to create a "sense of an ending" that neither falsifies his moments of crisis nor reduces his discoveries to analytical propositions that merely repeat in the predicate what is already contained in the subject.

Hamlet is a play that achieves as much lyric anxiety as tragic catharsis; and "Lycidas," like most classical elegies, is a lyric that achieves as much tragic catharsis as lyric power. For the catharsis of classical elegy the elegiac anatomies of Donne's two *Anniversaries* and the elegiac testaments of the *Pearl* poet and Tennyson's *In Memoriam*, which is in some ways the last medieval and first modern elegy, substitute the comfort of a theological or moral consolation. The greatest of the English medieval elegies, *Pearl*, combines the theological explanations of Augustine's *Confessions* with the absorption and ecstasy of a dream. Its consolations are to the catharsis of "Lycidas" what intellect is to emotion: it delivers the mourner's grief, which is wayward and unstable, over to the intellect of a tutor or instructor, who stabilizes.

The view that elegy must be a proper object of religious contemplation brings us from pastoral to medieval forms. In theologizing death, the *Pearl* poet is the first to acknowledge that only God or the Holy Spirit can determine the aesthetic forms best able to channel divine power. Hence elegy may be magical in its origins but not magical in its poetic nature. To have sanctity like the Cross is to be given a head start. But there are other objects, like the mourner's "pearl of great price," that only the elegist can make the bearer of power. The pragmatic end of ensnaring the mysterious higher force leaves the *Pearl* poet free to determine the confessional shape of his elegy, however constrained he may feel as a result of his daughter's death. The elegy produced becomes a proper object of religious contemplation but also a work of deep expressive power.

"In my end is my beginning": The Making of an Elegist

Logically, an elegy like *Pearl* moves toward its own origin. Just as the last link in the poem's concatenating chain, the word "pay" (l. 1212), reaches back to attach itself to the use of "paye" in line 1, so there is an important sense in which the elegy's end is also its beginning. Before he can tell the story of his grief and consolation, the speaker's theological conversion must allow his identities as a mourner and an elegist, as a grieving father and a consoled poet, to converge. Only then can he exchange his identity as a bereft father for his new identity as a poet.

In any confessional elegy the self that was, the self as the joyless jeweler or bereft father, must be integrated into the new self, the self that is, just as the movement forward in time must integrate the end of the elegy in its new beginning. Such is the logic of typological readings of Scripture, where Christ is both the fulfillment of a promise and an origin: "In the beginning was the Word." In elegies featuring weak mourners, the process is aborted: there is no death of the old self, and so the self that *is* remains the self that *was*, a self incapable of writing the story of its own regeneration.

The mourner's progress in *Pearl* is the growth in faith and understanding of an initially wayward pilgrim, torn between a mourner's theology of hope and a personal confession of incomprehension and despair. Like the elaborately linked chain words, which face two ways at once, each advance in the mourner's theological understanding is also a partial retreat. As we turn on the repeating rhyme in the eighth and ninth lines of each stanza, we tremble for a moment on a brink. Poised between joyful remembrance and the dread of loss to come, we can either look back or forward like the rhymes. Such, too, is the precarious balance of the mourner's psyche. Will he falter? Or will he come to welcome as kindred royalty the Prince who has stolen the pearl to enrich his treasury? Rivalry should no more exist between the mourner and Christ than between different persons of the Trinity.

Pearl's theology of reserve tries to honor Augustine's injunction to see through a glass darkly, *per aenigmate*. The headstrong father wants to see face to face: he hopes to dive into the river and be instantly reunited with his daughter. But it is hard to be rash and impulsive—"in a mad porpose" (l. 267), as the daughter says—if one is composing in the demanding alliterative verse perfected by the mourner. His desire for quick election and his sudden gusts of feeling make the firm control of the difficult rhyme scheme, refrains, and linking sounds, like the constraints of a strict theology of reserve, all the more imperative.

If the elegy were less riddling, its grievous reticence would be less heartbreaking. When the loss of the child becomes too painful to bear, the father puns on words like "spot," which help activate the mind and subdue his feelings. Even when death intrudes into the "spote" or place of purity, "wythouten spot" (ll. 12–13), the rhymes seem to conceal the change. By continuing the same sound pattern, the chiming of "synglere" and "erbere" (ll. 8, 9) half conceals the lines' shocking disparity in sense. By punning on "forser" (l. 263), which could mean either coffin or jewel box, the daughter later pokes fun at her father. As a connoisseur of gems, he should have recognized a jewel box when he saw one. Though the precision in logic justifies a fine discrimination of tones, it is no wonder the riddle has sometimes been misread. It is almost as though the mourner wants to misread it himself.

The theological debate at the center of the elegy functions as a kind of generalized tmesis, preventing any premature convergence of the father and his daughter. Like Hopkins' mourner in *The Wreck of the Deutschland*, the father cannot bless God until he understands Him better. Love of God must wait upon a fuller knowledge of God. But the daughter reminds her father that to see only with the outward eye of sense is incompatible with faith, which must hazard and venture greatly if great rewards are to be won. Each plays a game of verbal tennis with the phrase, "joyleȝ juelere" (l. 252), bandying it back and forth, and often returning it with a spin. The "joyleȝ juelere" would be less joyless, the daughter chides, if he were more gentle, better versed in the ways of heaven's courtesy. Even when the pace picks up, and the ball passes swiftly from one side of the net to the other, ill will is held in check by the intricate word links and by the daughter's efforts to tutor the mourner in theological mysteries. In acquiring the identity of a precocious but wrongheaded pupil, heretical in his impulses, the father has to be instructed in the theological distinction between righteousness and innocence, in the doctrine of unequal ranks and equal rewards, and in the difference between the graceful courtier and the gracious God of Christianity.

As the autobiography of a mourner, *Pearl* uses its backward motion to advance simultaneously to a climax of conversion. A forward motion that is at the same time recapitulatory is best described as a spiral. The verse form in *Pearl* might be thought to begin and end arbitrarily like Dante's *terza rimas* in *The Divine Comedy* (*Aba, Bcb, Cdc* . . .), where the *A* and the last *Z* rhymes appear only twice. Instead of formally concluding in the last stanza, however, *Pearl* rounds back, as we have seen, to its beginning by repeating the link word "pay." The linear form turns out to be circular, a recapitulation in disguise. It traces out spatially the same pattern that the drama of death, conversion, and consolation presents temporally, and which biblical theology may duplicate in its own drama of death and resurrection.

In dramatic monologues the speaker at the end is also the same person who speaks at the beginning. Withheld or aborted conversion is the genius of the genre. But in an elegiac confession like *Pearl* or *In Memoriam* the author at the beginning is also the person the mourner has *become*. The author and the persona, the elegist and the mourner, are the same only because beginning and end coincide. The successful elegist can say: I am what I am, but I was not always so. The speaker in a monologue can make the first statement, but not the second.

Though the autobiography of a mourner, like any autobiography, demands conversion, it might equally well be said that the nature of mourning itself gives rise in some elegies to the autobiographical form. Because the movement forward in time culminates in a conversion, and conversion implies the destruction of a previous self, such destruction repeats the radical breaking up that takes place at death. Will the breakup of the old self lead to a breakdown or a breakthrough? Though the mourner wakes up on the same grave mound where he fell asleep, and though his visionary journey seems to possess in retrospect only the shimmering mystery of a mirage, he has, in fact, come a long way. His mind is no longer filled with the horror of decay. Rejoicing instead in the glorious destiny of his lost pearl, the mourner now addresses his former rival, Christ, as his best friend. He even accepts the loss of his daughter in the spirit of resignation every strong mourner hopes to attain. As a pilgrim in understanding, the mourner has also learned to discipline his affections, which are too wayward and rebellious. The large and encompassing vista of *Pearl*'s last retrospect represents a breakthrough because it dramatizes a breakup, not between the mourner and the pearl, but between his former querulous self and his new self as an accepting mourner. Though all elegists are mourners, not all mourners qualify, like the *Pearl* poet, as successful elegists. Since the father is ready at the end to record his vision, *Pearl* is partly the story of the making of an elegist, partly a story of how the elegy itself comes to be written.

The Theology of Ends: Anatomy and Confession

Donne's anatomy of loss in his two *Anniversaries* would be unintelligible to the *Pearl* poet. As C. S. Lewis says, a medieval elegist would not have understood "the thesis—in cold prose it is mere raving—that the death of Elizabeth Drury was a more or less cosmic catastrophe" (1964, 208). Beneath the differences, however, lie many similarities, for both poets believe in a "theology of ends," a phrase whose meaning hinges on a pun. The final cause or purpose of life, its teleological end, is also its end in a literal sense. The termination of life and the aim of life are one. This is because each end is also a new beginning, disclosing at the center of each life, and at the center of history itself, a superintending pattern or design. The teleology that gives retrospective form and meaning to the raw data of experience in *Pearl* and *The Second Anniversary* is also the same paradox of ends, the same "firmness" at the center, which makes the lover's "circle just" in Donne's "A Valediction Forbidding Mourning" (l. 35), allowing the speaker to end where he began. In a theology of ends, as in a Platonic theory of knowledge as anamnesis, the normal relation of cause and effect is reversed. At the end of *The Second Anniversary*, Donne is to Elizabeth what John the Baptist is to Christ. The type is related to its antitype, not as cause to effect, but as effect to cause. In rounding back to the genesis of all things, to a Proclamation that has been working secretly in the elegist and that can use him as its trumpet in the final line, Donne shows that if the antitypes did not exist in Christ and Elizabeth, then there would *be* no types in himself or John the Baptist. By looking back from the vantage point of the second poem, the elegist can discern the same silent operations of God's plan that Augustine and the *Pearl* poet were able to see in the random events of an unregenerate life.

Though Donne shares a medieval sense of the mystery of death and decay, his words in *The First Anniversary* no longer bear evidence of occult power. Instead, they anatomize the sickness of a world from which the pastoral elegist's quasi-magical force has ebbed away. Donne first uses the word "anatomy" in its strict medical sense. He performs a kind of autopsy, dissecting Elizabeth's bodily and spiritual parts. But he also uses "anatomy" in the sense Robert Burton and Northrop Frye deploy it: his "anatomy" of decay is an exhaustive treatment of a single topic. What has decayed is nothing less than the medieval and early Renaissance faith in a sovereign power installed behind the world. We might say that Donne's metaphysical conceits are to a symbol like the pearl what his anatomy of loss, with its patient induction of instances, is to the figures of similitude in a pastoral elegy like "Lycidas." Though fictions of lost coherence dominate *The First Anniversary*, the chimera of a star's influence being imprisoned in an herb, charm, or tree (ll. 393–94) is now recognized as a chimera. "The art is lost, and correspondence too" (l. 396). The anatomist's simple comparison by standard units of measurement reveals that life is shorter than in the age of Methuselah. Though Donne deplores the new philosophy's inductive methods, he uses its most important tools—measurement and spatial arrangement—to anatomize and perhaps even hasten the decay he laments—the decay of teleology, the theology of ends.

But Donne's *Second Anniversary* reveals that teleology is still alive and well. Though the methods of judgment and analysis that abound in *The First Anniversary* are not abandoned, each trope drawn from geometry or physiology presupposes a logically ordered sequence from unstable ellipsis to stable cube, to stabler Elizabeth; or from angular rectangle to smooth circle, to even smoother prototype (ll. 141–42). Because each space in the continuum must be occupied, since "all must full or not coherent be," as Pope will say in *An Essay on Man* (I, 44), the ordered arrangement of the vertebrae of the spinal column or the celestial bodies threaded together on the string of Elizabeth's soul substitutes for action at a distance a complete sequential chain. The image is serial rather than circular. But it is teleological and one-directional, like an arrow. And vestiges of a circular return survive in the spacing out of widely separated terms. Like pseudo-Dionysius in his *Celestial Hierarchies*, Donne prefers the longest possible chain of intermediaries. As C. S. Lewis says, "the Divine splendor . . . comes to us filtered, as it were, through the Hierarchies. . . . Devolution or delegation, a finely graded descent of power and goodness, is the universal principle" (Lewis, 1964, 73).

Convinced that we are still deceived by false similitudes, Donne attempts a Baconean critique of resemblance.

> When wilt thou shake off this Pedantery,
> Of being taught by sense, and Fantasy:

> Thou look'st through spectacles; small things seeme great,
> Below; but up unto the watch-towre get,
> And see all things despoyld of fallacies:
> (*The Second Anniversary,* ll. 291–95)

By being prisoners of pedantry, we allow the idols of our tribe to produce spontaneous fictions. To rid ourselves of our idols we must ascend to a vantage point from which it becomes possible to see that, like a circle that ends where it begins, a truly representative sign must double back on itself. It must represent its own representative function as well as the world it is too often presumed to represent transparently.

Donne's best metaphor for this duplicating function is the line that, in passing once through the center of a circle, also touches the circumference at two points.

> Know that all lines which circles doe containe,
> For once that they the center touch, do touch
> Twice the circumference; and be thou such.
> (*The Second Anniversary,* ll. 436–38)

It is just as impossible to dissociate the centrifugal force of *The First Anniversary*'s anatomy from the centripetal pull of a theology of ends in Donne's *Second Anniversary* as it is to dissociate the two points of intersection on a circle's circumference from the point at the center through which each line must pass. The near chiasmus ("center," "touch," "touch," "circumference") also allows Donne to *use* as well as *mention* the idea of touching: with the sundering of the grammatical subject, "all lines," from its principal verb "do touch," two predicates do actually touch at the center.

Each line inside the circle passes through the middle. Focusing truth at one discontinuous point or center, like an aphorism, it honors the teleological principle of a superintending end or final cause. But in intersecting the circumference at two opposite points, each line also represents the difficult feat of translating into sequence truths that come to the seer discontinuously. Donne can use the double intersection to show that, because God's mysteries are withheld from prophets who try too hard to turn discontinuous vision into sequence, they are never fully knowable. Every attempt to wrestle with the necessary angel of continuity denies the unnameable essence of what the seer tries to name aphoristically, in isolated oracles or visions.

To see God face to face is not just to see an object; it is also to observe the knowing principle, the power that lets us know that we know. We not only see God; we also see what lets us see, the enabling medium of light—the means of seeing itself.

> Onely who have enjoyed
> The sight of God, in fulnesse, can thinke it;
> For it is both the object, and the wit.
> (*The Second Anniversary*, ll. 440–42)

Similarly, a sign that represents an object should also represent its own contribution to the act of representing: How far does it refine or impair our capacity to know?

One of Donne's best critics, Louis L. Martz, complains that *The First Anniversary* has no unifying focus, because Elizabeth Drury's death has "nothing to do with the sense of decay in the poem" (1962, 158). It seems to me, however, that if Elizabeth's death is not the efficient cause of the world's decline, but merely one more symptom of it, this absence of connection is not the "central inconsistency" that Martz perceives (158) but rather an "illustrative failure." It is a striking instance of ruin, of a world crumbled all "in pieces, all coherence gone" (*The First Anniversary*, l. 213). Though Donne may be guilty of a fallacy of imitative form, in an anatomy of decay one would not expect "the joints between sections and subsections" to be seamless. Nor would one expect "the parts" to "fuse" together "into an imaginative organism" (Martz, 1962, 161). By contrast, in *The Second Anniversary*, Donne puts teleology to the test. In replacing anatomy with confession, or what Martz calls the traditional "self-address of religious meditation" (165), Donne asks how possible it is for anyone who has attained maturity to resemble the emblem books of virtue. Like the scholar-gipsy in Arnold's "Thyrsis," Elizabeth Drury in *The Second Anniversary* has already become a legend. She is an emblem that seems just to have escaped from a treatise by Plato or a tract by a Cambridge Platonist like Glanvill: she is called a "worthiest booke" (l. 320), and the progress of her soul is praised as a Platonic "patterne" or type (l. 524). As in the "Funerall Elegie," the poet challenges future generations to emulate Elizabeth's virtue. It is not enough that the book with blank pages, still to be inscribed with virtuous examples, should represent a story that has ended ("A Funerall Elegie," ll. 99–102). As a still unfinished chronicle, it must also represent its typological function: its capacity to complete its meaning in the lives of future readers.

When taken together, Donne's two *Anniversaries* avoid both idolatry and skepticism. Using analysis and inductive sampling to combat the presumption of any prophet who tries to substitute his own word for God's Word (*The Second Anniversary*, ll. 511–12), Donne also avoids skepticism by using his theology of types to focus, limit, and define. He minimizes neither the sense of the limitless nor our sense of the comforting limitation afforded by an emblem book or typological code, both survivors of older, more teleological habits of language and knowing.

> Thou are the Proclamation; and I ame
> The Trumpet, at whose voice the people came.
> (*The Second Anniversary*, ll. 527–28)

In making God both the represented Word and the Word that represents, Donne demotes Elizabeth to a mere sign of the Word, and Donne himself is assigned the even lesser function of being a mere trumpeter or herald. Though the elegist's words are at least twice removed from their authenticating source, their continuum implies progressive acts of knowing. Because it ascends from lower to higher representations of the Word, Donne's theology of ends repeats its beginning on a higher plane: it traces an ascending circle or spiral.

From Augustine to Tennyson: Progress by Reversion

Behind both Donne's *Anniversaries* and Tennyson's *In Memoriam* it is possible to see traces of the great precursor text of Augustine, the confessional form that Donne and Tennyson both appropriate and rewrite. But as the venerable similitudes of the pastoral elegist yield to the cold intelligence of Donne's dissection of decay in the two *Anniversaries*, we can watch the older mythological space begin to separate from the scientific space of the new astronomy. Donne never quite recovers from the post-Copernican realization that, in Northrop Frye's phrase, "such words as 'sunrise' and 'sunset,' though metaphorically efficient, had become 'only' metaphors, and that, so far as they were descriptive, what they described was illusory." And Tennyson never quite recovers from a Darwinian awareness "that divine creation, as generally conceived, was an illusion projected from the evolutionary operations within nature" (1982, 14). As the confession of a mourner, *In Memoriam* differs from both Augustine's *Confessions* and Donne's *Anniversaries* in another respect. The speaker in a confession usually takes two steps forward for every one step backward; his progress by reversion is designed to secure the proper balance of closure and delay. *In Memoriam* reverses this formula: for every one step forward the elegist inches two steps backward. When progress is retarded, the mourner turns into a victim of melancholia and depression. Nothing has quite prepared Tennyson for the disappearance of an important part of his inner world. Its abrupt termination is like the death of God, an outcome no one could have predicted or foreseen.

Since *In Memoriam* has as much in common with Augustine's *Confessions* as it has with "Lycidas," a brief consideration of some of the confession's defining features should help clarify the poem. Just as

Augustine and Bunyan (in *Grace Abounding*) use biblical situations to order their present experience, and just as Dante uses the history of Israel as a figure of his own pilgrimage in *The Divine Comedy*, so Tennyson keeps referring his personal experience in *In Memoriam* to Hallam's life, death, and afterlife as a kind of continuing Bible or paradigm of his own spiritual history. An obvious example of this practice is Tennyson's habit of observing the anniversaries of Hallam's death and of reorganizing the calendar into the first, second, and third Christmas, spring, or other season after the event. This new ordering of his life is as meaningful in Tennyson's history as the renumbering of the years in the Christian era after the birth of Christ, for both events signify a new inflection of time.

Another characteristic of confession is its use of a second person, or "mediator," who helps make accessible to Augustine or Tennyson the truths he is trying to reach. Tennyson's views of immortality, art, and love are determined for him in advance by the man he "held as half-divine" (14.10). There is even evidence that Tennyson undertook the writing of his confessional elegy because it records the kind of "imaginative woe" intriguing to Hallam, the author of *Theodicaea Novissima*, who was skilled in theological argument and "loved to handle spiritual strife" (85.54). Equally important is the pattern of conversion in confessional writing. The conversion may be explicitly religious, as in Augustine's conversion from pagan rhetoric to Christian theology in his *Confessions*, or only implicitly so, as in Tennyson's climactic experiences in sections 95 and 130 of *In Memoriam*.

Confessions also tend to be circular in form, ending where they begin, though on a higher plane. The resolutions of the speaker's problems are often evident, at least by analogy, at very early stages of the confession. A trivial example is Newman's youthful practice of crossing himself when entering a darkened room in his *Apologia*. The significance of the gesture is clear to Newman only in retrospect, after his conversion to Catholicism. Just as Augustine finds unsuspected relations between rhetorical words and the theological Word, so Tennyson discovers in the very language he must use an important principle: the truth of the "lucid veil," of a meaning that "half reveal[s]" and "half conceal[s]" itself (5.3–4). The image of the circle even appears in section 130 of *In Memoriam*, which James Richardson convincingly calls "the true climax of the poem" (1988, 89).

> I prosper, circled with thy voice;
> I shall not lose thee though I die. (*In Memoriam*, 130.15–16)

In section 131, as another critic points out, "the circles of section 130 have yielded to the living will, which cuts like a vector through time."

Yet even then circularity still abides in the reasoning, "which asks for a faith in the future time when faith will be justified" (Peltason, 1985, 162).

The circular form of the confession is matched by "the circling of the syntax," which Richardson describes as "a kind of encirclement in elegiac flux" (1988, 6). He shows how *In Memoriam* is an elegy, not of "conclusiveness" but of "endless ending," in which "each stanza trails off, so markedly that more than one section . . . could end with a fine elegiac fade after *any* of its stanzas" (3, 7). The paradox of an "endless ending"—or of a circle that is always on the point of closing—accurately describes *In Memoriam*'s retarded motion and its reversal of the confession's normal pattern of progress by reversion. Marxist theories may help us understand Gray's "Elegy Written in a Country Churchyard," whose mute inglorious Miltons are marginal figures, far removed from the centers of political power. Marx's mourners are rational but not free. By contrast, Tennyson's mourner is fixated and obsessed, politically free but not wholly rational. This is why a psychoanalytic study of his grief, along the lines Freud attempts in *Mourning and Melancholia*, may best illuminate *In Memoriam*'s constant circling motions, which are one of this elegy's oddest mutations of an important feature of an Augustinian confession.

According to Freud, melancholy is object-specific, whereas melancholia is free-floating and difficult to ascribe to any particular loss. Freud believes that the only external misfortune to which victims of melancholia attribute their distress is poverty. Interestingly enough, it took Tennyson at least eighteen years to withdraw his love from Hallam and transfer it to Emily Sellwood. But the only explanation he offers hides as much as it reveals: he kept saying he was too poor to marry. It was once assumed that Tennyson was shattered by Hallam's death and never recovered from the shock. It was even suggested that Tennyson's search for a wife was really a search for an effective substitute for Hallam. More recent scholarship suggests that Hallam depended on Tennyson as much as Tennyson depended on Hallam (Kolb, 1981, 32), and that, like his sister Emily, Tennyson was quite capable of assimilating Hallam's loss (McKay, 1988, 150–51). The poet suffers from melancholia because his grief is related to some unconscious loss. Common traits characterize both grief and melancholia: painful dejection, loss of interest in the outside world, inability to love. But melancholia differs from mere grief or melancholy in one important way: the loss its victims suffer is a loss inside themselves. Creeping "like a guilty thing" to the dark house in Wimpole Street (*In Memoriam*, 7.7), Tennyson's mourner experiences a fall in self-esteem. But because he has committed no crime, his self-accusations seem unwarranted. We can make sense of these accusations only if we see them deflected from their true referent: nature's betrayal of the heart that loved her. Until Hallam died, Tennyson lived in the fond haven of an unreal paradise; he thought he was climbing an "altar-stairs / That slope through darkness up to God" (*In Memoriam*, 55.15–16). Now he wakes up in shock to find himself on a wild, careening roller-coaster, doubtfully teleological and frightening to contemplate.

Melancholia has its own distinctive language in *In Memoriam*. Its meters are self-retarding, and tend to be simultaneously expansive and diminished. While recurring apostrophes to yew trees, to the dark house and burial ship, are composing obsessive litanies, a more frugal music is constantly being broken off by dashes and ellipses that bring language to a standstill.

> No more? A monster then, a dream,
>   A discord. (*In Memoriam.* 56.21–22)

> I can but trust that good shall fall
> At last—far off—at last, to all, (*In Memoriam*, 54.14–15)

> O life as futile, then, as frail!
>   O for thy voice to soothe and bless!
>   What hope of answer, or redress?
> Behind the veil, behind the veil. (*In Memoriam*, 56.25–28)

The short tetrameter quatrains have the brevity of epitaphs. Delivery is halting, the silences long and weighted, and as rhythm slackens even the syntactic structures begin to break down. In section 95, for example, is the flame in the urn, like the "far-off . . . brook" (l. 7), being heard? Or is line 8 offered as a discrete unit of sense, as another bare jotting in a parataxis of impressions, each isolated like an epitaph in its strict autonomy?

> By night we lingered on the lawn,
>   For underfoot the herb was dry;
>   And genial warmth; and o'er the sky
> The silvery haze of summer drawn;

> And calm that let the tapers burn
>   Unwavering: not a cricket chirred;
>   The brook alone far-off was heard,
> And on the board the fluttering urn. (*In Memoriam*, 95.1–8)

Expansive appositions and nonrecoverable elisions are signs of melancholia: they testify to either too much speech or too little.

So word by word, and line by line,
     The dead man touched me from the past,
     And all at once it seemed at last
The living soul was flashed on mine,

And mine in this was wound, and whirled
     About empyreal heights of thought,
     And came on that which is, and caught
The deep pulsations of the world,

Aeonian music measuring out
     The steps of Time—the shocks of Chance—
     The blows of Death. At length my trance
Was cancelled, stricken through with doubt.

Vague words! (*In Memoriam*, 95.33–45)

Either there is too sudden a surge of words and energy, as the mourner crosses the breaks between two successive quatrains, or too complete a suspension of the neural flow, too sudden an arrest of the verse's pulse and the mourner's vital signs as grammar contracts at the end of the quoted passage to a two-word exclamation.

Equally erratic are the wild fluctuations between expansive and elliptical styles in section 56 of *In Memoriam*. The series of subordinate clauses modifying "Man" (l. 9), which remains suspended for three stanzas without a verb, produces one of the most desperate moments in the elegy.

        And he, shall he,

Man, her last work, who seemed so fair,
     Such splendid purpose in his eyes,
     Who rolled the psalm to wintry skies,
Who built him fanes of fruitless prayer,

Who trusted God was love indeed
     And love Creation's final law—
     Though Nature, red in tooth and claw
With ravine, shrieked against his creed—

Who loved, who suffered countless ills,
     Who battled for the True, the Just,
     Be blown about the desert dust,
Or sealed within the iron hills? (*In Memoriam*, 56.8–20)

The repetitive contrasts, accumulative doubts, and hysterical predicate of the quoted sentence mount in a crescendo of fear that is typical of the manic phase of depression and melancholia. The anxious insistence of the subordinate clauses brings the tempting slip into a frantic acceleration and tripling of the relative pronoun: "Who rolled . . . / Who built . . . / Who trusted" (ll. 11–13); "Who loved, who suffered . . . / Who battled" (ll. 17–18). The final fearful decline into fragments without verbs—"No more? A monster then, a dream, / A discord" (ll. 21–22)—wrecks the harmony of the "mellow music" (l. 24). The section ends in a cacophony of disintegration, subsiding in the final breathless phrases, "Behind the veil, behind the veil" (l. 28), to a momentary stasis of chord and discord, expectation and distress.

Estranged, retarded, constantly on the point of being swallowed up by dashes and ellipses, the depressed language of *In Memoriam* is often marked, however, by increased cognitive power. Though the mourner may seem overly ingenious in comparing Hallam to a helm ("I sit within a helmless bark," 4.3) or in likening emotional to financial loss by punning on "The far-off interest of tears" (1.8), his verbal brilliance helps activate his mind, delivering his grief, which is unstable, over to the intellect, which stabilizes. For every pun the mourner actually makes, there are many more "antipuns" that raise the specter of some ghastly shadow-meaning, which is then fenced off. For example, the fantasy of crushing nature, "like a vice of blood, / Upon the threshold of the mind" (3.15–16), conjures up the hyperlucid image of clamping nature in a vise, then crushing out her lifeblood.

> And shall I take a thing so blind,
>> Embrace her as my natural good;
>> Or crush her, like a vice of blood,
> Upon the threshold of the mind? *(In Memoriam, 3.13–16)*

Because of the grotesque power of the antipun in "vice," a bride who is carried across the threshold of her future home seems to be murdered by her husband at the very moment he ought to embrace her. The world "hold" that embeds itself in "threshold" intensifies the holding power of a vise. If Tennyson had said "as in a vice of blood," instead of "like a vice," the pun would have worked. Instead, he clamps off the pun by turning "the vice of blood" into a simile, into one more distemper that he has to fend off, just as he fends off the pun. Menaced by the violence of these shadowy meanings, the mourner uses his antipuns and puns to quarantine the infection before it can spread.

The frightening power possessed by Tennyson's vision of God as a "wild poet," working "without a conscience or an aim" (34.7–8), is partly a result of the mourner's depicting as an inhabitant of the outer-world an inner "dis-ease," his own "unquiet heart and brain" as a poet (5.5). This psychic mechanism of "projective identification," analyzed by Melanie Klein, is found in its crudest form in Browning's Caliban, who associates an unwanted element, a brute force that he himself exercises over crabs, with an inner figure, an "I" rather than a "he." This first-person Caliban is then expelled from consciousness and projected onto a savage god, a tyrannical force in the outer world called Setebos. Because Tennyson's "wild poet," like Caliban's Setebos, is projected from the speaker's consciousness, it has special, threatening knowledge of him. Materializing in the lightning and thunder, the figure Caliban has expelled becomes a persistent, looming menace. Similarly, in *In Memoriam* predestinating gods and other hostile powers seem to possess Tennyson's inmost secrets: they gain unlimited power over him. Since God's wild poetry is also a poetry of Tennyson's own making, and since he cannot at times make sense of it, the mourner, like many victims of melancholia and depression, is constantly on the verge of mental collapse, constantly on the verge of losing his own mind.

As a figure who has first taken up residence inside the mourner before being projected outward, Hallam, too, exists as a probing spectator. From the vantage point of "A higher height, a deeper deep" (*In Memoriam*, 63.12), he can penetrate the mourner's inmost defenses and reserves. Hallam is privy to the secret that, by identifying with his sister's "widowed heart," Tennyson has been initiated into the *amor socraticus*, a kind of Platonized homosexual love for Hallam that is a direct result of introjection—of taking into his own person both the dead man and his bride-to-be, Tennyson's own sister. It is easy to see why the mourner's progress is retarded, why he continues to back away from a discovery he keeps creeping toward: "Behold me, for I cannot sleep, / And like a guilty thing I creep / At earliest morning to the door" (*In Memoriam*, 7.6–8). If he has so totally identified with Hallam that he secretly and guiltily loves the woman Hallam has loved, is it any wonder that his search for truth seems programmed to fail? Incest laws alone would discourage discovery of his secret.

The critical event in Victorian elegy is often a questioning or testing through speech of an apostrophe to some dead friend. Section 90 of *In Memoriam* takes the convention of the verse epistle or love poem, in which a speaker is addressing some intimate correspondent, and transgresses the code by removing the addressee.

> Ah, dear, but come thou back to me!
> > Whatever change the years have wrought,
> > I find not yet one lonely thought
> That cries against my wish for thee. (*In Memoriam*, 90.21–24)

When Tennyson starts reading Hallam's letters in section 95, he is almost afraid his correspondent will start talking back. He plugs his ears, and allows silence to become a defining feature of the genre. Some-times, as at the end of "Thyrsis," the person addressed does finally reply. But what Clough says is audible only as a whisper. Gradually, however, in its search for its lost correspondent, *In Memoriam* does try to restore its own version of Descartes' formula: "I speak and you hear me, therefore we are" (Kristeva, 1986, 45). At the climax of section 95 talking breezes and ghostly flowers, capable (it seems) of weirdly easy metamorphoses, help the mourner assimilate his dread. The newly dead, like Wordsworth's Lucy, seem merely asleep. And once Hallam has been dead a while, he begins communicating with the mourner through the supernatural agency of the breeze and through his "silent-speaking" letters. The silent speaking of the dead is also the condition of the heartbroken elegist, whose words, after speech, reach into the si-lence. Purged of his guilt, the former victim of melancholia finds that everything he says is chastened by the active silence of his dead friend. Restoring the patterns of progress by reversion, including the images that repeat, repeat, and repeat again, but finally with some relieving difference, the mourner is at last able to take two steps forward for every one step backward. He turns his melancholia into potentially consolable grief by allowing his words to look back and forward at once, incorporating like the two outer rhymes of *In Memoriam*'s tetrameter quatrains both a morbid persistence of the past into the pre-sent and a hope for future life.

> So be it: there no shade can last
> > In that deep dawn behind the tomb,
> > But clear from marge to marge shall bloom
> The eternal landscape of the past; (*In Memoriam*, 46.5–8)

Leading Life Backwards: Retrospective Form

A confessional elegist like the *Pearl* poet or Donne can see in retrospect that he ends where he begins: he traces an ascending circle or spiral. The same circular pattern survives in *In Memoriam* and *Four Quartets*, but its trace is fainter and sometimes even evaded or broken down. In both cases the elegist may have to live backwards, from the vantage point of a privileged moment. Only then does he discover that the moment of death must be every moment, because only such a mo-ment can precipitate a crisis in identity. And only such a crisis can dis-close to the mourner that every end is also a new beginning. The pil-grim on his circular journey is not what he has already done, but what he is about to make of the rest of his life. The past is prologue. So far he has been writing the cover and title page; now he is to start writing chapter 1.

Merely to lead life forward is to give it a tragic linear perspective. Until we give life retrospective form by leading it backwards, the outline of a circular journey will not appear. Inspired by Dante's treatment, for example, Tennyson's "Ulysses" glosses the Homeric story from a linear, Christian standpoint, which is the perspective of death. In the epic Ulysses' journey is circular. It returns to where it originated, in Ithaca. But both Dante and Tennyson transform Ulysses' circular journey into linear disaster. In Dante's poem Ulysses' descent into hell is a literal descent into a region of the Inferno. Hell is also a figurative descent of each character, like each mourner in an elegy, into the deepest region of the self. The self-retarding movement of many elegies has a dual effect. Loops, detours, and digressions impede advance and may turn mourning into melancholia. But because the elegist's habit of turning upon himself, questioning his own most cherished axioms, may strengthen resolve, we can see in retrospect that the linear journeys of strong mourners are sometimes circular ones in disguise. *In Memoriam* and *Four Quartets* offer teleologial critiques of linear categories. Their beginning presupposes a moment of conversion that turns the confession of doubt into a profession of faith, the truant into a pilgrim, and the wayward mourner into a poet. When the pilgrim reaches the "end" of his journey—both its terminal point and its goal—the "end of all [his] exploring / Will be to arrive where [he] started," as T. S. Eliot says, "And know the place for the first time" ("Little Gidding," V.27–29).

As a confessional elegy, *In Memoriam* tends to be circular in form: like Augustine's precursor text, it ends where it begins. The final verb in Augustine's *Confessions* is a sesame word. Adapting a quotation from Matthew (7.7), "only then will the door be opened to us," the ending circles back to the prayer for openness in the fifth section of the first book: "My heart has ears ready to listen to you, Lord. Open them wide (*aperi eas*), and *whisper in my heart, I am here to save you.*" Just as the final opening is present at the start, so in *In Memoriam* the events that occur do not acquire their identity from themselves alone, but also reflect the temperamental secrecy and reserve of the autobiographer who experiences them. Tennyson discovers very early in his elegy, in words that "half reveal / And half conceal" their meaning (5.3, 4), a verbal analogue of an important truth. This is the truth of the "lucid veil" (67.14), the truth that the sacramental breeze and flowers of section 95 are an adjective of spirit, hiding the face of God even as they reveal His presence.

Since the conclusion seems the natural outcome of the opening, the circular form gives to the conclusion what Frank Kermode has called "the sense of an ending" (1966, i). But the confessional form has another property: despite this sense of an ending, it is also open-ended. Even in *Pearl* and Donne's *Anniversaries* the progressive disclosure of an end that is all along implicit never predictably determines the elegy's outcome. But in contrast to earlier confessional elegies, *In Memoriam* tries to do contradictory things; in controlling grief, it tries *not* to make the reader feel that art is controlled. Instead of being given a simple or a single coherence, the reader is asked to resolve disorder by organizing the coherences of pastoral elegy, philosophic treatise, lyric sequence, and autobiographical poem. Perhaps the best evidence of *In Memoriam*'s open form is its apparent instability. The design is visibly strained beyond the point of unity; fragmentation lurks in every section. The peril of generic experimentation, the uncertainty of logic, the restless search after vision, the vagrant asides—all these are expressed as powerfully by the broken forms of *In Memoriam* as if the poem were another cry from the heart, like "Break, break, break."

At first glance the retrospective form of *Four Quartets* is even more circular than *In Memoriam*. Eliot both mentions and uses the idea that "Home is where one starts from." In a sentence that repeats, with the elements reversed, the sentence with which "East Coker" began, the conclusion exemplifies the circuitous return it describes: "In my end is my beginning." And as the last movement of the last quartet rounds back to the rose garden at the beginning of the poem, Eliot's "circuitous journey through his remembered past . . . ends," as M. H. Abrams says, "in the recognition of the garden and home he had started from" (1971, 322). A prose paraphrase of *Four Quartets* confirms Abrams' definitive account of how the poem enacts its statement that "the way forward is the way back." But an actual reading of *Four Quartets* also belies that account. Reading the poem is neither difficult nor easy: it is uneasy. The reader's need to hold in the mind patterns that are continually being broken down and transformed denies him the comfort of a single coherence or retrospective form.

A theology of ends allows the *Pearl* poet and Donne to end where they began, but on a higher plane of knowledge. Though the circular journey in *Four Quartets* is also spiral, Eliot's ascent is curiously muted. His reluctance to force his patterns or to falsify his beliefs allows him to write beautifully about the heartbreaking waste of heightened consciousness. It cannot translate itself into anything else. And yet we are astonished, I think, that poetry of such heartbreaking loveliness can refuse to convert itself into the simple consolations and coherences that the extremities of Eliot's pain and suffering clearly seek. "The crying shadow in the funeral dance" and "The loud lament of the disconsolate chimera" ("Burnt Norton," V.21–22) may decisively reverse the "old chimera of the grave" that haunts Stevens' elegist in "Sunday

Morning." But even as Eliot transfers what is spectral and illusory from the resurrection story to the pointless frenzy of the funeral dance and the mourner's loud laments, his imagination seems all on the side of the "Shrieking voices" that attack the Word. Something is ill about the heart. His skeptical reminder of the way even words "slip, slide, / Decay with imprecision" ("Burnt Norton," V.15–16) is subtle but conclusive. The doubts that scold, mock, or merely chatter, but always assail us ("Burnt Norton," V. 17–19), clearly reveal the paradox involved in the movement of the elegiac passages toward the defeat of their own generic promise. Eliot's removal of his own suffering consciousness from the kinds of comfort that patterns normally provide in verse seems to me a profound moral achievement. But "like all such achievements in great art," as John Bayley observes of Shakespeare, "it makes absolutely no parade of its own moral nature" (1981, 183).

The *Pearl* poet may be baffled, but he has no trouble guessing the identity of his transformed daughter. Guessing the identity of Eliot's compound ghost, however, is another matter. The ghost's final disclosure is concerned with the problem of closure, of how to culminate and then conclude. The speech itself, however, does not conclude; it is broken off by the breaking of day. And though the phantom master offers "a kind of valediction" ("Little Gidding," II.95), we are never told what he says. Oddly enough, what should be "a crown upon" a "lifetime's effort" (II.77) refuses to culminate. Grammatically, the final revelation seems an afterthought, introduced anticlimactically in a short subordinate clause: "unless restored by the refining fire / Where you must move in measure, like a dancer" (II.92–93).

Guessing the mentor's identity is a critical activity Eliot has encouraged. But he has also ensured that the pursuit will fail. Though Yeats and Dante, the two most popular candidates for the ghost, fail to meet the test in several ways, they also encourage readers to believe that a solution to the mystery exists just beyond their mental reach. Yeats's use of the dancer and the dance and his horror of being fastened to a dying animal provide a link between the refining fire of art and the anatomy of aging. But as Eliot's contemporary, Yeats is too young to be a mentor who rebukes his pupil for neglecting the master's "thought and theory" (II.59). Dante, by contrast, is ancient and venerable enough to be a mentor, but there is nothing pertinently Dantesque about the ghost's disclosure of the gifts reserved for age. Perhaps a more plausible mentor than Dante or Yeats is Eliot's intellectual father, F. H. Bradley. His "thought and theory," which the poet is rebuked for having "forgotten" (II.59), were the subject of the young poet's doctoral dissertation. And, like the phantom master, Bradley has been concerned, in Eliot's view (1932, 455), "To purify the dialect of the tribe"

(II.75). What matters is not a conclusive identification of the phantom master as Yeats, Dante, or F. H. Bradley, but a demonstration that, since several identifications seem equally plausible or implausible, none is completely convincing. Paradoxically, the more precise and convincing a demonstration becomes, the less precise and convincing it will also have to be. For one of the ghost's defining properties is that he *cannot* be defined: he is someone Eliot has "forgotten" and has only "half recalled" (II.40). Like Eliot's elegiac verse, the compound ghost remains a marvel, unlimited and undiminished by anything we are tempted to say about it.

Instead of providing one clearly realized retrospective form, *Four Quartets* offers "hints and guesses, / Hints followed by guesses" ("The Dry Salvages," V.29–30), and meanings that will not quite formulate. Even when the timeless appears to intersect time, Eliot is careful to place that intersection at a point on the horizon that seems always to recede. When Incarnation is experienced, it is only as a "gift half understood" ("The Dry Salvages," V.32), and in a context that seems just as appropriate to Krishna's experience as to Christ's. "Every quality in relation," says F. H. Bradley in analyzing relation and quality in *Appearance and Reality*, has "a diversity within its nature." The harder we try to relate qualities, the more "we . . . are led by a principle of fission which conducts us to no end" (1893, 26). The roses in "Burnt Norton," for example, have "the look of flowers that are looked at" (I.29), and yet "the door" "Into the rose-garden" is "never opened," so the flowers are never seen (I.13–14). To explain the odd relation of being simultaneously looked at and not seen, Eliot has to introduce in the "Late roses filled with snow" ("East Coker," II.7) a second relation. Like the roses in the garden, the roses filled with snow combine contradictory qualities. They show how it is possible to be simultaneously seen and unseen by being simultaneously in and out of time. We can see roses bloom in early winter; but we cannot see how these roses are literally tumbled at the same time by the hollyhocks of high summer ("East Coker," II.5–6). To perform such a visual feat, we must be both inside and outside of time. And such a paradoxical relation is possible only if past and future are reversible, with the result that death is not what we think it is.

Eliot explores the alternative possibility in his striking figure of the "Royal Rose" pressed between leaves of an unopened book, which recalls the unopened door to the rose garden.

> I sometimes wonder if that is what Krishna meant—
> Among other things—or one way of putting the same thing:
> That the future is a faded song, a Royal Rose or a lavender spray

Of wistful regret for those who are not yet here to regret,
Pressed between yellow leaves of a book that has never been opened.
("The Dry Salvages," III.1–5)

To call the past "a faded song" would be commonplace. But Krishna reminds Eliot that it is just as logical to identify time with the song as with the person who originally heard the song. If so, the song that has faded for its hearer, like water that has flowed by an observer as he stands on the bank of a stream, more accurately describes time future than time past. "The only wisdom we can hope to acquire," Eliot warns, "is the wisdom of humility: humility is endless" ("East Coker," II.47–48). Words of humility may initiate and sustain discourse. But only some vision outside of words, some vision of a future that is also "a faded song," can end it. The tentative "I sometimes wonder," like the halting dashes and self-deprecating asides, remind the reader that if such a vision exists, it belongs not to Eliot or other elegiac poets but only to the Word. Eliot himself can never hope to fix that Word and never hope to speak it in his poem.

The Paradox of Proof: Logical Coercion and Free Assent

Because Aristotle organizes nature into substances and their properties, which are the very categories he uses to explain art, his famous statement that art should imitate nature is really a *petitio principii* in disguise: art is said to imitate a nature that is already an organized version of itself. It might be said that all so-called proofs about axiology and the fate of the dead are involved in a similar paradox: the conclusion they presume to reach is already assumed in the premise. Circular reasoning will not convince a skeptic who disallows the opening premise. But a chain of propositions too weak to induce assent by themselves may produce belief when the ends of the chain are joined together to form a circle. Tennyson and Browning both ask: To what degree are our beliefs about the afterlife grounded in a chain of rational argument? And to what degree are they postulates of faith, or forms of free assent to an explanatory circle or web?

Paradoxically, what is desirable for a rational explanation of death—some grounding of a conclusion in logical inference or deduction—is undesirable for faith, since any logical demonstration compels agreement and makes the free assent of faith impossible. As Browning's Bishop Blougram asserts, "With me, faith means perpetual unbelief" ("Bishop Blougram's Apology," l. 666). Conversely, what is desirable for faith—some loosening of the links in an argumentative chain—is undesirable for a logical explanation of death, since any breakdown in an inferential chain makes it impossible to ground a conclusion in the evidence available. How can the elegist adjust the claims of grounded belief and free assent? How can he offer a theological or moral explanation of death without bludgeoning an impartial observer into accepting some foreseen conclusion that follows inescapably from the argument's premises?

There would be nothing mysterious about death and about doctrines of the afterlife if a causal relation held between beliefs and facts. But in Tennyson's poem, "The Two Voices," despair is right to insist that "the grounds of hope" are never "fixed" (l. 227). A grounded assertion compels agreement and is incompatible with either faith or free assent. Tennyson's skeptic overstates his case, however, when he concludes that hope is groundless. Belief is not just the predilection of a sanguine temperament, an optimist whose biochemical "elements were kindlier mixed" (l. 228). The difference lies in a capacity for vision. Unlike the skeptic, the believer "owns the fatal gift of eyes, / That read his spirit blindly wise, / Not simple as a thing that dies" (ll. 286–88). His "eyes," like his words, look two ways at once. "Own" might be a synonym for "possess." But it could also mean "admit." Is belief's inward seeing a misreading of the world, a fatal form of solipsism? Or does it fatefully decipher the code, solving the riddle of fate itself by discovering, among other things, that the blindly wise spirit is lord and sovereign over outward sense? The prophet-like seer may be a proud possessor of wisdom withheld from the skeptic. Or he may be half shamefully conceding the fatality and blindness of his so-called gift.

Blind to the senses, hence blind to the fact of death, the knowledge of the seer is self-reflexive. Whether he is "blindly *wise*" or reads in a blind way or fashion, the seer, like his oxymoron, perilously straddles the space between grounded beliefs and free assents. An assertion that is grounded wholly in the evidence of the senses, like the skeptic's, may try to coerce agreement by disallowing free assent. But an assertion that is blind to sensory evidence, like the seer's, may wisely preserve the value of free assent only to find its own beliefs are groundless.

The skeptic in "The Ancient Sage" reminds us that we may all be in possession of more bitter knowledge than we want to be. The shocking reminder that the dust of the beloved is "greening" in the rose tree's "leaf" and that "Her blood is in [its] bloom" (ll. 165–66) puts us all at the mercy of harsh powers in nature. If "the world is dark with griefs and graves" (l. 171), then we are not free agents after all, but a doomed procession of phantoms, passing from nothingness into nothingness.

> For all that laugh, and all that weep
> And all that breathe are one

> Slight ripple on the boundless deep
> That moves, and all is gone. ("The Ancient Sage," ll. 187–90)

The shock comes in the pause at the end of line 188, where we hang for a moment, despite the absence of punctuation, uncertain what trope will be used to cap the third use of "all" in two short lines. All things human are *what*? One ocean? One body? No. Only one slight ripple. When magnitude reappears in "the boundless deep," it has been shifted away from everything that breathes, which now constitutes the merest "ripple," to the all-obliterating element, the annihilating ocean itself. Vacancy looms in the second-syllable caesura in line 190, which swallows up the "Slight ripple" as abruptly as the alarming paratactic syntax—"That moves, and all is gone"—cuts off the reader's breath, bringing all motion to a stop.

Socratic dialectic sometimes seems coercive, a substitute for a wrestling match. But Tennyson's poetry of debate shows that arguments about the afterlife may have a higher function than coercion. The Ancient Sage wants to save not only himself but also the world from nothingness, and "the boundless deep" is his medium. Through moral action and the will to believe, he turns the "deep" into a testing ground, a place of probation, where he can prove his beliefs in the only sense of "proof" that matters. Only propositions we already believe, trivial facts like the date of Hallam's death, are capable of proof. When the mourner in *In Memoriam* wonders aloud, for example, whether his desire for immortality derives from love, he is not trying to prove anything (55.1–4). Attempting something less rigorous but potentially more valuable than proof, he is trying to explain the inherent probability of a God of love's granting his wish to be reunited with Hallam. By testing his courage and faith, an explanation's value will be intrinsically greater the less capable it is of strict demonstration or proof.

In his elegy *La Saisiaz*, Browning tries to discover, like Tennyson, how far a belief in the afterlife can be grounded in argument without becoming coercive, and so eliminating the free assent of faith. If Reason had its way in its intellectual skirmishing with Fancy, rational argument would be as coercive as the dialectic of Socrates, a contest of wits in which the stronger competitor wins. But Fancy values a less coercive method: it tries to reconstruct with the heart what its adversary has overthrown with the head. It is not rational necessity but moral need that drives Browning to believe in God. As a postulate of natural theology, used to explain the physical world, the idea of God is the supreme *petitio principii*, as useless as the hypothesis of ether in explaining light. Browning needs a dying God, a God who is both suffering and self-sufficient, whose weakness is his strength ("Saul," l. 308). If there is no such god, then his imagination of love is an anomaly or contradiction. And so a longing to assign finality to the universe, to make its creator conscious and personal, "a Man like to me" ("Saul," l. 310), leads Browning to posit two indubitable axioms or "facts," as he calls them: Descartes' axioms that both his soul and God exist. Fancy believes that even teleologically directed inquiries that build surmises on these two axioms or "facts" may be of value. Surmises about "earth, heaven, hell" (l. 465) and rewards in a world to come may be ennobling as the architect of our moral nature and designer of our final cause or end. A Kantian God of conscience, the author of the moral order, who exists in embryo in the Lutheran notion of faith, may not be capable of proof. But Browning believes there is more intrinsic value in Fancy's rearing an airy "superstructure" (l. 518) in support of such a moral order than in Reason's forging a chain of arguments to enslave rather than free each inquirer.

Browning's metaphor for the form of argument that compels assent is the chain of flawlessly connected links. Remove one link in the chain, and the whole argument unravels.

> . . . Not so loosely thoughts were linked,
> Six weeks since as I, descending in the sunset from Salève,
> Found the chain, I seemed to forge there, flawless till it reached
> your grave,— (*La Saisiaz*, ll. 606–8)

When Browning says the forged chain was "flawless," does he mean that the links were so securely joined that they carried him right to the edge of the grave and presumably beyond? Or is the emphasis on "till"? Was the forged chain "flawless" only "till" it met the assault of death, at which point its links broke and fell apart? If the chain is as unstable as the meanings in this passage, it seems to be more "filmy" (l. 609) than "flawless."

Any argument about the immortality of the soul that tries to build its conclusions inductively on indisputable axioms may be less like a book of proofs in Euclid than a tower of Pisa. Remove one bottom brick, and the whole building crumbles. Surmises about the afterlife must match the tremulous hopes of Browning's inquirer. The breaks in his life and thought coincide with the fearful pauses created by the multiple dashes and caesuras that suspend speech at the precise point Browning hopes to resume it with Anne Egerton Smith: "Therefore,— dared and done today / Climbing,—here I stand: but you—where?" (ll. 138–39). Three dashes in one and a half lines come close to a record, even for Browning. Breaks in the chain of argument are matched by ellipsis, contraction in the grammar, and removal of prepositional phrases in hyphenated, kenning-like word pairs: "pilgrim-foot" (l.

325), "tangle-twine" (l. 94), "heart-deeps" (l. 116). Though such syntactical compression often makes the serpentine eight-beat lines more tortuous, they remind us that a truly unbroken chain forged in the spirit of Euclid would betray the temper of the inquiry by forcing the mourner to accept the results of a logical demonstration.

As the explanatory model of the buried root, "stocked with germs of torpid life" (l. 615), is allowed to replace the flawlessly linked chain of a proof, it is recognized that tangled threads or knots, highly inconvenient in a logical argument, may be desirable as a means of meshing and reinforcing the threads of an explanation, which resemble the root system of a plant. *La Saisiaz* abounds in such tangles and knots; it is an extraordinarily dense and digressive poem, full of self-retarding loops and detours.

> No, the terrace showed no figure, tall, white, leaning
> through the wreaths,
> Tangle-twine of leaf and bloom that intercept the air
> one breathes,
> Interpose . . . (ll. 93–95)

The sequence of negatives and trailing appositional phrases branches out and spreads, "intercepting" Browning's meaning as the leaves intercept the air. The elegy creates a whole receding vista of interceptions, as the verb in the relative clause finds itself mirrored in "Interpose," the principal verb of the sentence. Only after digressing for another twelve lines can Browning bear to confront the harsh truth that the same negative construction tries to veil for a second time: "yet she violates the bond, / Neither leans nor looks nor listens: why is this?" (ll. 106–7).

Elsewhere an opening conditional phrase arouses a desire for resolution that is then delayed by a profusion of parallel conditional clauses that run contrary to fact (ll. 319–34). The long awaited apodosis—"I must say—or choke in silence—" (l. 333)—is too desolating to voice. Its arrival is deferred by an interruption that exhorts the speaker to be clearer (l. 326), by digressions fenced off by dashes (ll. 331–34), and even by a parenthesis nested inside a concessive clause (ll. 327–30). In conferring meaning only retrospectively, after considerable time has passed, the suspended syntax imitates the way Browning explains his digressions and asides only at the end of his elegy, where he tries to show why the branching roots of a plant may better describe his chosen method of inquiry than the linked chain of a logical demonstration. Browning is less concerned with proving anything than with explaining how belief in the soul's immortality might be possible, despite apparent excluders. If such a belief disconcerts the skeptic by encouraging a triumph of hope over expectation, then it is doing, I suspect, what all true belief or faith ought to do. The problem, of course, is that the same could be said of even the most irresponsible surmise. A philosopher's confidence in a laboriously constructed argument for the soul's immortality may pale beside a prophet's saving faith in a single insight that transforms our understanding. But unfortunately there are no rules for having insights. Though one prophet may be worth a thousand philosophers, the prospect of every scholar setting up as a prophet does not inspire confidence. To support his claim, half prophetic and half polemical, Browning shows that, though immortality is a mere surmise, and not a fact, it can be grounded in the holiness of the heart's affections. The ground of a loving mind and temper still leaves room for the free assent of faith.

Strictly speaking, however, *La Saisiaz* is an elegy of hope: it does not celebrate that hypostasis of things hoped for that the writer of Hebrews identifies with faith (Hebrews 11.1). Browning's final "hope"s, hovering somewhere between a stammer and a trumpet flourish, try to establish the necessary equilibrium: "So, I hope—no more than hope, but hope—no less than hope . . . " (l. 535). More important than proving the soul is immortal, which would be more than hoping, is to see how immortality is possible, which is no less than hoping. Not knowing where (or what) the dead Miss Smith is, or whether the word "where" even applies to her, Browning switches from faith to hope as the real basis of his coda. To see how immortality can be grounded in Browning's love for his dead wife, Elizabeth, despite its inaccessibility to logical proof, is not an act of faith in the biblical sense at all. It is a celebration of hope—a rather modest hope that facts and surmises may fit together. Browning's demonstrations in the elegy may be less rigorous and more circular than proofs. But because they do not merely prove something we already believe (like Browning's claim to have talked with Miss Smith on Mount Salève before she died), these demonstrations are intrinsically more valuable than proofs. The claims the elegist can prove tend to be more trivial than the claims he wants explained.

The final optatives are a variation of the funeral benediction "rest in peace." But in the name of *not* disturbing his wife's grave, they forbid discovery: "Rest all such, unraised forever" (l. 617). Browning is resolved to leave more unsaid than he says, and his final words acknowledge his reserve: "Least part this, then what the whole?" (l. 618). If Browning were less reticent, he might have made the ground of his faith too explicit, leaving less room for free assent. Had he been more reticent, his beliefs might have seemed groundless. His achievement in *La Saisiaz* is to substitute for the proofs of a logically constructed argument the explanatory power of a buried love whose full "resurrection" cannot be permitted for fear of triggering psychic shock.

Though Browning's crises of faith in *La Saisiaz* consist of a circle, it is not a vicious circle. On the contrary, it is an example of the circle that is contained in any explanatory web that allows for free assent, as opposed to the logical coercion of an inductive proof consisting of a connected chain of statements. Because all propositions in an explanatory web contain each other, an explanation, unlike a proof, always implies a circle. The retrospective form revealed by such a web—a version of the confessional elegist's circuitous return, the snake with its tail in its mouth—may become glaringly clear, but only if we take a hermeneutical leap, a leap of faith, which allows us to establish all its explanatory statements together.

Confessional Elegy and the Theory of Genre

To compare pastoral elegies of any historical period is to exercise critical judgment. Conscious of an acknowledged similarity between "Lycidas" and "Adonais," or between "Adonais" and "Thyrsis," I tried in chapter 1 to fine-tune our awareness of equally important distinctions, which is the function of judgment as opposed to wit. The present chapter reverses that method. For pragmatic purposes I have tried to *desensitize* elegy, making students of the genre less aware of differences. I have attempted, one might say, a form of "wit-criticism" by positing unsuspected similarities among poems as apparently dissimilar as *Pearl*, Donne's *Anniversaries*, *In Memoriam*, and *Four Quartets*.

Whether students of elegy should use their judgments or their wits is not a philosophical or a theoretical question, but a practical one. The wit-critic's search for circular patterns in elegies, and for the progress by reversion that often accompanies them, is in keeping with structuralism's search for underlying patterns that allow the critic to perform specific operations on poems. Rather than say that *Four Quartets* or *In Memoriam* is a confessional elegy, let us propose a pragmatic thought-experiment: let us explore what one of these poems is like when we read it in terms of the circular, self-retarding, or other features associated with confessional genres.

Let us recognize, too, that all similarities soon reach the limits of their explanatory power. As Adena Rosmarin says, "genres can never be perfectly coincident with texts unless we posit as many genres as texts—at which point we fall back into a Crocean world, into treating each text in isolation" (1985, 45). The medieval confessions of Augustine and the *Pearl* poet have important successors in Donne's *Second Anniversary*, *In Memoriam*, and *Four Quartets*. But there are breaks in this tradition as well as continuities. A grief that is free-floating rather than object-specific generates a diffusive melancholia in *In Memoriam*. And sometimes only the faint vestige of a circuitous theology, whose end is contained in its beginning—"I am Alpha and Omega, the beginning and the ending" (Revelation 1.8)—survives in the necessarily circular reasoning that allows Tennyson's Ancient Sage or Browning's elegist in *La Saisiaz* to assert the free assent of faith.

Most critics regard periods like the Romantic, the Victorian, and the modern as necessary fictions. We cannot write a literary history of a genre without periodizing. Even if we want to deny the idea of a unified period, we require the concept to refute it. The genre "Victorian elegy" or "modern elegy," then, is not to be taken as a historical class, but rather as a classifying statement or proposal. And even in crossing traditional historical boundaries, the text called "confessional elegy" is always understood to be different from the particular poem a student of the genre happens to be reading. Affinities at once surprising and just, like the unsuspected similarities between *Pearl* and *Four Quartets*, are the most persuasive. But often an apparent similarity or family resemblance masks a more profound and striking difference. Though a prose paraphrase of *Four Quartets*, for example, assimilates its circular form to the testaments of mourners like the *Pearl* poet, Donne, or Tennyson, the more attentively we read Eliot the more the circular pattern seems to break down or elude him. Sometimes a poet's paradoxical task is to indicate the boundaries of a genre by obliterating them. Simultaneously drawing attention to the circular form and evading it, Eliot does not so much impugn this feature of confessional elegy as create an impression of a distinctly poetic text, one that seems alive and subtle precisely because it eludes a reader's generalizing grasp.

3 ❧ Epistemology and Paradox: Berkeley, Kant, Foucault

I begin this chapter by tracing, to Berkeley's axiom that to be is to be perceived and to Kant's Platonic axiom that the noumenal world cannot be known directly, two of the seismic shocks that occur in eighteenth-century and early Romantic thought. A tremor from the first shock survives in Gray's "Elegy Written in a Country Churchyard," where it deeply affected Dr. Johnson. Hopkins received a comparable shock from the second seismic wave, which put human nature into a "tremble," he claims, in Wordsworth's "Ode: Intimations of Immortality." In Wordsworth, as in such philosophers of the noumenal world as Plato, Hopkins says "human nature . . . saw something, got a shock; wavers in opinion, looking back, whether there was anything in it or no; but is in a tremble ever since" (1938, 147–48; letter to Canon Dixon, Oct. 23, 1886). Moving in the final section of the chapter to the Victorian and modern periods, I associate with Darwinian speculations that man is a cosmic accident, a mere anomaly of the moment, Foucault's disturbing prediction that humanity itself is a recent invention, only tentatively set in place and in danger of disappearing. I show that such speculations seem confirmed by a gradual disappearance of the subject in late nineteenth-century and modern elegies.

My approach to elegies in this chapter supplements the diachronic model of Philippe Ariès, who traces changing attitudes to death from classic to modern times, with Foucault's synchronic model. Substituting for traditional cultural history a program of cultural archaeology, Foucault replaces the triangle of author, work, tradition with the triangle of text, discourse, culture. Both Ariès and Foucault try to chart changing ideologies. But Foucault sees culture as a system of hidden epistemes, or axioms of knowing, like the subjectively framed cognitions I associate with Berkeley and Gray, and with Kant and Wordsworth. One advantage of searching for such hidden axioms is that they keep us close both to the structure of thought and to the language that a critic of elegies needs to foreground.

The Fault Lines of Elegy: Seismic Shocks

Gray's "Elegy Written in a Country Churchyard" is located on a fault line separating the older elegiac anatomies of Donne from a more reflexive mode designed to map the mind of a self-conscious knower. George Berkeley names the epistemological space peculiar to many Romantic and post-Romantic elegists when he announces that to be is to be perceived. And J. F. Ferrier refines Berkeley's axiom when he speaks of the minimal unit of cognition as the world "*mecum*" (1854, 93), "the object with the addition" of the "I's self-conscious response." It is only a short step from Gray to Romantic lyrics of loss like Wordsworth's "Tintern Abbey," which, as John Hollander points out, "is both the mind's picture of the scene and the poem's picture of the mind" (1975, 282).

According to Berkeley, the universe would not exist without a human or divine consciousness to perceive it. Like the falling tree in the earless forest, the only reality is what a mind perceives to be real. As one commentator says, "black holes only exist because we observe them into existence" (Thomas, 1992, 28). Like Berkeley, the Romantic poet tells himself, in his pride, that he is the thinking part of the universe, the earth's awareness of itself. Since the poet, in Shelley's phrase, is "the eye with which the Universe / Beholds itself and knows itself divine" ("Hymn of Apollo," ll. 31–32), the power that Milton has called "both the eye and the soul . . . of this great world" (*Paradise Lost*, 5.171) has now been transferred from an external object, the sun, into a quality of the poetic mind itself. This cultural change is part of "the great process of Internalisation," as C. S. Lewis calls it, according to which "item after item is transferred from the object's side of the account to the subject's" (1964, 215).

A second seismic shock originates in Kant, who makes reality less and less accessible by separating the noumenal from the phenomenal world in his first *Critique*. In the new post-Kantian world the supernatural is real and art may bear witness to its power. But though the natural supernaturalism of Romantic ideology requires aesthetic objects, as it requires nature, to make available some special revelation, many nineteenth-century elegies are emblem poems with a difference. In his "Ode: Intimations of Immortality," for example, Wordsworth, no longer fully conscious of "the glory and the dream," glimpses it only intermittently, as a sublime but elusive power. "Two things fill the mind with ever new and increasing admiration," Kant confesses at the end of his second *Critique*: "the starry heavens above and the moral law within." To preserve a valuable cargo of belief from theological shipwreck, many Romantic and post-Romantic elegists recover in Kant's "starry heavens" the trope whereby the natural creation declares God's glory. But just as Kant exalts the "moral law" above the stars, so elegists like Wordsworth and Tennyson discover that, whereas the "view of a countless multitude of worlds" may annihilate their importance as animal creatures, the human consciousness reveals to them "a life independent of animality and even of the whole sensible world" (Kant, 1923, 260).

Another legacy of Kant's teaching is that, even though truths of the Pure Reason, including truths about the immortality of the soul and the existence of God, are inaccessible, there are moral and practical reasons for acting as if these beliefs were true. Elegies by D. G. Rossetti, Morris, and Swinburne can at least simulate an aura of the supernatural by creating atmospheres charged with awe. And in filtering the most harrowing "Calvaries" of human "Love" through a theological veil (lyric 322, l. 28), even Emily Dickinson seems to express some sympathy for Feuerbach's claim that the predicate of biblical theology, "love," should become the subject of a new anthropological religion, and that what is now subject, "God," should be relegated to the predicate as a mere god-like attribute. Like D. F. Strauss's critical theology and Hans Vaihinger's Kantian philosophy of "as-if," elegy may be governed increasingly by supreme fictions. According to Strauss, everything happens *as if* the elegist and his public were linked by a community of belief, even though there is nothing to believe in but community itself. Swinburne's elegy on Baudelaire and D. G. Rossetti's sonnet "The Hill Summit" celebrate a religion with a priest and congregation but no god. Dismantling all the ideologies of elegy as "objectless" (except presumably his own ideology), I. A. Richards denies that Shelley believes in immortality at all; in "Adonais" he merely creates the aesthetic effects of such belief (Richards, 1924, 279–80).

Scholars have already traced a line of descent from Kant's *Critique of Judgment* to the ascendancy of doctrines of art for art's sake. It seems equally plausible to associate this phenomenon, including what Ortega Y Gasset calls the "de-humanization of art" (1968, i), with nineteenth-century and modern speculations about humanity's fragile foothold on the evolutionary scale. Darwinian thought sets a clear precedent for Foucault's claim that "man is an invention of recent date. And one perhaps nearing its end" (1973, 387). Challenging both Kant's axiom that the human consciousness is more sublime than nature and Berkeley's assumption that without a perceiver the whole universe would break down in disorder, Darwin and his modern descendants remind us that, in the scale of evolution, we are still new to the earth, a fragile species, "at risk of fumbling," as Lewis Thomas says, and "in real danger at the moment of leaving behind only a thin layer of our fossils, radioactive at that" (1992, 25).

Berkeley and Gray: Is Death Conceivable?

When applied to elegy, Berkeley's new axiom of knowing—*esse est percipi*—produces the paradox of the absent mourner. We continue to exist as long as a sympathetic mourner remembers us. But what happens when the graveyard empties and there is no one left to read our epitaph? Berkeley's answer is as surprising as it is famous, and helps explain why Dr. Johnson found it "vain to blame and useless to praise" Gray's "Elegy Written in a Country Churchyard."

> There was a young man who said, "God
> Must think it exceedingly odd
> When he finds that this tree
> Continues to be,
> When there's noone about in the quad."
>
> "Dear sir, your astonishment's odd.
> God's always about in the quad;
> And that's why this tree
> Continues to be,
> Since observed by,
> Yours faithfully, God."

If we find Berkeley's solution more ingenious than convincing, we must still concede that as long as we continue reading a poem like Gray's "Elegy" we are duplicating an important operation inside the poem itself, and are functioning to that degree as a version of Berkeley's God.

For Gray's "Elegy" paints a picture of how the portrait of the rural dead comes to be painted. Substituting for Johnson's elegiac portraits in "The Vanity of Human Wishes" what Foucault has called the "representation of a representation," Gray's poem introduces an operation of thought, the generous response of an observer, which, when applied to a given situation (the apparent oblivion of the unhonored dead), reinstates the very kind of situation to which it was applied. Just as interesting to Gray as the elegist's tribute to the unhonored dead is how his elegist's own death may be commemorated by a sympathetic observer, the "swain" of line 97, and how the swain may be commemorated by another commemorator, including successive readers. This process without limit resembles the dizzying replications Foucault discovers at the center of classical representation (1973, 3–16). It anticipates the paradoxical conclusion of Berkeley's nineteenth-century disciple, J. F. Ferrier, who argues that, since the dead can never be removed from a perceiving consciousness, they prove "this great law of human thought —the natural inconceivability of death" (1842, 819).

In Gray's "Elegy" the speaker's representations of the country churchyard have their own sealed-in equivalents in the inquiry of the kindred spirit and the sympathetic rejoinder of the hoary-headed swain (ll. 96–97). Is the elegist the observer or the subject? For a moment he seems to switch places with the unhonored dead, walking through the picture frame to become the subject of a second representation. An example of Thomas De Quincey's well-known characterization of the "Piranesi effect," Gray's "Elegy" also illustrates the *mise en abyme* discussed in recent French theory. As one critic explains, the reduplicative power of the *mise en abyme* "uncovers a frame within a frame in endless replication—the Kantian and painterly 'parergon' . . . that one can also think of in more homely terms as the Dutch-cleanser, Quaker-Oats, or Morton-Salt pictorial recursions of American commercial packaging" (Joseph, 1992, 92).

As Gray moves irresistibly from a landscape before the eye to a landscape in the mind, he finds that the people he wants to commemorate may be too obscure to represent. If they are prey to "dumb Forgetfulness" (l. 85), how can their celebrant himself be anything but mute? His elegy seems constantly on the verge of running out of subject matter. To prolong his portrait he must momentarily allow his mute inglorious Miltons to come alive and speak. Freed from temporal and spatial constraints by a chain of timeless infinitives, the guiltless Cromwells step right out of their picture frame, striding across history in the elegy's first bold crossing of the break between stanzas.

> The applause of listening senates to command,
>   The threats of pain and ruin to despise,
> To scatter plenty o'er a smiling land,
>   And read their history in a nation's eyes,
>
> Their lot forbade:
> ("Elegy Written in a Country Churchyard," ll. 61–65)

Before the long delayed apodosis is allowed to return them to their frame, the spilling of grammar over the boundary between stanzas must make us more appreciative of "circumscribed" living (l. 65).

Sometimes we seem to pass imperceptibly from one picture to another. The absence of a second frame around Gray's portrait of world-historical criminals makes possible, for example, the elegy's only use of two-way grammar.

> Far from the madding crowd's ignoble strife,
>   Their sober wishes never learned to stray;

> Along the cool sequestered vale of life
> > They kept the noiseless tenor of their way.
> ("Elegy Written in a Country Churchyard," ll. 73–76)

Do lines 73–74 attach themselves grammatically to the infamous oppressors of humankind? In wading "through slaughter to a throne" and shutting "the gates of mercy on mankind" (ll. 67–68), do these oppressors never learn to stray from the strife? Or are we to take "sober wishes" without any benefit of irony? The comma after "strife" suggests that line 73 is not an adverbial phrase modifying "stray," but an adjectival phrase in apposition to "wishes." The "sober wishes" are the "wishes" of the poor, and we have slipped, almost imperceptibly, into the picture space of a very different portrait.

At the end of the elegy Gray dramatizes the pain and risk of leave-taking.

> For who to dumb Forgetfulness a prey,
> > This pleasing anxious being e'er resigned,
> Left the warm precincts of the cheerful day,
> > Nor cast one longing lingering look behind?
> ("Elegy Written in a Country Churchyard," ll. 85–88)

As we linger fondly over the hypermetric last line, the falling dactyls add regret to the backward-reaching intimacy of a final weighted gesture. With the slow departure of life from the twilight world of the opening stanza, the stage empties for everyone but the elegist. Now it seems to empty even for us. For having been drawn into the elegy by a rhetorical question, "For whom to dumb Forgetfulness a prey . . . ?" the reader now finds it hard to resist identifying with Gray's elegist, who invokes himself two quatrains later in a phrase of approximately the same syntactic shape: "For thee, who mindful of the unhonored dead" (l. 93). The apostrophized "thee," we discover in the next line, is the speaker himself. But it is unusual to address oneself as "thou." Before we register the true meaning, we may surmise that, in imitating an epitaph inscription that hails a passer-by from the grave, the elegist is now addressing *us*.

What was lacking for the submarine gem or desert flower (ll. 53–56)—a sympathetic witness—is now supplied by each reader. The "voice of Nature" that cries out from the tomb is a voice that seeks attentive response. Even a "frail memorial," whose "uncouth rhymes" (l. 79) recall Milton's "uncouth swain" in "Lycidas," invites a sympathetic observer to infer that the unhonored dead are virtuous, without being tempted to ask Wordsworth's subversive question: "Where are all the *bad* people buried?" (1974, 2:63). The epitaph's moving tribute to the elegist, the "youth to Fortune and to Fame unknown" (l. 118), celebrates qualities that do not act well. But Gray makes his undramatic subject moving by unobtrusively contrasting it with behavior that is actable but vicious. To the swain the dead elegist is merely an anonymous eccentric. But he fondly seeks him out, and regretfully notes his absence from familiar places: "Another came; not yet beside the rill, / Nor up the lawn, nor at the wood was he" (ll. 111–12). The three negatives ring out like a knell. Like Swift's self-portrait at the end of the satirical verses on his death, or Pope's self-eulogy in the "Epistle to Dr. Arbuthnot," Gray's epitaph invites us to weigh silently our impressions of private virtues. If Gray's elegist, like the unhonored dead, is difficult to commemorate, it is not because he has tried to play an obscure or remote historical role, but because he does not understand the nature of playing a role at all.

The epitaph's closing quatrain becomes suddenly reticent, as if the eulogist has already said too much. Enclosed in parentheses, the death youth's "trembling hope" is made even more tremulous by its tenuous grammatical connection with the rest of the stanza.

> No farther seek his merits to disclose,
>   Or draw his frailities from their dread abode
> (There they alike in trembling hope repose),
>   The bosom of his Father and his God.
> ("Elegy Written in a Country Churchyard," ll. 125–28)

Only in this last parenthesis does Gray begin to intimate the hidden truth that elegiac crossings are always fraught with risk. Nothing is certain. To be reticent about the merits of the dead allows one to be equally silent about their failures. If the youth had frailities, epitaphs are not the place to record them.

In a handsome tribute Dr. Johnson praises as original Gray's idea that the best protection against insult and oblivion is some representation in sculpture or words to which a sympathetic observer may generously respond. "I have never seen the notions in any other place; yet he that reads them here, persuades himself that he has always felt them" (Johnson, 1906, 2:464). No wonder the notions strike Johnson as original. For the idea that an object is inseparable from a sympathetic perceiver represents a new theory of representation and perception. It coincides with Berkeley's new axiom of knowing: "to be is to be perceived." To be a village Hampden or a little tyrant of the rural fields is to lack a theater like Cromwell's—a world-historical stage on which to perform. And spectacle for its own sake reaches a zenith of absurdity in the arrogance of Gray's desert flower, "born to blush unseen" (l. 55), or in the "gem of purest ray serene" (l. 53), wasted in the darkness of an unfathomed ocean cave. Without observers, the world becomes a play without an audience. If "every bosom returns an echo" to the sentiments of Gray's poem (Johnson, 1906, 2:464), it is because the sentiments of each reader are an important part of what the elegy represents. In the youth's epitaph every kindred spirit finds the representation of a representation. We find a mirror of the tribute some future elegist may pay *us*.

A similar theory of knowing and perception informs Wordsworth's representation of the conditions of representing in "Tintern Abbey." The reciprocity of mind and nature, observer and observed, is recognized at that moment in the poem when Wordsworth discovers that nature can never exist wholly as spectacle, as an object of purely aesthetic devotion, blind to its own darker side. Pure spectacle isolates the scene or person to be observed; incapable of seeing anything itself, the scene as spectacle is already half unhinged from a picture's necessary complement, a perceiving subject. And the perceiver of such a landscape is himself half blind or dead, since in trying to detach himself from the spectacle, he is trying to represent less than can be represented. The minimal unit of knowing, we discover, is what J. F. Ferrier calls "the world *mecum*," the object in union with a perceiving subject. Because the mind partly creates and partly perceives its world ("Tintern Abbey," ll. 105–7), each picture of the Wye Valley is both a picture *in* Wordsworth's mind and a picture *of* his mind—a representation of an observer's way of representing change.

Though a strangeness like absence or death can be felt to inhabit the spaces between words and lines in "Tintern Abbey," Wordsworth knows that a sympathetic observer who is faithful to Berkeley's axiom of being can fill the void with cherished presences. The greatest of the poet's losses will be the absence of Dorothy. But as long as he can represent some future condition of his sister's representation, his ending is not despair. And so in saying to Dorothy, like a voice from the grave, "Nor . . . / . . . wilt thou then forget / That on the banks of this delightful stream / We stood together" (ll. 146, 149–151), Wordsworth draws upon the auxiliary verb of prophecy and volition to reach into the future and to commemorate by an odd kind of inverted déjà vu his sister's future commemoration of a love which, after his death, she alone will be able to keep alive in the "dwelling-place" of memory.

If virtue is never unremembered and God is the ultimate absentee mourner, then Berkeley's axiom *esse est percipi* can be generalized into an even bolder paradox: Ferrier's claim that death is not conceivable. The inconceivability of death can mean one of two things. It may mean that death is a threshold experience: being outside life, it cannot be moved forward in time. To place death inside life, as a painful experience, rather than on the boundary of life, is to forget that, though the *idea* of death affects the way we live, the *phenomenon* of death brings experience as such to an end. Alternatively, we may say that death is inconceivable because of Berkeley's paradox: neither as an idea nor as a phenomenon, is death capable of being detached from a perceiving subject.

In the first case, since death is not an experience as such, it would seem impossible to have a clear intuition of the difference between events in the lives of ghosts and flesh-and-blood people. The events in such lives are surely different, but not decisively different. What kind of relational failure, for example, would entitle the child in Wordsworth's "We Are Seven" to conclude that two of her sisters and brothers are dead? Since life, unlike a chain of linked events, is not essentially relational, it is possible that death is inconceivable because we have no clear intuition of the kind of relational failure that would entitle Wordsworth's child to detach her dead siblings from her own consciousness of them by proclaiming they are no longer members of her family.

The impossibility of doing so brings us to the second reason why death may be inconceivable. And this involves a form of Berkeley's and Ferrier's paradox, the curious fact that we are continually trying to know *less* about death than it is possible to know. Since the atoms or building blocks of knowledge are "the things, or thoughts *mecum*" (Ferrier, 1854, 93), the moment we try to detach death from our consciousness of death, making it into an idea rather than an experienced phenomenon, we are trying to perform an epistemological operation that is not, strictly speaking, possible. "Try to flood your consciousness with the image of non-consciousness," as Unamuno says, "and you will see the difficulty. We cannot conceive of ourselves as not existing" (1972, 43). In order to think of its own annihilation, the mind must sever itself from a framing consciousness. But the mind itself is just such a frame: to conceive its destruction, it must detach itself from itself. As Shelley asks in "Adonais": "Shall that alone which knows / Be as a sword consumed before the sheath / By sightless lightning" (ll. 177–79)? If the preposition "before" is construed temporally, then the annihilation is inconceivable, because how can lightning consume a sword until it first burns through its protective sheath? And if "before" is construed spatially, so that we imagine the sword placed outside or in front of the sheath, then destruction is equally inconceivable. For how can any contained consciousness, which is by definition "sheathed," be possibly conceived as sheathless? Since "that alone which knows" is both container and contained, any attempt to remove the sword from its sheath simply encases the sword in a nesting structure of new sheaths.

The inconceivability of removing death from a containing consciousness helps explain the paradox of "an immortal sickness which kills not" in *The Fall of Hyperion: A Dream* (l. 258). The poem's containing frame is the dreamer's experience in the garden before he drinks the elixir. Inside that outer frame Keats places the dreamer's visions in the sanctuary, culminating in his "view of sad Moneta's" skull (l. 275), which frames events originally presented without any framing consciousness in the first *Hyperion*. Though perhaps only Moneta or Christ can maintain the same intense interest in universal death that each individual takes in his own death, Keats shows how Moneta's transformation of her deathward progression is, at least in principle, possible. Deathward declensions are reversed (they "progress to no death"), when the framing of a frame inside a frame allows Keats to revive the force of Berkeley's paradox by showing how death is inconceivable. Nothing, including the dreamer's own annihilation, can be divorced from folds within folds of his own containing consciousness.

Kant and Wordsworth: Can a *Real* Reality Be Known?

Behind the veil of phenomena Kant's practical reason discovers moral consciousness and God. And his aesthetic faculties discover a "purposiveness without purpose," not a humanly useful creation, but one that exists autonomously, for its own sake, suggesting design and intention yet eluding these things. Paradoxically, the more meaningful and teleological our knowledge becomes, like the "shadowy recollections" that are still "a master light of all our seeing" in Wordsworth, the less we are able to know, at least directly. The shadow of Kant's paradox falls across the whole nineteenth century, and Northrop Frye puts it this way: "The world that we see and understand is not the noumenon, the world in itself, but only the world as phenomenon, as adapted to our categories of perception and reasoning. The inference is that *real* reality, so to speak, cannot be known" (1968, 84).

Kant's paradox encourages the Romantics to create a flexible language of symbols. They may even affirm that Kant's noumenal world is a world of mystical identity. Though we generally know flowers and grains of sand only as phenomena, if we could know them as they really are, we would "hold Infinity in the palm of [our] hand," as Blake boasts, "And Eternity in an hour" ("Auguries of Innocence," ll. 3–4). Because Wordsworth is more cautious than Blake, he finds it more difficult to close the gap between the noumenal world that lies naked under the clothes of phenomena in a work like *Sartor Resartus* and the clothes that both conceal and reveal that nakedness. Romantic nature represents a reality it does not fully exhaust. But unlike Tennyson's phantom Nature, "A hollow form with empty hands" (*In Memoriam*,

3.12), Wordsworth's "clouds of glory" are a symbol of what is really there. With their keener sense of the limitations of ordinary experience, Victorian elegists like Tennyson and Arnold are likely to be warier, more critical of the entombment of noumena in "Shades of the prison-house" that "begin to close / Upon [Wordsworth's] growing Boy," obscuring the "trailing clouds of glory" that he brings "From God, who is [his] home" ("Ode: Intimations of Immortality," ll. 65–66, 68–69).

Behind the world of representation, the objective world in which pure reason sees the objective counterpart of itself, Kant discerns, like Wordsworth in his "Ode: Intimations of Immortality," traces of a divine spark, "the visionary gleam" that is always on the point of taking flight from the world. Just as Kant's unconscious will discovers God, so his aesthetic faculties discover a sovereign spirit delighting in its own free play and design. Such is the elusive "glory" that hovers like a "purposiveness without purpose" over Wordsworth's ode. This power may not exist in the same sense that the setting sun and meanest flower exist. But it is a fiction we enter into "as if" it were true, an imaginative and poetic premise. If we accept it, we do so tentatively, as a form of the kind Kant calls teleological, relating to purpose and ultimate design.

I have no direct evidence that Wordsworth, like his friend Coleridge, had firsthand knowledge of Kant. Yet Wordsworth's celebrated saying that the eye both creates and perceives its world ("Tintern Abbey," ll. 105–7) enshrines a cornerstone of Kant's so-called Copernican revolution in philosophy—his new axiom of knowing that our judgments of the world are both synthetic and a priori. Certainly the play of "glory" in Wordsworth's ode exhibits a formal purposiveness of the kind Kant describes, for it excites our "cognitive power without being limited to any definite cognition" (Kant, 1914, 71). Syntactic hovering allows Wordsworth's first use of "glory" to waver in emphasis between "The glory . . . of a dream" and "the glory of a *dream*" (l. 5). Are the glory and freshness celebrated for their dream-like lucidity? Or is the rhyme of "dream" and "seem" meant to suggest the shimmering illusion of a mirage? The wavering makes the vision playful and tremulous, like an optical illusion or trompe l'oeil: now we see the glory and now we don't. As Kant says, the elusive gleam may seem "contrary to purpose." Yet "objectively, as requisite for the estimation of [the glory's] magnitude, it is purposive" (1914, 122). "Waters on a starry night" present harmony; Wordsworth rightly calls them "beautiful and fair" (ll. 14–15). But a sublime glory is not like that. It uses conflict and elusiveness to surpass "every standard of sense" (Kant, 1914, 110).

Once "a glory" has passed away, it is harder to associate it with a specific item like a "meadow, grove," or "stream." And the cognate phrase, "a glorious birth" (l. 16), is equally indefinite. After describing the "Waters" as "beautiful and fair," we half expect Wordsworth to say that the sunshine is fair, too. But the adjective "glorious" is transferred from its expected antecedent to a strange new referent. What exactly does the sun give birth to? To day, a life, the planets? We are invited to run up and down a scale of marveling, as Wordsworth leaves us trembling on the brink of at least three threshold states. When the fourth use of glory is assimilated by alliteration to a fitful "visionary gleam," it is no longer linked to "dream" by the preposition "of" but by the correlative conjunction "and."

> Whither is fled the visionary gleam?
> Where is it now, the glory and the dream?
> ("Ode: Intimations of Immortality," ll. 57–58)

Hendiadys stabilizes the two-way flow of a "glorious dream" and a "dreamlike glory" into a parity of marvels: a single but elusive "glory-dream." By presenting a sensory whole that draws two singular grammatical forms into its orbit ("Where *is it* now?"), Wordsworth is trying to show that nature is sublime and glorious only "in those of its phenomena whose intuition brings with it the idea of their infinity." And, as Kant says, "this last can only come by the inadequacy of the greatest effort of our imagination to estimate the magnitude of an object" (1914, 117). That inadequacy explains why the feeling of the sublime is also a feeling of pain.

But though pain arises from the want of accord between the pure reason and the aesthetic faculty, Kant believes we are also exhilarated to discover that some ideas exceed our greatest faculty of sense. Any "falling" away of sense may seem a "failing." But Wordsworth discovers that even the vacancy produced by a "falling" away can produce the fullness of a "visionary gleam" (l. 57). Peal away the husk around "misgivings" and "Blank" (l. 146), for example, and we find that "misgivings" dislodges "givings," and that "Blank" links up with its earlier near-rhyme "thanks" (l. 142), to yield benediction and praise. We tremble before such discoveries "like a guilty Thing surprised" (l. 149), because we had not expected to extract out of "Blank misgivings" (l. 146) such bounteous "thanksgivings." Such lexical treasures are an undeserved gift. Like our "High instincts," "first affections," or "shadowy recollections" (ll. 148, 150–51), they are received with pleasure as a glorious surprise.

Kant discloses a final paradox, that "the feeling of the sublime in nature is respect for our own destination" (1914, 119). There is nothing behind the veil that is not already in front of it. This paradox explains why, even as shades close in upon the youth, the glory remains undulatingly alive in Wordsworth's strange use of prepositions and conjunctions.

> But he
> beholds the light, and whence it flows,
>   He sees it in his joy;
> ("Ode: Intimations of Immortality," ll. 70–72)

The untroubled conjoining of the noun "light" and the adverbial clause "whence it flows" implies that the origin and destiny of light are as lucidly beheld as the light itself. Though the phrase "He sees it in his joy" might simply mean that he beholds the vision "joyfully," the prepositional construction intimates something stranger. In experiencing joy the youth is also beholding the light, since light is the truest emanation of a joyful soul. The glory that is "the fountain light of all our day, / . . . a master light of all our seeing" (ll. 153–54) is also the self-delighting mind, free and playful, in its most radiant form. This paradoxical discovery helps justify the penultimate use of "glory."

> Thou little Child, yet glorious in the might
> Of heaven-born freedom on thy being's height,
> ("Ode: Intimations of Immortality," ll. 123–24)

The daring figurative transfer of "might" to a nonphysical attribute of the child, its "heaven-born freedom," explains the power of the child's present experience to permeate and radiate its future and also to qualify Kant's stricture that "the inscrutableness of the idea of freedom quite cuts it off from any positive presentation" (1914, 144).

"In our mind," Kant boasts, "we find a superiority to nature even in its immensity. While the might of nature makes us recognize our own impotence, considered as beings of nature, it discloses to us a faculty of judging independently of, and a superiority over, nature" (1914, 125). Wordsworth's final use of "glory" in the ode helps sustain this paradox.

> Though nothing can bring back the hour
> Of splendour in the grass, of glory in the flower;
>   We will not grieve, . . .
> ("Ode: Intimations of Immortality," ll. 179–81)

The fine wavering in lines 64–66 between the glory's betrayal of the exile and the exile's betrayal of the glory is repeated now in the double sense of "in." The glory that resides *in* the flower is a splendor that the mourner once *gloried in*. The rippling waves of rhyme, assonance, and alliteration breathe life into the lost vision, beautifully reversing the impact of the elegist's lament. Because the poet cannot previsage a loss of glory, or a suspension of the tremulous states of consciousness that give the word its meaning, he finds he cannot really imagine an eclipse of the celestial light that is the truest emanation of an awakened self. Wordsworth wants the excitement of this discovery to spread like a shock wave or tremor. Even when the fitful gleam seems to tremble out of sight, the long wave of the poet's fluctuating moods remains unbroken. It has been said that the greatest elegiac ode of the nineteenth century is incorrectly named: it is not an elegy about immortality at all. But when Wordsworth lifts Kant's veil, he finds there an image of himself. We survive the death of our natural bodies as a "glory" we have made and helped commemorate. As Kant says, our feeling for the sublime in nature is a feeling for our destination; in Frost's words, "it is most us."

Foucault and Stevens: Can the Subject Disappear?

In his *Critique of Judgment* Kant discloses behind the veil of phenomena the teleological operations of a self-conscious mind. In *The order of Things* Michel Foucault takes the rending of the veil one step further. Behind the subject he discloses pure aesthetic design, behind the oracular poet a word made object. Just as Kant discovers behind nature a "purposiveness without a purpose," so Foucault discovers behind each writer or speaker a self-sustaining system of signs, like the bytes in a computer, which will doom humanity to "dispersion when language regains its unity" (1973, 386). Foucault formulates the paradox this way: he predicts that just as the Romantics celebrated in the death of representational language the birth of self-consciousness in man, so future structuralists and semioticians—the heirs of the Symbolists and formalists—will reverse the process by celebrating the rebirth of an "imperious unity of Discourse" as the death of man.

Before I try to defend the paradox of a sign that effaces all trace of its human origin, I shall cite some well-known arguments against it. How can words be freed, we might ask, from the speakers who use and reinvent them? If writers are not the primary shapers of their works, can they be held accountable for what they say? And are critics not then free to make a poem mean anything or nothing according to whim? Like Hans Vaihinger, a nineteenth-century disciple of Kant, we might accept the fiction of an autonomous language "as if" it were true, the way we might accept one of Kant's regulative truths. Yet if language does not exist for the sake of something other than itself—for a poet's or a reader's sake, say—how can it be said to exist for its own sake either? Moreover, contrary to Foucault, George Steiner contends that man and language die together. If, in Adorno's phrase, there is "no poetry after Auschwitz," then no elegies can be written. Or if they are, they must be composed of broken words and negations. How can an elegist like Geoffrey Hill write on the holocaust without being implicated in the horrors he writes about? He speaks of the tongue's atrocities, as if words themselves had lost their innocence and "the living truth [were] no longer sayable" (Steiner, 1967, 52).

Nietzsche's insight that God and language die together also refutes Foucault's paradox. In Nietzsche's aphorism, we cannot get rid of God until we get rid of grammar. Only as we discard the Renaissance and medieval figures of similitude and the later classical tropes of representation can we discard the God they were designed to name. In his lecture given at Mount Holyoke College, "Two or Three Ideas," Wallace Stevens confirms Nietzsche's thesis. The gods are destroyed when their aesthetic becomes invalid. And as Eliot argues in "Second Thoughts about Humanism," the death of the gods is in part our death, too. A time of disbelief is precisely a time when the frequency of a detached style, a style that is just made up of words, is greatest. But far from endorsing Foucault's uncritical apology for such a style, Stevens is a formalist who wants to expand the power of formalism to include what is often considered its opposite: a power to invent supreme fictions, to be an architect of both humanity and its new gods.

Foucault's hermetic poet is a fashioner of self-contained verbal forms: he is a renewer of words rather than a changer of worlds. As an elegist, Stevens combines both kinds of poetry. The sealed-off, self-reflexive forms of "The Owl in the Sarcophagus" are to the vatic utterances of "The Auroras of Autumn" what structuralism is to hermeneutics. In the former, "language itself speaks and so offers itself as an object of experience" (Bruns, 1974, 2). In the latter, the poet's power "extends . . . beyond the formation of a work toward the creation of the world" (1). Few elegies are more hermetic than "The Owl in the Sarcophagus," Stevens' "mythology of modern death," and few are less accessible. The poem's "inventions of farewell" (I.10), sleep, peace, and the spirit of valediction, lead a fugitive half life; they are essences without existence, as Santayana would say. "Nothing is ever present to me except some essence; so that nothing that I possess in intuition, or actually see, is ever *there*" (Santayana, 1955, 99). Few readers would fail to identify Santayana as the subject of Stevens' elegy, "To an Old Philosopher in Rome." But would anyone know that "The Owl in the Sarcophagus" was written for Henry Church if Stevens had not said so? The absence of a paraphraseable content in the poem—at least any I would feel confident about summarizing—lends an odd, whimsical rightness to the witty remark Stevens made to Frost on a Florida train trip: "The trouble with your poetry, Frost, is that it has subjects."

Sleep, the first of the "inventions," is evoked in a seamless grammatical unit, knitting together six tercets, as if raveling up syntactically the sleeve of care.

> There he saw well the foldings in the height
> Of sleep, the whiteness folded into less,
> Like many robings, as moving masses are,
>
> As a moving mountain is, moving through day
> And night, colored from distances, central
> Where luminous agitations come to rest,
> ("The Owl in the Sarcophagus," III.1–6)

"Foldings" and its cognate alert us to the self-enfolding of sleep, a mirroring surface on which we see "the meanings of its folds" reflected, "As on water of an afternoon" (III.10, 12). Reflecting the power of the transformed observer, whose "wild-ringed eye" perceives these things, sleep also fulfills in a double sense, both consummating the purpose or end of sleep and "filling full" the lungs of sleep's deep breather.

> Then he breathed deeply the deep atmosphere
> Of sleep, the accomplished, the fulfilling air.
> ("The Owl in the Sarcophagus," III.17–18)

Peace, the second of the elegist's "inventions," is just as self-reflexive. Transformed by the brightness of his own "brilliant height," like a sun irradiated by its own fire, Peace flourishes the world in a double sense. He causes the world to flourish, or break into flower. But he also makes strokes or flourishes with it, as though he were brandishing a weapon. Though few transformations could be more magical, few forms of magic are as hermetical or self-enclosed.

> This is the figure stationed at our end,
> Always, in brilliance, fatal, final, formed
> Out of our lives to keep us in our death,
> ("The Owl in the Sarcophagus," IV.22–24)

Stevens even manages to impart an exciting tautness of implication to the phrase "Out of our lives." Life is the material cause of Peace, but Peace is also external to or *outside of life*. As in Yeats's petition to be taken "out of nature' ("Sailing to Byzantium," l. 25), the preposition "in"—"in our death" (IV.24)—exerts a backward force on "Out," inviting us to take the word more literally than we had planned. When the elegist tells us that Peace is attired in "a robe that is our glory" (IV.27), we are asked to construe "our" as both a subjective genitive that attires us in our own glory and as an objective genitive that derives our glory from the robe. If Peace were not guarding the dead, as a genius of the infernal shore, he would have no glory. Light flows in two directions at once: it is as true to say that a light emanating from our death confers glory on Peace as it is to say that Peace is the king, the "candle by our beds," who confers glory on *us*.

Stevens' last "invention of farewell," the spirit of valediction, is the most elusive of the three. Like Keats's Moneta, whose visage progresses "deathwards to no death," this third "monster of elegy" reveals its secrets only at the moment of change or breakup, just as electron volts emitted at the speed of light are said to reveal the atom's structure only when the atom itself is breaking down.

> She held men closely with discovery,
>
> Almost as speed discovers, in the way
> Invisible change discovers what is changed,
> ("The Owl in the Sarcophagus," V.6–8)

In conjunction with these bold claims of discovery, Stevens uses the qualifier "Almost"—"Almost as speed discovers"—to create a tremor of nuance and delicate discrimination. Instead of coming totally into focus for the mind, these tremors gesture at distinctions that elude the mind and that tend to expire just beyond its grasp, "on the edges of oblivion" (V.15), like the spirit of valediction herself. Surviving intact, however, is the elegist's exact apprehension of what remains unattainable for him, something that escapes into the empty space beyond the dash "in the silence that follows [the spirit's] last word—" (V.18).

Made out of marvels rather than marble, the three "monsters of elegy" (sleep, peace, and valediction) are fugitive, self-created essences, miracles of self-enfolding and self-division.

> This is the mythology of modern death
> And these, in their mufflings, monsters of elegy,
> Of their own marvel made, of pity made,
> ("The Owl in the Sarcophagus," VI.1–3)

Inhabitants of what Santayana calls the "realm of essence," these self-reflexive and hermetic forms are "monstrous" because fabulous, like centaurs: they are an indelible background for all the transitory facts of mere existence. The moment Stevens tries to envisage the relations among the "monsters of elegy" in the mind that begets them, their kinship is bound to seem incestuous. For the process of procreation is more like cloning than a form of adult procreation. Since one of the brothers is said to be a father, he must be a monster in the Oedipal sense, both the mother's husband and her son. As a mind-begotten fiction, "the mythology of modern death" may seem as monstrous as incest once we try to conceive it. But the conquest of death still requires the elegist to contemplate the "supremest images" of death, "The pure perfections of parental space" (VI.6). To entertain these pure images is to embrace more than a shadow world of hermetically sealed fictions. It is to move into a world of eternal possibilities that are not the opposite of life but only the opposite of successful imaginations, of intuitions that have guessed some principle of experience.

As in one of M. C. Escher's drawings of a hand drawing a hand, there is always something hermetic about an elegy that uses self-enfolding forms. How, for example, are we to visualize the cosmic marvel of the dead man's apotheosis in "Cortège for Rosenbloom"? When the mourners turn the corner of a line, they "turn," not up the street, as we half expect, but "Up the sky."

> Rosenbloom is dead.
> The tread of the carriers does not halt
> On the hill, but turns
> Up the sky.
> They are bearing his body to the sky.
>
> It is the infants of misanthropes
> And the infants of nothingness
> That tread
> The wooden ascents
> Of the ascending of the dead.
> ("Cortège for Rosenbloom," ll. 11–20)

Is the last phrase a subjective or objective genitive? Are the dead ascending a ladder, or are they themselves the ladder that is climbed? The receding prepositional phrases may yield only the commonplace tautology: the dead ascend a ladder. But the ladder of the dead may itself be ascended in an oddly regressive use of the objective genitive that defies precise visualization. As casually as the pallbearers shed their misanthropy to recover the radical innocence of "infants," bearing [the] body into the sky," we are invited to imagine the ascent of an ascending, as if one moving stair or ladder were riding over another.

Comparably hermetic and self-enfolding is the apotheosis of Canon Aspirin in *Notes toward a Supreme Fiction*. In his dream the aspiring canon not only *sees* ascending wings but also *becomes* them: "he was the ascending wings he saw" ("It Must Give Pleasure," VI.10). In enlarging himself "to include the things / That in each other are included" (VI.19–20), the canon is not just envisaging the traditional subject of elegiac transformation, or any subject at all. Instead, his apotheosis becomes an event, an epiphany of what may *become* a subject. Because the canon is flung at the speed of light to the central point of naked-ness, to the "point / Beyond which thought could not progress as thought" (VI. 15–16), and where, instead of being contained, he him-self becomes the container of the "whole" (VI.20), his transformation is as marvelous as Lycidas's apotheosis, and just as cosmological.

Sometimes Stevens' hermetic self-enfoldings seem to retreat endless-ly, like clouds drifting in space, or like the noun "meanings," which is repeated a half-line later as "half-meanings."

> Like watery words awash; like meanings said
>
> By repetitions of half-meanings. Am I not,
> Myself, only half of a figure of a sort,
>
> A figure half seen, or seen for a moment, a man
> Of the mind, an apparition apparelled in
>
> Apparels of such lightest look that a turn
> Of my shoulder and quickly, too quickly, I am gone?
> ("Angel Surrounded by Paysans," ll. 16–22)

An apparition "apparelled in / Apparels" seems to be dressed in itself somehow, or else folded in clothing that wraps nothing at its center. Though such fugitive phantoms enjoy only half a life, we are awed by the ease with which they jump the breaks between stanzas and lines, as irrepressible and Phoenix-like as the elusive serpent shapes in "The Au-roras of Autumn."

Occasionally a poem as self-enclosed as a haiku may convey all the appalling heartbreak of quick dissolution and early death. Wonderfully alive to the interplay of singular and plural forms, "Man Carrying Thing," for example, celebrates the delicate singularity of the one storm "we must endure all night" (l. 10). Even as the peaceful drift of singulars into a dissolving plural makes us half in love with easeful death, as in Frost's snow poems, each framed couplet composes a tiny fragment, a stay against confusion, as perfectly fashioned though as fragile as a snowflake or haiku.

But such achievements in elegy are rare. It is more common for a hermetic, self-enclosed "invention of farewell" like "The Owl in the Sarcophagus" or "To an Old Philosopher in Rome" to impress the reader as a triumph of formal discipline. The "kind of total grandeur" that Santayana achieves "at the end" of his life is inseparable from the "grandeur" that Stevens achieves at the end of his elegy. "An inquisitor of structures," the elegist arrives at truth by an ascetic practice that Stevens himself compares to a state of chastity prolonged into late ado-lescence. Such austere exercises may lack the power to wound, touch, or even move a reader. But even in writing an Oedipal incest story in "The Owl in the Sarcophagus," Stevens shows how self-enfolding hermetic forms can be perverse as well as witty, as debasing as they are exhilarating, and as destructive as they are fitfully sublime.

Stevens comes closest to validating Foucault's paradox about a disappearing subject in elegies like "The Death of a Soldier," where sense data, in acquiring a life of their own, inhibit the elegist's power to shape or control his materials. When the repeated verb "stops" refuses to stop, in momentary defiance of its meaning, the poem's only runover between stanzas allows the elegist to relax his will by hovering uncertainly for a moment, without any clear sense of where he is going.

> Death is absolute and without memorial,
> As in a season of autumn,
> When the wind stops,
>
> When the wind stops and, over the heavens,
> The clouds go, nevertheless,
> In their direction. ("The Death of a Soldier," ll. 7–12)

For any preconceived direction the poet might wish to impose, the wayward clouds begin to substitute their own motions. The best comment on this "conclusion in which nothing is concluded" comes from Richard Poirier: "The voice drifts away from the narrative and argumentative assertiveness of the first two stanzas and solicits the reader to meander with it. . . . Stevens has phased the poem into a mood wherein the human will, instead of registering its supposedly inherent resistance to self-dispersal, simply relaxes into it" (1987, 216–17). The loss of volition marks a deathward decline and an abdication of the words' responsibility to offer any of the elegy's traditional consolations.

As volition is erased like Foucault's "face drawn in sand" (1973, 387), the human subject seems to preside over its own disappearance. But is contemplation of our self-destruction still not a human act? Only human creatures know they are members "of a fragile species," as one commentator says, "the youngest creatures of any scale, here only a few moments as evolutionary time is measured" (Thomas, 1992, 25). Because we are "the self-conscious children at the edge of the crowd," we alone among the animate creation know that our absence or disappearance has "Itself to be imagined" (Stevens, "The Plain Sense of Things," l. 14). In his Mount Holyoke lecture, Stevens claims that "to see the gods dispelled in mid-air and dissolve like clouds is one of the great human experiences" (Houghton Library typescript, fMS Am 1333.5, 4). Is the spectacle of our own dissolution not just as human and just as great?

Though it is hard to imagine either words or events that remove all trace of a human subject, it must be conceded, in fairness to Foucault, that in an age of computer language and artificial intelligence, which includes Foucault's own project of cultural archaeology, it is easy to cite evidence of art that is inhuman, "not only because it contains no things human," as Ortega Y Gasset explains, "but also because it is an explicit act of dehumanization" (1968, 22). As an invention of bourgeois ideology and liberal humanism, the idea of humanity may be as vulnerable to obsolescence as any other ideology. We can witness its death, not just in modern elegies on the holocaust, but also in the oddly infernal elegy Swinburne writes for Baudelaire. Here language takes on the distinctly infernal quality to be found in any elegy that short-circuits the relay of words through concepts back into sensory objects. Swinburne manages to outwit death by turning Baudelaire into a pure precipitate of language. He distills Baudelaire, the giver of Symbolist words, into his own gift of form.

To dehumanize subjects and turn the words that describe them into sensory wonders, it is not necessary to alter their inherent structure. All Swinburne has to do is dive beneath the level observed by natural perspective, becoming momentarily an anatomist of bosoms, or what one commentator calls "a new Columbus discovering hemispheres" (Ortega Y Gasset, 1968, 36).

> Hast thou found place at the great knees and feet
> Of some pale Titan-woman like a lover,
>> Such as thy vision here solicited,
>> Under the shadow of her fair vast head,
> The deep division of prodigious breasts,
>> The solemn slope of mighty limbs asleep,
>> The weight of awful tresses that still keep
> The savour and shade of old-world pine-forests
>> Where the wet hill-winds weep? ("Ave atque Vale," ll. 58–66)

Though the "solemn slope of mighty limbs asleep" is as pastoral as it is erotic, not even the pun on "slope" can prevent the Swiftian blowup from introducing a stroke of broad parody against the great analogy connecting the female body to the *hortus conclusus* in the Song of Songs.

Whenever pre-Raphaelite and Symbolist elegists sunder syntax or make repetitive use of an alliterative pattern, they increase the chance of turning words into objects. Though both habits persist in the elegiac verse of Ezra Pound, he also transforms them, as in the familiar eighty-first section of *The Cantos*. Pound's injunction, "Pull down thy vanity," expresses the secret truth that we all live in perpetual risk of being dehumanized. Unlike an animal or bird that is always sure of being a mere "beaten dog" or "swollen magpie" (ll. 152–53), man the creator can never take his humanity for granted. For his identity as artist, architect, or fashioner of worlds is never given; it is always in the process of being made. Pindar's heroic imperative, "Become what you are," is echoed in Pound's celebration of the artists who "have gathered from the air a live tradition" (l. 167). Instead of producing an idolatry of the word, as in lesser late Victorian verse, the primitive form of wisdom Pound enjoins releases an energy that is no longer expended with a further end in view. Because such disinterestedness is compatible with deep passion and commitment, its pure projected detachment, "cold / And passionate as the dawn," in Yeats's phrase ("The Fisherman," ll. 39–40), is not to be mistaken for the indifference that parodies disinterestedness or for the anxiety that profanes concern.

For the Romantics, individual experiences and words come first: grammar follows the lexicon. But Foucault's paradox about the disappearing subject reminds us that in purist and structuralist thought the reverse is true. In Booleian logic and the formal mathematical systems of Whitehead and Russell, the grammar and codes precede the lexicon. The formal interweaving of sleep, peace, and the spirit of valediction in Stevens' elegy "The Owl in the Sarcophagus" is the mythological equivalent of this reversal. Though Stevens' elegy on Santayana, "To an Old Philosopher in Rome," has its priest-like celebrant, its rite, the church-like "architecture" of its bed and "ambered room" and even its congregation of "moving nuns," it retains all the form of a theology without any of its content. Its inquisition of structures is not to be mistaken for an inquisition of religious beliefs. As purist art, such elegies occupy a spiritual territory segregated from the workaday world. In one respect, they signal a return to the closed, ritualistic, sacred space of "Lycidas" and *Pearl*. Yet the claim of such poetry to authority, to be holier or more sacred than other elegies, is not supported by any theological or metaphysical claim. The rituals of classical elegy always revolve around a god or the apotheosis of some hero. But in purist elegy god and the hero have departed. Language is left to generate its own quasi-divine power.

When the disappearance of the subject and the absence of teleology are celebrated as a virtue, the value of aesthetic activity becomes its very pointlessness. Glorying in such inutility and reduced ambition, Oscar Wilde is the first English critic to throw over art's absence of point the halo of the sacred. Now the more arbitrary the sacred sign, the purer the faith, because only God can guarantee it. In "Easter 1916" almost anyone, from a madman to a drunken lout like Mac-Bride, can be made a hero, not because all things are equally noble, but because they are equally indifferent. MacBride is exalted only in a Nietzschean sense. As an Irish martyr, he stands beyond good and evil, transfigured by a transvaluation of values. In such an elegy death provides a fresh start: it breaks with all determined values and introduces randomness—the shuffle before another deal. Purist elegy demystifies the sacred by dramatizing the separateness of two levels. All that is necessary is to break the cycle, to stop Ixion's wheel.

In "Easter 1916" the "stone" that troubles "the living stream" is a metaphor for the word made object: Is such a fixity a consummation to be wished, or is it synonymous with death?

> Hearts with one purpose alone
> Through summer and winter seem
> Enchanted to a stone
> To trouble the living stream.
> . . . Minute by minute they live:
> The stone's in the midst of all. ("Easter 1916," ll. 41–44, 55–56)

The frightening side of the stone is disclosed in the poet's next breath. By transmuting change into permanence, the martyrs' sacrifice may "make a stone of the heart" (l. 58). It may destroy the affections, achieving the fixity of a memorial at too high a price.

It is easy to be lulled asleep by the heroic muster call of proper names· "I write it out in a verse— / MacDonagh and MacBride / And Connolly and Pearse" (ll. 74–76). But just when the elegist's mind is being numbed by incantation, his critical faculties return to check the drift into reverie.

> What is it but nightfall?
> No, no, not night but death;
> Was it needless death after all? ("Easter 1916," ll. 65–67)

Though the political martyrs seem from the beginning of the elegy to belong to a secret and elite group, the ordinariness of their lives is mocked by the dull shape of the repeating rhymes and identical phrases.

> I have passed with a nod of the head
> *Or polite meaningless words,*
> Or have lingered awhile and said
> *Polite meaningless words* ("Easter 1916," ll. 5–8, my emphasis)

A "terrible beauty" attaches to MacBride and his fellow patriots, not because they belong to a class of special people, but because they represent the special class of martyrs. Their purity would be less inviolable if it were not so arbitrary.

Even the elegy of abomination falls into Foucault's purist category.

For this category may require something human to die so that something less contaminated, more debased but also more sacred, can be put in its place. As Julia Kresteva explains in *Powers of Horror: An Essay on Abjection*, sacrifice and abomination "reveal their true interdependence at the moment when the corpse topples from being the object of *worship* over to being the object" of defilement, the body held in abjection and contempt (1982, 110). Such an object is the fantasized corpse of Sylvia Plath's father, with a "stake" driven through its "fat black heart," in her elegy "Daddy" (l. 76). Plath's portrait of her father has to be offensive enough to arouse outrage and dismay. But her hatred of the "Panzer-man," however brutalized, still preserves intact the *force* of what she loathes. The father whom she wants to kill is still a holy figure. Though he is a fallen god in whom the sentimental has been purified by irony and emptied of its human content, the religion of abomination in which he plays the role of victim clearly overlays a religion of the sacred.

4 ❧ The Paradox of the Unspeakable: Speaking by Being Silent in Romantic Elegy

Classical elegists differ from other people in what they know, Romantic elegists in what they do not know. The strong mourners of classical elegy remind us that death may make all things new, and that only weak mourners are destroyed by it. The estranged and silent mourners of Romantic elegy remind us that nobody knows what death means. Mourners who profess to speak about its mystery are in danger of profaning it. Classical elegists have come to possess eloquence and acquired skills, but Romantic elegists may pride themselves on their silence and artlessness. Their unjaded vision would be spoiled by training, which would prevent further education. Like children who have failed to socialize their imagination, Romantic elegists prefer to be shy and reclusive. They would rather be Wordsworth's reticent elegist in the Lucy poems than an eloquent mourner like Donne.

In such elegists silence and reserve are more than a stylish aesthetic of despair. As for Augustine, time moves toward eternity the way each syllable in their sentences moves toward the silence of the period at the end. We have to linger over the dashes and caesuras, over the periods and ellipses, listening there for meanings that are otherwise inaudible. Geoffrey Hill speaks well of the "ambivalent power" of the short word in Hopkins (1984, 101). As grammar fragments, the soul is revealed in its "most frightful splintering" (98). Auden's elegiac ballad, "As I Walked out One Evening," and Hopkins' elegy, *The Wreck of the Deutschland*, share no discernible Romantic ideology. But because both poems alternate predictably between expansive and elliptical styles, they are united by a family resemblance discernible in the zero values of disjunction and elision.

As Kierkegaard understands, the paradox of the unspeakable is a form of irony, a way of speaking without saying anything. And irony seems the only possible response to the necessary scandal of Romantic culture. I am referring to the scandal that, though nineteenth-century culture cannot deny art's centrality to its most original claim (that each perceiver is an artist and builder, a self-conscious fashioner of worlds), neither can it deny the marginal status of many artists, including the solitary mourners of many Romantic elegies. Since all the estranged elegist can do is wait for an undeserved grace of intuition, for a spark from heaven, like Arnold's scholar-gipsy, he may often feel like a leech gatherer during a season of drought. Art is central and serious, but how can Romantic culture come to terms with an enterprise so fraught with risk? Though Wordsworth in *The Recluse* (ll. 786–94) applies the same panoply of venerative terms to the poet's mind that the Middle Ages and the Renaissance reserve for God alone, a silence of melancholy must descend on the Romantic elegist when he reflects that, whatever the fortune of the humanity he helps create, his own achievements are short-lived and precarious.

Most medieval, Renaissance, and Augustan elegies use theological and moral explanation to console the mourner. But many Romantic and post-Romantic elegies present death as a wild and terrifying phenomenon. What begins in Gray and Wordsworth as a dramatization of the consciousness that rims the inner self ends in Tennyson and Pater as confrontation with a very strong form of nothingness. The Romantic elegist's assurance is founded on what Wordsworth calls the lordship of his mind over "outward sense" (*The Prelude*, 12.222). But as Harold Bloom says, "any sublime that founds itself upon the power of the mind over a universe of death must smash itself to fragments on that rock of otherness constituted at last" by our own death (1987, 133). Silence seems the only possible response to the elegist's discovery that the universe of sense is also a universe of death. When he thinks he is safely on the ground, he looks down and realizes he is standing on a girder, thousands of feet above an abyss.

Though it is difficult to use the terms "classical" and "romantic" responsibly, it is impossible to do without them. I have been trying in the preceding paragraphs to distinguish between a romantic and a classical sensibility that corresponds in a rough way to the distinction that is often made between the Romantic age and the classical culture that precedes it. I realize, however, that this is not the precise use of "classical" I developed in chapter 1, where the terms "pastoral" and "classical" are often used interchangeably. It is possible to speak of a classical pastoral elegy like "Lycidas" or of a romantic classical elegy like "Adonais," just as it is possible to speak of a classical confessional elegy like Donne's *Second Anniversary* or of a romantic confessional elegy like *In Memoriam*. In courtesy to the reader I should explain that when I speak of a Romantic or post-Romantic elegy I am referring to poems written during or after the historical period we usually call Romantic, the period 1780 to 1830.

I have already discussed *In Memoriam* as a confessional elegy, and I shall have more to say about it in chapter 7. Considered as a whole, *In Memoriam* does seem to me to have more in common with an Augustinian confession than with a classical elegy like "Lycidas." I would be the last to deny, however, that an individual lyric like section 86 of *In Memoriam* has more concentrated cathartic power than lyric angst. It makes far more sense to compare it with a pastoral elegy than with a confessional poem. A lyric like number 7, the "Dark house" elegy, is best explicated in terms of the brokenness and breakthrough I associate with modern elegy. Many individual lyrics of the poem are Romantic elegies of reserve, and I want to consider them in that context in a moment. The conclusion would seem to be that individual elegies fall into all the categories I discuss in this book. Overall, the poem, I would contend, is a confession. But just as individual lyrics can belong to more than one genre or category of elegy, so critics are surely free to discuss them in more than one context.

The episteme, which Michel Foucault proposes as a new taxonomic category, has the value of aligning the style of an elegy with a historical period's epistemological premises, with its most pervasive axioms of knowing. These can be studied in the figures of similitude common to pastoral elegy, or in Berkeley's and Ferrier's new axioms of cognition, which help foreground the elegist's self-conscious mind, as we saw in chapter 2, even eclipsing in importance the person who is mourned. This chapter examines a third axiom, the Romantic premise that because we can know the truth but never speak it, an elegy should be one part speech to three parts silence. As developed by Wordsworth, Berkeley's *esse est percipi* is a Romantic premise, too. It asserts the faith that, by birth and by nature, we are all artists, architects, fashioners of our own humanity and values. Perhaps we should say that Berkeley's axiom is to Romantic epistemology what doctrines of silence and reserve, as developed, for example, in John Keble's theology of reserve in *Tract 89*, are to Romantic and post-Romantic theories of symbolism and signs. As a poet of withheld meanings, an elegist is often a master of what Tennyson oxymoronically calls "silent-speaking words" (*In Memoriam*, 95.26). But a silent-speaking word is a paradox few readers can assimilate. To the degree that a word speaks its silence would seem to be illusory, and to the degree that it is silent it is incapable of speech.

In the context of section 95 of *In Memoriam*, a fine example of the Romantic elegy of reserve, the phrase "silent-speaking words" refers to the dead Hallam's letters: "And strangely on the silence broke / The silent-speaking words, and strange / Was love's dumb cry" (*In Memoriam*, 95.25–27). The words may be "silent-speaking" because Tennyson pronounces them subvocally. More probably, they are said to be silent because the voice of the friend who must be imagined speaking them is estranged by the medium of the written word. Not only must this voice be elicited from words as they appear to the eye on the written page; it must also be elicited as the voice of someone who speaks from the far side of silence, having died since the letter was written. Eric Griffiths has argued that all good poetry stages "small imaginative drama[s] about speaking, a drama on the page for the voice elicited from the page" (1989, 71). This is particularly true of elegies, where the poet is often inviting the reader to help him elicit a voice from beyond the grave. What Wordsworth calls a "strange half-absence" can be created by a skewing of the lines, or by creating a rhyme to the eye but not to the ear, or by suggesting "a compact the voice cannot speak and the eye cannot fulfill."

In the quoted passage Hallam's words break "on the silence," and their breakage coincides with both the slight breaking of the voice at the end of the poetic line and with the breaking of emotion on the hard edge of print. The elegist speaks of silence and also uses silence to speak. "In *letters*," as Tennyson confides to Emily Sellwood before their marriage, "words too often prove a bar or hindrance instead of a bond of union" (Lang and Shannon, 1981, 1:173). As evidence of such a hindrance, Tennyson's lines about the letters' "silent-speaking words" are fraught with tonal indecision and semantic ambiguity. Are Hallam's words "broken" by the silence, as the voice itself seems to break down or fail because of the letters' absence of any indicated gestures and tones? Or does "break" convey a contrary meaning? In "breaking out," as from a prison, do the words elicit what C. S. Lewis memorably calls "the rough, sharp, cleansing tang" (1961, 19) of a dead person's voice, which may remain clear and distinct long after the visual memories fade?

To what degree does Tennyson's paradox of a "silent-speaking word" antecedently exist in nineteenth-century elegies? And to what extent is it a construction of the generic critic or literary historian? Taxonomies and epistemes presumably correspond to historical realities. But did the idea of a "silent-speaking word" or of a "printed voice" actually exist until Tennyson and Browning found names for it? Perhaps that question is less important than another more pragmatic one: What is the consequence of a literary critic's entertaining the idea of a family of poems to which elegies by Wordsworth, Hardy, Patmore, Dickinson, all belong? In discussing "family resemblances," Wittgenstein reminds us that members of a family need share no common essence; it is enough that they share a network of similarities (1972, 32, prop. 67). But because most critics of genre share a distaste for induction, "direct observation of texts is the most unusual method of classification," and, as David Perkins reminds us, "it is also the least effective, if effectiveness is measured by acceptance" (1992, 69). This anomaly becomes intelligible if we recall that a critic never knows what to look for in poems until he entertains some premise about their axioms and genre. What "family resemblances" does a theory of silence or reserve allow a critic of Romantic and post-Romantic elegy to discover? And why should the mark of "truth-saying" be the oxymoron or riddle that allows the elegists to reveal and conceal their meanings simultaneously?

Elegiac Riddles: Audacities of Reserve

As Timothy Peltason has said, "restraint can be another form of audacity in the Romantic tradition" (1985, 46). The riddler's reserve may hide a truth that does not bear talking about. Or it may allow a mourner, reticent by nature, to overcome reserve by lavishly praising the dead while seeming to talk about something else. Wittgenstein assumes that riddles are unanswerable by definition and hence do not exist, since "if a question can be framed at all, it is also *possible* to an swer it" (1961, 149, prop. 6.5). But like a paradox, which can reveal most when it holds something back, a riddle, I think, is meant to be solved. Certainly, the riddles in most elegies are transparent enough. Though the speaker pretends to be puzzled by the mourner's "riddle of [his] loved Lionesse" in Spenser's "Daphnaïda" (l. 177), and though the dreamer in Chaucer's *The Book of the Duchess* pretends not to guess the riddle of the chess game in which the black knight loses his queen, there seems to be a touch of genius as well as ingenuousness in such puzzlement. Everywhere Chaucer's dreamer turns, in both literature and dreams, he finds a version of his own story written. Alcione is a bereft lover like himself, and so is the black knight. It seems unlikely that a mourner so attuned to grief as the dreamer would not recognize a fellow mourner when he meets one. Even in apologizing to the knight for troubling him, the dreamer obliquely alerts us to his true motive.

> I am ryght sory yif I have ought
> Destroubled yow out of your thought.
> Foryive me, yif I have mystake.
> (*The Book of the Duchess*, ll. 523–55)

In Middle English the force of the prefix "des" is intensive. To "destrouble" is not to free from trouble, as in the verb "dispossess," but rather its opposite, to trouble further or vex. Yet having raised the more logical possibility—"to distract from trouble"—the dreamer cannot wholly retract that meaning now. His apparent failure to guess the black knight's secret and solve the riddle is really psychological discernment in disguise. It helps the black knight overcome his natural reserve by unburdening his heart in praise of the queen while ostensibly amplifying the riddle, making it easier for the dreamer to guess its meaning.

The effect of a riddle is often the opposite of what it seems to be. The lost queen in the chess game allows the riddler to draw a circle of words around his meaning, not because he is indifferent to a loss that he makes the subject of an intellectual game, but because he suffers from an excess of concern. We make riddles about losses we cannot bear talking about, and also about things we love, things that we want to turn over with fond and exact scrutiny. The knight can be most eloquent when he speaks obliquely. But even then, despite the great dignity of his encomium, he grieves because of his radical failure to inscribe in words his dead wife's worth: "Allas! myn herte ys wonder woo / That I ne kan discryven hyt!" (ll. 896–97). "Menen" can mean "say" or "mean" in Middle English. Because the knight always means more than he can say about his loss, the dreamer is tempted to say more about the folly of grieving for such loss than he has any right to mean: " 'Why so?' quod he, 'hyt ys nat soo. / Thou wost ful lytel what thou menest' " (ll. 742–43). Only at the end of the elegy do the knight and the dreamer learn to mean exactly what they say and say exactly what they mean. Five exchanges take place in three short tetrameters, and the two speakers even mark their new-found intimacy by sharing a poetic line.

> "Allas, sir, how? what may that be?"
> "She ys ded!" "Nay!" "Yis, be my trouthe!"
> "Is that youre los? Be God, hyt ys routhe!"
> (*The Book of the Duchess*, ll. 1308–10)

Rising above confusion and misunderstanding, these lines have all the heartfelt simplicity of literalness. After the baffled efforts to communicate through riddles, the simplicity of the exchange represents a triumph of reserve and tact over the natural defects of language.

As well as dwelling lovingly on an object, an elegiac riddle may draw words around something it is afraid to face directly. The second quatrain of Wordsworth's elegy, "A Slumber Did My Spirit Seal," assumes the form of a riddle: What could happen to Lucy that would vindicate everything trite and sentimental that the lover says about her in the first quatrain, but with a total reversal of all his words imply? The riddler is not just being reserved; he is using silent-speaking words to hide something obscene, a horror that will not bear talking about.

> A slumber did my spirit seal;
>   I had no human fears:
> She seemed a thing that could not feel
>   The touch of earthly years.
>
> No motion has she now, no force;
>   She neither hears nor sees;
> Rolled round in earth's diurnal course,
>   With rocks, and stones, and trees.
> ("A Slumber Did My Spirit Seal")

The slight flicker of hesitation after "feel" (l.3), which would be lacking in a prose version of the lines, is the pause of revulsion, as the jealous lover shrinks from naming the defiling touch of her body by his rival's hands. What Lucy feels is something as immediate as a physical touch, the touch of a hand, and yet as strange and uncanny as the touch of time, which is not warm, like a lover's touch, but cold. "Earthly" means earth-centered and earth-anchored, not merely *of* the earth but also *on* the earth and *in* it.

One might have thought the elegist takes grim satisfaction in Lucy's punishment for allowing herself to be seduced by an earthly rival, especially after the elegist has just boasted of how invulnerable and pure she was. But these thoughts are too painful to utter: they expire in the pauses and empty spaces created by the heavy sixth-syllable caesura in line 5 and by the use of emphatic end-stopping and four negatives: "No motion has she now, no force; / She neither hears nor sees" (ll. 5–6). In imitation of Lucy's suspension and loss of motion, the words seem to falter before coming to the edge of a poetic line, where they are left trembling for a moment, suspended. Just as the peace of a graveyard is often disturbingly at odds with the agitations that shake a mourner's heart, so Lucy is securely and restfully enclosed within a turning world that, in its strenuous rotations, is the opposite of restful. The elegy's magnificent tranquilizing evocation of the grave, however, mutes the agitation and subdues the rough diurnal motions of the earth. Though violence survives in the harsh spondees—"No motion," "no force," "Rolled round" (ll. 5, 7)—it is also tamed by Lucy's marvelous metamorphosis.

At the end of the elegy the energetic forward movement is recovered in a network of prepositions and conjunctions that spin a protective web for Lucy: "Rolled round in earth's diurnal course, / With rocks, and stones, and trees." The rough earth is now more than a lusty lover.

It is also in full possession of the force and motion Lucy has lost, but which it now restores to her as her vigorous protector. The masculine rocks and stones and the thrusting trees roll her round in a consummation that seems never to end. Their strenuous at-onement will last as long as the earth continues to hurtle through space. Interpreted literally, the phrase "Rolled round in earth's diurnal course" (l. 7) describes the time during which the woman is physically embraced by the earth in its daily orbit. But the preposition is also spatial: to be rolled around is also to be turned around *inside* the earth. The grimness is sealed off, as it were, by the riddle of an aggressively intrusive earth—by its power, not merely to enter the woman, but also to have the woman enter *it*. As the sexual identities of a lover and his beloved are momentarily reversed, the oddness is made even stranger by the unpacking within "diurnal course" of puns on "urn," "die," and "corse." Wordsworth estranges the most commonplace phrases, a cliché like "touch of time" or "earthly years," making them unobtrusively odd, surprisingly fresh and alive. Even the dual invasion of the woman by the earth and of the earth by the woman is made to repeat the earth's daily invasion of the regions of outer space. Having hurtled through space while being herself invaded, Lucy experiences the kind of calm vertigo that hurricane victims are said to feel when they find themselves at the still center of a storm and live to tell of their ordeal.

For a comparably riddling evocation of the grave we have to turn to the elegiac coda of Tennyson's "Tithonus," which contrasts the brutal indignity of becoming "earth in earth" with the splendor of renewing one's beauty "morn by morn." Turning to earth is partly a matter of Tithonus's turning courteously to Aurora, to compliment her great beauty, even though he will no longer be there to see or praise it.

> Thou seëst all things, thou wilt see my grave:
> Thou wilt renew thy beauty morn by morn,
> I earth in earth forget these empty courts,
> And thee returning on thy silver wheels. ("Tithonus," ll. 73–76)

What audacities of restraint! The fact that Tithonus can be obliquely insulting, using his exquisite politeness to mask a touch of bold yet riddling insolence, belies T. S. Eliot's strictures against the dissociation of sensibility in nineteenth-century poetry. Here "the intellect [seems] immediately at the tip of [the elegist's] senses," as Eliot requires (1932, 210). For the understated and delicate turn within the word "returning," which refers both to Aurora's coming back and to her turning on and betraying Tithonus, is reinforced by the similar yet different senses of the two paired phrases. "Earth in earth" matches "morn by morn" grammatically, but masks a profound disparity of meaning.

Though a riddling elegy like "A Slumber Did My Spirit Seal" distracts the mourner from an outrage too brutal to face directly, the poem is too short to achieve the lucid dignity of the knight's riddling tribute to his dead duchess in Chaucer's elegy. For audacities of reserve that combine the elisions of Wordsworth's elegy with the reticent praise of Chaucer's, we have to turn to two elegies by Coventry Patmore and Thomas Hardy. Curious as it may seem, the riddling indirection that puts reason and sanity at risk in Patmore's "Departure" and Hardy's elegy "Without Ceremony" is more vivid and memorable than anything either elegist can say less obliquely.

The repetition of the frightening circumstances of the wife's departure in Patmore's poem (ll. 6–9, 27–30) seems at first to add few clues about the purpose of her journey. But the redundancy is apparent, not real. For the second time the leave-taking is described it is slightly altered. The first account is circumstantial. It takes place on a "July afternoon" (l. 4), just before the wife's departure on a journey the poet is expecting her to take (l. 10). If this is a riddling way of describing death, the little domestic drama between the offended husband and his thoughtless wife casts a glimmer of lightness and social comedy over the event. So finely poised between elegy and domestic comedy is this circumstantial narrative that each time we read the poem it seems to offer a different facet to the mind. But the second time the event is described (ll. 27–30), slight changes in the repeated elements turn the separation of leave-taking into a separation that is final. The "journey of so many days" (l. 8) now becomes the more absolute "journey of all days" (l. 29). By turning the impulse to berate, to feel anger at his wife for dying, into a contest in gentility, like the exchange that Chaucer dramatizes between the dreamer and the black knight, Patmore is able to blunt the pain. The riddle is not so sustained that Patmore can lavishly praise his wife, like the black knight, while pretending to talk about something else. Yet, ironically, the wife's only defect in social tact, the suddenness of her going, turns out to be her most gracious act of all. For in leaving the mourner with the only "loveless look" (l. 31) she ever gave, she is sparing him the pain of words. Such is the audacity of the mourner's own restraint that he manages to praise his wife while seeming to rebuke her. "It was not like your great and gracious ways!" (l. 1), he chides her, conscious all the while that she displays in dying both a bolder discourtesy and a finer tact than any she has shown in life.

Like Patmore's "Departure," Hardy's elegy "Without Ceremony" is a riddling lyric of reserve, stoically restricted in means and spoken by a mourner who has put away the genre's traditional consolations. After the memory of familiar farewells in the first stanza, and the homely observation that the trunks have been prepared, Hardy has a glimpse of a break that is absolute, which he describes despairingly, and with the rare—and hitherto disguised—finality of a going that is "for ever" (l. 12).

> So, now that you disappear
> For ever in that swift style,
> Your meaning seems to me
> Just as it used to be:
> "Good-bye is not worth while!" ("Without Ceremony," ll. 11–15)

As if to temper his audacity, however, in disclosing a break that is "for ever," Hardy uses riddling two-way syntax to leave the speaker poised between the shock of death and a mere style of disappearing, a manner that is simply in character. To cross the boundary of the poetic line is to recognize the finality of a logic that binds the words "for ever" to the verb. But to hover over the slight break at the end of line 11 is to soften the blow by attaching "For ever" to the adverbial phrase, "in that swift style" (l. 12), to the mere habitual manner of the going. Grammatically, the second line may be construed as an adjectival phrase in apposition to the pronoun "you" (l. 11). This less alarming possibility absorbs the terror, affording an easy transition to the hint of relief, as of a burden lifted, in the last two lines.

A Grievous Reticence: Wordsworth's Unheard Words

For Wordsworth's mourners, as for Patmore's and Hardy's, language is only the trace of something unsayable, and therefore "unceremonious," something that the elegist who honestly charts the truth of his feeling can never quite put into words. Full of unheard words, Wordsworth's elegies dramatize three kinds of silence. Sometimes the sudden stoppages, elisions, and dashes express a mere depth of reserve. When Wordsworth's mourner says that Lucy "is in her grave, and, oh, / The difference to me" ("She Dwelt among the Untrodden Ways," ll. 11–12), he seems reluctant to define that "difference" for fear of profaning something he alone can value. More disturbingly, silences may express the blankness of mere emptiness and loss. After his son's disgrace, Michael is mute. It is as impossible to speak about the scandal as it is to look directly at death or the sun. A third possibility is that the unheard words express "Thoughts that . . . lie too deep for tears" ("Ode: Intimations of Immortality," l. 205). The elegist is silent, not because his heart is too empty to say anything, but because it is too full. He seems to understand everything until he comes to put it into words, and that may betray his want of understanding.

When the first kind of silence combines with the third, the traces of a poem's elegiac origin may be momentarily effaced. In the sonnet "It Is a Beauteous Evening, Calm and Free," where the poet's heart seems too full for speech, it may come as a shock to realize that the young girl seems most alive when described as a soul that has passed into paradise. To be laid in Abraham's or Arthur's bosom (l. 12) is a benediction usually reserved for people like Falstaff after they have died: "Nay, sure, he's not in hell: he's in Arthur's bosom, if ever man went to Arthur's bosom" (*Henry V* 2.3.9–10). Because the silence of reserve alternates with a silence of amazed possession and plenitude, it is also easy to read "The Solitary Reaper" without registering its affinity to an epitaph inscription: "Stop here, or gently pass" (l. 4).

Though Geoffrey Hartman has shown that Wordsworth's best elegies often approach the mute concision of an epitaph, in his "Essays upon Epitaphs" Wordsworth himself carefully distinguishes between the two modes of composition. What is laboriously carved on stone should have the status of a fixed feeling, whereas a feeling too transitory or poignant to be inscribed on stone may be entertained as a fugitive impression in an elegy. In one case, however, the *Excursion*'s chronicle of the dalesman who lost his hearing as a young child, Wordsworth does acknowledge that he has used as his source "a concise Epitaph" found "in one of the most retired vales among the Mountains of Westmoreland." Like an epitaph, the chronicle imitates the loss it commemorates by using strong caesural pauses and breaks between lines. And what begins as a silence of loss and dispossession ends as a silence of plenitude and restored possession.

> Beneath that Pine . . .
> . . . a gentle Dalesman lies,
> From whom in early childhood was withdrawn
> The precious gift of hearing. (*Excursion*, VII, 395–99)

When combined with the slight pause, even at the end of the unpunctuated third line, the hyperbaton allows us to hover for an instant on the brink of loss. We half expect to hear that "The precious gift of life" has been withdrawn. But Wordsworth reaches that end by a less direct route. At first the loss of hearing tolls like a knell: "the bird of dawn / Did never rouze this Cottager from sleep" (ll. 402–3). Placed at the head of a line, the resounding negative prevents the bird from "dawning" for the youth by demoting the word "dawn" to terminal position. When the poet proclaims that the "valley was to him / Soundless, with all its streams" (ll. 401–2), the early-breaking caesura has the effect of withdrawing sound prematurely, as if gently preparing for a withdrawal more absolute, "the profounder stillness of the grave" (l. 465).

Yet by placing the adjective "Soundless" and the past participle

"Upheld" at the head of lines, Wordsworth uses parities of syntax and rhythm to establish links between them.

> And this deep mountain valley was to him
> Soundless, with all its streams. *(Excursion,* VII, 401–2)

> Yet, by the solace of his own calm thoughts
> Upheld, he duteously pursued the round
> Of rural labours: (*Excursion,* VII, 414–16)

The withdrawal of sound becomes the calm that upholds, the source of repose and "pure contentedness of mind" (l. 472). As in "Monologue of a Deaf Man," the work of a modern British poet, David Wright, whose deafness places him in a comparably odd relationship with language, we are made to feel that "The injury, dominated, is an asset" (l. 18). The elegist's office is hallowed by the deaf man's life, which is already a perfect poetry of silence, as well "composed" as Wordsworth's elegy.

If a poem is written "at the side of a grave," Wordsworth believes it should retain some trace of its impromptu composition. The discipline of verse may even dry up the current of genuine feeling in an epitaph. Matthew Dobson's pathetic lines for his daughter Eliza would have been less intense if they had been written in verse instead of prose.

> She is gone—my beloved Daughter Eliza is gone,
> Fair, chearful, benign, my child is gone.
> Thee long to be regretted a Father mourns,
> Regretted—but thanks to the most perfect God not lost
> For a happier age approaches
> When again my child I shall behold
> And live with thee for ever. (*Essays upon Epitaphs,* III, 218–24)

Each time the subject is repeated, it is lovingly amplified: at first the lost child is a mere indefinite "she"; then she becomes "my beloved Daughter Eliza"; and finally she is "my child." But the mourner seems too stunned to speak. He composes in fragments, and is incapable of assimilating his loss. The tremor of open vowels, including the three wailful "gone"s, sends a quaver of barely suppressed emotion down the first two lines. Repeating the terminal words without variation, then turning on the past participle "regretted," Dobson seems too dazed to revise his halting syntax, which breaks apart at the dashes, as the father's heart breaks with grief. Since nothing can assuage the pain, it is affecting that the places of fracture should be allowed to show through, like a broken bone protruding through a wound.

In his third "Essay upon Epitaphs" Wordsworth argues that the

Duke of Ormond's feeling that he "preferred his dead Son to any living Son in Christendom" was "natural and becoming," but because it deserved "no enduring place in the mind," its display on a gravestone would have given the wild and wayward sentiment the wrong kind of permanence. Since the feeling retains "the infinitude of truth," however, Wordsworth chooses to preserve it in "The Two April Mornings." The dead are irreplaceable. What more is there to say? Matthew gives voice to this painful truth, not by proclaiming it publicly on an epitaph, but by stumbling on it, almost by accident, and then by expressing it obliquely: "I looked at her, and looked again: / And did not wish her mine!" (ll. 55–56). "The sublimity of the sentiment," as Wordsworth says in his essay, "consists in its being the secret possession of the Father." It is the elegy's unheard thought, conveyed at first only by a sigh, which Matthew declines to explain, and whose meaning he shares with the poet only in the last line he speaks. The feeling is so secret and wild a possession, so untameable, like death, that the old schoolmaster almost takes it to the grave with him.

> Matthew is in his grave, yet now,
> Methinks, I see him stand,
> As at that moment, with a bough
> Of wilding in his hand. ("The Two April Mornings," ll. 57–60)

At the beginning three halting caesuras in a single line—"And Matthew stopped, he looked, and said" (l. 3)—insinuate a faltering at the brink. Yet the rhythms in the rest of the first quatrain are brisk and buoyant. Only the phrase, "The will of God be done!" (l. 4), seems solemnly in excess of what the rising sun would seem to warrant. Though the claim that the one April morning is the "very brother" of the "other" seems vindicated by the lodging of "other" within its rhyme word "brother" (ll. 26, 28), the interplay between singular and plural forms—between "a day" and "thirty years" (ll. 23–24)—helps expose the converse fallacy of accident. Things that appear similar under accidental circumstances may not be similar in their essential natures. The dead Emma is not the young and blooming girl Matthew sees, and the April mornings are decidedly two, not one.

Silences of reserve and silences of self-reproach and guilt are often hard to tell apart in this poem. We hear both kinds of silence in the quatrain that culminates in the first mention of the daughter's grave.

> With rod and line I sued the sport
> Which that sweet season gave,
> And, to the church-yard come, stopped short
> Beside my daughter's grave. ("The Two April Mornings," ll. 29–32)

Despite the sweetness of the season and the pleasure of angling, "sued" sounds harsh and angry. In retrospect Matthew arraigns or sues the pleasures that have surprised him, crept up on him, even as he edges toward his daughter's grave. Because there is no punctuation at the end of line 31, which is broken by three caesuras and an ellipsis before "come," we seem to stumble, then fall over the line ending, as Matthew falls over the grave. The father trembles for an instant at the edge of some grievous reticence, something he is either too reserved or too ashamed to mention.

But once Matthew discloses the nature of his loss, his love swells out beyond all measure.

> Nine summers had she scarcely seen,
> The pride of all the vale;
> And then she sang;—she would have been
> A very nightingale. ("The Two April Mornings," ll. 33–36)

We are mildly surprised by the nonsequitur. Having lamented the brevity of her nine short summers, Matthew might be expected to say, "And then she died." But "then" is not a specifically temporal adverb. It seems to function as a synonym for "moreover," as if he were trying to amend the harshness of his first "Beside"—"Beside my daughter's grave" (l. 32)—with a more consoling use of the same word: "And beside, she was a lovely singer." Yet no sooner is loss replaced by eulogy than the magnitude of the loss comes back to immobilize the father. The line breaks in the middle. When he returns to speech on the far side of the dash, he beautifully combines the impulse to praise with a grave acknowledgment of a loss that is absolute.

The allusion to the guilt-ridden Macbeth—"Duncan is in his grave" (*Macbeth* 3.2, 22)—dramatizes the magnitude of what the elegist has tried to repress. As in the Lucy poem ("But she is in her grave, and oh, / The difference to me!"), the restoration of the words behind the words shows that the agitation abides, especially since its wildness is merely touched in passing, so painful is the wound. Because the elegist is remembering an event Matthew remembered, the doubling of the memory might seem at first to displace the pain by safely distancing the event. But we wonder how safe the elegist really is. Will Matthew stay safely in his grave, or will he roam out of it, to haunt the poet? There are silences of dispossession and loss in this elegy that no silences of reserve can permanently suppress. We know there is more delusion than understanding in Macbeth's picture of Duncan sleeping well while he himself continues to defy death. And we discover there is more delusion than understanding in Matthew's surmise that a living girl can ever take the place of his dead Emma. When the dazed and numb repetition, "I looked at her, and looked again" (l. 55), seems to freeze the mourner, he breaks the ice jam with a heartfelt though seemingly cruel rejection: "And did not wish her mine!" (l. 56). Each woe, he learns, is flat and final, because each loss is irreplaceable. Just as Emma will not stay securely in her rocky cave, but continues to tease and pain her father by assuming the guise of a blooming girl, so Matthew seems to stand before the elegist now. As Macbeth is haunted by Duncan's ghost, so Wordsworth, we feel, will be haunted by Matthew's.

Like "The Two April Mornings," the sonnet "Surprised by Joy" is an elegy of shocks and aftershocks. Like tremors of an earthquake, the silences of loss, rapture, and reserve spread out from the epicenter of the poem's four gaping dashes.

> Surprised by joy—impatient as the Wind
> I turned to share the transport—Oh! with whom
> ("Surprised by Joy," ll. 1–2)

Strangely enough, the transport of sudden rapture produces less of a jolt than the transport of the mourner's grief. The first transport is dramatized by the dash before "impatient" and the second by the dashes before the soul-wrenching "Oh! with whom" (ll. 1–2) and the self-reproachful "But how could I forget thee?" (l. 6). The pattern of a shock followed by aftershocks more wrenching is repeated for a final time in line 11.

> —That thought's return
> Was the worst pang that sorrow ever bore,
> Save one, one only . . . ("Surprised by Joy," ll. 9–11)

Ironically, the threefold repetition of "one" and its cognate "only" betrays the singularity of what the elegist wants to say. Constrained to draw a circle of words around his "heart's best treasure" (l. 12), he finds her "heavenly face" (l. 14) as darkly veiled as his own deep silences of loss and reserve. Equally withholding is the elegiac narrative poem, "Simon Lee, The Old Huntsman," where the words we most want to hear must be provided by the "silent thought" of each reader (l. 66).

Even when there is no generic veiling, and the title of a poem like "Elegiac Stanzas" introduces death as its explicit subject, Wordsworth still manages to compose a poetry of silent or withheld meanings. "I love to see the look," the elegist confesses (l. 50). He sees in Peele Castle something that seems to look back at him: the seeing is oddly multiple. Such two-way viewing is implicit in the tricky genitive phrase in line 2: "Four summer weeks I dwelt in sight of thee." Is the poet viewing the castle, or is the castle looking at *him*? "I saw thee every day" (l. 3) makes the language run for a moment on one track only. But two-way syntax keeps alive the possibility that the real sleeper is the gazing poet, who seems enchanted, half entranced, by his vision. As a human gaze is replaced by a painter's gaze, the shimmering sfumato produces a haze of illusion, which the elegist tries to dignify as a "consecration" and a "Poet's dream" (l. 16).

By the end of the elegy, however, this consecrating eye is said to be blind, and the inward eye has disclosed beneath the glassy mirror of the deep a very different depth.

> A power is gone, which nothing can restore;
> A deep distress hath humanised my Soul.
> ("Elegiac Stanzas," ll. 35–36)

Wordsworth likes to think he is a stoic, "Cased in . . . unfeeling armour" (l. 51), like the "huge Castle, standing here sublime" (l. 49). But he is too human for that. The blind spot at the center of stoicism is the injunction to escape fate by willed indifference. Though fate is to be borne stoically, it may not be in the stoic's power to will anything, including a sturdy resolve to welcome "fortitude, and patient cheer" (l. 57). Language keeps betraying Wordsworth, deforming what he thinks he is saying. But in betraying him, the silences of rapture, dispossession, and reserve are also saving him, making him fully responsive to the crisis. The tension between what is said and what is withheld, between the language of the living and the silence of the dead, accounts for the revelatory power of Wordsworth's best elegies. Evasion of dark truths extends even to Wordsworth's oblique naming of his brother, who is obscurely evoked as "Him whom I deplore" (l. 42). He laments his brother's drowning, but is also tempted to upbraid him for destroying a perfect picture. The odd use of "deplore" alerts us to the elegist's complex response to the claims of both his illusions and his visions, his blindness and his insight, the thoughts he voices and the more affecting and disturbing ones he often leaves unsaid.

The Muteness of Mourners Who Refuse to Act a Part: Dickinson and Rossetti

The use of silence in nineteenth-century elegy culminates in the art of Emily Dickinson and Christina Rossetti, not because these elegists are just silent or reserved by temperament, but because they do not seem to understand the nature of playing a part at all. As a religious poet, Rossetti should be overflowing with God's love. But her heart is wounded, and she suffers from exhaustion, depletion, and diminished hope. To fill the void she experiments with roles: she becomes the cold and scornful spurner of proffered love; the rejected wooer; the weary traveler, inquiring about food and shelter at the journey's end. When death arrives, Dickinson, like Rossetti, may turn to a literal down-to-earth world to domesticate her grief. With housewifely instinct, Dickinson puts love away, like a dish, until eternity. But it is not enough to become an officious housekeeper, using the bustle about the house to ward off fear of the unknown. Sooner or later death makes role-playing impossible and irrelevant. It suspends the poet's power to terminate or even coherently develop the story line she begins. There are no conventional roles the elegist can adopt in response to death or God's summoning of her, because there is something about the experience that defeats eloquence and that produces in many dramatic readings the subtlety of the off-key note. Each elegist learns to relax and be patient, even to forsake the safety of role-playing. Like George Herbert's actors, she may be saved when she is brave enough to be vulnerable, to relax her defenses, and let God or death do his part, too.

Though silence must weigh heavily upon the strangeness of death, not to speak at all is to stop being meaningful. To bring muteness to life as imaginative decorum, as a principle of tact or reserve that refuses to trespass on too private a domain, Dickinson experiments with roles that are as whimsical, elusive, and untheatrical as possible. In lyric 272 it is difficult to say precisely what mask the poet has donned. At first we assume she is a gamester who has beaten someone at cards· "I breathed enough to take the Trick" (l. 1). But as we swing on to the next line, the removal of air and the simulation of breathing reveal that the opening use of "breathed" is more literal than we allowed: the poet breathed enough to seem alive, then promptly expired. The flicker of hesitation as to whether the breathing itself constituted the trickery or whether she was alive enough to win less deviously, as one might win a trick in a game of bridge, establishes a much closer connection between breathing and trick-taking than we first suspect.

> I breathed enough to take the Trick—
> And now, removed from Air—
> I simulate the Breath, so well—
> That One, to be quite sure—
>
> The Lungs are stirless—must descend
> Among the Cunning Cells—
> And touch the Pantomime—Himself,
> How numb, the Bellows feels! (lyric 272)

What some lover of the dying poet should have done in life can now be done only in death by a grim coroner who, in a kind of autopsy that is artfully deferred by the sundering of the indefinite "One" from its principal verb "descend," begins to touch and feel the inmost cells of her body. The surprising possibility that this deathbed intimacy is the trick she has played on her would-be lover attenuates the role-playing, making it as problematic as possible, even as the suspicion is allowed to linger on as the elegy's unsettling afterthought.

In one of Dickinson's most famous elegies, "Because I could not stop for Death" (lyric 712), the speaker is presumably too distraught or preoccupied to visit her friends. So a kindly friend must be courteous enough to stop and wait for her. But her friend is no ordinary friend. And he has power to alter all future roles she plays.

> Because I could not stop for Death—
> He kindly stopped for me—
> The Carriage held but just Ourselves—
> And Immortality. (lyric 712, ll. 1–4)

The preposition "for" hovers between two contradictory meanings. Could she not stop "because of" death? Does anxiety about her impending death make her too busy to pause? Or is she too preoccupied to wait for Death or include him in her schedule? As we round the corner of the first line, we realize that parallel syntax—"for Death," "for me"—probably dictates the second of these two possibilities. But the line also reinstates the first possibility at the very instant it seems to rescind it. For if Death is gracious enough to pause for Dickinson, then her inability to stop because of her overriding preoccupation with death is a preoccupation all too quickly justified by Death's courteous attentions to *her*.

The elegy's central passage on passing rides with ease across four successive stanzas, crossing centuries with as much facility as it gently transfers its energies from one quatrain or one line of verse to another. Just as gentility and tact are used to domesticate the strange, so sun and people are allowed to shuttle back and forth, as if the most familiar and awesome objects were passing each other on a crowded thoroughfare. As in lyric 1129, "Truth's superb surprise" (l. 4) requires us to register both the female concern for fashion and the shock of her final dwelling place. Scruples about the delicate fabric of her "Tippet" and the gossamer thinness of her gown are finely expressed, but not without a touch of *superbia*. The pride has to be tamed by deferred recognition of the oddly constructed house, whose subterranean cornice and scarcely visible roof hold their own "superb surprise" in reserve.

Philip Larkin complains that Dickinson rarely brings her magnificent openings to a successful conclusion. "Too often the poem expires in a teased-out and breathless obscurity" (1983, 194). But the breakdown that Larkin objects to may be hard to distinguish from a breakthrough. To inaugurate a poem successfully may be to take refuge in role-playing. By the end of the lyric, however, the poet may find herself transported into a world where no roles can be played. To object to the obscurity of the poet's endings is to object to mysteries that cannot bear acting or being talked about. Because Dickinson's imagination of death is often at work, less in what she says and sees than in what her imagination causes her to cancel or suspend, she finds she must often write as a De Saussure, a semiotician of heavenly hurts.

> Heavenly Hurt, it gives us—
> We can find no scar,
> But internal difference,
> Where the meanings, are— (lyric 258, ll. 5–8)

Cristanne Miller has written well about Dickinson's uncanny anticipation of Derrida's idea of *différance* (1987, 102). Like the "Slant of light" (l. 1), even the rhymes and meter are slanted away from the hymnal's "common measure." But "listens" is still close enough to "Distance" (ll. 13, 15) to allow us to measure the angle of slant. One way of deferring the "indifference" of terminal events while intimating what they mean is to move from more to less concrete sensations. The heavenly hurt, a sensation like touch, is first apprehended visually. Later, it seems to be a fugitive sound, something elusive that the landscape listens for, but something that we, like the shadows, can hear only when we hold our breath during one of the four caesural breaks in the lyric's closing stanza.

The language that betrays the elegist least is the language that is most elliptical, most broken by dashes and parentheses. In lyric 193, for example, so minimal a sign as a line ending, a dash, a punctuation mark, can become a formidable boundary for Dickinson, as challenging to cross as the divide of death: "I shall know why—when Time is over— / And I have ceased to wonder why—" (ll. 1–2). When using words like "death" or "grave" in her letters, Dickinson almost always punctuates them with a dash. "I hoped to write to you before, but Mother's dying—almost stunned my spirit." "The illumination that comes but once paused upon her features, and it seemed like hiding a Picture to lay her in the grave—" (Houghton Library Autograph file, TL. to Louise Norcross). Anyone who has studied Dickinson's autograph letters to Thomas Higginson will also realize how much more teased-out and breathless her poems appear when jotted down in short two- or three-syllable lines (Houghton Library autograph file, A. L. to T. W. Higginson, 1880 and 1882). Such verse is elliptical and concise to the point of extinction. It declines from the modest to the minimal. As in lyric 303, where we descend from two four-syllable lines—"Present

no more," "Upon her Mat" (ll. 4, 8)—to a mere two-syllable one—
"Like Stone" (l. 12), we are made to realize that exclusion is a form of
austere destitution, perhaps another form of dying itself.

Everything in these poems and letters serves to mute the force of
death. We pause at its brink then half recede from its edge. The last
stanza of lyric 465 is typical. Containing the most dashes, six in all, it
allows the speaker and her reader to edge closer and closer to a pause
that leaves us breathless and suspended.

> There interposed a Fly—
>
> With Blue—uncertain stumbling Buzz—
> Between the light—and me—
> And then the Windows failed—and then
> I could not see to see— (lyric 465, ll. 12–16)

The last contraction is grammatical. As the resources of language fail,
the elegist is reduced to a stammer: "I could not see to see—." Even at
the end, however, as she loses the capacity to perceive anything physically, death is deferred by one last recursive effort, by one desperate
final attempt to inch two steps back for every one step forward.

Christina Rossetti's elegies, like Dickinson's, combine the familiar
and the strange, the whimsical and the serious, the spinsterish and the
sad. However firm and confident the acting of a role-player may be at
the beginning of an elegy, death soon erodes any notion of playing out
that role in a single consistent spirit. Rather than contemplate the facts
of sexual giving and taking on which she fancies her happiness depends, Rossetti often casts asceticism as the new romance. The two
spinsters, Emily and Christina, are outlandishly romantic figures, revel-
ling in exotic touches even while using homely details to domesticate
death and fear of the unknown.

Since it is easy to stretch a definition of "elegy" to the breaking
point when comparing poets whose favorite theme is death, I want to
narrow the discussion by showing how death defeats role-playing in
each poet's verse. Death may make it difficult for Dickinson and Rossetti to strike a correct attitude or tone, or even to come to a decisive
understanding of the world that supersedes all "befores" and "afters"
in Rossetti's lyric "Praying Always." Just as Rossetti's poem explores
the mystery of a time beyond the grave by considering altered meanings
of the preposition "after," so in her lyric, "Before the ice is in the
pools," Dickinson teases mystery out of several temporal uses and a
possible spatial use of the word "before."

> Before the ice is in the pools—
> Before the skaters go,

Or any cheek at nightfall
Is tarnished by the snow—

Before the fields have finished,
Before the Christmas tree,
Wonder upon wonder
Will arrive to me! (lyric 37, ll. 1–8)

Will "Wonder upon wonder" come to the poet as she stands "before" or in front of the tree? Or is "before" another temporal conjunction ("Before the tree is cut down and decorated"), with an ellipsis understood after "tree"? Transports of feeling occur in the places of fracture or elision, in the rift of anticipation created by the dashes after "pools" and "snow," for example, or in the rift created by the oddly unfinished intransitive force of the verb "finished" in the fifth line: "Before the fields have finished." Like Hopkins or Donne, Dickinson seldom strikes the reader as a simple or uncomplicated poet. As in *In Memoriam* 123.8—"Like clouds they shape themselves and go"—even a simple and abbreviated use of "go," coming abruptly at the end of the second line, can harbor double meanings of setting forth to skate or of disappearing altogether.

Rossetti's poems, by contrast, are often so ingenuous that a reader may miss their ingenuity. In "Praying Always," the plain honesty of statement, intimating an almost mute depth of feeling as "Day-fall" begins (l. 8), may seem at first too ordinary and obvious.

After midnight, in the dark
    The clock strikes one,
    New day has begun.
Look up and hark!
With singing heart forestall the carolling lark.

After mid-day, in the light
    The clock strikes one,
    Day-fall has begun.
Cast up, set right
The day's account against the oncoming night.

After noon and night, one day
    For ever one
    Ends not, once begun.
Whither away,
O brothers and O sisters? Pause and pray. ("Praying Always")

As we enter the third stanza, however, we realize that "After noon and night" is not just another adverbial phrase like "after midnight" (l. 1) or "after mid-day" (l. 6). Because this third phrase is introduced by a nontemporal preposition, by an "after" *after* all befores and afters, its summons seems to speak to Rossetti, like Arthur Hallam's summons to Tennyson, from "that deep dawn behind the tomb" (*In Memoriam*, 46.6). Only by following the progress of a simple preposition like "after" or "before" can a reader begin to see how Rossetti and Dickinson fashion a complex play of meaning out of the most minimal elements of prosody and grammar.

Rossetti's apparent ordinariness and simplicity often disguise complications we had not at first anticipated. Her elegiac sonnet, "After Death," for example, seems obvious enough until we realize that the speaker dies somewhere during the sestet: "once dead / He pitied me" (ll. 12–13). Disturbed by a vision of her own funeral, as her sheet turns imperceptibly into a shroud and her bed into a coffin, the speaker at first overhears her male friend, and in the silence she knows that he weeps. But the most affecting gestures are all imaginary. Far more is conveyed by what the friend does not do than by what he does.

> The curtains were half drawn, the floor was swept
>   And strewn with rushes, rosemary and may
>   Lay thick upon the bed on which I lay,
> Where through the lattice ivy-shadows crept.
> He leaned above me, thinking that I slept
>   And could not hear him; but I heard him say,
>   'Poor child, poor child': and as he turned away
> Came a deep silence, and I knew he wept.
> He did not touch the shroud, or raise the fold
>   That hid my face, or take my hand in his,
>   Or ruffle the smooth pillows for my head:
>   He did not love me living; but once dead
>   He pitied me; and very sweet it is
> To know he still is warm though I am cold. ("After Death")

There may be a touch of subterfuge in the speaker's pretending to sleep and not to hear her friend. And even in the poem's sestet, where the scene seems to switch from her deathbed to the interior of her coffin or somewhere beyond it, she indulges a hint of self-satisfaction in her exemplary behavior: "and very sweet it is / To know he still is warm though I am cold." But elsewhere in the sonnet, though the speaker is an actress cast for a part in some play, she seems not to understand the nature of playing a part at all. Nor does her friend behave any more theatrically. The negatives fall with appalling force: "He did not touch . . . or raise . . . / or take . . . / Or ruffle . . . / He did not love me living" (ll. 9–12). Every imagined scenario is a rejected scenario. And yet into the friend's two repeated phrases, "Poor child, poor child" (l. 7), which are the only words he speaks, words memorable in context but barely meaningful, Rossetti manages to gather all the powers of language.

By the end of the elegy, with the cruel admission she was never loved, the coldness of the grave has returned, and the speaker's diction has been purified of all false or wrong surmise. What arrests this progress is the silence of the friend. There is no question of the poet's coming into the presence of his love. But there is no clear absence of affection either. Because his response may be pitying, or just noncommittal, it inhibits pathos by preventing Rossetti from playing a single dramatic part either as the betrayed woman or the romantically remembered friend. Several scenarios seem to have been superimposed, and a resourceful reader may want to reconstruct a palimpsest of narratives. But since no one scenario is privileged, and Rossetti appears to have transgressed elegiac conventions by speaking from inside the coffin or from the far side of it in the second stanza, she, like her speaker, does not seem to have been made for the dramatic art of writing elegies at all. When death threatens to dissolve her identity, instead of inventing a new dramatic role, she learns what it means to renounce role-playing altogether. Nonplaying is not just a prelude to nonbeing, but a prelude to a whole new conception of what living and dying might be like.

After donning a traditional mask at the beginning of her sonnet "Remember," the mask of the admonitory dying person, Rossetti discovers that the most exquisite and refined torture is, not to be forgotten by her beloved, as Cathy imagines in *Wuthering Heights*, but to inflict suffering on *him*.

> Remember me when I am gone away,
>   Gone far away into the silent land;
>   When you can no more hold me by the hand,
> Nor I half turn to go yet turning stay.
> Remember me when no more day by day
>   You tell me of our future that you planned:
>   Only remember me; you understand
> It will be late to counsel then or pray.
> Yet if you should forget me for a while
>   And afterwards remember, do not grieve:
>   For if the darkness and corruption leave
>   A vestige of the thoughts that once I had,
> Better by far you should forget and smile
>   Than that you should remember and be sad. ("Remember")

By the middle of the sonnet tactful concern for the lover displaces any self-centered desire to live on in his memory. But as Rossetti begins to experiment with phrases that have two-way meanings, vestiges of the mask she has abandoned can be found lingering on. "Only remember me; you understand / It will be late to counsel then and pray" (ll. 7–8). If the phrase "you understand" modifies "remember me," it is harsh and admonitory. But if it attaches itself to the clause "It will be late to counsel then," as it is invited to do syntactically and by the semicolon after "me," then the tone is gentle and commiserating. Because it is possible to solicit contradictory tones from the printed words, it is hard to assign any single dramatic attitude to this speaker. Such an elegist is devoid of studied eloquence, as an angel might be. Her reticences are the silence of a speaker who forgets how to act conventional dramatic parts. Using her lean diction to fashion a poetry of "sumptuous Destitution," to borrow Dickinson's phrase (lyric 1382, l. 7), and abandoning many conventional roles, the poet has not the time to reassemble her sense of self and the language that goes with it. Because such speakers may even be at a loss for ordinary studied consistency, in Rossetti's elegies, as in Dickinson's, we may often learn the difference between life as a series of roles to be performed, a play to be arranged, and life as a mere abbreviated interval between our coming hither and our going hence.

Sound, Sense, and Silence: The Underthought of Elegy

When the odd assortments of sound and sense in a poem send a reader in search of its silent or unspoken meanings, the interplay between what is heard and what is intimated or half said creates a polyphony that gives the poet a chance to speak with a divided mind upon a subject. In "Stanzas from the Grande Chartreuse" the brisk jog-trot of Arnold's tetrameter couplets—"The bridge is crossed, and slow we ride, / Through forest, up the mountain-side" (ll. 5–6)—flatly contradicts the sense: I assume that the lines are metrically defective. But when Arnold creates a polyphony of voices by allowing the bracing meter of his concluding stanza in "Dover Beach" to be teasingly at odds with its despairing sense, I should like to reach a different conclusion. Because the counterpointing is subtler, I am tempted to infer, not that the sound refuses to echo the sense, but that the sound is echoing a hidden sense or "underthought," a silent meaning that the critic may try to make more audible.

Consider Claudio's mediation on death in *Measure for Measure*. There is a wild abandon at the center of his speech, a sense of vastness, created in part by patterns of diverging alliteration and by spacious runovers, which contrast dramatically with the sudden constriction of consonants and harsh successive stresses at the end of the passage.

> Ay, but to die, and go we know not where;
> To lie in cold obstruction and to rot;
> This sensible warm motion to become
> A kneaded clod, and the delighted spirit
> To bathe in fiery floods, or to reside
> In thrilling region of thick-ribbed ice;
> To be imprisoned in the viewless winds,
> And blown with restless violence round about
> The pendent world; or to be—worse than worst—
> Of those that lawless and incertain thought
> Imagine howling,—'tis too horrible!
> The weariest and most loathed worldly life
> That age, ache, penury, and imprisonment
> Can lay on nature is a paradise
> To what we fear of death. (*Measure for Measure*, 3.1.118–32)

" 'Tis too horrible!" Claudio says. And in a bald paraphrase of the passage death *is* horrible. Yet the expansive sound patterns and suspended syntax do create an attractive option, a release from the prison of "age, ache, penury," which works against the stated sense. For the speaking voice the prospects of life after death are magnificently liberating, and acquire a touch of Lucretian grandeur. The skewing of sound and sense sends us in search of a hidden and unstated meaning: the "under-thought" that there are worse things than dying, and that Claudio is rationalizing his fear of death. Sound and sense are allowed to pull apart, but only so they can be made to work together again at the level of the silent and unheard meaning, at the level of the subtext, if you will.

I hope this digression makes clearer what I am going to argue about Arnold and Hardy. Though the final stanza of Arnold's "Dover Beach" has always impressed me as one of the great elegiac passages in English, a prose paraphrase suggests that Arnold's bleak farewell to illusion is too unrelievedly desolating to qualify as poetry of the highest order. How does Arnold manage to counterpoint the sound and sense of his verse? And how does that counterpointing send us in search of a silent or unstated thought that makes the ending bracing rather than defeatist?

> Ah, love, let us be true
> To one another! for the world, which seems
> To lie before us like a land of dreams,
> So various, so beautiful, so new,
> Hath really neither joy, nor love, nor light,

Nor certitude, nor peace, nor help for pain;
And we are here as on a darkling plain
Swept with confused alarms of struggle and flight,
Where ignorant armies clash by night. ("Dover Beach," ll. 29–37)

The stanza opens with resurgent tenderness and hope. At first huddled together as if adopting a defensive posture against the naked solitude ("love," "let us"), the alliterating sounds widen out, in an expansive gesture that seems to embrace the whole world. The lover's apparition exalts and ennobles him. But such splendor of the heart cannot allay anxiety, and almost every phrase discloses a threatening shadow-side. After the auxiliary verb of illusion, "seems," the infinitive "To lie" (l. 31) evokes a double sense of lying "before us" in a gesture of repose and of lying in the sense of hiding the truth. Is Arnold deceiving his bride on their honeymoon about his love affair with Marguerite, whom the glimmering lights off the French coast may bring to mind in the first stanza? Instead of exposing everything in an act of faith, Arnold and his bride may be concealing something through deceit and falsehood. The dream of variety, beauty and novelty is then no longer a mere semblance or illusion: it becomes an outright deception or lie.

Like the abrupt reversal of "joy," "light," and "love" into their fearful antonyms at the middle of the stanza, the axis is likely to reverse polarity at any moment. As the sea of faith has ebbed, God may not really have died. He may merely have been entombed in a dead religious language. If this is so, then perhaps He can come to life now in Arnold's appeal to his bride. Yet what assurance is there that Arnold can be any truer to *her* than to his lost Marguerite? That dark fear may linger on as the coda's unspeakable underthought. We can feel it in a sudden constraining pressure: in the shrinking of the final line to four feet and in the noose-like constricting of the closing couplet, which seems slipped without warning around the victim's neck.

But so far I have told only half the story. Because a simple sturdiness opposes the impulse to dissolve in the nighttime air, a slow-wheeling drift into the void is also countered by an equally slow-wheeling but obdurate resistance to death, as of an heroic call to arms. The melancholy, long, withdrawing roar of the penultimate stanza, which establishes an enchanting vowel music to lull the mind into oblivion, like one of Frost's snow poems, is now confronted with firm resistance. Since the sound is subtly at odds with the primary sense, however, a reader hears no dull tramp of stoic fortitude, but an exquisite interlacing of parallel syntactic units and the motions of a freely fluid verse. Nor is Arnold ever allowed to sink smugly into shallow pessimism. An echo of Newman's Oxford sermon on "Faith and Reason" (1839), which ends with Thucydides' account of the "night battle, where each fights for himself, and friend and foe stand together" (1887, 201), reverses the import of the lover's plea to his bride by summoning up Arnold's true subject. The poem's unspoken underthought is the trauma of pointless conflict, in which each disputant fails to understand what his adversary means, and in which theological language may even displace or elide a painful drama of estrangement and loss, including Arnold's own separation from Marguerite. The allusion to Newman shakes the listener out of complacent doubt and skepticism by urging him to avoid the night battles of logomachy and to define his words strenuously and lucidly. Hard work and honesty are called for: suicide on the darkling plain would be ignoble only if Arnold or Newman thought it was adequate.

When sound provides a supplement of feeling not strictly connected with his grief or despair, Hardy, like Arnold, can use it to control or shape, instead of merely succumb to, his bafflements of mood. Sometimes a buoyant refrain in a poem like "During Wind and Rain" seems to pull against the bleak sentiment it appears to express. As a result, a bald paraphrase of such a poem may subtly falsify the slightly different experience we have in reading it.

In the final stanza of "In Death Divided" sound and sense work together to evoke a sense of doubleness. And that doubleness is reinforced by the way the stated sense of the passage and what the eye sees on the page begin to pull apart.

> The eternal tie which binds us twain in one
> No eye will see
> Stretching across the miles that sever you from me.
> ("In Death Divided," ll. 23–25)

"No eye will see." But the eye does see. In the final line all that severs "you" from "me" is the preposition "from." The long hexameter speaks of severance and division. But in the final phrase the two pronouns all but fuse in an empathic merging of persons. Even as sound and sense combine to evoke a sensation of sudden compression after strain and separation, the "eye"'s contradiction of what is said about the "eye" creates the chance for a polyphony, the opportunity for a divided sensibility to speak with two minds about a subject.

In Hardy's elegy "Without Ceremony" the brisk motion of the trimeters and tetrameters is at odds, not with the implicit sense of the poem, but only with the gravity and ceremony we expect to find in an elegy. When sound seems to work against the sense, it sends us in search of a different meaning. The real discourtesy is death's, and in sparing her husband the ceremony of a protracted farewell Emma's abrupt departure may have been her most courteous act of all. Is it possible to find a similar undercurrent of sense in "A Broken Appointment"? In creating the cruel woman in his own best image—as someone who might have been compassionate and kind—is Hardy suggesting that by sparing him the pain of words the woman's breaking their appointment was really kindness in disguise? Though Hardy protests that the loss of the woman's "dear presence" was less wrenching than the loss of imagined qualities of "high compassion" and "pure loving-kindness" (ll. 3, 5, 6), the epic enlargement generated by the spacious runovers and the Miltonic device of framing a noun between two adjectives ("human deeds divine," l. 12) creates a strong counterfeeling of how such qualities might have ennobled a lover. Unless I am seriously misreading the lyric, these imagined qualities continue to linger on as a kind of absent presence for the speaker. The bitter force of the poem depends on the withdrawal of the very qualities its epic manner evokes, on the undoing of the very detail it seems to present. In "The Going" the main sense is desolating. But there is also an undertow of hope, a desperate feeling that the moment of the wife's "great going" might still be delayed, if only by a deferral of the words: "close your term here" (l. 4). Often the force of the elegy comes from the disparity between the oddity of what is said—"I / Saw morning harden upon the wall" (we see "morning" but hear "mourning")—and the emotional truth of what is felt (ll. 9–10).

Though Hardy's elegy "During Wind and Rain" reaches sublime heights, and has power to chill and ravish readers, its meanings often jar so strangely with the sounds we hear that we are never quite sure whether the "blithely breakfasting . . . / Men and maidens" (ll. 15–16) are being mocked or mourned. Like the gay gardens and neat pathways, the symmetrical grammar and phonetically paired lines seem touchingly at odds with the eerie, reverberating, reproachful lament that passes like a shudder down each stanza's tremor of open vowels, then mounts to a surge of terror in the harshly stressed and alliterated final lines. Equivocations about a society Hardy finds both brittle and charming express themselves in savage switches of tone. As the literal down-to-earth world asserts its counterpower, a dark principle that is unaware of the other discourses going on around it makes the gentility of the courtly world suddenly hollowed out and vain. A blight that sickens and makes rotten, inducing something close to physical nausea by ripping dead roses from walls (l. 21), is also wrenchingly at odds with the high decorum and formality of Hardy's verse.

In the final stanza, for the first time in the lyric, the rhymes in the first and last lines are faintly dissonant. "Ploughs" is slanted away from its rhyme word "house": heard in one tone, the relentless effacements are a deserved reversion of decadence to Huxley's "cosmic process"; heard in another tone, they are a heartrending dramatization of the breaking points of the human voice: "Ah, no; the years, the years." Torn between primitive exultation and a cry of pain, the speaker finds his emotional attachment to the dear dead people is strongest when he is about to settle his score with them. His allegiances must be divided before he can find the heart to write. He has to disclose how pitilessly the raindrops plough down their names on the granite headstones before he can be moved to pity them. It is as if the elegist must lose his voice to find it. The final words seem torn out of him with the greatest reluctance, almost against his will. So tense and heart-wrenching is the polyphony of voices in this extraordinary lyric that one of its best recent commentators, David Gewanter (1991, 203–6), proposes to recast the whole elegy, not just as a chorus of discordant voices, but as a ballad with two speakers.

Polyphony takes a different form in Hardy's elegy "At Castle Boterel," which makes explicit the disparity between the possible meaninglessness of something that was said—a mere piece of nonsense perhaps—and the emotional truth of words we are not allowed to hear.

> What we did as we climbed, and what we talked of
>> Matters not much, nor to what it led,—
> Something that life will not be balked of
> Without rude reason till hope is dead,
>> And feeling fled.
>
> It filled but a minute. But was there ever
>> A time of such quality, since or before,
> In that hill's story? ("At Castle Boterel," ll. 11–18)

What gives "quality" to such a moment is the affective power of the words behind the words. As in Browning's poem "By the Fireside," which Hardy quotes in *Tess of the d'Urbervilles*, it is important that the actual conversation *not* be heard. Even when Hardy speaks, his words have a habit of looking two ways at once. What are we to make of the phrase "since or before / In that hill's story" (ll. 17–18)? Is the hill the recorder, like the primeval rocks in the next stanza? Or is Hardy chronicling the *hill*'s story? Perhaps the possessive is both a subjective and objective genitive, and the story narrated *by* the hill is also a story *about* the hill. In any case, as Hardy bids farewell to the young Emma's "phantom figure" (l. 28), it is hard to tell who is more benighted, the poet or the ghost. Because the contracted "sinking" (l. 33) is lodged within the sound patterns of line 31—"and I look and *see* it there, shr*inking*, shr*inking*"—even language seems to turn against the elegist as we watch the sinking feminine rhymes loosen his foothold and pull him down toward the edge.

In "Rain on a Grave" Hardy never allows his subversive underthought to surface. He prefers to replace the discourtesy of death, in dishonoring the fastidious woman, with a more attractive picture of the daisy-covered mound.

> Soon will be growing
>   Green blades from her mound,
> And daisies be showing
>   Like stars on the ground,
> Till she form part of them—
> Ay—the sweet heart of them,
> Loved beyond measure
> With a child's pleasure
>   All her life round. ("Rain on a Grave," ll. 28–36)

Nature has a kind of lover's quarrel with the woman. They mend their differences only when she consents to become, not just a portion of the star-like daisies springing from their mound, but also "the sweet heart of them" (l. 33). The phrases "sweet heart" and "ground" (ll. 31, 33) have internal plasticity. "Sweet heart" easily contracts into "sweetheart," and "ground" contains "round." They can and do change their shapes, whereas the repeated "them" (ll. 32–33) and "there" (ll. 22, 24–25) have only an external plasticity. Phonetically intractable, they seem incapable of verbal change. The possibility of being ravaged or violated in the privacy of an erotically secluded place is the elegy's unspeakable underthought. As in Wordsworth's Lucy poem, it will not bear talking about. But the touch of horror that resides in the very softness and pleasure of the trap is partially canceled in Hardy's elegy. It is offset by the boisterously innocent pleasure of a child, which in an overflow of feminine rhymes and a resurgence of a buoyant dance-like rhythm, quite at odds with the grimness of what is said, is able to unite high and low, as the flowers combine "stars" and earth in a sweetness "beyond measure."

Even when Hardy's skepticism deviates into simple unbelief, as in "God-Forgotten" and "Unknowing," which read like versified footnotes to Herbert Spencer's treatise "The Unknowable," the lilt or simple monotony of the lines may still be used to comment obliquely on the pessimism's lack of profundity. What is said trippingly or buoyantly can be beguilingly at odds with how it is said. It is as if the poet knows the pessimistic profundity is not really profound. When substance and manner tug in opposite directions the poet may be using an equivalent of the novelist's unreliable narrator to distance himself from the "message." According to Housman, poetry is not the thing said but the way of saying it (quoted by Ricks, 1987, 166). In Hardy's finest elegies it is surely both together. The lilting rhythm and jaunty rhymes of the refrain—"Ah, no; the years O!" ("During Wind and Rain," ll. 6, 20)—are not simply saying in their own medium what the diction is saying. Like the refrain from *Twelfth Night*, "With hey, ho, the wind and the rain" (v.i. 399, 403, 407, 411, 415), the exuberant "no"s and "O"s are telling something teasingly at odds with what they are saying, and I think more profound.

Zero Values of Disjunction and Elision

When elegies aspire to silence, they aspire to the integrity of a blank page or void. Since no poem can be composed entirely of pauses filled with words, zero values of disjunction and elision are most likely to appear in elegists like Auden and Hopkins who allow an expansive appositional style to contract suddenly to one-word petitions or short asides. To hear what they say we may have to linger over their dashes and caesuras, over the parentheses that Coleridge calls the drama of reason, or over their exclamations or splintered cries.

In *The Wreck of the Deutschland* Hopkins uses an expansive style to give God a spacious dwelling place in language. But alternating with his sundered syntax and figures of dilation is an austere use of dashes and ellipses, which propel him toward sudden stoppages and breaks. As grammar fragments and language almost grinds to a halt, Hopkins uses five lines of poetry to concentrate two extremes of discourse.

> But how shall I . . . make me room there:
> Reach me a . . . Fancy, come faster—
> Strike you the sight of it? look at it loom there,
> Thing that she . . . there then! the Master,
> Ipse, the only one, Christ, King, Head:
> (*The Wreck of the Deutschland*, 28.1–5)

First, the language falls apart into grammatical fragments, loosely bound by spatial and temporal connectives like "there," "look at it," "then." Such language, a version of Roman Jakobson's "similarity-disorder," is marked by a loss of the all-important nouns and subject words. A moment later the disappearance of deictics and the multiplication of nouns that were formerly missing produce the opposite danger, a species of Jakobson's "contiguity-disorder." The record needle sticks in the groove, and all Hopkins can do is stammer out six different names for the same thing.

As long as Hopkins petitions God in poems like "Myself Unholy" and "Nondum," he must present Christ as a dash or caesura, as a silence of emptiness or absence. But in *The Wreck of the Deutschland*, where Hopkins supplements Christ's silence with the silence of his own self-effacement and humility, dashes, hyphens, and caesuras mark off the silent spaces where God can at last make His long-delayed entry.

> A vein for the visiting of the past-prayer, pent in prison,
> The-last-breath penitent spirits—the uttermost mark
>   Our passion-plungèd giant risen,
> (*The Wreck of the Deutschland*, 33.5–7)

"The uttermost mark" is literally the dash that precedes the phrase—the mark of ellipsis and caesura. It is the place of fracture, where life breaks apart after being all but exhaled through the hyphens that divide the monosyllables in the compound phrase "The-last-breath penitent spirits." God lives in that break: He comes to life in it, even as He came to life from a tomb.

Like Hopkins, Auden allows some of his elegies to alternate between a clipped, oracular style, where death is confronted in what is elided or displaced, and a more expansive language. Sometimes, as in his elegy for Yeats, the two styles come together, often in the same line. Though the obituary plainness of the January scene seems capable of endless elaboration, it is conveyed with a disturbing economy of words and gestures.

> He disappeared in the dead of winter:
> The brooks were frozen, the airports almost deserted,
> And snow disfigured the public statues;
> The mercury sank in the mouth of the dying day.
> What instruments we have agree
> The day of his death was a dark cold day.
> ("In Memory of W. B. Yeats," ll. 1–6)

The weather report is straightforward, but its laconic simplicity allows elided meanings to filter through. We hear them in the euphemism of the opening verb, "He disappeared," in the telegraphic style that leaves more implied than it says, and in the stanza's single metaphor, which turns the death of the day into the death of a patient. The final line is at once an example of a terse modern style and, in its alliteration, monosyllables, and climactic triple stresses, a Tennysonian contrivance, reminiscent of the mourner's disillusion in *In Memoriam*: "On the bald street breaks the blank day" (7.12).

For a more sustained alternation of expansive and elliptical language we must turn from Auden's elegy on Yeats to one of his most powerfully elegiac ballads, "As I Walked out One Evening." The ballad gently subverts the lover's boast that his "Love has no ending" (l. 8) by making his defiance of closure coincide with the end of a poetic line and quatrain. Though there is no break after the second "I'll love you" in stanza 3, the line ending creates a brief pause. In that breathing space the reader has leisure to guess what platitude the lover will think of next. He might try to imitate the Prayer Book and say "I'll love you / As myself" (ll. 9–10). Instead, the lover says something at once more trite and more marvelous. In substance, he utters a commonplace: "I'll love you forever." But the hyperbolic conceit into which he translates the adverb "forever" makes each new wonder seem as natural as it is surprising.

> I'll love you, dear, I'll love you
>   Till China and Africa meet,
> And the river jumps over the mountain
>   And the salmon sing in the street,
> ("As I Walked out One Evening," ll. 9–12)

Mountain-jumping rivers generate the idea of river-jumping salmon with some display of logic. But they are also a surprise. For these salmon sing where no fish can hope to survive—in the city street, where "crowds upon the pavement" have already been harvested like wheat. As in Tennyson's line, "Man comes and tills the field and lies beneath" ("Tithonus," l. 3), we are tempted to place the milling urban crowd "*under*" the pavement rather than "upon" it.

The unobtrusive shock of the ocean's being folded and hung up to dry, like linen, depends on our expectation of some grander outcome. "I'll love till the ocean" does what? The slight pause on the edge of the line ending invites readers to provide an answer to that question.

> I'll love you till the ocean
>   Is folded and hung up to dry
> And the seven stars go squawking
>   Like geese about the sky.
> ("As I Walked out One Evening," ll. 13–16)

An apocalypse of singing salmon in the previous stanza may lead us to expect: "I'll love you till the ocean surrenders its dead or meets the Alps." Auden jolts the reader by domesticating the mystery. But instead of evoking the idea of apocalypse only to rescind it, he allows the idea to resurface in the spectacle of an ocean that has been dried out at the end of time, like the sea in Revelation, when the deep will give up its dead.

Like the life that leaks "Vaguely . . . away" in stanza 8, something heroic and ennobling drains away in the empty space between the fifth and sixth stanzas. The time that has undergone a marvelous expansion, encompassing the drying up of oceans at the end of recorded history, now contracts to nothing: "O let not Time deceive you," the whirring clocks warn the lover, "You cannot conquer Time" (ll. 23–24). As Auden allows the leisurely expansive movement of his love song to be replaced with harsh ellipses, even his language becomes death-like. The removal of a single syllable from the spectral phrase, "naked *is*," generates the rhyme word "kiss." Wasted by disease, the emaciated lover finds that his own words are wasted.

> In the burrows of the Nightmare
>   Where Justice naked is,
> Time watches from the shadow
>   And coughs when you would kiss.
> ("As I Walked out One Evening," ll. 25–28)

The use of "is" to carry the metrical stress is distressing to the ear. It is a deadly thing to do, as deathly as the tubercular coughing that replaces the expected "kiss."

Even the expansive love song signals the move toward abrupt stoppages and breaks. Early in the song "sing" harks back to "evening," its rhyme word in the preceding stanza (ll. 1, 6). The love song seems to find rhymes in everything, even in terminal words like "evening" that are not expected to rhyme. By the end of the song, however, only imperfect rhymes are allowed to join the lovers by spanning space and time in a magnificent sweeping arch.

> For in my arms I hold
> The Flower of the Ages,
>   And the first love of the world.
> ("As I Walked out One Evening," ll. 18–20)

The desperate arch of rhyme—"hold" and "world"—that the lover tries to build between himself and "The Flower of the Ages" sends out its own distress signal. At the zenith we are already halfway to the nadir, to that low point of dyslectic rhyme, the deathly coupling of "naked is" with the alliterative "cough-kiss."

The collapse of the arching rhymes is matched by the collapse of other arches: Cupid's bow is broken by the sundering of the threaded dances, and time breaks the "brilliant bow" traced out by the arched back of the diver.

> Into many a green valley
>   Drifts the appalling snow;
> Time breaks the threaded dances
>   And the diver's brilliant bow.
> ("As I Walked out One Evening," ll. 33–36)

Inverted word order and the pause after "valley" allow the verb "Drifts" to literally drift across the line break, filling up the space before we know it is there. The snow proves most "appalling" in its power to surprise us with three different meanings of that adjective. Snow literally blanches the valley, turning its verdure white; it buries the green earth, until life itself seems borne off beneath a pall; and it terrifies by its power to whiten. We can see the face turn white, drained of blood, just as the green valley changes color.

Sometimes slight pauses or tremors at the center or end of lines cause the elliptical and expansive styles to converge. Stressed monosyllables momentarily crowd together in the noun "teacups," for example, before dispersing themselves over a wider expanse of sounds.

> And the crack in the teacup opens
> A lane to the land of the dead.
> ("As I Walked out One Evening," ll. 43–44)

Even the momentary hovering of the voice over the noun "blessing," which comes at the end of a line, evokes a trembling of innocence on the edge of experience: "Life remains a blessing / Although you cannot bless" (ll. 51–52). The pause at the end of line 55 prepares for an even sharper blow when crookedness, we discover, is an attribute of the lover's own misshapen heart.

Alternating between caesural and appositional styles, the ballad combines ellipsis and amplification. As language falters, halts, then threatens to stop altogether, Auden surrounds the void with expansive apostrophes and exhortations: "O look, look in the mirror," for example, or "O stand, stand at the window" (ll. 49, 53). A phrase like "I'll love you, dear, I'll love you" (l. 9) seems to multiply its parts automatically, as if sustained by a power that carries the speaker over the break between stanzas (ll. 12–13). At the opposite extreme time seems to run down and disappear through one of the many empty spaces that keep opening up between words and lines. These tiny fissures are the poetic equivalent of the cracks in the teacup, and they break discourse apart, crowding the elegy with unsaid thoughts about lost virginity or sexual impotence, as "Jill goes down on her back" (l. 48) or the "brilliant bow" collapses (l. 36). Such thoughts will not bear talking about, and Auden half buries them in elliptical metaphors that equate milling urban crowds with wheat, or in debasing alliterations that couple "coughs" with "kiss" (l. 28)—a rhyme that seems to follow with death-like rigor once we witness the mechanism of its production: the elision of the syllable "ed" between "naked" and "is" (l. 26). Equally austere are the syntactic patterns that contract to discrete one-line units:

It was late, late in the evening,
    The lovers they were gone;
The clocks had ceased their chiming,
    And the deep river ran on.
("As I Walked out One Evening," ll. 57–60)

With the emphatic end-stopping, rhetoric seems to shrink to nothing, like the vanished lovers. As an expansive celebratory style alternates with a stripped, emaciated one, compressing all meaning to zero values of disjunction and elision, we can feel the ground of the loss, its buried life, in metaphoric displacements and deletions. But nothing can translate it. It is like walking on silence.

Silences of Plenitude and Emptiness

Earlier in this chapter I distinguished between silences of emptiness in Wordsworth's elegies and silences of plenitude—moments when there are no more words, but only the dashes or elisions that mark an amazed possession of all words. In the elegies of Amy Clampitt, a contemporary American poet, both kinds of silence reappear. Only now it is harder to tell emptiness and plenitude apart. Though Clampitt uses an elliptical style to register the shock of the violent termination of life in "The Dakota," she faces in the suspended grammar and the dashes of her elegy both a plenitude and an emptiness. In the assassination of John Lennon there is an obvious senselessness and emptiness, too painful at first to face. But there is also, more surprisingly, a plenitude of earlier expressions of loss, an embarrassing abundance of words that Clampitt feels qualms about using. In a longer elegy, "What the Light Was Like," a more expansive style allows Clampitt to move with assurance toward lucid threshold states. Her intimations of a cross-over and a breakthrough help her inscribe some portion of a world outside familiar waters, at the frontier of the harbor. She takes us to "a restricted area, off limits for all purposes but puffins'" (l. 61), and invites us to chart for ourselves the terra incognita that lies just across these borders. But what do we find when we get there? A silence of emptiness or a silence of plenitude? Clampitt shows us that the prospect of lifting the veil can be just as terrifying as living with illusion.

As a belated immigrant to realms of feeling occupied and expressed before her, Clampitt finds that the allusiveness of her elegy for Lennon is part of her problem. Conceding that her poem's "most telling lines . . . are lifted almost bodily from 'Eleanor Rigby,' recorded by the Beatles in 1966" (Clampitt, 1983, 139), she is struck by the way grief "repeats itself: there's nothing / more original that it can do" ("The Dakota," ll. 16–17). Like the biblical Koheleth, whose doctrine of vanity repeats a repetition of the Buddha, Clampitt fears that her most authentic griefs are derivative. If there is nothing new under the sun, including the thought there is nothing new under the sun, then an elegist may feel that her problem is one of plenitude rather than emptiness. There are already too many songs and poems expressing how she feels.

The holes created by the dashes and suspended grammar at the center of her elegy are like the bullet hole that ends John Lennon's life.

> Grief for a generation—all
> the lonely people
> gone, the riffraff
> out there now mainly pigeons—
> steps from its limousine
> and lights a taper
> inside the brownstone catacomb
> Of the Dakota. ("The Dakota," ll. 1–8)

We have rapidly to construe the grammar at line 5: "Grief for a generation . . . / steps from its limousine." The shock of confronting the deferred predicate prepares for the even greater shock of the assassin's bullet. The most important meanings are swallowed up by empty spaces: they are swiftly silenced and elided. But death is not the only elided element. Also elided is the thought that, in being shot down, a spokesman for a generation's grief is immediately transformed into both the commemorated victim and the commemorator, who wrote his own memorial fourteen years earlier in a popular song.

> Pick up
> the wedding rice, take out
> the face left over from
> the funeral nobody came to,
> bring flowers, leave them woven
> with the lugubrious ironwork
> of the Dakota. Grief
> is original, but it
> repeats itself: there's nothing
> more original that it can do. ("The Dakota," ll. 8–17)

If the real funeral is always the one "nobody came to" (l. 11), a funeral of the heart's private grieving, where no floral tributes are found, then all rites of mourning are as oddly "lugubrious" as the flowers woven into the ironwork or the tapers lit in the catacombs of the New York hotel. The most moving gestures are the most irrelevant, because they are mere repetitions of repetitions, like the confessed inadequacy of the elegy's "most telling lines."

For a more spectacular elision of its subject, we must turn to one of Clampitt's more expansive elegies, "What the Light Was Like," a poem that swivels on the hinge of a leisurely chiasmus. The voyage out in the boat is not followed by the anticipated voyage home. And so the pilgrimage out of life can best be intimated by displacement. What is it like to travel out beyond familiar compass points and landmarks into unfamiliar territory? Though there is something ominous about the poet's report that her unnamed friend had gone out at dawn one morning in October, the fact to be communicated is deferred for ten whole stanzas. The elegy takes a detour around the bleak truth that the friend went out one morning never to return. Stanzas 7 to 16 function as a tmesis, an interposed roadblock—the separating middle terms of a narrative of pilgrimage, like Ulysses' voyage in Dante and Tennyson.

We are assured at first that everything is "as usual." The repeated phrase, used anaphorically at the head of successive tercets (ll. 19, 22), mutes the strangeness, focusing instead on the ordinary and the familiar. Even awesome or estranging impressions affirm continuity: if the surge of burning sun, turning the whole ocean into fool's gold over molten emerald, is present as a core of amazement, it is still a day-after-day amazement. Only imperceptibly, as the boatsman, steering straight into the sunrise, shrinks from view, does the hold of familiar landmarks begin to relax and lessen. At last even the spired town, a diminished compass point, becomes as feeble a tie as an apron string, despite all efforts to retain and fix it.

Like any voyage into death, "What the Light Was Like" is a boundary poem. But boundaries tend to break down and erode the more closely we approach them. In all the "ungirdled wallowing and glitter" (l. 30), we seem to be headed for the mouth of a volcano, where opposites are hard to keep separate, and where what we love most is the same as what we fear most (ll. 31–32). As the juxtaposed participles "burning," "turning," execute an exuberant chiasmus, the elegist shows how exhilarating it can be to turn on the pivot of a repeating suffix: "straight into the sunrise, a surge of burning turning the whole ocean iridescent" (l. 25). But what happens when a boundary experience cannot be reversed? What happens when the boundary itself is crossed, and no return to restricted zones is possible? As in Frost's poem "Birches," no one wants to travel too far out: at some point it is comforting to initiate the countermovement of the returning pendulum or arc.

The voyage we anticipate ought to trace a perfect chiasmus: items seen on the voyage out should be seen once more, though this time in reverse order. We reach a crisis when chiasmus fails, when we miss the anticipated reversing motion, as things begin to "wander into shorter focus / as, around noon, you head back in" (ll. 39–40). At first our expectations seem to be fulfilled: the lighthouse, the rock pile of Cranberry Point, the huge boat hulls, the radar gadget, the inner bar, all seem to trace out the second arc of an expanded chiasmus. But there is one asymmetry and distress signal, all the more unsettling because everything else is so normal and expected, so predictably chiasmic. Without warning, the pronouns suddenly change: the third-person pronoun used to describe the boatman who sets out is replaced by an unfamiliar second-person pronoun.

> we heard how *he'd* gone out
> at dawn, one morning in October, unmoored the dinghy and rowed
> to *his* boat
>
> as usual. ("What the Light Was Like," ll. 17–19)
>
> Out there, from that wallowing perspective, all comparisons amount
> to nothing,
> though once *you've* hauled *your* last trap, things tend to wander into
> shorter focus
>
> as, around noon, *you* head back in: . . .
> . . . then *you* see the hamlet . . .
> . . . and *you* detect among the
> chimneys and the TV aerials,
>
> *yours.*
> ("What the Light Was Like," ll. 38–40, 42, 48–49, my emphasis)

The strange "you" seems addressed to us now, the readers. Though the voyage home ends when the boatman picks out the familiar chimney and television aerial, that boatman is not the friend who initially set out, but Everyman, oneself, the reader, who is no longer able to maintain a comfortable distance from the action of the elegy.

We stare beyond the boundary, past the familiar compass points and restricted areas, and what we glimpse is unnameable, a mystery, like Carlyle's signless Inane, although we may be tempted to call it God.

> maybe, out there beside the wheel, the Baptist spire shrunk to a com-
> pass-point, the town an interrupted circlet, feeble as an apron-string,
> for all the labor

> it took to put it there, it's finding, out in that ungirdled wallowing
> > and glitter,
>
> finally, that what you love most is the same as what you're most
> > afraid of—God,
> in a word, ("What the Light Was Like," ll. 28–32)

For an instant the elegist seems to back off from the brink, from the frightful precipice of the dash. For what can cross the magnitude of that mark? The dash is the elegiac chasm, the divide, but also the dividing force itself: "—God, / In a word" (ll. 31–32). Yet "God" is an inadequate word for what the elegist wants to say. What matters is the merging of opposites like love and fear, birth and death, as the end of life turns into the last of our new beginnings. Death as the end of a trajectory is replaced by death as a question: What does death mean? Our experience of boundaries is threatening, not because it is the end of life, but because it is the most important moment *in* life. Like the syntactic silence that ends a sentence and gives it meaning, death is the pause of the dash and caesural break after the penultimate syllable in line 31. It is the instant of retrospect but also the instant of looking forward, which confers meaning or absence of meaning on everything that went before or comes after.

At the end of the elegy we retrace the voyage out, but this time without the comfort of chiasmus.

> When, on the third day, his craft was sighted finally, it had drifted,
>
> with its engine running, till the last gulp of fuel spluttered and ran
> > out,
> beyond the town's own speckled noose of buoys, past the furred crest
> > of Schoodic,
> vivid in a skirt of aspens, the boglands cranberry-crimson at its foot,
>
> past the bald brow the sunrise always strikes first, of the hulk of
> > Cadillac,
> ("What the Light Was Like," ll. 54–58)

After taking us fifty miles beyond familiar landmarks (l. 60), the elegist tries to imagine the imageless condition of being beyond all boundary lines, outside all restricted areas and limits. Perhaps that is what death is like.

> I find it tempting to imagine what,
> when the blood roared, overflowing its cerebral sluiceway, and the
> > iridescence

of his last perception, charring, gave way to unreversed irrevocable
                                                                    dark,
the light out there was like, that's always shifting—from a nimbus
                                                          gone berserk
to a single gorget, a cathedral train of blinking or the fogbound
                                                              shroud

that can turn anywhere into a nowhere.
("What the Light Was Like," ll. 62–67)

We know that the vision finally ebbed. But did it ebb because of a plenitude of light, a halo gone berserk, like the somersaulting grandeur of the ocean at sunrise? Or because of a void of emptiness, a background of "unreversed, irrevocable dark" (l. 64)? For many Romantic and post-Romantic elegists, as for the ancients, "dreams" seem "to loom and vanish" there "against a background of immutable ebony" (Flaubert, 1919, 220. Steegmuller, 1982, 20).

Clampitt's elegy, "What the Light Was Like," originally averts its gaze from the hole or void to be found at the center of many elegies. This empty place, which Dr. Johnson associates with "the horror of concluding," is as specific as the bullet hole that ends John Lennon's life in "The Dakota." Gradually, however, as "What the Light Was Like" unfolds, and we are invited to explore boundary or threshold states, death becomes a worded mystery, an ineffable quantity like love, which the elegist must work at the height of her power to put into words. The climax of the poem is not an original uttered word, guaranteed by a voice that speaks it from the whirlwind or the sky, like the strange voice that talks to Tennyson at the climax of *In Memoriam*: " 'The dawn, the dawn,' and died away" (95.61). In Clampitt's elegy every intimation of unmediated being or plenitude has its countervailing intimation of absence or emptiness. Like the deconstructionists, Clampitt conducts her own critique of Western culture's infatuation with some absolute proximity of voice and being. She knows that anything she may say about filtered light in a cathedral, the searing flame of a hummingbird's throat, or "a nimbus gone berserk," is likely to founder on spurious axioms of presence.

Elegy and Silence: The Romantic Legacy

One legacy of the Romantic movement is that, because a truth expressed is nearly always a lie, the best elegies are one part speech to three parts silence. As Wordsworth observes in his "Essay upon Epitaphs," the elegist must somehow convey that "the sublimity of [a] sentiment consists in its being the secret possession" of the mourner

(1974, 2:88). Tennyson's staged deaths in "The Lady of Shalott" or "The Passing of Arthur" contrast with the silent performances of mourners who, like many mourners in Dickinson's and Rossetti's elegies, do not seem to understand the nature of playing a part at all. In Frost's "Home Burial," a post-Romantic elegy that I discuss in chapter 6, the stage on which conventional mourning takes place is suddenly withdrawn from us. The reader is as unnerved as the husband by the silence out of which the wife's sense of wrongness arises at the beginning and to which it returns at the end. Seldom do the silences in poetry give such a sustained impression of being outside elegy and art altogether, beyond the reach of traditional consolation.

Sometimes the silences of extremes—of plenitude and emptiness— suddenly converge in a phrase like Amy Clampitt's "—God, / In a word" ("What the Light Was Like," ll. 31–32), which is doubly broken by a dash and a line break, or in Hopkins' desolating line: "They fought with God's cold—" (*The Wreck of the Deutschland*, 17.1). Silences and modal verbs, and sudden alternations of an expansive and elliptical style, slam human powers against inhuman or superhuman ones—forces deadly and unremitting. It might be thought that only in a post-Romantic world of skepticism and doubt, where God and nature are at strife, is the elegist's silence, like Christ's silence before His accusers, a mark of truth-saying or integrity. But as Eric Griffiths reminds us, a world in which nothing unequivocally indicates God's providence is not a modern conception at all: the silence of a God who cannot love anyone because He *is* love dates back at least as far as Augustine (1989, 349).

Among the elegists considered in this chapter, Hardy may seem the outsider, the poet to whom family resemblances least apply. But that is mainly because his restraints are less audacious, his reticences and silences more discreet. The genteel diction of "During Wind and Rain," for example, is inseparable from what is archaic in the past, from what now seems dead and done with.

> Clocks and carpets and chairs
>   On the lawn all day,
> And brightest things that are theirs . . .
>   Ah, no; the years, the years;
> Down their carved names the rain-drop ploughs.
> ("During Wind and Rain," ll. 24–28)

Hardy seems to take pleasure in a refrain, "Ah, no; the years, the years," that he can imagine himself singing, like the "Treble and tenor and bass" (l. 3), but that is too desolating to hear spoken out loud. The silence of print even allows us to imagine as mastered or subdued an impulse to berate, transformed now into nostalgia or even fondness for the vanished "Men and maidens" singing "their dearest songs" (ll. 1, 16). In Hardy, as in earlier Romantic elegists, it is often difficult to imagine a voice for the words we read silently. The absence of any single way of hearing the refrain—"Ah, no; the years O! / And the rotten rose is ripped from the wall" ("During Wind and Rain," ll. 20–21)—is what has most precisely to be imagined. Do we hear pity or revulsion in the speaking voice, or is the tone just noncommittal? Because it is difficult to read such lines aloud without dishonoring or putting into jeopardy a complex dual allegiance that allows Hardy to hover between the sardonic and the wistful, the indignant and the sad, the silences in his best elegies are often the silences of an achieved absence of voice.

Using the transformation of Wordsworth's Lucy or the sudden departure of Hardy's and Patmore's wives to draw a circle of words around their meaning, many Romantic and post-Romantic elegists speak obliquely or in riddles. The boldest words in Dickinson, Rossetti, and Arnold are usually the words we do not hear: they form part of the elegy's subtext. The distance between these elegists and Milton is as thick as the distance to the next star. Their silences, evasions, and multiple time frames, even in a profoundly simple elegist like Wordsworth, have almost nothing in common with the triumphal simplicities of "Lycidas." To reach the buried truth in Wordsworth's elegy "The Two April Mornings," readers have to dig through four strata of rock. Beneath the upper layer of present narrative lies the time period of Matthew's death, and below that the events of the two April mornings, separated by an interval of thirty years. Even when we reach the two wild lines out of a private heart near the end of the elegy, we have to dig below their naked exclamation—"I looked at her, and looked again: / And did not wish her mine!" (ll. 55–56)—to unearth the father's unspeakable underthought: his wayward feeling that he prefers his dead daughter to any living girl in Christendom. For Milton's single narrative frame at the end of "Lycidas" Wordsworth has substituted four separate frames.

Unfolding by surprise, Romantic elegies betray our expectations. When their losses cannot be ritually absorbed, they induce a strong shock or tremor that draws us into the action of the elegy; the mourner's losses become our losses, too. Though the opposite of obvious, the sense of fulfilled expectation in "Lycidas" partly removes us from the events, leaving us spectators of a play that has all the cathartic power of a short tragic drama. Instead of leaving us emotionally detached, however, there are few experiences more powerful, moving, or memorable than reading "Lycidas." Even to hear the elegy read aloud at a funeral service, as I did in the late 1960s when a close friend and several of my students died in a fire at Cornell, is an experience that can etch us sharply and deepen us. The elusive Romantic elegists might seem to respond more powerfully and deeply to deaths that are not staged but painfully literal—deaths that catch us offguard. But Milton, perhaps because he is a more spectacular and theatrical elegist than most of his successors, has power to turn the most ordinary analogies between the drowned man and the sun into figures of such renovating power that I, like Paul Elmer More, "can never peruse the climax of the poem without a thrill such as scarcely any other verses in the language excite" (1961, 93).

5 ❧ The Paradox of Veridiction: Breakdown and Breakthrough in Modern Elegy

As students of elegy we are concerned with what A. J. Greimas calls the marks of "truth-saying" or "veridiction" in poetry. The hallmark of truth-saying in pastoral elegies is a quasi-magical performative use of words that allows the elegist to achieve maximum cathartic effect with a minimum of material. In confessional elegies, by contrast, lyric anxiety is a mark of truth: use of an expansive appositional style allows an end that is perfectly foreseen to be endlessly delayed as well. When Romantic elegists discover a passion in restraint, silence or reserve replaces amplification as a signature of truth. Wordsworth's lines—"I looked at her, and looked again: / And did not wish her mine" ("The Two April Mornings," ll. 55–56)—are immediately intelligible, because their naked exclamations come straight from the heart. But often we have to guess what a truncated poetic line or stammer, a suddenly reticent rhyme or rhythm, manages to leave unsaid.

Modern elegy takes this reticence one step further. The slight impediments to speech become more pronounced and audible. They become open sites of fracture and breakdown. Instead of being interpreted as mere restraints, as meanings half said or intimated, these breaking points dramatize the way a tactical stumble or ellipsis may turn the breakdown of language, a potential awkwardness or stammer, into a moment of breakthrough instead. Breakup itself becomes a sign of veridiction whenever the hesitations or ambivalences of a self-divided mind are interpreted as a positive quality, as a mark of superior alertness or discernment. If one axiom of modernism is that there are no truths outside the creative power of our own subject lenses, then to succeed in saying so is also to fail. For if it is true that no marks of veridiction in modern elegies are really true, something is true after all. If it is false, then again something is true. The paradox of veridiction consists in this: even in denying a truth-claim we presume to make one.

Places of Breakup: A Divided Mind

The elegiac poetry of Yeats and Larkin comes to life in places of fracture or breakup, and in lines that look two ways at once. Some of Yeats's most broken, halting lines remain stuck in the throat.

> I had thought . . .
> . . . to have brought to mind
> All those that manhood tried . . .
> With some appropriate commentary on each;
> Until imagination brought
> A fitter welcome; but a thought
> Of that late death took all my heart for speech.
> ("In Memory of Major Robert Gregory," ll. 89–96)

James Richardson has written well of the way Yeats can turn "potential awkwardness into an asset" (1988, 183). He shows how awkwardness may be a kind of grace, and how an elegy can grow "proudly silent" by qualifying its own momentum. The two semicolons near the end of Yeats's elegy for Gregory seem to stop the speaker in his tracks, almost bringing the poem to a halt, as he falters in his capacity to find words. If thought of Gregory has taken all "his heart for speech," perhaps he is still holding something back, keeping his most important meanings in reserve. At the middle of his penultimate line Yeats awkwardly admits that the original plan for his poem has broken down. But that breakdown is also a breakthrough, for the hesitations and awkwardness are a part of the elegy's unquestionable strength. Yeats's broken, contingent conduct of his elegy is the perfect way of expressing the broken, contingent nature of every life. Without the heavy caesural pauses and the unpredictable shift in direction, the passion might dwindle, and the conclusion of the elegy would be much less powerful than it is.

To show how Yeats discovers the elegy's way of unfolding as he writes, we have to see how he keeps using two-way meanings to create a flicker of alternative possibilities:

> And now their breathless faces seem to look
> Out of some old picture book;
> I am accustomed to their lack of breath,
> ("In Memory of Major Robert Gregory," ll. 43–45)

Are the "breathless faces" rapt with the ardor of new discovery? Or are they literally dead, without any trace of breath? Before the phrase "lack of breath" (l. 45) restores the shadow of the banished meaning, the "breathless faces" (l. 43) have power to evoke life at the very moment death is being acknowledged.

Repeated in seminal contexts, "courtesy" and its opposite are just as effective in breaking down univocal meanings and creating a divided response. Lionel Johnson is said to be "courteous to the worst" (l. 19). Death, by contrast, is "discourteous" to the best, to "Our Sidney and our perfect man" (ll. 47–48). The "discourtesy" of Gregory's death has made Yeats discourteous, too, since his plan to commemorate his other friends has broken down. The "fitter welcome" he wanted to extend to them is uncivilly withheld. Though "courtesy" denotes gracious concern, it also evokes as a shadow-meaning the tenure in medieval law by which a husband holds property inherited from a spouse. Gregory cannot share in that tenure; premature death has deprived him of his due. Embroidered upon an archaic legal meaning of "courtesy," the incivility is both a breach of decorum and a breach of law.

In the penultimate stanza the slow unfolding of one of the elegy's few metaphors consumes all its forces, as if the poem, like Gregory's life, "had finished in that flare."

> Some burn damp faggots, others may consume
> The entire combustible world in one small room
> As though dried straw, and if we turn about
> The bare chimney is gone black out
> Because the work had finished in that flare.
> Soldier, scholar, horseman, he,
> As 'twere all life's epitome.
> What made us dream that he could comb grey hair?
> ("In Memory of Major Robert Gregory," ll. 81–88)

The "measureless consummation" Lionel Johnson merely "dreamed of" (l. 24) is now beautifully achieved. But while Yeats speaks of death as if it were "life's high meed," its zenith, the high point Johnson could never reach, "flare" also contains an antipun on "flair." Has Gregory's life mere flair or finish, or is it finished in the sense of being perfectly consummated? There can be no direct collision of mere elegance with moral consummation, because what is not fully admitted into the elegy is not there to be collided with. One cannot do battle with a phantom. And yet a phantasmal shadow-meaning is allowed to linger. Even as Gregory dies into life, finishing in a "flare," Yeats continues to divide his allegiances and balance his values. Any residual distrust of virtuosity is effectively discharged by Yeats's phrase "As 'twere all life's epitome" (l. 87), which both fleetingly recalls and discredits Dryden's dilettante, Zimri, "A man so various, that he seemed to be / Not one, but all mankind's epitome" ("Absalom and Achitophel," ll. 545–46). But what does the perfection of Gregory's "secret discipline" consist in? Is it the mere courtesy of the courtier? Is it the flair or aesthetic finish of the artist, inseparable from his "stern colour" and "delicate line" (ll. 67–68)? Or is the "secret" something sturdier, more fully human, less cloistered and fugitive—a legacy likely to deepen rather than diminish with time?

In their blend of colloquial speech and vision, few of Yeats's elegiac lyrics dramatize more poignantly the conflicts of a divided mind than "The Folly of Being Comforted" and "The Arrow." In the second of these poems the poet's heart is driven wild, not just by the thought that the man is in love and loves what vanishes, but by the excluded thought that when the woman was young no man could look on her and retain his composure. We half expect Yeats to say, "There's no man may look upon her" (l. 3) and not declare her more beautiful than ever. But the arrow that has lodged in his marrow is sharper than that: "This beauty's kinder, yet for a reason / I could weep that the old is out of season" (ll. 7–8). "The Arrow" allows only one of two possible meanings a collidable reality. But at the end of "The Folly of Being Comforted" two opposed meanings are invited to wed and bed, and the result is open war.

In this more complex poem the principal speaker plays a game of verbal tennis with the one who "is ever kind," a Polonius-like comforter, whose sententious platitude, "Time can but make it easier to be wise," is thrown back at him with a spin: "Time can but make her beauty over again" (ll. 4, 8). Even the comforter's tender diminutives—the "threads of grey" in the "well-belovèd's hair" and the "little shadows" that "come about her eyes"—are picked up and reversed in the lover's heartfelt protest: "No, / I have not a crumb of comfort, not a grain" (ll. 2–3, 6–7). Any speaking aloud of Yeats's lines is in danger of betraying their complex ambivalence and deeply reticent power to say opposite things at once.

> One that is ever kind said yesterday:
> "Your well-belovèd's hair has threads of grey,
> And little shadows come about her eyes;
> Time can but make it easier to be wise
> Though now it seem impossible, and so
> Patience is all that you have need of."
>   "No,
> I have not a crumb of comfort, not a grain.
> Time can but make her beauty over again:
> Because of that great nobleness of hers
> The fire that stirs about her, when she stirs,

Burns but more clearly. O she had not these ways
When all the wild summer was in her gaze."

O heart! O heart! if she'd but turn her head,
You'd know the folly of being comforted.
("The Folly of Being Comforted")

Is the lover celebrating in the subtle motions of the fire a great and noble beauty that time has indeed "made over"? Or is he lamenting the loss of a more breathtaking beauty, "when all the wild summer was in her gaze"? When she turns her head, will she reveal a beauty that richly compensates for any loss, or will her face be lined and haggard? Even in pronouncing the words of the title, the lover seems to speak with a forked tongue: Is he a fool for seeking comfort where no comfort is needed? Or is he foolish for trying to pretend that nothing has been lost? Good critics of a poem like "The Folly of Being Comforted" justify the value of sudden breaks in the argument and two-way meanings by fostering ambivalence in their critical response. To hover like Yeats's speaker between consolation and inconsolability may be the best way of remaining self-divided and so critically aware.

Yeats's lover no doubt wants to say that the conflict envisaged by his false comforter remains a possibility only in a world of speculation. The war between the ravages of age and the wild summer of youth is evoked only to be excluded by the beauty that the woman's great nobleness refines. Yet no sooner has the conflict been banished than it comes back to obsess the speaker. The first exclamation, "O she had not these ways" (l. 12), breaks the poem apart. As "the wild summer" goes up like flame from a collapsing funeral pyre, the two kinds of beauty approach each other from opposite directions, and in the concluding lines they seem headed for direct collision. Though the phrase, "O heart! O heart!" (l. 13), conveys sudden access of emotion, there is no clue comparable to the phrase "I could weep" from "The Arrow" (l. 8) to indicate whether the lover is consoled or inconsolable. Indeed the absence of any such indication is what each reader needs precisely to imagine.

The break in feeling that occurs after the first exclamation in "The Folly of Being Comforted" is hard to miss. But often Yeats uses two-way grammar to signal such a break less openly.

Everything that man esteems
Endures a moment or a day.
Love's pleasure drives his love away,
The painter's brush consumes his dreams;
The herald's cry, the soldier's tread

Exhaust his glory and his might:
Whatever flames upon the night
Man's own resinous heart has fed.
("Two Songs from a Play," ll. 25–32)

Just when we may feel that Yeats is retreating into easy aphorism, the double meaning of the last two lines alerts us to a disturbing break or division in his thought. Is "heart" or "flames" the subject of the verb "fed"? Is the nighttime spectacle feeding the "resinous heart," or is the heart feeding the flames? The two-way flow of words allows Yeats to combine the same apparently contradictory theories of determinism and self-making that Henry Adams combines in his essay, "The Rule of Phase Applied to History" (1909), a work we know Yeats admired. The determinism is implicit in Adams' teaching that, at ever accelerating rates, a mechanical phase of history, supposed to have lasted from 1600 to 1900, has been replaced by an electric phase, which is fated to be superseded by an even briefer ethereal phase. In a world where the blood dripping from Dionysus's heart is already the "Odour of blood when Christ was slain" (l. 22), the future exerts a backward pressure on the present. To prevent such a self-repeating cycle from seeming completely rigged, Yeats asserts the countertruth that each reader, like each poet, is also a creator who answers the determinism by authoring it: his "resinous heart" continues to feed the flame. As Adams explains, the mind cannot "reach anything but a . . . reflection of its own features," because man's "thought" is continually "projecting its own image . . . into the unknown" (1909, 295–96). A deep break or divide allows double meanings to grow out of the center of a poem in which "the virgin" is at once Athena and Mary, and "the peace of Augustus," as one critic says, "both a moment of high civilization and the moment of a fatal relaxation of control, a dropping of 'the reins of peace and war'" (Brower, 1954, 786).

Unless Yeats can master his bitterness against rivals like MacBride, his plaintive verse is in danger of losing its humanizing character. But the opposite risk is just as pressing. The jaunty unconcern with which the grave-diggers in "Under Ben Bulben" thrust the dead "Back in the human mind again" (l. 24) betrays Yeats's alarm at the threat posed to time, history, and personal identity by a collective unconscious. Resisting the urge to regress to magic, or to any eternal return of the cycles in the anima mundi, Yeats prefers the temporal breaks and unique one-way departures of the elegist.

Like Yeats, Philip Larkin delights in "Taking both voices in old arguments" ("'Under a splendid chestnut tree,'" l. 37). In "Poetry of Departures," for example, Larkin half admires the audacity of people who make sudden breaks in their lives. Yet the implied meaning is that sudden breaks are death-like. Larkin even uses the word "epitaph" (l. 2) to sum up the behavior of the man who *"chucked up everything / And just cleared off"* (ll. 3–4). Larkin's allegiances in "Church Going" are equally divided. Having viewed the church with "awkward reverence" (l. 9), he suddenly affirms, without apparent irony, "A serious house on serious earth it is" (l. 55). Does the compulsion to be serious overtake the poet? Or is Larkin overtaking the compulsion by allowing it to gravitate to the ground of the half-comic superstition that the dead may teach the living? He probably means the former, but seems to say the latter.

As deeply divided in his allegiances and use of breaks as Yeats, Larkin concedes that "no word can be spoken of which the sense / Does not accuse and contradict at once" (" 'There is no language of destruction,' " ll. 9–10). No sooner does Larkin assert that death cannot be invoked than he proceeds to invoke it, first as a cloud, then as something more minimal: a shadow to grow silent in.

> For in the word death
> There is nothing to grasp; nothing to catch or claim;
> Nothing to adapt the skill of the heart to, skill
> In surviving, for death it cannot survive, . . .
> (" 'And the wave sings because it is moving,' " ll. 25–28)

Even in saying that the "keys" to meaning cannot be recovered (l. 29), Larkin half recovers them by speaking with a forked tongue. Ostensibly, the meaning of line 28 is that the heart cannot survive death. But what if the pronoun "it" is merely intensive, a repetition of the noun "death"? If there is nothing to grasp in the word "death," then it has no referent and cannot survive. It becomes a fiction, however supreme, something man has "made up . . . / Out of his bitter soul" (Yeats, "The Tower," III.29, 31).

Many of Larkin's lines move in two directions simultaneously.

> And saying so to some
> Means nothing; others it leaves
> Nothing to be said. ("Nothing to be said," ll. 16–18)

These concluding words both mention and use the idea of ending speech when there is nothing left to say. But the two kinds of "nothing" mask a profound disparity of meaning. Sometimes words and sound assert one thing, and their appearance to the eye something else.

> In times when nothing stood
> but worsened, or grew strange,

> there was one constant good:
>   she did not change. (" 'In times when nothing stood,' " ll. 1–4)

Metrically, the contraction of three trimeters to a strongly stressed dimeter allows the last line to function as a refrain—a place of return, where sound reinforces sense. But to the eye the indented last line also qualifies what it says—"she did not change"—by becoming the only line to change appearance visually.

Open to every pull and counterpull, Larkin finds his poetry moving toward the breakup Yeats describes in "The Second Coming": "things fall apart; the centre cannot hold" (l. 3). But out of these divided allegiances and lifelong quarrels with himself his best poetry is born. Before the soul can pass from a re-creative, through a plaintive, to a genuinely human phase of living, it must, in Yeats's words, "lie down where all the ladders start, / In the foul rag-and-bone shop of the heart" ("The Circus Animals' Desertion," ll. 39–40). Larkin's equivalent of Yeats's "shop" is what Derek Walcott finely calls "the rubbed, worn-out familiarity" (1989, 40) of a poem like "Home is so sad." Touched to poetry like a glowing coal, the sadness at the heart of domesticity shines from the closing lines:

> You can see how it was:
> Look at the pictures and the cutlery.
> The music in the piano stool. That vase. ("Home is so sad," ll. 8–10)

Though Larkin does not expect us to be deeply moved by losses that are not unusual, he alone seems capable of expressing "that element of tragedy which lies," as George Eliot's narrator says in *Middlemarch* (bk. 2, chap. 20), "in the very fact of frequency."

Like Frost's poem "The Home Stretch," "The Whitsun Weddings" explores moments of both rupture and continuity. Marriage and funeral rites are oddly commingled.

> The women shared
> The secret like a happy funeral;
> While girls, gripping their handbags tighter, stared
> At a religious wounding. ("The Whitsun Weddings," ll. 52–55)

Since the bride will remember her initiation as a near death (l. 62), we squint at the phrase "religious wounding," wondering for an instant if the rites have been transposed. Though a sexual initiation may inflict injury, only the religious ecstasy of a St. Theresa is usually said to wound. Like the oxymoron of "a happy funeral" (l. 53), the poet's own response seems ambivalent. The "squares of wheat" into which the "postal districts" are "packed" (l. 70) seem as ripe for reaping as Auden's crowds upon the pavement, which are compared to "fields of harvest wheat." Is it life or death that Larkin sees? Is the moment of "frail / Travelling coincidence" (ll. 74–75), of brief coming together followed by a quick dispersion, an end or a beginning? George Eliot says that marriage is a "great beginning," but in *Women in Love* D. H. Lawrence expresses the countertruth that marriage is just as likely to be the end of all experience as the beginning. Only Larkin's poetry of honorable equivocation and divided sensibility is able to half say or intimate that marriage is both of these things simultaneously.

Rituals, we are told, have power to change. But even "change" in Larkin is a loaded word: "and what it held / Stood ready to be loosed with all the power / That being changed can give" ("The Whitsun Weddings," ll. 75–77). The married couples have a power to change the world, to create something that did not exist before. But "change" can also mean a mere passing away, a dispersion. Though the arrow-shower is a sexual dying, it may be a dying to rise or only a dying to fall. Like the family's hopes in "Home is so sad," "A joyous shot at how things ought to be, / Long fallen wide" (ll. 7–8), will the sense of falling away bring a real break? Or will the end of the train journey, like the end of the poem, be "the end of an event / Waving good-bye / To something that survived it" (ll. 31–33)?

Often the places of fracture or breakup in Larkin's poems are hard to tell apart from affirmations of continuity and renewal. In his poem of ritual passing, "Arrivals, Departures," we hear, almost in the same voice, the call to "come and choose wrong" and the elegiac warning "O not for long," as if the antiphon were already contained in the refrain (ll. 9, 12). Christopher Ricks has noticed that "it is hard to say where the ending" of some of Larkin's poems "begins" (1987, 275). Initiated slightly before the end, this poem's conclusion starts, not with the last stanza, but immediately after the "rising": "And so we rise. At night again they sound" (l. 10). What starts off as a repetition— "again"—turns out to be a breaking point or fracture, a reversal of everything waking and arrival stand for.

Breakdown or Breakthrough? From Elegy to Apocalypse

We have seen that moments of fracture or breakup in modern elegies can be moments of breakthrough, too. One of the barriers a poet may break through is the barrier of genre itself. At its outer limits an elegy may turn into an apocalypse, which is a lament, not just for a dead person, but for the passing of a world. When the universe goes to war, and stars send down their spears, what happens to the individual mourner? Will he survive the wreck of nature, as Tennyson predicts in section 123 of *In Memoriam*, or will his light, too, be blotted out?

Usually a breakthrough prevents a breakdown. But in the great chorus on death in *Murder in the Cathedral*, T. S. Eliot finds the reverse may be true. As the chorus breaks through one illusion after another, it brings its own unsettling vision of what lies naked under the veil of phenomena. Beyond the visible agents of death, beyond the cramped thin spondees of "The white flat face of Death," and even behind the Last Judgment itself, stands the great reflexive image of the Void, collapsing everything inside it like a black hole or burned-out star.

> And behind the Judgment the Void, more horrid than
> > active shapes of hell;
> Emptiness, absence, separation from God;
> The horror of the effortless journey, to the empty land
> Which is no land, only emptiness, absence, the Void,

This vision of the chorus immediately preceding Becket's martyrdom is apocalypse with a difference. For the spectacle of linking "nothing with nothing" on the far side of what "we call death" is a breakthrough that is also a breakdown of all the chorus hopes for. Instead of disclosing any "deep dawn behind the tomb," this breaking through the veil is a fate worse than death, since it betrays our expectation that the suffering will end with Becket's murder. The archbishop's martyrdom seems to be the only way out of a play that has been ready to end from its first act. But the comfort we expect to find in "what beyond death is not death" is cruelly withdrawn at the culminating moment. The uncertainty about what the chorus will find behind the veil allows the play to roll across and crush the very patterns that permit the mind to isolate, limit, and possibly comprehend the mystery.

Remove the mask from the white flat face, and we find another face: the face of God and His divine judgment. So far so good. But remove the mask form God's face, and we enter the no-man's land behind it. In a demonic version of looking into Moneta's skull, like Keats's dreamer, but finding vacancy instead of plenitude, the chorus watches the skull split apart with pain, only to disclose inside the skull a new version of its own splitting. The agents of hell repeat the same pattern: they grow in power only to dissolve in dust. First the belly, the fingers, the skull itself, are split. Then the mind is assailed by psychological terrors, in which even the footfall and the shadow are divided from the fury they portend. Each painful sundering is folded inside some more horrendous replica of itself, in a regress of awesome interminability. The terror is compounded by the self-enfolding tropes, which allow the mind to step through skull after skull, behind face after face, to confront the spectacle of uniting nothing with nothing, in a kind of malignant solipsism. Impervious to grace, the noumenal world stirs Eliot's imagination to a vision of ineradicable absurdity. It is a nightmare of perversity and horror.

Even when modern elegists discover, like Sartre, a more meaningful relation between nothingness and being, they may commemorate in the simple onset of night the passing away, not just of people, but of whole worlds and suns. Archibald MacLeish in "You, Andrew Marvell" greatly enlarges the scope of conventional elegies by allowing a breakdown in grammar to match the breakdown of life, as night usurps day. The poem consists of incomplete infinitive phrases, trailing away at the end in a series of triple dots.

> And here face down beneath the sun
> And here upon earth's noonward height
> To feel the always coming on
> The always rising of the night
>
> To feel creep up the curving east
> The earthy chill of dusk . . .
>
> To feel how swift how secretly
> The shadow of the night comes on . . .
> ("You, Andrew Marvell," ll. 1–6, 35–36)

Marvell's worried awareness of Time's winged chariot hurrying near conveys the panic-stricken sense of the transience and hence the seriousness of pleasure. MacLeish magnifies this sense of panic to include a sense of the transience, and hence the seriousness, not just of pleasure but of life itself. Is the breakup of light a breakdown or a breakthrough? What is discovered in the final ellipses? The infinitive phrases that are left suspended in space hover in force between verbs and nouns. The adverb "always" in the third and fourth lines makes us aware of the "coming on" and the "rising" as an event. But so palpable is its power that MacLeish also manages to reify it into a substance or thing, a shadowy force whose swift and secret coming on also contains a mystery that the exotic place names—"Ecbatan," "Kermanshah," "Baghdad," "Palmyra," "Lebanon," and "Crete"—help create and sustain.

Equally alarming and apocalyptic is the onset of night in Hopkins' "Spelt from Sibyl's Leaves," where the triple dots in the first line acquire the same annihilating power as the ellipses that conclude MacLeish's poem.

> Earnest, earthless, equal, attuneable, / vaulty, voluminous, . . .
> stupendous
> Evening ("Spelt from Sibyl's Leaves," ll. 1–2)

Even in filling the first line with no fewer than seven adjectives, two of them polysyllabic, Hopkins seems to be subsiding involuntarily into an abyss of darkness. It is as though a host of unnamed attributes has been drained away through the caesuras and triple dots, like stars that have just disappeared down a black hole.

> Evening strains to be time's vast, / womb-of-all, home-of-all,
> hearse-of-all night. ("Spelt from Sibyl's Leaves," l. 2)

The grammatical sundering of "time's" and "night" evokes an impression of magnitude and possible breakthrough. But the swift transit from womb to home to hearse enacts the rapid expansion and quick collapse of a whole universe. When the suspended referent is supplied in the noun "night," it simply flaunts the power of the hearse to break down and then swallow up not only the three parts of the compound in which it appears, but also the whole triad of compounds, including the womb and the home, of which it forms the final, all-devouring element.

As in poems by MacLeish and Hopkins describing the onset of night, the elegiac power of Wallace Stevens' "The Auroras of Autumn" is most apparent when Stevens is transforming it into something else: into an apocalyptic poetry of star wars and cosmic inquisition. Just as a poem can belong to more than one genre, so an elegist can be treated in more than one context. In chapter 3 I discussed Stevens' hermetic elegies, and in the next chapter I shall have something to say about the elegiac coda of "Sunday Morning." Now I want to show how Stevens tries to turn breakdowns into breakthroughs by making change a congenial as well as a deathly subject.

Like many great elegists, Stevens makes us feel the very moment of change, of breakdown or breakthrough, by keeping us in touch with both old sensations and the advent of something unforeseen and new. He is a master of the receding prepositional phrase, as it retreats farther and farther from the word it modifies, down a corridor of other receding phrases: "Whether fresher or duller, whether of winter cloud / Or of winter sky, from horizon to horizon" (II.10–11). He also estranges the familiar by developing a wavering feel for the interplay of definite and indefinite articles. The definiteness of "The flowers," "The wind," "the solid of white" is diffused by an elusive shimmer of indefinition, by "a white / That was different," "a kind of mark," "an aging afternoon" (II.5–9, 12, 14). Is something new coming into focus, or is something familiar fading away? Are we witnessing a breakthrough or a breakup?

Metamorphosis is always a congenial subject for a poet who is trying to move from elegy toward apocalypse. Few readers will be changed so deftly as the repeating elements in Stevens' poem. But if we live long enough, we shall all be changed by time. And the great oxy-morons of change in "The Auroras," oxymorons of "frigid brilliances" and polar "enkindlings," enlarge the transformations by keeping us in touch with both the old polar coldness and the new flares, even using words like "gusts" and "sweeps" to animate the Arctic world of "ice . . . and solitude."

> He observes how the north is always enlarging the change,
>
> With its frigid brilliances, its blue-red sweeps
> And gusts of great enkindlings, its polar green,
> The color of ice and fire and solitude.
> ("The Auroras of Autumn," II.21–24)

The earlier tercets have been withholding and austere. Meanings seem excluded by an "extremist" in excising, whose "exercise" (II.15) even yields by excision the excluded word "excise." Now, by contrast, there is something lavish, almost flamboyant, in the display. "Frigid bril-liances" are striking and fine, though not miraculous, since even glitter-ing diamonds may emit cold light. But the last two conjunctions are something else. It seems as if the polar caps can be felt as warm grass and that the very glaciers sustain life-giving green. As warm as fire yet as austerely durable as cold diamonds, the poetry is animated by sweeps of wind and great enkindling gusts. Instead of taking us outside of nature, however, Stevens transforms scenes that are unremittingly natural, sometimes even commonplace, into apocalyptic poetry of rav-ishing and fierce simplicity.

As a prophetic poet, the oracle in whom vision takes place, Stevens takes care in canto 4 to make his supreme fiction of a bushy-browed father, who sits in space, a figure of paradox and cosmic wit. Ironically, the providence of Stevens' sovereign power may be annihilation in dis-guise, for the father's beneficence is hard to distinguish from cruelty and caprice.

> He says no to no and yes to yes. He says yes
> To no; and in saying yes he says farewell.
> ("The Auroras of Autumn," IV.5–6)

In sanctioning the spirit of denial that annihilates God, the father seems to consent to his own disappearing act. But how can the poet of farewells say good-bye to God, and so dissolve the idea of a sovereign ghost, without dissolving the idea of his own ghost, too? To dramatize the high unimaginability of God's relation to a world He has created but refuses to govern, Stevens uses hyperbaton—"Of motion the ever-brightening origin / Profound" (IV.21–22)—to place the originating cause, not at the expected head of the line but at its end, where Omega turns out to be Alpha, spilling over the break between stanzas and worlds.

As inquisition of a sovereign power turns into apocalypse, into an annunciation of disaster and a possible twilight of the gods, the poet, like the scholar of a single candle, is afraid of being burned up and consumed.

> He opens the door of his house
>
> On flames. The scholar of one candle sees
> An Arctic effulgence flaring on the frame
> Of everything he is. And he feels afraid.
> ("The Auroras of Autumn," VI.21–24)

When runovers magnify and exalt the whole frightening spectacle, even the hackneyed "side-wise" becomes "wide-wise," as if direction itself were swallowed up in an engulfing amplitude.

> Splashed wide-wise because it likes magnificence
> And the solemn pleasures of magnificent space.
> ("The Auroras of Autumn," VI.10–11)

Sometimes a line ending allows the oracular poet to create a momentary ambiguity about how a fluid syntax is to deploy its elements.

> Nothing until this named thing nameless is
> And is destroyed. ("The Auroras of Autumn," VI.20–21)

The slight pause at the end of the line may invite us to conclude that the "named thing" is nothing until it becomes nameless. But as we round the corner of the line, we may wish to reconstrue "this named thing nameless" as a kind of Miltonic deity, framed oxymoronically by two adjectives, and conclude that its creation is followed by its decreation: it *is* and is *destroyed*. Though tautology is the most withholding of tropes and the copula the most exiguous of verbal forms, the repetition of "it is, it is" allows the Orphic poet to affirm that existence is the essence of the sovereign power.

> It is like a thing of ether that exists
> Almost as predicate. But it exists,
> It exists, it is visible, it is, it is.
> ("The Auroras of Autumn," VIII.13–15)

As in Anselm's ontological proof of God's existence, existence is said to be the thing's defining property, something that abides "Almost as predicate," even though it is no more substantial than a superannuated fiction or myth, and no more palpable than ether.

The annunciation of disaster at the elegiac climax of the poem has all the simplicity of literalness. Disaster "may come tomorrow in the simplest word" (IX.22). But the annunciation has all the suggestiveness of a symbolic drama, too, because of the simile comparing the glittering belts of the stars in the constellation Orion to "a great shadow's last embellishment" (IX.21). "Disaster" conjures up apocalypse, or the falling away of stars, in a wonderful revival of the word's Latin etymology. Placing slight pressure on words like "glittering," which suggests a littering of light but also a gilding, a trace of both guilt and gilt, Stevens manages to be original with a minimum of change.

> The stars are putting on their glittering belts.
> They throw around their shoulders cloaks that flash
> Like a great shadow's last embellishment.
> ("The Auroras of Autumn," IX.19–21)

By masking the Latin *bellum* with the French *belle*, even "disaster" is made to seem innocent. But there is an unsettling ambiguity in the phrasing. Does the indefinite "It" denote an unspecified annunciation? Or does it hark back grammatically to the "disaster" of the fifth preceding line?

> It may come tomorrow in the simplest word,
> Almost as part of innocence, almost,
> Almost as the tenderest and the truest part.
> ("The Auroras of Autumn," IX.22–24)

The promise of breakthrough in the midst of breakdown is partly a matter of the fond and caring turn on "Almost," and of the lingering alliteration of "tenderest" and "truest." No longer a Paterian affectation, a promise of delicate discrimination that is then withheld, the threefold use of "Almost" hints at reserves of anguish and intelligent effort behind the attainment of any great simplicity and innocence. But though such a conquest may be more heroic, its risks are also more deadly than the star wars of Orion. Indeed, the phrase "simplest *word*" lodges a "sword" inside it. Like a weapon encased in its sheath, "the tenderest and truest part" of this apocalypse may be the most lethal of all.

"The Bléssed Break": Three Elegies on Civil War

One mark of truth-saying in modern elegies is the presence of what Robert Lowell in his poem "For the Union Dead" calls "the bléssed break." In this poem and in two other elegies on the American Civil War, one by Allen Tate and the other by Walt Whitman, I want to show how the places of fracture are also "breaks" in the sense of strokes of luck or good fortune, opportunities to recover a wholeness that has been lost. The breaks may be places of breakthrough that allow warring factions to be united, as T. S. Eliot says, "in the strife which divided them" ("Little Gidding," III.25). These elegists often use puns or two-way meanings the way Yeats and Larkin do, to fold the factions in a single party. Alternatively, they may use self-reflexive images to split an object in two, allowing it to look at a portion of itself, as if dramatizing the fact that a nation torn by civil strife is still oddly two *and* one.

Lowell's elegy "For the Union Dead" distinguishes between two kinds of break. One may break *out* of the deathly circle, like a fish or reptile breaking out of its prison: "Everywhere, / giant finned cars nose forward like fish" (ll. 64–65). Or one may break *through* a barrier, as Colonel Shaw and his regiment seem to break forth into a new dimension. The excitement and agitation of the second kind of break—the breakthrough as opposed to the breakout—cause the "bell-cheeked Negro infantry" (1. 22) to tremble into life. Their fitful half-life refuses to subside. Like "the tingling Statehouse, / shaking over the excavations" for an underground garage, the Civil War relief of Shaw and his regiment is made to seem tremulous by the antipun evoked in the "plank splint." Propped against St. Gaudens' statue, the "splint" itself seems "split" by the quake set off by the nearby excavations (ll. 20–24). Such tremulous meanings, like the tremors released by the quake, help sustain the life-like illusion: "at the dedication," Lowell reminds us, "William James could almost hear the bronze Negroes breathe" (ll. 27–28).

The best comment on the structure of Lowell's poems comes from Randall Jarrell: they "understand the world as a sort of conflict of opposites," he says. "In this struggle one opposite is that cake of custom in which all of us lie embedded like lungfish. . . . Struggling within this like leaven, falling to it like light, is everything that is free or open, that grows or is willing to change" (1953, 208–9). In Lowell's elegy "For the Union Dead," the violence of this struggle survives mainly in the antipuns: in the gaunt "waist" that flickers in "wasted" and in the "fray" that lingers in the "frayed" flags that turn the graveyards of the ever slimmer and ever younger "abstract Union Soldier" into a patchwork quilt of green and white squares.

> On a thousand small town New England greens,
> the old white churches hold their air
> of sparse, sincere rebellion; frayed flags
> quilt the graveyards of the Grand Army of the Republic.
>
> The stone statues of the abstract Union Soldier
> grow slimmer and younger each year—

> wasp-wasted, they doze over muskets
> and muse through their sideburns . . .
> ("For the Union Dead," ll. 41–48)

To be "wasp-waisted" is to be insect-taut and slender. But it is also to be wasted to the waist, lean as a compass needle, like the tense and hungry colonel, who is ready to break through everything that is "closed, turned inward, incestuous" (Jarrell, 1953, 208).

In the "giant finned cars" that "nose forward like fish" (l. 65), Lowell seems to witness a metamorphosis of the savage reptiles that have stepped out of their abandoned "South Boston Aquarium" (l. 1). But such a breakout is not a breakthrough. Only Shaw's heroic decision "to choose life and die" can take him out of bounds.

> Colonel Shaw
> is riding on his bubble,
> he waits
> for the blesséd break.
>
> The Aquarium is gone. Everywhere,
> giant finned cars nose forward like fish;
> a savage servility
> slides by on grease. ("For the Union Dead," ll. 61–67)

The "break" is doubly "blesséd": it is a "break" or opportunity, but it is also a "break" in the literal sense, a word that introduces a break between stanzas. Placed at the point of fracture, the word "break" blessedly frees the colonel from the servility around him. Unlike the "bronze weathervane cod" that has "lost half its scales" (l. 3), the colonel is a moral weathervane, a compass needle that still knows how to point. Encapsulated in self-concentrated, end-stopped lines, he stays taut and vigilant.

> He has an angry wrenlike vigilance,
> a greyhound's gentle tautness;
> he seems to wince at pleasure,
> and suffocate for privacy. ("For the Union Dead," ll. 33–36)

But just as he seems on the point of suffocating in his bubble, he is said to be "out of bounds" (l. 37). Released by "man's lovely, / peculiar power to choose life and die" (ll. 37–38), he achieves the freedom of riding buoyantly across the break between lines. That graceful run-on replaces the violence of a mere breakout with the mystery of a breakthrough: a leap to a new dimension.

To fold the factions in a single party in his "Ode to the Confederate Dead," Allen Tate experiments with wordplay and puns. Even as the

mind is made to wage war against shadows of its own casting, it begins
to rediscover in the brokenness of words, in their puns and antipuns, a
version of Lowell's "blesséd break."

> Row after row with strict impunity
> The headstones yield their names to the element,
> The wind whirrs without recollection;
> ("Ode to the Confederate Dead," ll. 1–3)

"Impunity" is not usually "strict"; what is strict is impunity's antonym,
punishment. And so there hovers spectrally over "impunity," like a
ghost over a corpse, the grim antipun of "impugn-ity." The brokenness
is repaired, but only in the republic of the grave, and only by a power
that proves all too strictly punitive.

It is not just two-way meaning per se that marks both the breakup
of words and a "blesséd break"—the chance to realize the potential
unity of language. The elegist also insists that the same person, the
same apostrophized "you," should take both sides of a conflict: first
the natural point of view and then the theological one.

> You shift your sea-space blindly
> Heaving, turning like the blind crab.
>
> You know the unimportant shrift of death
> ("Ode to the Confederate Dead," ll. 23–24, 36)

In reviving the theological word "shrift," Tate makes it echo its paired
word "shift." Often the orders of nature and grace are hard to keep
separate. At first the "collect" in "recollection" (l. 3) seems evoked
only to be fenced off. But then the liturgical sense of "collect," a devo-
tional reading, resurfaces in the second next line as "sacrament."

> In the riven troughs the splayed leaves
> Pile up, of nature the casual sacrament
> To the seasonal eternity of death;
> Then driven by the fierce scrutiny
> Of heaven to their election in the vast breath,
> They sough the rumour of mortality.
> ("Ode to the Confederate Dead," ll. 4–9))

The excluded liturgical meaning also reappears in the theological word
"election." Is "the vast breath" only the whirring wind, or is it the
breath of God? And does a "seasonal eternity" evoke only a commonplace event, the annual death of nature, or is it the oxymoron it seems
to be? Reverberations are sustained by the repetition of sounds in the
phrase "ru*mour* of *mor*tality," which revives the strange, echoing force
of "rumour." As Lewis Thomas well observes, the word "is never used

for something you heard . . . , unless that something is itself a rumor, a rumor of a rumor in effect" (1990, 44–45). Behind the "sough" or sigh of the driven leaves, we also hear the seeding of "to sow." When even the wind becomes humanized through the inspired perversity of the pun, we are reminded how elegies on civil war can be deeply irenic by grounding a logomachy (or civil war of language) in harmless word-play and games.

As Tate explains in his essay, "Narcissus as Narcissus," the elegy's self-reflexive images establish the macabre solipsism of a civil war, of a body divided against itself and feeding parasitically off its own substance. Wherever the observer turns in the graveyard he finds, not the expected vacancy, but an astonishing image of himself: "The brute curiosity of an angel's stare / Turns you, like them, to stone" (ll. 19–20). The death-like power of self-reflexive forms is also dramatized in the jaguar, destroyed by its own reflection in the water. As the animal "leaps / For his own image in a jungle pool" (ll. 83–84), his war with shadows kills him. The solipsist's self-inflicted violence, his oddly spectral form of shadow boxing, is also the breakup of a civil war, the insurrection of a body against itself.

For a bolder and more inclusive use of self-reflexive language we must turn from Allen Tate to an earlier Civil War elegist, Walt Whitman. I realize that the appearance of Whitman in a discussion of modern elegy may seem anomalous. But he writes, as Christopher Ricks has said of Marvell and the Ulster poets, out "of an imagination of civil war" (1987, 51), and is more obsessed by self-reflexive forms that most elegists. In a beautiful passage about passing, for example, in his great elegy on Lincoln, Whitman turns the passing of the funeral cortège into the rite of passage of a whole nation. Oddly enough, Lincoln's coffin is said to be its own observer, as if an object on display were momentarily to become a part of the waiting crowd.

> Coffin that passes through lanes and streets,
> Through day and night with the great cloud darkening the land,
> With the pomp of the inloop'd flags with the cities draped in black,
> With the show of the States themselves as of crape-veil'd women
> standing,
> With processions long and winding and the flambeaus of the night,
> With the countless torches lit, with the silent sea of faces and
> unbared heads,
> With the waiting depot, the arriving coffin, and the sombre faces,
> With dirges through the night, with the thousand voices rising strong
> and solemn,
> With all the mournful voices of the dirges pour'd around the coffin,

> The dim-lit churches and the shuddering organs—where amid these
>   you journey,
> With the tolling tolling bells' perpetual clang,
> Here, coffin that slowly passes,
> I give you my sprig of lilac.
> ("When Lilacs Last in the Dooryard Bloom'd," ll. 33–45)

As the coffin takes the place of the mourner's eyes and ears, the effect is one of awed transposition. The expansive passage of verse is literally a passing over, a gentle but inexorable transfer of energies. The hope is that such a transfer can occur without violence or injury, that it can be as natural as a seasonal change. There is a haunting interminability to the way in which grief can see itself replicated in a vista of receding views. What grief beholds is always an image of itself, a reflection of breakup, as if the grieving person were split in two, divided from himself, like a coffin looking at its own interment in a graveyard, or listening to the dirge chanted around it, including its own lament for Lincoln.

Given his subject, the death of the Civil War leader, Whitman is deeply concerned with the possibilities of breakthrough and the union of warring elements.

> O powerful western star!
> O shades of night—O moody, tearful night!
> O great star disappear'd—O the black murk that hides the star!
> O cruel hands that hold me powerless—O helpless soul of me!
> O harsh surrounding cloud that will not free my soul.
> ("When Lilacs Last in the Dooryard Bloom'd," ll. 7–11)

Because of the reiterated apostrophes, we tend at first to take the phrase "O helpless soul of me!" (l. 10) as an oracular use of the possessive case, as a solemn way of saying "my helpless soul." If so, then each dash is a place of fracture or breakup, and Whitman looks in vain for some equivalent of Lowell's "bless'd break." But if we construe the phrase "soul of me" as "the quintessential me," "the essence of me," then "the black murk" hiding the star becomes the soul's own content, as the elegist swoons helplessly before his own reflected image in a mirror. If the halting apostrophes were not so dark and menacing, there would be something half preposterous about them. For in a real sense, the "cruel hands" that "hold" the mourner "powerless" (l. 10) are his own. Like a nation torn by civil war, Whitman is in danger of disappearing in the "murk" of his own darkest imaginings.

To appreciate the full self-reflexive power of a passage we may have to proceed to its short, compressed end, then circle back to the beginning to take the journey for a second time. As the corpse in canto 5, for example, journeys among the spears of wheat "uprisen" from their shrouds (l. 29), its own shroud journeys among a version of itself that is unobtrusively transformed.

> Amid the grass in the fields each side of the lanes, passing
> the endless grass,
> Passing the yellow-spear'd wheat, every grain from its shroud in the
> dark-brown fields uprisen,
> Passing the apple-tree blows of white and pink in the orchards,
> Carrying a corpse to where it shall rest in the grave,
> Night and day journeys a coffin.
> ("When Lilacs Last in the Dooryard Bloom'd," ll. 28–32)

The expansive, periodic sentence structure does not allow us to register the full shock of the change until we come to the short last line: "Night and day journeys a coffin" (l. 32). And then we realize that the shrouded coffin does not simply pass other shrouds. Though all flesh is grass, and the grass the coffin passes may seem at first to be "endless," "every grain" of "yellow-spear'd wheat" is also said to have broken out of "its shroud" (ll. 28–29). The prospects of breakthrough are greatly enhanced by Whitman's becoming increasingly attuned to the power of a "blesséd break" in short, contracted phrases. Coming after long liturgical chants, such short phrases often acquire the ritual force of an invocation—"Come lovely and soothing death" (l. 135)—or of a dedicatory offering—"A sprig with its flower I break" (l. 17).

A shrouded corpse's journey through miniature transformations of a shroud is subtle but decisive. Though displaying a touch of genius rather than ingenuousness, such details often require Empsonian attentiveness to discern. Sometimes we may wonder if Whitman has combined the happily deliberated and the unplanned. We saw a moment ago that after apostrophizing the coffin for seven lines in canto 6, Whitman seems to forget he is already addressing the coffin, and exhorts it to contemplate "the waiting depot, the arriving coffin, and the sombre faces" (l. 39). Is the self-reflexive effect only the result of a memory lapse or a mistake in grammar? How much is planned and how much is merely accidental felicity?

Occasionally Whitman's two-way syntax allows us to make the language self-enfolding if we choose; the option is ours.

> All over bouquets of roses,
> O death, I cover you over with roses and early lilies,
> But mostly and now the lilac that blooms the first,
> Copious I break, I break the sprigs from the bushes,
> With loaded arms I come, pouring for you,
> For you and the coffins all of you O death.
> ("When Lilacs Last in the Dooryard Bloom'd," ll. 49–54)

The first phrase might be a simple ellipsis for the expression used in the next line: "I cover you over with bouquets of roses." But the removal of the preposition "with" allows death to stand over the roses, which are themselves strewn over death. The moment we try to bury death, it keeps disinterring itself to entomb its own entomber. Though the caesural breaks between successive uses of the verb "break"—"Copious I break, I break" (l. 52)—holds out the prospect of a "blesséd break," the odd inversion of normal word order, which puts "all" after the noun it most logically modifies (l. 54), allows the adjective to attach itself to "death" as well as "coffins." In collapsing the plural "coffins" into an all-encompassing singular, "For you . . . O death," Whitman shows how easily death divides again and multiplies.

Only a knowledge of death that is endlessly self-replicating can master death's power to be simultaneously many and one, like a cancerous cell or a nation torn by civil strife. "I knew death," Whitman boasts, "its thought, and the sacred knowledge of death" (l. 119). Using the grammatical object to mirror its verb, the phrase "to know . . . knowledge" may be an innocuous use of cognates. Or it may be boldly regressive. If "the sacred knowledge of death" is construed as a subjective genitive, then the grammar confers on the knowing mourner whatever knowledge death possesses. The whole spectacle acquires a recessional quality, as the all-encompassing perspective of the coffin's camera eye, roving over America, is passed on to the mourner and the reader. Difficult distinctions between a mere conceptual "thought of death" and a "knowledge of death" that is either self-conscious— "I know that I know"—or else self-replicating—"what death knows I also know" (ll. 119–21)—become unexpectedly concrete when Whitman turns the contrast into two comrades, whose hands he holds as he walks between them.

> Then with the knowledge of death as walking one side of me,
> And the thought of death close-walking the other side of me,
> And I in the middle as with companions, and as holding the hands of
> companions,
> I fled forth . . .
> ("When Lilacs Last in the Dooryard Bloom'd," ll. 120–23)

Moving relentlessly toward larger enfoldings of all lovers and comrades in itself, endlessly dividing and endlessly recomposing, death becomes hard to distinguish from the liquid billowy waves of Whitman's lines, "always alike in their nature as rolling waves," as one critic says, "but . . . never having the sense of something finished and fixed, always suggesting something beyond" (Traubel, 1906, 414).

Paradoxically, when the poet's eyes were open they were bandaged by his power to see (ll. 169–70). Sight becomes insight only when Whitman learns that the self-divisions of civil war contain the possibility of a "blessèd break." The healing occurs when the elegist begins to experience in the final canto death's capacity to absorb all breaks and divisions in itself. As he abandons finite verbs in the last stanza, Whitman replaces them with a timeless infinitive—"Yet each to keep and all" (l. 198)—and with a retrospect of cherished memories, all syntactically equivalent. The elegist turns breakdown into breakthrough by cultivating some of the self-reflexive and regressive paradoxes that Christopher Ricks associates with "an imagination of civil war," which is an imagination both victoriously and "desolatingly two and one" (1987, 51, 55).

Broken Rhymes and Recovered Wholes: Marks of Veridiction in Geoffrey Hill

As elegists keep testing the conventions, little cracks or fissures begin to break apart what A. J. Greimas calls the marks of "truth-saying" or veridiction in their language. It might be argued that, as students of elegy, we should be studying the history of these fractures. Unlike Dr. Johnson, for example, the modern elegist is no longer concerned with producing the greatest resonance with the fewest words. In Johnson's elegy "On the Death of Dr. Robert Levet," the hallmark of truth-saying is an antithetical rhetoric—"Obscurely wise, and coarsely kind"—which a later age will find too patterned and sententious to be trusted. The eighteenth century assumes that a judicious mind, constantly in search of the isthmus of some middle state, can best express itself in a rhetorical seesaw, finely suspended on a fulcrum of shared truth at the center. By contrast, in Tennyson's "The Ancient Sage" the boundary conditions expand: one mark of "veridiction" is the use of "counterterms" like faith and doubt, life and death, to conduct "border-races, holding each its own / By endless war" ("The Ancient Sage," ll. 250–52). As the double irony of the nineteenth century replaces the single irony of its predecessor, a simultaneous endorsement of contrary codes proclaims that a truth in elegy is one whose opposite is also true. Such an elegy never argues or refutes: it only includes.

Even emblems may bear the mark of truth, not just in George Herbert's verse but in modern poetry as well. Oddly self-authenticating is the crescent shape of John Hollander's poem, "Last Quarter," where the "C" of the opening parentheses turns out to be inseparable from the reversed "C" of closure. Since "openings / stand only for / closings" (ll. 18–20), it is hard, as in some of Larkin's poems, to keep endings and beginnings separate. The curved "C" of the last-quarter moon is not only "the bold crescive" sign "of becoming," but also "our cupped left / hands held out / sickle-like" in a gesture of death (ll. 9–10, 21–23).

Often prophetic or millennial discourse aspires to truth-saying by speaking of future events in a historic present tense: "Hence forth thou art the Genius of the shore, / In thy large recompense" ("Lycidas," ll. 183–84). In Dryden's ode to the memory of Anne Killigrew, where a levitating angel seems to be performing a ballet over our heads on the ceiling of a baroque church, even a generalized hieratic gesture may bear the stamp of truth. Another mark of veridiction is Tennyson's use of biblical quotation—"He is not here" (*In Memoriam*, 7.9)—to project an authoritative biblical voice through a confessional, lyric one. Since elegies explore the only really invisible world, the world across death, an elusive icon like the Holy Grail in the elegiac passing of Tennyson's Galahad or like Arnold's elm tree in "Thyrsis" should be able to "declare its own truth-saying," in Greimas's phrase (1989, 655), by keeping itself veiled or hidden, like a repressed truth in psychoanalysis, a parable in the Gospels, or an esoteric figural meaning in a typological reading of Scripture. Alternatively, an elegy like *The Wreck of the Deutschland* may perpetuate the alarming and disruptive force of biblical prophecy by using splintered syntax. The harder Hopkins' nun struggles to apprehend a God who seems also to be her enemy, the more the elegist's words begin to falter, halt, then stop altogether. In Hopkins' poem, as in many of the modern elegies discussed in this chapter, the place of fracture or breakup becomes itself the site of truth.

Modern elegists tend to substitute for the classical elegist's paradox of power, for the confessional elegist's paradox of ends, and for the Romantic elegist's paradox of the silent-speaking word, the civil wars of a self-divided mind, whose warring allegiances are united, as T. S. Eliot says, "in the strife which divided them" ("Little Gidding," III.25). But how exactly are we to interpret Eliot's paradox? Are we *united* in the strife, and somehow made one? Or are we touched only by the genius of warfare, united only by our fighting? If the latter, then perhaps only "the constitution of silence" and the silence of the grave can "fold" the many "in a single party" ("Little Gidding," III.41–42).

The "antiphonal style" of the modern elegist is more than just a war of words. As Geoffrey Hill explains, it is a self-critical style that bears the stamp of truth by turning upon itself, allowing the poet to revise his most cherished premises. Alert to every pull and counterpull, the elegist must display "radical rectitude" in his decision to dramatize the conflicts "within the texture of [his] own work, since nothing else would serve." Even "his parentheses are antiphons of vital challenge" (1984, 93). Only when an antiphonal style comes under pressure may it break into an open war of opposites—into an insurrection of the self, a civil strife.

In his volume of essays, *The Lords of Limit*, Hill analyzes the self-divided, antiphonal styles of Hopkins and Arnold (1984, 93–102). To show how Hill turns moments of breakdown into moments of breakthrough in his own elegy, *The Mystery of the Charity of Charles Péguy*, I want to experiment with some of the rhetorical methods Hill himself deploys in his critical essays. Operating as an antiphonal voice in his own chorus, as it were, Hill's elegist turns breakdown into breakthrough in two main ways: by recovering an original language of nature, in which all words are equivalent in meaning, and by transforming broken rhymes into whole or perfect ones.

Since rhyme effaces the singularity of what is proper to a person named Jaurès or a farce entitled *Sleepers Awake*, there is something death-like and killing about the near-rhymes of "Jaurès" with "stares" and of "smoke" with "*Awake*" (1.1–4). On the other hand, when the elegist wants to sound prophetic, collapsing the pull and counterpull of an "antiphonal style" into an easy aphorism, he occasionally recovers the power of "truth-saying" that an eighteenth-century elegist like Dr. Johnson associates with a fluent use of couplets.

> History commands the stage wielding a toy gun,
> rehearsing another scene. It has raged so before,
> countless times; and will do, countless times more,
> in the guise of supreme clown, dire tragedian.
> (*The Mystery of the Charity of Charles Péguy*, 1.5–8)

Even chiasmus becomes a mark of truth, comprising an arc—"before, / countless times; . . . countless times more"—which is supported at both ends by a pillar of rhyme.

I realize that in their sheer diversity most modern elegies resist explanation by a single controlling idea or metaphor. Robert Lowell's idea of a "blessèd break" will take us only so far. And I am under no illusion that broken rhymes and recovered wholes can explain the power of Geoffrey Hill's elegy. Indeed were any single explanation possible, it would probably be undesirable, for there is a peril of monotony in such an exercise. An intense reading of *The Mystery of the Charity of Charles Péguy* is unlikely to have much extensive power beyond the poem itself. And the more elegies a single critical idea is able to explain, the less agile and supple each reading is likely to be.

In order to do deathly things to language, broken rhymes must work in alliance with other poetic elements. One of these elements is the deadly pun that turns the unreeling of the newsreel into the downward reeling motion of the French army on its way to Verdun.

> The brisk celluloid clatters through the gate;
> the cortège of the century dances in the street;
> and over and over the jolly cartoon
> armies of France go reeling towards Verdun.
> (*The Mystery of the Charity of Charles Péguy,* 1.29–32)

Other puns are less lethal. Because the shell-shocked comrades, in their sudden sagging and crying have lost the power to "stand," a literal pressure is exerted on the commonplace figurative force of the verb, saving it from cliché.

> Must men stand by what they write
> as by their camp-beds or their weaponry
> or shell-shocked comrades while they sag and cry?
> (*The Mystery of the Charity of Charles Péguy,* 1.14–16)

The elegy stages swift progressions in shock and intimacy. The near-rhymes of the third quatrain, whose imperfection and blur are meant to mime the imperfect ghosting of Caesar's ghost by mountebanks and actors, modulate in the fourth stanza into the perfect couplets of "incite" and "write," weaponry" and "cry." Actors mime in innocuous ways, but mountebanks kill in the name of justice. Was Brutus himself a martyr or a mountebank? And as Eliot's Becket ponders in *Murder in the Cathedral,* what sets a true martyr apart from a spurious one? Such questions might be inscribed as epitaphs on the graves of both Jaurès and Péguy, for Hill might have said of this elegy, as he said of his "Annunciations: II," "I want the poem to have this dubious end; because I feel dubious; and the whole business is dubious" (quoted by Ricks, 1987, 287).

Such openness and uncertainty allow the military metaphors buried in phrases like "embattled hope" and "braving an entrenched class" to spring unexpectedly to life. Even Péguy's army cape, worn at first as a mere mannerism, is fated to become less affected at the Marne. The imperfect rhymes that distort "guard" in "beard" and that muffle "cape" and "hope" mock the mere "ghosting" or miming of heroic postures.

> Would Péguy answer—stubbornly on guard
> among the *Cahiers,* with his army cape
> and steely pince-nez and his hermit's beard,
> brooding on conscience and embattled hope?
> (*The Mystery of the Charity of Charles Péguy,* 1.17–20)

How, then, can we hope to cross the divide between mere "embattled hope" at the end of stanza 5 and the "Hope" that at the end of the next quatrain is said to be "a little child," the second of Paul's three Christian virtues? Though Péguy is dignified as a loser, each seminal phrase is oxymoronic: "Footslogger of genius, skirmisher with grace / and ill-luck" (2.5–6). Just as Newman draws on military metaphors to make potentially arid controversies in theology as exciting as he can— "Froude was a bold rider, as on horseback, so also in his speculations" (1968, 43), so Hill does everything in his power to make Péguy's unromantic story as romantic as possible.

As a cross between Yeats's "Easter 1916" and Arnold's "Dover Beach," Hill's elegy both commemorates martyrdom and mourns for a world that has ceased to believe anything. Wandering between two worlds like Arnold, the "out-manoeuvred man" (2.2) has suffered the displacement of his manhood, just as "man" seems displaced from the adjective preceding it. Only with a return of old allegiances and values do the heroic couplets return in phrases like "centurion" and "hard-won" to norms that enact their meaning by *seeming* "hard-won."

> The sun-tanned earth is your centurion;
> you are its tribune. On the hard-won
> high places the old soldiers of old France
> crowd like good children wrapped in obedience
> (*The Mystery of the Charity of Charles Péguy*, 2.9–12)

The stable repetitions—"the old soldiers of old France"—evoke a vision of order all but vanished, though momentarily revived in the couplet that rhymes "obedience" with "France." Only "good children" can be wrapped in such obedience, which may seem equivalent to "sleep" (2.13). Yet the vision is not childish. As Coleridge would say, it is what child-like vision might become if it were carried alive, like Wordsworth's genius, into the strength of manhood, where Memory and Imagination are allowed to harvest the field (2.16).

Even as the red beets mingle with the red blood and "a terrible beauty is born," as remote as possible from the pallid statues that adorn the graves, we are never spared the antiphonal voice of a skeptic or heckler who schools us in the arts of agility and surprise, in subversive wordplay and cogent asides.

> Such dreams portend, the dreamer prophesies,
> is this not true? Truly, if you are wise,
> deny such wisdom; bid the grim bonne-femme
> defend your door: 'M'sieur is not at home.'
> (*The Mystery of the Charity of Charles Péguy*, 3.37–40)

The turns on "true" and "wise" submit the prophet's dreams to exact and fresh testings. Even the concluding phrase looks two ways at once. To say monsieur is "not at home" is to invite the bonne-femme of skepticism to bar the door against belief or faith. But like Renan, who slept with a revolver under his pillow for fear of a revelation, the bonne-femme is gently mocked. As in Hallam's removal from the empty house in Wimpole Street (*In Memoriam*, 7.9), it is also possible to hear in her words an echo of the angel's words to Mary in the first three Gospels: "he is not here."

A cleric manqué, Péguy is an advocate of "adjectival religion." Removing the adjective from its traditional referent, he attaches it to his "true domaine" (3.19), a scholar's paradise, reminiscent of the paradise that Santayana inhabits in Stevens' elegy. Turning the field of battle into a field of grain, ripe for harvest, the editor's and poet's proofs become a field of discourse. At home with terse Latinists, and schooled in "the hard rudiments of grace" (3.35–36), Péguy the poet must still be as strictly bound to the discipline of his alexandrine as a Frenchman is to the justice meted out in the Napoleonic Code. Like Santayana, the dead man is an "inquisitor of structures," reducing disorder to something simple and patterned, like a book of hours or a stack of printer's proofs. "The lean kine" emerging at dawn (4.8), like the phosphorescent shapes glimmering in twilight at the climax of *In Memoriam*, also beckon the elegist toward some vision of boundlessness, an admittedly imageless vision of "the radical soul—instinct, intelligence, / memory, call it what you will" (5.6–7). At this critical juncture Hill does something unique in the poem. For the first and last time he allows the run-ons to cross the divide, not merely between stanzas, but also between the fourth and fifth cantos.

Reaching back into history, Hill's imagination of "the radical soul" must include the three wise men on their march to Bethlehem, seraphim looking toward Chartres, as well as hedgers and ditchers. And though we can scramble the letters in "scarred" to produce "sacred," the same word also generates "scared": "Here the lost are blest, the scarred most sacred" (5.40). In such phrases Hill tries to collapse all words into units of equivalence. He wants to restore the original, undifferentiated language of a "poem-universe" that contains inside itself all that can be said. But we recall how fleeting and precarious such successes are when the next lines temporarily abandon the near-rhymes, assonances, and consonances that occur elsewhere in the canto.

> odd village workshops grimed and peppercorned
> in a dust of dead spiders, paper-crowned
> sunflowers with the bleached heads of rag dolls,
> brushes in aspic, clay pots, twisted nails;
> (*The Mystery of the Charity of Charles Péguy*, 5.41–44)

"Fatal decencies" generally teach us the discipline of form: we become "lords of limit" (4.2), and hence "lords / over ourselves" (5.57–58).

But here the patterns are just sufficiently ordered for anarchy to impinge. Nothing can connect "dolls" and "nails." And "peppercorned" and "paper-crowned" compose a fantastic alliteratively disordered variation of the unities and rhymes we half expect to find.

Even when decay sets in, however, the active grammar keeps alive the possibility of a reversing flow. Double meanings grow from the repeated phrase, "dispense with justice," which can denote either just dispensation or a total abeyance of justice.

> To dispense, with justice; or, to dispense
> with justice. Thus the catholic god of France,
> with honours all even, honours all, even
> the damned in the brazen Invalides of Heaven
> (*The Mystery of the Charity of Charles Péguy*, 6.1–4)

Moreover, the sudden reordering of meaning with the wordplay on "even" and the rearrangement of commas remind us that, if all honors are "even," in the sense of equal, then all people, including the damned, have to be honored. Does such inclusive tolerance not offend a true "lord of limit" (4.2)? Sometimes the active grammar discloses that a seemingly quiet word is really an explosive one. We are shocked, like Péguy, when words are taken literally and "the metaphors of blood begin to flow" in actual streams. "Flow" rhymes perfectly with "show" (6.45,48). But is the convergence of rhymes, like the convergence of word and deed, a loss or a gain? We want our metaphors to be blooded, to be endowed with life. But when they become occasions for violence and war, the two-way flow of language reverses the promise that each fall may be a prelude to redemption, a restoration "beyond the dreams of mystic avarice" (6.28).

Some patterns affirm only heartbreak and terror. But others point the elegist toward an elusive lodestar for his faith. The first kind of pattern survives in the metaphors of situation in 1.23 and 4.21–22, which find their logical completion in 7.25–26, where Péguy's hostile eyes, caged behind the glass of his pince-nez, and the sound of breaking glass that haunts him through life, become the picture of the purblind Saul, "groping in the dust / for his broken glasses." The second, more bracing kind of pattern subsists in the stubborn endurance of the root word "dur"—the pain of what is hard and arduous—in the chain "duration," "endurance," "obdurate."

> their many names one name, the common 'dur'
> built into duration, the endurance of war;
> blind Vigil herself, helpless and obdurate.
> (*The Mystery of the Charity of Charles Péguy*, 7.22–24)

The Indo-European root for "dur" is *deru*, originally meaning something solid, true, enduring. In forging consolation out of endured pain, the sufferers who perpetuate Christ's Passion by becoming, like Péguy, the "labourers of their own memorial" (7.20) seem engaged in an enterprise that is comparable to Hill's. Sometimes both kinds of pattern converge in a single passage. In 7.28–30, for example, the faltering and reforming and eventual vanishing into smoke of the battle line become a literal faltering and reforming of the poetic line, which rides defiantly across the break between stanzas.

> The line
>
> falters, reforms, vanishes into the smoke
> of its own unknowing;
> (*The Mystery of the Charity of Charles Péguy*, 7.28–30)

In dehumanizing death, canto 8 also brings about a death of language. Reduced to stump-toothed, ragged-breathed throngs, the "lords of life" find that their words, like their bodies, have been turned to dust, to mere reified signs, without any of the performative power of the opening phrase, "Dear lords of life" (8.1), an echo of Hopkins' petition "Mine, O thou lord of life, send my roots rain" ("Thou are indeed just, Lord," l. 14). As language coarsens, words become nameless gobbets thrown up by the blast, indistinguishable from the exploded bodies, detonated into unidentifiable bits. Sundered from their contexts in ecclesiastical and Roman oratory, yet spilling over the spaces between stanzas, like corpses disgorged from a trench, the verbal tags "servitude et grandeur" and "vos morituri" (8.7–8) suffer the fate of "Amor" and "Fidelitas" (8.14–15), mere war words, sounds devoid of meaning, stamped into featureless mud as obsolete mottos.

Yeats says that at the moment of "black out," death becomes a "Heaven blazing into the head" ("Lapis Lazuli," l. 19). But what happens when the blaze goes out? Does the failing flame resemble Wordsworth's failing sense, when the light goes out but with a flash that reveals the invisible world?

> The blaze of death goes out, the mind leaps
> for its salvation, is at once extinct;
> its last thoughts tetter the furrows, distinct
> in dawn twilight, caught on the barbed loops.
> (*The Mystery of the Charity of Charles Péguy*, 8.21–24)

Our expectations are betrayed. We are promised a moment of nirvana-like illumination, but then the revelation is withheld. Not only do the soldiers die; so do their heroic commonplaces, their hollowed-out words. Nothing seems predestined or fated, because nothing has a teleology or end. A death that impales its victims on barbed loops is a mere parody of "Heaven blazing into the head." Its "irony of advancement" masks the desolating truth that "we / possess nothing" (8.27–28).

"Advancement" finally comes in canto 9 when the elegist celebrates the dead man's power to make his own paradise. To commemorate Péguy in his true home, Hill must discern his essential quality, his "true tempérament de droite" (9.2). Since Péguy's defeat and affliction are inseparable from the lost cause of France, only an ancient Gallic landscape of green branches can effortlessly translate the true landscape of Péguy's mind into cross-hatchings of twigs and light and "small fish / pencilled" deftly into a lucid "stream" (9.3–5). Though the thunder portends violence, intimating that "Bismarck is in the room" (9.24), the threshing and casting of the chestnut trees seem to inaugurate a moment of vision or revelation, like the annunciation of disaster at the climax of "The Auroras of Autumn," or the incremental gathering of forces in section 95 of *In Memoriam*.

Instead of the expected annunciation, however, all we hear is Rimbaud's desolating phrase: "je est un autre" (9.32). Even the anticipated grammar breaks down. The communication of the dead, says T. S. Eliot, is tongued with fire beyond the language of the living. But Rimbaud's communication, his "fatal telegram," floats past Péguy "in the darkness," because it is "unreceived" (9.32–33). Outwardly, everything seems lost. The lines of men that in 7.28–29 had faltered and vanished into smoke, seem totally erased now. To find consolation we must read the elegy back from its ending. Logically, it is a drama of eulogy and elegy moving toward its own origin: " 'in memory of those things these words were born' " (10.44). Only the elegy's last words, by rounding back on its first words, can explain the poem's origin: the mourner's transformation into an elegist by the sweetness of a grief that devours sorrow only to make it more rending and acute (10. 26–27).

To understand "the heart / of the mystère" (9.13–14) instantaneously and as a whole, Hill keeps using hyphenated compounds to collapse all words into units of equivalence. Such phrases as "dawn-masses," sounding "fresh triumphs for our Saviour crowned with scorn" (9.7–8), are electric with energy. They do not allow us to sort out atomic impressions of the hunt, dappled light, and sacramental celebration. Instead, by dropping connectives and using hyphens, Hill allows a crowd of images and visions—a dream of "warrior-poets" and of an "androgynous Muse / your priest-confessor, sister châtelaine"

(9.18–20)—to rush all at once to the point of his pen. For a comparable recovery of an undifferentiated whole, preceding the division into
subject and object, noun and verb, we must turn back to the opening
lines of "The Windhover," where, instead of separating out his impressions of color, light, and aerial motion, Hopkins communicates a
parataxis of highly charged sensations: a prince-like bird drawn by a
chariot of dappled light, a spacious riding-of-the-rolling-level-under-
neath-him-steady-air.

In modernism a divided or broken consciousness becomes a mark of
"truth-saying." It is a desirable quality, a respect for the conjunction of
many forces of life. Because the extermination camps and other atrocities of this century make war and the inadequacies of life to our conception of life central concerns, modern elegies tend to be split and
discontinuous. "Between the idea / And the reality / . . . Falls the Shadow" (T. S. Eliot, "The Hollow Men," V.5–6, 9). A sign of superior
awareness, the two-way meanings explore the pull and counterpull of a
divided consciousness, and express a dominant axiom of modernism itself. The one mark of "truth-saying" that survives intact is an antiphonal style that honors the forces of resistance and the undertow of
skepticism in an elegy, while using other devices to lift the poetry above
internal strife and the perplexed persistence of despair. Jostling elements that share the same space may at least be locked together in hyphenated compounds or in what one critic calls "the hook-and-eye grip
of the possessive case" (Schneider, 1968, 35): "our heart's charity's
hearth's fire, our thoughts' chivalry's throng's Lord" (*The Wreck of the
Deutschland*, 35.8).

More binding are the phonetic couplings of alliteration and wordplay in elegies by Robert Lowell, Allen Tate, and Geoffrey Hill, who establish momentary unities of sense and sound. Warring elements can be
folded into patterns of approximately the same semantic size and
shape, as in the line just quoted from *The Wreck of the Deutschland*.
Alternatively, Hill may precipitate whole or perfect rhymes out of a solution of broken or imperfect ones. Or out of contending parts that
have broken away, like planets from a sun, a holophrase or compound
can recover so undifferentiated a whole as Hill's "dawn-masses" or his
"androgynous Muse," a "priest-confessor, sister-châtelaine" (*The Mystery of the Charity of Charles Péguy*, 9.7, 19–20). Often the difference
between breakdown and breakthrough is as precarious or slight as a
play on altered senses of a root like "dur" (7.22–24). Sometimes just
an interval, a span of timed thought, will tease new meaning out of a
recurrent image of brokenness. An example is the sound of breaking
glass, which Péguy remembers as a form of breakdown, but which Hill
transforms into the breakthrough of conversion, into the searing "light

from heaven" (Acts of the Apostles 9.3) that leaves Saul blind, "groping in the dust / for his broken glasses" (7.25–26). The modern elegist plays with such images of brokenness, with broken words and broken rhymes, and may with grace or good luck transform the place of fracture into the "blessèd break" of a recovered whole or saving anagram, where "the lost are blest, the scarred most sacred" (*The Mystery of the Charity of Charles Péguy*, 5.40).

6 ❧ Does Good Therapy Make Good Art? The Paradox of Strong and Weak Mourners

It might be thought that the best elegies combine maximum emotion with maximum control. But an elegy that detaches a mourner from his grief by substituting the impact of bad news for a tremor of emotion that passes through him like a wave, may be less affecting as poetic art than an elegy that is less successful in completing the work of mourning. Weak mourners may dominate so direct and poignant an expression of grief as Henry King's "The Exequy" or the elegy that Randall Jarrell calls one "of the most moving and appalling dramatic poems ever written" (1953, 29–30), Frost's "Home Burial." Conversely, strong mourners quite capable of blunting death's impact turn up in defective elegies like Browning's "Prospice," where the bumptious husband seems to bounce out of his moral gymnasium into the silence of eternity. Unlike "Prospice," Tennyson's elegy for Sir John Simeon resolves nothing. But it is a teasingly strange and honest poem that touches the heart and enters the mind like a revelation of the moment.

Paradoxically, strong elegies often feature weak mourners, and vice versa. Is the tough-minded husband who represses what he feels and who tries to speed up the process of mourning in "Home Burial" a stronger or a weaker mourner than his tender-minded wife, who is bent on reforming the world's way of grieving? How are we to tell strong and weak mourners apart? Our discoveries are often counterintuitive. We expect elegies to be bracing rather than defeatist, but have to concede that psychological values are a poor criterion of aesthetic values. We may prefer elegies that impart the immediacy of a physical sensation. Yet an elegy that excludes us from intimacies of consciousness may intimate distresses that are more poignantly felt than any sensations of empathy we prove upon our pulses. Though we value elegies that have more tragic catharsis than lyric angst, we recognize that melancholia has its own power and that grief therapy is a dangerous basis for a theory of art.

Strong and Weak Mourners: Which Appear in the Best Elegies?

Peter Sacks has shown that many elegies perform a psychological function—what Freud calls "the work of mourning." But because a bad elegy like "Prospice" may perform the work of mourning more efficiently than a good elegy like *In Memoriam*, strong mourners alone do not guarantee a successful work of art. According to Julia Kristeva, melancholy is an unmanly, peculiarly feminine form of grieving: a species of incomplete or aborted mourning. Yet the melancholia that spreads like a black sun over Henry King's "widowed heart" in his touching poem "The Exequy" does not make that remarkable elegy any less powerful as poetry. What makes an elegy good or bad art is not necessarily what makes it a fine or a flawed spiritual accomplishment or an efficient means of purging grief.

Death is always a brutal assault, and even in the elegy of a strong mourner like Ben Jonson, who writes as a kind of Roman stoic, it is allowed to do deathly things to language. Not until Hopkins allows a line ending to break apart the word "astray" in "Spelt from Sibyl's Leaves" will the sundering of a word by a line ending be so boldly conceived as in Jonson's ode to Cary and Morison.

> Where it were friendships schisme, . . .
> To separate these twi-
> Lights, the *Dioscuri;*
> And keepe the one halfe from his *Harry.* ("To the Immortall
> Memorie, and Friendship . . . of Cary and Morison," ll. 90–94)

> For earth / her being has unbound, her
>   dapple is at an end, as-
> tray or aswarm, all throughther, in throngs;
> ("Spelt from Sibyl's Leaves," ll. 5–6)

The splitting of "twilights" inflicts a deadly wound. The shock is akin to civil war: two words seem to fight within the bosom of a single state. Though death, the original schismatic, always precipitates an insurrection in the self, seldom has that breakdown been so dramatically portrayed as in the breaking of a word by a break between lines. Yet even in death the two friends, Cary and Morison, are united by the break that divides them. If "twi" is a prefix meaning "two" or "half," then the unnatural sundering emphasizes the atrocity of the act. But "twi" also has a root meaning "twin." Death is a hyphen, with power to both split and bind the friends.

Equally shocking is the enjambment that splits the proper name, Ben

Jonson, leaving the given name suspended at the end of the counterturn and the surname stranded at the head of the stand (ll. 84–86). In one critic's words, this assault on language is "a kind of pun by discovery. . . . The line ending 'Ben' . . . is for a coterie reader; with the addition of the *contre-rejet*, it becomes more properly public" (Hollander, 1975, 142). What is also unexpectedly affecting, giving the poem a depth of personal power that helps Jonson become a strong mourner, is his comforting assurance that the dead youth still lives in memory with Ben.

> And there he lives with memorie; and Ben
> > The Stand
> *Jonson,* who sung this of him, e're he went
> Himselfe to rest . . . ("To the Immortall Memorie," ll. 84–86)

We may wonder for a moment if Jonson is talking of his dead son, Benjamin. As we round the corner of the counterturn into the stand, we discover that he is leaping the present age to imagine the reader's own memory of the elegist. But until then the double possibility is in keeping with the persistent perplexity and the undertow of reluctance in the arguments. The style is self-critical, allowing the elegist to return upon himself, revising his first thoughts or premises.

> Alas, but *Morison* fell young:
> Hee never fell, thou fall'st, my tongue.
> Hee stood, a Souldier to the last right end . . .
> ("To the Immortall Memorie," ll. 43–45)

The play on "fell" and "fall" introduces the needed antiphonal voice. Self-correction lifts the elegist above the retarded motions of despair. Morison fell literally, as a soldier might, but he did not fall in the sense of "fail." He never missed the mark, or fell short in performance and attainment. Standing "to the last right end," Morison's life does not seem unduly amputated, partly because its "right end" coincides with the anticipated ending of the poetic line on the right side of the page.

The power of poetry's measures and answered syllables to delineate "the lines of life" (l. 64) is nowhere better "proved" than in the contraction and expansion of Jonson's own lines.

> A Lillie of a Day
> Is fairer farre, in May,
> Although it fall, and die that night;
> It was the Plant, and flowre of light.
> In small proportions, we just beauties see:
> And in short measures, life may perfect bee.
> ("To the Immortall Memorie," ll. 69–74)

The "Lillie of a Day" is confined to a mere trimeter, a sad contraction. But it dramatizes metrically the claim that the measures of a good life, like the measures of a fine poem, are assessments, not of length or size, but of "how well / Each syllab'e answer'd, and was form'd, how faire" (ll. 62–63). Though Jonson is a strong mourner who never minimizes the breaks in continuity, he also beautifully develops the thought that, because the two friends are united even by the schism that divides them, their perfection is a quality of proportion, of the aptness of what is done and wrought in season.

The death of Jonson's first son produces a death of the self. As energy starts to fail before the poet can make it to the end of a line, the late-breaking eighth-syllable caesuras do deadly things to language.

> Farewell, thou child of my right hand, and joy;
>   My sinne was too much hope of thee, lov'd boy,
> ("On My First Sonne," ll. 1–4)

The constant precariousness of life, its tragic tendency to pull away and slip over the edge, is intimated by "the couplet's identically delayed caesurae," which "give the last foot in each line ('and joy,' 'lov'd boy') a fragile and tragic detachability," as Peter M. Sacks finely says (1985, 120). Combined with the harsh spondees, the later caesural breaks are like knife wounds, cuts inflicted on the body and soul of the world.

> For why
> Will man lament the state he should envie?
> To have so soone scap'd worlds, and fleshes rage,
>   And, if no other miserie, yet age? ("On My First Sonne," ll. 5–8)

Because each knife would also cuts the father's heart, he must bring the war inside himself to a peaceful resolution if he is to remain a strong and resourceful mourner.

Though pride enters the elegy in the father's boast about his best piece of poetry, he tries to distance that pride by putting the words in the mouth of his dead son. The daring ventriloquism, which allows the father to speak through the corpse, half restores the boy to life. For a moment he imagines the youth being asked a question, and responding in the words of an epitaph inscription:

> . . . and, ask'd, say here doth lye
>   Ben. Jonson his best piece of poetrie.
> For whose sake, hence-forth, all his vowes be such,
>   As what he loves may never like too much.
> ("On My First Sonne," ll. 9–12)

The final vow is both a dedication and renunciation, balancing the harrowing conflation of valedictory and baptismal rites in the opening line. Though the knell-like "Farewell" tolls incongruously in its baptismal context of lengthening out the proper name by stating its meaning in the first line, it also prepares for the desolating vow at the end, where renunciation of too intimate an attachment to things we love seems to "exact" too much of the father: it makes an inhuman demand of him. Is Jonson's vow never to "like too much" the people he "loves" not as contradictory as saying he will love God but not like him? Even if "like" is construed as "thrive," is it not blasphemous to assume that God would be jealous of anyone who prospers? Out of his warring words Jonson seems to be piecing together the thought that love is a response of total commitment and dependence, whereas liking is response to someone's singularity. A father may love a son whom neither he nor anyone else could possibly like.

The benediction that begins in prayerful submission, "Rest in soft peace," reverses itself in midcourse by boasting of the poet's own power, as a lesser God, to beget people as well as poems. Such is Jonson's strength as a mourner, however, that he can allow his presumption to carry him to the threshold of blasphemy before saying farewell to all such vanity in a final vow. Even in rounding back to his introductory "Farewell," and saying good-bye to his son, this strong mourner seems to recover a portion of what he has lost. For when his son is asked a question, what is more natural than that he should say something in reply? The phrase, "and, ask'd, say" (l. 9), establishes a perfect reciprocity, a beautiful and moving continuity of relation, which allows the father to take leave of his son in lines that, for all the pathos of their distance, retain the intimacy of a shared conversation, one that seems to go on after the poem, like the child's life, has formally concluded.

A strong mourner like Jonson would rather fight a civil war of self-definition, precipitated by a conflict between his identities as a proud poet and a submissive Christian, than possess no identity at all. A weak mourner, by contrast, allows his identity to dissolve. He is pulled down by the undertow that threatens to sink even Jonson when he cries out in grief: "O, could I loose all father now" (l. 5).

Henry King's "The Exequy," an elegy for his wife, is a sustained exercise in such sinking. Exhausted by complaint, the husband impatiently awaits his own dissolution. Having internalized the dust, he then projects it as a sexual rival, as a lover of his dead saint. So unwilling is this weak mourner to relinquish his identity as a husband that he even turns his own imagined funeral into a ghastly marriage of his "body to that dust / It loves so much" (ll. 86–87). Is it any wonder that King, a dean of Rochester and bishop of Chichester, was unwilling to publish the poem during his lifetime?

"The Exequy" reflects the influence of many Renaissance and seventeenth-century spiritual treatises which, instead of preparing the dying for death, as in the Middle Ages, "teach the living to meditate on death" (Ariès, 1981, 301). King, however, subverts the spirit of these treatises by using his meditation on death, not as a means of living better, but as a means of imparting to life the backward motion of a crab (l. 22). Though King feels uneasy, and admits parenthetically, in one of those asides that Coleridge calls the drama of reason, that he may be guilty of some crime, the only offense he seems to recognize is his consent to live apart from his wife, instead of dissolving with her.

> Dear (forgive
> The crime), I am content to live
> Divided, with but half a heart . . . ("The Exequy," ll. 117–19)

Not only does King mention the idea of division: he also uses it to divide the past participle "Divided" from its infinitive "to live." Even the vocative "Dear" is divided from the personal pronoun "I" by a deft insertion of the bracketed petition "(forgive / The crime)," which is also broken at its center by another break, the division between lines. Though all the breakage and division produce a state of protracted civil war, there are moments when the mourner relaxes his will and seems to speak directly from the heart: "Dear loss!" (l. 7), "My little world!" (l. 55), "meditate / On thee, on thee" (ll. 8–9). It is partly because the mourner who envisages his funeral as a wedding seems to be acting out a stage-tragedy death, that the husband who mourns his "little world" gives the impression of acting no part at all.

As in King's "The Exequy," the mourners in Donne's "A Nocturnall upon S. Lucies Day" and John Clare's "Love and Memory" have so identified with another's annihilation that they, too, have become the quintessence of nothing. In Clare's elegy a death of the self brings a death of language in its wake. As the lover's identity dissolves and he laments his "being is gone," the bonds of syntax slacken, dissolving any stable antecedent for the pronoun "one" (l. 87).

> Yet thy love shed upon me
> Life more then [sic] mine own
> And now thou art from me
> My being is gone
> Words know not my grief
> Thus without thee to dwell
> Yet in one I felt all
> When life bade me farewell ("Love and Memory," ll. 81–88)

Does "one" denote the singularity of the beloved? Does it hark back two lines to the phrase "my grief"? Or does it reach forward to attach itself to the mourner's last farewell? The totality of the loss seems appropriately conveyed by a use of "one" that refuses to remain singular. In the one valediction, as in the one grief and the one woman, the mourner knows all of leave-taking, loss, and love that anyone can hope to know. Indeed, for a weak mourner like Clare, Donne, or King the emotional overload proves too great. As the mourner who depersonalizes himself allows the bond of being to slacken and unravel like his words, he begins to project his own nothingness back upon the world. The decay of language and the world, which run down like a clock, is more deeply terrifying because it seems to pry into the most secret recesses of the mourner's soul.

Death the Phenomenon and Death the Idea

When we test the assumption that strong mourners like Ben Jonson write better elegies than weak mourners like Henry King or John Clare, we find that the evidence disproves the theory. One way to refine the theory before discarding it altogether is to say that what we really value in "The Exequy" or "Love and Memory" is a mourner's ability to share with a reader all the intimacies of a grieving consciousness. If these intimacies can be preserved, will they not produce better art than an elegy that takes a distant or detached view of death? To put the question another way: Will a mourner like Donne who experiences death as a particular phenomenon not write better elegies than a poet like Dryden or Pope, who tends to experience death as a generalized idea, as an event that may still make a strong impact on the poet, but that fails to induce a tremor of self-concern?

Pascal says that "it is easier to endure death without thinking about it than the thought of death without the danger of dying" (Ariès, 1981, 22). The first alternative describes death the phenomenon; the second describes the idea of death. When Rilke says that rightly to celebrate death is also to magnify life, he may mean that any *idea* of death exerts a large and growing influence over the process of living. The more completely the idea of death exercises this influence, the more completely a strong mourner like Dryden or Pope is able to tame or familiarize death. By contrast, Donne and Shakespeare, like many Romantic elegists, often respond with a tremor to the phenomenon of dying itself. In taking the internal view and trying to keep death alive as a strange and terrifying *phenomenon*, Donne runs the risk of being merely a weak mourner like Henry King. But if Donne can master death the phenomenon, recovering his balance at the penultimate moment, he may turn out to be a stronger mourner than elegists who convey only the *idea* of dying.

The difference between the idea of death and death the phenomenon can best be clarified by comparing elegies of mediated grief with elegiac passages from sonnets by Shakespeare. In sonnet 73, "That time of year thou mayst in me behold," Shakespeare allows us to feel intensely what the aging poet has to endure. In line 12 the palsied speaker hovers over each caesural pause, tremulous with indecision: "When yellow leaves, or none, or few, do hang." The labored and irresolute uttering of the words is astonishingly at one, not only with the absurd indignities of age, but also with the reader's pained and sympathetic hearing of them. Even in sonnet 129, when Shakespeare bewails, not a literal death, but a figurative death of the spirit, the words have an extraordinary physical immediacy that compacts a sense of riot and madness in the blood with a sense of pained and heavy breathing.

> Th' expense of spirit in a waste of shame
> Is lust in action; and till action, lust
> Is perjured, murderous, bloody, full of blame,
> Savage, extreme, rude, cruel, not to trust; (ll. 1–4)

One remembers the sonnet as a sort of taste in the blood or an agitation of the nerves. A tightening in the throat seems followed by a protracted exhalation.

In Dryden's elegy on Anne Killigrew, the onslaught of smallpox is presented as an assault from outside, as an attack of a deadly but external foe. By contrast, Donne, like Shakespeare, registers the tremors of death the phenomenon. In his "Hymne to God my God," for example, death is as immediate as an experience of headache or fever; there is nothing external or detached about it.

> That this is my South-west discoverie
> *Per fretum febris,* by these streights to die
>
> I joy, that in these straits, I see my West,
> ("Hymne to God my God," ll. 9–11)

The puns' desperate zigzags catch in their network the frenzy with which a half-crazed mind tries to make its pain more bearable. As a stay against delirium, the first use of *febris*—*Per fretum febris*—seems wholly a product of Donne's raging fever; as his mind wanders, so does his language. But *febris* means "strait" as well as fever. And in entering the strait gate, he unexpectedly completes his south-west passage, his entry into terra incognita, which is also his voyage into death. Just when we assume he has finished with the pun, it emerges again in line 19: "All streights, and none but streights are wayes to them." In pointing Donne to God, these puns, we hope, will ease his pain. But because the thickening of the wordplay, like the perilous thickening of the blood that seems to clot about the heart, only compacts the fever, there seems little prospect of relief.

Perhaps because intimacies of consciousness are valued as a signature of truth in contemporary writing, we tend to prefer Donne's elegies to Dryden's or Pope's. But the distinction between death the phenomenon and death the idea may be just as treacherous a basis for a theory of art as the distinction between strong and weak mourners. If we try to identify good elegies with poems that present death the phenomenon and bad elegies with poems that present a more detached and impersonal view, we are in for some surprises.

At first glance, a comparison of Dryden's and Donne's elegies may confirm our preconceptions. In his ode to the memory of Anne Killigrew, it is far easier for Dryden to ease the pain than it is for Donne, partly because Dryden, unlike Donne, is not writing about himself. To attenuate the sensation of being in pain, which afflicts Donne like a knife wound and makes him sick with fever, Dryden joins the literal locomotive force of "promotion," a "moving forward," to the figurative sense of the word, as if Anne were skipping grades or graduating early: "Thou youngest virgin-daughter of the skies, / Made in the last promotion of the blest" (ll. 1–2). Dryden omits all inward experience of what Anne's "promotion" might be like. He offers none of the immediacy of being in ecstasy, nothing of the tremor that even Richard Crashaw in his over-ripe "Hymn to Saint Teresa" manages to impart to the melting, dart-killed soul, exhaled "to heaven . . . / In a resolving sigh" (ll. 116–17).

Even the lines expressing Dryden's greatest empathy with Anne are curiously devoid of feeling.

> So cold herself, whilst she such warmth express'd
> 'Twas Cupid bathing in Diana's stream.
> ("To the Pious Memory of . . . Mrs. Anne Killigrew," ll. 86–87)

Her achievement seems an oddity, almost a perversion of nature. Because it is prurient for Cupid to bathe in the same stream as the naked Diana, we are tempted to say of Anne what Dryden says of her paintings: "So strange a concourse ne'er was seen before" (l. 125). In the absence of genuine solicitude or empathy there is often only amused bewilderment, yielding at moments to some exasperation and impatience: "What next she had design'd, Heaven only knows" (l. 146). Even the irony of the brother's being wrecked, not by storms at sea, but by the wreck of his sister's face, conveys a generalized truth about unforeseen outcomes rather than a shared experience of loss. For the phenomenon of grieving Dryden substitutes the mere idea of grieving, as if our capacity to empathize with or imaginatively embrace pain were itself seriously damaged or impaired.

If we turn from Dryden to Pope, our distrust of generalized gestures may also be confirmed. Wordsworth dislikes Pope's epitaphs, because he feels Pope "forgets it is a living creature that must interest us and not an intellectual exercise" (Wordsworth, 1974, 2:77). For the "language of affectionate admiration" that Wordsworth recommends in an elegy (p. 80), Pope substitutes in his "Elegy to the Memory of an Unfortunate Lady" a barrage of rhetorical questions. His tone is hectoring and inquisitorial:

> What beck'ning ghost . . .
> Invites my step, and points to yonder glade? (ll. 1–2)
>
> Why dimly gleams the visionary sword? (l. 4)
>
> Is it, in heav'n, a crime to love too well? (l. 6)

By the time we reach the end of the elegy, however, confidence in our theory begins to erode. The most powerful lines in the elegy are a direct result of Pope's external point of view. If the poem were less detached, it would be much less moving than it is. Pope evokes a sense of being outside, of what it is like to be excluded from the terrible distress and estrangement of the lady's tragedy. Just as there can be no fatal glissade from empathy to sympathy for someone who has taken her own life, so there is a deliberate precluding of the reader's own sympathy for Pope.

> Poets themselves must fall, like those they sung;
> Deaf the prais'd ear, and mute the tuneful tongue.
> Ev'n he, whose soul now melts in mournful lays,
> Shall shortly want the gen'rous tear he pays;
> ("Elegy to the Memory of an Unfortunate Lady," ll. 75–78)

There is pathos in the very distancing of pathos, the fencing off of any generous tear. The elegy could not be written with less detachment, because it is at least as much about feelings from which we are excluded as it is about those we are invited to share. The most potent lines come at the end, and depend on the view from outside and the feeling of being excluded. What is most intensely felt depends on our feeling so little—on a failure of sympathetic feeling and a breakdown of empathy.

I have been testing the theory that the best elegies present an internal point of view. A superficial comparison of Dryden's and Donne's elegies may initially confirm the theory, but the distancing of pathos to create pathos in the last part of Pope's elegy calls the theory into question, and Dr. Johnson's most elegiac poem demolishes the theory altogether. I realize that, unlike his elegy on Robert Levet, Johnson's poem, "The Vanity of Human Wishes," is not a conventional elegy. Some readers may object to its inclusion in this study. As I argue in the next chapter, however, the elegiac power of a poem may be most transparent when it transgresses generic norms. Ostensibly, Tennyson's verse epistle to Dufferin is a letter of thanks to a friend; in fact, it is an elegy, and contains some of the most moving lines about death that Tennyson wrote. In theory, "The Vanity of Human Wishes" is a satire, an imitation of Juvenal. In practice, it is an anatomy of disappointed ends, an elegiac meditation on vanity in the biblical tradition of Koheleth. One reason we may miss the poem's affinities with elegy is its deliberate exclusion of sympathetic trespass. Because Johnson the moralist precludes our sympathy for wrongheaded victims with whom we might otherwise feel sympathy, he may seem at first too detached to grieve. When Johnson observes a helpless victim engulfed in waves, he is always looking on from the shore. Readers are as incapable of sharing the terror of the drowning man as they are powerless to stay the current that is carrying him down to his death. Yet Johnson's "extensive view" of disappointed hopes in no way diminishes the power of his poem. Just as the withholding of pathos generates its own pathos in Pope's elegy, so the tremor of emotion with which Johnson confronts his own fate at the end of "The Vanity of Human Wishes" would be inconceivable apart from his use of the generalized idea of vanity elsewhere in the poem, which is designed to exclude us from just such intimacies of anguish and pain.

Johnson's elegiac retrospects are not unfeeling: he invites us to experience events intensely, but only from outside and at a distance. When the licentious beauty is destroyed, we feel less empathy for her than for her detractors.

> Now Beauty falls betrayed, despised, distressed,
> And hissing Infamy proclaims the rest.
> ("The Vanity of Human Wishes," ll. 341–42)

Though the missed anguish of the fallen beauty may make us miss a heartbeat ourselves, the hissing sibilants invite us to share the *detractors'* experience rather than *hers*. The woman's distresses are still felt, but they are unshared, fenced off, as it were, so that Johnson can inhibit grief and better enforce his strong moral and theological views.

So as our theory breaks down, we are left in a bind. How can a poet who offers a generalized *idea* of vanity and death generate more depth of feeling than Donne, who in "A Hymne to God my God" offers a more vivid picture of death the *phenomenon*? The learned Johnson, the only English poet on whom the Muses have conferred a doctorate, takes a more scholarly—a more detached and external—view of his subject. And yet in writing an imitation of Juvenal he manages to write a more powerfully elegiac and a more personal poem than any of the more confessional elegists considered in this section. Perhaps the only rule for writing a good elegy is that there is no rule. Though I suspect a moving elegy will always elude a theorist's generalizing grasp, in Johnson's case the restraint of an aloof anatomy and a scholarly imitation seems to be another form of passion. Feeling suddenly overflows in the short concluding prayer and confession, which are the testaments of a man in spiritual extremity. Johnson's faith is not easily won. He is able to arrive at a center of truth only because he finds himself forced into ever darker, more forbidding corners of a world where phantoms betray each wanderer in the mist and most people consume their lives in chasing shadows. The solution Johnson finds is the last refuge of a skeptical and critical mind in retreat from a series of alternative positions, successively found untenable.

The vanity of life was an old and commonplace thought even when the author of Ecclesiastes came to formulate it. To make his meditation on disappointed ends as strange and powerful as the biblical Koheleth did, Johnson not only writes out of spiritual extremity; he also puts unexpected pressure on his diction. The sinking or falling motion of a heavy object is concentrated, for example, in the Latin verb *precipitates*, to fall upon and consume: "And restless fire precipitates on death" (l. 20). When the fire, after melting down its victims, causes solid forms to "precipitate" (which is the chemical meaning of the verb), death becomes as vivid to the senses as a corpse liquefied by heat. "Ignorance sedate" (l. 345) is another active phrase. Both "sedative" and "sedate" come from the common Latin roots *sedare* ("to settle," "allay") and *sedere* ("to sit").

> Must helpless man, in ignorance sedate,
> Roll darkling down the torrent of his fate?
> ("The Vanity of Human Wishes," ll. 345–46)

Since ignorance is sedate only because it is sedated, we are not surprised when the anchorage of "sedate" in its root *sedere* is wrenched suddenly out of place by man's precipitous forward lurch from his throne.

Sometimes language as well as fortune turns against a victim. First a mere nod of Wolsey's head can "turn" the "stream of honor" (l. 103). Later, wherever he "turns, he meets a stranger's eye" (l. 111). With this turn in the fortune of the verb, language itself becomes an adversary as it does for a later churchman, Archbishop Laud, for whom Johnson reserves one superbly reticent pun: "Nor deem, when Learning her last prize bestows, / The glittering eminence exempt from foes" (ll. 165–66). "Glittering eminence," indeed. Though Laud was not a cardinal like Wolsey, "glittering eminence" reflects the shine of the prelate's "glittering plate" (l. 114). The word has a precise ecclesiastical as well as a more generalized figurative force.

Often when we assume a word has sunk into oblivion, like all the other mirages in the poem, it unexpectedly reappears.

> On every stage the foes of peace attend,
> Hate dogs their flight, and Insult mocks their end.
> Love ends with hope, the sinking statesman's door
> Pours in the morning worshiper no more;
> ("The Vanity of Human Wishes," ll. 77–80)

Not even the use of "end" as an end word succeeds in burying it. It surfaces two words later in the arresting phrase, "Love ends with hope." That sounds at first as if love ends *in* hope, a trite if reassuring thought. But the pun on "morning," which reads at first like a misprint for "mourning," makes the implication far more disturbing: the end of hope is also the end of love, which does not outlast the hope of profiting from it.

We learn in the coda that only religion can build a ladder on which wavering man, deluded by wavering optical phenomena and wavering caesural pauses, can mount securely from the scorching "torrent" (l. 346) to the fires of "sacred presence" (l. 357). What secures the ease of the turn to God and the safety of the swivel is the firmness of the rhymes and the near chiasmus.

> Implore his aid, in His decisions rest,
> Secure, whate'er He gives, He gives the best.
> ("The Vanity of Human Wishes," ll. 355–56)

The completeness of this turn is signaled by a host of other reversals in the coda. Usually Johnson is contemptuous of enthusiasm, but now he praises strong devotion and fervor (ll. 358–59). The prayer is remarkable in view of the way even benign exhalations of prayer are perverted earlier in the poem into enthusiastic storms and tainted gales. Shakespeare's Prospero says that, in piercing heaven, prayer may assault "Mercy itself and [free] all faults" (*The Tempest*, "Epilogue," ll. 17–18). But in Johnson the military force of the metaphor comes disconcertingly alive. In the neighborhood of words like "invade" and "alarms" (ll. 41–42), the "general cry" that "assails . . . the skies" (l. 45) is fiercely militant. The poet is already preparing for the striking reversal of the coda, where the strategist who practices his military arts, even against God, finds that he, not God, is the target of a "secret ambush" (l. 354).

A reversal will not seem striking until we place it in context. In his elegy on Dr. Robert Levet, Johnson claims that sudden death may be a blessing: "Death broke at once the vital chain, / And freed his soul the nearest way" (ll. 35–36). This has always seemed a striking claim to me, because it breaks radically with medieval aversion to sudden death—"*Amarae morti ne tradas nos*" (Ariès, 1981, 13)—a tradition Johnson would be familiar with from its survival in the litany of *The Book of Common Prayer*: "from plague, pestilence, and famine; from battle and murder, and from sudden death, *Good Lord, deliver us.*" Similarly, I find it odd that Johnson should warn us of the dangers of a "specious prayer" (l. 354) at the very moment he invites us to pray. To "pour forth" one's "fervors" might be unremarkable in a Methodist. But this injunction comes from a poet who is just about to invoke the aid of heaven against the charms of false similitude, the baleful fantasies that make a man mad. In advocating a pouring forth of that fervor whose predominance over reason had at other times struck him as a degree of insanity, he is praying like a lunatic not to be mad. The author of *Rasselas* is not noted for according a high place to happiness. But now he praises "celestial Wisdom" for making "the happiness she does not find" (ll. 367–68). Though a final chiasmus clinches the argument—"These goods He grants, who grants the power to gain" (l. 366)—the reversing alliterative pattern is persuasive primarily because everything the poet prays for reverses something he once stood for. If he were not so terrified of death and madness, so eager to melt "with unperceived decay" (l. 293) and glide away unnoticed, his confession would be much less wrenching and his prayer much less heartfelt than it is.

Though not formally an elegy, "The Vanity of Human Wishes" is the most profoundly moving meditation on death that Johnson wrote. The pathos of mortality and short-sightedness is built into its restrictive use of the heroic couplet. In Donne's anatomy of decay in *The First Anniversary*, rhetorical tropes like anaphora carry the reader across the breaks between couplets. But in Johnson's poem, despite "the extensive view" (l. 1) and miniature vistas of regress, which keep miming the tremulous hopes of fame's aspirants, who incessantly "mount, . . . shine, evaporate, and fall" (l. 76), we feel blocked in and checked on every front. Only the vantage point of Johnson's concluding prayer can replace with the surprise of a paradox the predictable ironies of fate and an almost morbid fear of dissipating life in chasing shadows. Like his heroic couplets, which (though regular and patterned) are the opposite of obvious, the paradox of an end that is also a new beginning comes only in the closing prayer. And it comes as a total surprise, reversing everything the disillusioned anatomist of vanity has come to stand for and expect.

To End a Poem as a Mourner Might Hope to Die

Consolation is to the mind what catharsis is to a mourner's affective life. An elegy that foregoes traditional religious consolation cannot dispense quite so readily with the catharsis that allows an elegist to end "With peace . . . / And calm of mind all passion spent" (*Samson Agonistes*, ll. 1757–58). Though good elegies may feature weak mourners and may even withhold sympathy from the dead, it seems safe to say that some vestige of pastoral elegy's therapeutic power, its capacity to provide catharsis or healing, will produce a better elegy than one in which this trace is missing. To support my claim I want to show how three modern poets, Wallace Stevens, Amy Clampitt, and A. R. Ammons, for whom the traditional consolations of "Lycidas" are presumably not available, still manage to find in the flight or descent of birds a natural, but essentially religious, version of the pastoral elegist's healing power. The birds' conduct of their flight helps the elegists make the conduct of their poems bracing rather than defeatist.

The annunciation of God's death at the end of Stevens' "Sunday Morning" is like hearing an opera by Wagner, wholly secularized and domesticated, then presented as a kind of lyric reverie by Virginia Woolf. In a twilight of the idols, made softer, more subdued by "Complacencies of the peignoir" (l. 1), the elegiac coda continues to build on the ruins of worlds it has demolished. Even as the slow-wheeling verse manages to mute the sense of closure by deferring it, there is a sense that steadiness and simplicity have been achieved at a cost, that they are a product of being "unsponsored," "free" (8.7), without God in the world. The descent "to darkness" at the end of the poem is muted by a final adverbial clause, which allows the "casual flocks of pigeons" to make a soft landing. The birds descend as the speaker might hope to die.

> Sweet berries ripen in the wilderness;
> And, in the isolation of the sky,
> At evening, casual flocks of pigeons make
> Ambiguous undulations as they sink,
> Downward to darkness, on extended wings.
> ("Sunday Morning," 8.11–15)

There are pauses both before and after the crowded accentual stresses in line 13, which give the birds leisure to hover, to gather up strength, like a slowly building wave, before releasing it in the "Ambiguous undulations" of the next line. With the disappearance of the gods there is a pathos of self-concern and a risk of self-pity in the coda. But the aphoristic weight and paratactic concision help ground the pathos, while the birds brace the romantic swell of feeling against a counterthrust of detached, natural observation.

Equally bracing and cathartic is the migrant bird's discovery of its lost flyway in Amy Clampitt's elegy, "A Procession at Candlemas."

> Memory,
> That exquisite blunderer, stumbling
>
> like a migrant bird that finds the flyway
> it hardly knew it knew except by instinct,
> down the long-unentered nave of childhood,
>
> late on a midwinter afternoon, alone
> among the snow-hung hollow of the windbreak
> on the far side of the orchard, encounters
>
> sheltering among the evergreens, a small
> stilled bird, its cap of clear yellow
> slit by a thread of scarlet—the untouched
>
> nucleus of fire, the lost connection
> hallowing the wizened effigy, the mother
> curtained in Intensive Care:
> ("A Procession at Candlemas," ll. 128–41)

The end of the elegy, in rounding back to its beginning, to "the mother / curtained in Intensive Care" (ll. 12, 140–41), traces in its own spiral structure "the stillness and the sorrow / of things moving back to where they came from" (ll. 143–44). The real redeemer is memory, especially the memory of women, who seem better equipped than men for an instinctual repossession of the "long-unentered nave of childhood." Compared to a migrant bird as it rides gracefully across the breaks between five successive tercets, memory finds among the snow-hung hollows of the windbreak a mirror image of itself: "a small / stilled bird, its cap of clear yellow / slit by a thread of scarlet" (ll. 136–38). The grammar that seems to lose itself in an appositional maze finally unravels in the word "encounters" (l. 135), which provides a long deferred principal verb for the subject, "Memory." At first an "exquisite blunderer" like the bird, the grammar seems to "stumble" into clarity. Its boldly self-reflexive conceit of a bird-like memory commemorating in a bird a replica of itself also allows the elegist to find a "lost connection" (l. 139). The slit of scarlet thread on the bird's cap is the missing "nucleus of fire" (l. 139), the element in nature that, as Frost would say, is "most us." Just as a dehumanizing male culture tries to tame fire, the carrying of new life, by inventing the insult of religion, the Mosaic insult, perpetuated in such feasts as the Virgin's Purification, the feast of Candlemas, so modern medical technology tries to anesthetize and tame death by curtaining the dying "in Intensive Care." Every culture lives by fictions, including supreme fictions that God "might actually need a mother" (l. 29). Though such fictions make the tender-minded happy, there is a need to refine them, making them worthier of tough-minded feminists who want "the terror and the loveliness entrusted / into naked hands" (ll. 27–28). The bird that carries the "nucleus of fire" liberates the mourner. It shows her how to repossess the past and make "the lost connection" (l. 139). These acts are peculiar, Clampitt thinks, to the feminine experience of mourning, because they are recoverable only by instinct—the way an "exquisite blunderer," some stumbling migrant bird, rediscovers a flyway it had forgotten it knew.

In A. R. Ammons' elegy, "Easter Morning," the momentary break in the flight pattern of "two great birds" provides a wholly secular equivalent of resurrection and rebirth.

> the first
> began to circle as if looking for
> something, coasting, resting its wings
> on the down side of some of the circles:
> the other bird came back and they both
> circled, looking perhaps for a draft;
> they turned a few more times, possibly
> rising—at least, clearly resting—
> then flew on falling into distance till
> they broke across the local bush and
> trees; ("Easter Morning," ll. 84–94)

To understand this "sight of bountiful / majesty and integrity" (ll. 94–95), we have to be sensitive to the way it works within the elegy as a whole. We have to see how it completes the meaning of earlier patterns of circling and hovering in the poem. So sustained at first is the war of impulses pulling the poet back and forth in opposite directions, just as the two great birds are pulled, that we are uncertain whether the grave of the dead child to which Ammons returns is the grave of an actual brother or of a self that, like Tennyson's Lady of Shalott, has failed to make the transition from innocence to experience.

> I have a life that did not become,
> that turned aside and stopped,

> astonished:
> I hold it in me like a pregnancy or
> as on my lap a child
> not to grow or grow old but dwell on ("Easter Morning," ll. 1–5)

Shockingly, the child that died in the elegist continues to stir his memory. Like the circling words, which must "return and return / to ask what is wrong, what was / wrong" ("Easter Morning," ll. 8–10), the elegist's mind is riveted obsessively on a loss it can neither understand nor accept.

Hovering on the terminal word "for," which is repeated at the beginning of the next line, Ammons uses the break between lines 57 and 58 to dramatize the oppression of the blank interval, the empty space at the center, which no words can fill with meaning.

> I stand on the stump
> of a child, whether myself
> or my little brother who died, and
> yell as far as I can, I cannot leave this place, for
> for me it is the dearest and the worst,
> it is life nearest to life which is
> life lost: ("Easter Morning," ll. 54–60)

Returning to the place he can never leave in memory, where his brother and relatives are buried, the speaker grieves for his own death, for his expulsion from the "home country" (l. 17), from his re-creative paradise. In a sense, however, he has never left the place. As a poet, he is still a child in spirit. The child is always stirring in his mind, sharing its grave with the "old man" who must survive on the inheritance that is left him. Only in the graveyard can the elegist brace for his own rite of passage, his need to "go on into change" with all its attendant "blessings and / horrors" (ll. 38–39). Without the stage properties of the stump and the home-country graves, it seems unlikely that the poet who both mourns and celebrates the funereal baptism of dying into life could bear to confront directly the pathos inherent in the simplest cycles of human change.

Before the poet can consecrate the dance of sap within the trees, or the formation of ripples round the ripplestone in the brook, he invites the reader to experience a double shock. For what seems at first to be a pleasant journey back to the family homestead to visit parents, uncles, and aunts, turns out to be a visit to their graves. Only the premature closure of the stanza's last line, amputated in its two-syllable brevity, can begin to inscribe the shock of the family's having made the journey into death.

> . . . mother and father there, too, and others
> close, close as burrowing
> under the skin, all in the graveyard
> assembled, done for, the world they
> used to wield, have trouble and joy
> in, gone ("Easter Morning," ll. 30–35)

Assembled in the graveyard, his kin seem as close to the elegist as a parasite burrowing under his skin, yet also as detached, in their strict autonomy, as the absolute grammar of the two concluding lines. Even the "empty ends" he crashes into, when drawn like Adam from his rural paradise, are made to sound emptier because of the silence created by the late-breaking caesura after "ends" (l. 51) and because of the removal of the word from its expected position at the end of a line.

> we all buy the bitter
> incompletions, pick up the knots of
> horror, silent raving, and go on
> crashing into empty ends not
> completions, not rondures the fullness
> has come into and spent itself from ("Easter Morning," ll. 48–53)

The elegy's second, more important surprise is the discovery that rightly to commemorate a rite of passage from the re-creative paradise into the world of experience is also to magnify that growth into life that robs death of its terror. In their self-retarding spirals and expansive run-ons, the lines describing the sudden arrest, return, and ascent of the birds show how dying into life—like any form of progress by retreat—can be

> . . . a sight of bountiful
> majesty and integrity: the having
> patterns and routes, breaking
> from them to explore other patterns or
> better ways to routes, and then the
> return: . . . ("Easter Morning," ll. 94–99)

Significantly, the breaking and affirming of a pattern are as true of the poet's conduct of his poem as of the birds' conduct of their flight. The gerund "breaking" marks a slight pause at the end of a poetic line; and when the birds "return," a new line returns with them. As the elegist learns of finalities beside the grave, he discovers that in every entrance on the new and the strange there is a chance for the ageless heart of the poet to recapture and transform experience by making it "fresh as this particular / flood of burn breaking across us . . . / from the sun" (ll.

102–4). As the phrases drift down one by one, with as steady but un-hurried a conclusion as any elegy can have, even the raw feeling of pathos and grief acquires something of the subtle scope and feel of a re-birth.

Gender Wars: Tough- and Tender-Minded Mourners

Since strong mourners appear in weak elegies and weak mourners sometimes appear in strong ones, perhaps our understanding of "strong" and "weak" has to be refined. If for "strong" we substitute the adjective "tough-minded," and for "weak" the attribute of being "tender-minded," perhaps some of the paradoxes surrounding the sub-ject will begin to disappear. A tough-minded mourner, like the husband in Frost's elegy "Home Burial," represses his feelings and refuses, un-like his more tender-minded wife, to take time out to grieve. If we equate toughness with strength, then we have to entertain a new para-dox: a tender-minded mourner like Amy may really be the opposite, a tougher and stronger mourner than her husband. Does this mean that a tender-minded mourner is likely to be featured in a stronger elegy than a tough-minded one? Or is it hard to decide which kind of mourner is right? If truth lies on both sides, then maybe the best elegies present a going by contraries, a marriage of minds, as in "West-Running Brook," where both tough- and tender-minded mourners can learn from each other.

The contrast between tough- and tender-minded temperaments orig-inates with William James, whom Frost jokingly describes as "the most valuable teacher I had at Harvard," though "I never had him" (Thompson and Winnick, 1971, 643). The gender wars that Frost pre-sents in many of his best elegies are an attempt to humanize a larger dilemma that James uses his celebrated contrast between tough- and tender-minded thinkers to dramatize. Every pragmatic critic of tradi-tional philosophy faces a problem, James says. If his language is too skeptical and tough, too purged of the idealist quest for "truth" or "good," he will not sound serious enough. But if his language is too tender-minded, too Emersonian and transcendentalist, his readers will find his manner boring and pretentious.

Though Frost was "almost a farmer," as Robert Lowell shrewdly observes, "there was always the Brahm crouching, a Whitman, a great-mannered bard. If God had stood in his sunlight, he would have el-bowed God away with a thrust or a joke" (Houghton Library, bMS Am 1905 [2812]). The battle in Frost's elegies between tough-minded men and tender-minded women is psychologically suggestive, but it is also as philosophically complex as the warfare William James describes between Hegelian idealists, who are "always monistic" and guided by abstract principles, and their adversaries, the "typical Rocky Mountain toughs in philosophy," who start from parts instead of the whole (1911, 12). The sexual politics becomes even more complex when Frost exposes the tough-minded man as the weak and vulnerable partner, which is exactly the way he presents himself in his correspondence with the formidable Amy Lowell.

As a political outsider, Frost lacks the power of his female counterpart: "I who am about to be thrown to the critics salute you!" he writes in a letter of November 18, 1923 (Houghton Library, bMS Lowell 19 [459]). He wants Lowell to review his poetry, but admits he has no right to ask, since he refuses to review anyone himself. Though Lowell can get Frost's work published, he cannot return the favor, even when he tries. Literary influence is so tied up with political influence that Frost punningly rejects both kinds as a disease. "They are good folks . . . worth influenzing . . . they all seem to want the influenza. Will you give it to them?" (Feb. 13, 1917). Frost is strongest when conceding weakness, and is most intimate with Lowell when admitting his friendships with women can never be as intimate as his male friendships. "The closest I ever came in friendship to anyone in England or anywhere in the world I think was with Edward Thomas, who was killed at Vimy last spring . . . I never had, I never shall have another such year of friendship" (Oct. 22, 1917).

In the politics of self-promotion Frost is clearly not Lowell's equal. Though he claims he is too poor to make the trip to Boston for a meeting of Lowell's Poetry Society, he detests the aloofness he seems to take pride in: "I hate to seem to stand outside of anything. . . . I am always grieved when asked if I belong to the Masons or the Rebeccas and have to say No" (May 14, 1916). To make his lack of social and political power less painful Frost will often joke about it. Any seeming token of his influence or power is really, he shows, a dramatization of its opposite. It might seem that his being asked to read poetry before the movies was a token of his local reputation. But, on the contrary, he jokes: "I was advertised first and invited afterwards. I wasn't there" (May 14, 1916).

Such reversals occur in Frost's poetry only when the clash of tough- and tender-minded temperaments threatens to break out into open hostilities, as in "Home Burial," where the reader seems dragged along in a state of increasing exhaustion, like the Fool in *King Lear*. "In the Home Stretch" tries to normalize the air of irrelevance and inadequacy that characterizes the nightmarish upside-down world of husband and wife in "Home Burial." When the wife in the former poem proceeds to extol the virtues of darkness, the mercy of some middle ground that hides from people knowledge of their ends and their beginnings, her husband good-naturedly invites her to renounce visionary vagrancy for more practical concerns. "Come from that window where you see too much," he gently chides, reversing Arnold's injunction to his bride in "Dover Beach," "And take a livelier view of things from here" ("In the Home Stretch," ll. 60–61). Though kind and solicitous, the man's tough-mindedness can be felt in his refusal to shrink from painful truths. How long is "the home stretch"? he wants to know. How many years does she see ahead for them? Reluctant to give an answer, the wife tutors her husband on the limits of knowledge, prompting him to formulate for himself the epistemological paradox: "I don't want to find out what can't be known" (l. 170).

The truth about the wife's apparent break with her past, which like every such break is an image of death, is what she and her husband agree to say about it. By placing the word "ends" at the beginning of a poetic line and by interrupting her thought with a midline caesura, the wife tries to justify her claim poetically: "Ends and beginnings—there are no such things. / There are only middles" ("In the Home Stretch," ll. 174–75). An idea is truest, as William James says, when it "performs most felicitously its function of satisfying our double urgency" to marry "old opinion to new fact" (1911, 63).

The wife is not as tender-minded as her husband seems to think: the future of this tough pragmatist will make itself true, have itself classed as true, by the way her anticipations of it work. In the economy of their marriage " 'End' is a gloomy word," the wife insists, because when the end is seen ahead as an inescapable fact it can no longer have the appeal of a desired destination. The wife's foreknowledge of her end is like her faith in her husband. Because she wants to leave room for the free exercise of love and making belief, she is reluctant to say exactly what the future holds. People who love each other are shy of predicting, because their belief in each other "knows it cannot tell." As Frost says in "Education by Poetry," "only the outcome can tell" (1968, 46). The wife's anticipation of the end is not the kind of communicable knowledge she can share with someone else, even with her husband, but the kind of personal foreknowledge that the pragmatist is able to believe into being: like all good poetry, it begins "in something more felt than known" (Frost, 1968, 45).

Perhaps the most poignant clash of tough- and tender-minded temperaments in Frost's poetry takes place in the exchange between the gently skeptical husband and the religiously inclined wife of "West-Running Brook." The war between the sexes creates a life within the words that is at once a recognition of the violence everywhere, a truce, and sometimes even a marriage in the best sense of that word. Though the husband tries to fend off the waving gesture that the wife ascribes to the wave, the poem forbids any separation of the two kinds of waving. For the wave's throwing backward on itself is indeed a kind of wave or gesture to humanity. It is an emblem of some power of "strange resistance" to the "cataract of death" (ll. 56, 58), some principle of novelty and freedom. Fred tries to turn the "waving" of the "wave" into an antipun, an inspired perversity on his wife's part, which he then combatively fends off. But, ironically, his own culminating discourse sustains his wife's defense of antipun: "It wasn't, yet it was" (l. 30). Though the figurative sense of the wave's being "waved to us" (l. 29) is banished, the total meaning is both "waving" and not "waving," for the exclusion of one sense of waving is itself part of the meaning. In the wave's waving to the wife even the skeptical husband finds a figure for his own pragmatic efforts to *make* something true, to find emotional and practical satisfaction in what he *says* and *does*. The common sense that resists the fantasies of the imaginatively vagrant wife helps Fred escape bewitchment. But his own appalling vision of a world on the edge, teetering on the brink of fragmentation and collapse, teases Fred out of any skeptical complacencies. Like James' pragmatic theism, the gesture of the wave running "counter to itself" (l. 39) helps Fred discover and proclaim, in a principle of flux and freedom that "is most us" (l. 72), a cosmological theory of human promise and hope.

In his impatience to run language back on its tracks, to "Get back to the beginning of beginnings" (l. 43), Fred even smuggles in two redundant uses of "from": "It is from that in water we were from / Long, long before we were from any creature," "It is from this in nature we are from" (ll. 40–41, 71). Impatience of the steps leads to an automatic doubling of the preposition "from" and the adverb "long." Sometimes the grammar is equally odd. Is "runs away," for example, a restrictive or nonrestrictive clause?

> Here we, in our impatience of the steps,
> Get back to the beginning of beginnings,
> The stream of everything that runs away.
> Some say existence like a Pirouot
> And Pirouette, forever in one place,
> Stands still and dances, but it runs away;
> It seriously, sadly, runs away
> To fill the abyss's void with emptiness.
> ("West-Running Brook," ll. 42–49)

The absence of a comma makes the clause in line 44 technically a restrictive one. But if the relative pronoun "that" modifies "stream" instead of "everything," then the idea of universal ebbing has not been evoked only to be rescinded. The more appalling possibility survives in the vision of the stream itself running away—the stream of everything that is. The only element that does not "run away," because of its stationary terminal position in successive lines, is the phrase "runs away" (ll. 44, 47–48).

The stream is the dividing element, the drowning element, but also the sustaining element: "It flows between us, over us, and *with* us" (l. 53). Its end product is nothingness. Yet it is resisted by itself. It is defeated by its own resemblance, by a counterprinciple within itself. If we advance by retrogression, by backward motions toward the source, then the cataract's war against life is moderated and tamed. "That is the sting of it," William James laments, "that in the vast driftings of the cosmic weather," as in Fred's "universal cataract of death" (l. 56), all life "seriously, sadly, runs away." Although many a jut of shore and many a buoyant wave appear "long lingering" before they "be dissolved—even as our world now lingers, for our joy—yet when these transient products are gone, nothing, absolutely *nothing*, remains to represent those particular qualities, those elements of preciousness which they may have enshrined" (James, 1911, 105). Frost mutes James' terror of death by allowing his poem to advance understanding between husband and wife by staving off or holding at arm's length the brutal war of words that drive husband and wife apart in "Home Burial." A contrariety of ideas becomes a marriage of ideas, a way of "going by contraries" (l. 7) instead of being destroyed by them. Unlike the "cataract of death," the contraries go *with* the partners, not *between* or *over* them. The fall of most things is a shrinking, a diminution, but a shrinking that has still sent "up a little," "Raising a little" (l. 63). We seem to hear "raising a little one," raising a family, but also the flicker of an antipun—an echo of that razing, of that sad and serious "running down," which allows us to be pushed to the side of our own lives to make way for the rise of a new generation.

The elegy "Home Burial" is Frost's most brutal and deeply affecting portrayal of the pain husband and wife inflict on each other in their marriage wars. Accusing the husband of being insensitive to their son's death, the wife shows what James means when he says that "each type"—the "tough-minded" pragmatist and the "tender-minded" idealist—"believes the other to be inferior to itself" (1911, 13). Were it not that his wife's belief is so harrowing and self-destructive, the tough-minded husband might disdain or even dismiss her irrational conviction that the energy with which he builds the coffin shows contempt for their son. His impatience and exasperated sense of irony, attitudes James discerns in the tough-minded temperament, survive even in the midst of his exquisite torture: "God, what a woman! And it's come to this, / A man can't speak of his own child that's dead" (ll. 69–70).

Though the wife wants her husband to verbalize his loss, to commemorate it in some less inscrutable way, he knows there is no pragmatic lexicon in which he can look up the meaning of death. Because words leave the heart of meaning untouched, the tough-minded husband concedes that words "are nearly always an offense": a loss so intrinsic does not translate, and a consolation expressed is usually a lie.

For her part, the wife insists on translating their loss into some appropriately grieving act, some proper ritual celebration. She cannot be reconciled to the tragic insufficiency of all efforts to deal pragmatically with death. Unless death has some consequence for life, the domesticity that is shaken by death's inscrutable strangeness seems too frail to survive. Precisely in insisting that death must make a difference, that it must be possible to wring some use or consequence from it, the tender-minded wife may seem tougher in the end, more rigorously pragmatic, despite some suicidal impulses, than her tough-minded husband.

At first the wife is so immobilized by grief that she hesitates to advance. When she takes "a doubtful step," she is said to undo it, until the pulse in the blank verse lines almost ceases to beat.

> . . . She was starting down,
> Looking back over her shoulder at some fear.
> She took a doubtful step and then undid it
> To raise herself and look again. ("The Home Burial," ll. 2–5)

She cannot even advance steadily across the line endings, but must replace a finite verb ("was looking") with a protracted and temporally arrested participle ("Looking back") or with an infinitive ("To raise herself and look again"). For one step forward Amy seems to take two backward. Such verse cannot really advance or go anywhere. The husband is stricken with the pathos of it, and tries to help. But the verse paragraph in which he tries to speak sequentially falls apart into one-line units, as if he were incapable of taking his eye off each particular gravestone in the family plot. The window may frame the whole of the graveyard. Yet there is no sense in which the verse paragraph can frame or easily accommodate the fractured multiplicities of the husband's thoughts. When he finally manages to cross the line endings, there can be no cutting off of the sequential flow, which must tell its tale regardless of what pain it may inflict.

> There are three stones of slate and one of marble,
> Broad-shouldered little slabs there in the sunlight
> On the sidehill. We haven't to mind *those*.
> But I understand: it is not the stones,
> But the child's mound—("Home Burial," ll. 26–30)

Later references to the "Three foggy mornings and one rainy day" that "Will rot the best birch" (ll. 92–93) make mud and ooze in connection with the dead boy inside the coffin all too harrowing for the grieving mother. In context, the association of ooze and mud with "slab," a muddy place, or wet and slimy matter, and by extension with a dull, slow, or untidy person, given to slabbering or slobbering talk, makes it difficult for the wife not to hear just such slabbering in her husband's dismissive words about the "slabs." The tiny markers gleam pure and sunlit. But the wife assumes they look oozy and trivial to the husband who resolves to overlook them: "We haven't to mind *those*." "Slab" flickers for an instant like a misprint for "slob," called up and held off—the perfect situation for that combative nonviolence that drives the two speakers apart, just short of coming to blows.

The multiple meanings of even seemingly innocent and casual phrases alert us to the silent thoughts and unheard words: "He said twice over before he knew himself: / 'Can't a man speak of his own child he's lost?'" (ll. 34–35). Is "himself" merely an intensive pronoun? Or is it reflexive—the object of the verb "know"? If the latter, then what does the daunting task of knowing oneself involve? Do these warring partners truly "know" themselves? Can they recognize themselves in each other's behavior? To speak is to wage a war of words. But to be silent may hide only deeper violences. To avoid war there may have to be truces or off-limit territories, neutral zones. "We could have some arrangement" (l. 50), the husband suggests, not to trespass verbally on each other's domain.

Just as the wife feels suddenly short of breath and claustrophobic, so she seems to lack the staying power to fill out even a short line of verse with a connected thought.

> Not you!—Oh, where's my hat? Oh, I don't need it!
> I must get out of here. I must get air.—("Home Burial," ll. 36–37).

Few poems can continue to unfold and still say so little. The pulse in such lines seems barely capable of mounting the hurdle of the line breaks. The beat is sustained only by a flutter of improbable hope—"I can't say I see how" (l. 48)—and sickening fears—"A man must partly give up being a man / With womenfolk" (ll. 49–50). The failing pulse and tempo of the verse enact the pain the husband feels in accepting the collapse into separateness.

> We could have some arrangement
> By which I'd bind myself to keep hands off
> Anything special you're a-mind to name.
> Though I don't like such things 'twixt those that love.

> Two that don't love can't live together without them.
> But two that do can't live together with them.
> ("Home Burial," ll. 50–55)

Amy and her husband were formerly the second kind of partners, people who cannot live together without crossing boundaries and sharing everything. Now they can share nothing. The composition of separate items into unity breaks down, as clauses that ought to be bound together grammatically are separated by periods. Instead of being joined by a comma, for example, even the concessive clause that fills line 53 is syntactically a mere fragment, divided by a period from the preceding line. Like good blank verse, people who are truly married need commitment to ampler unities that draw the component parts together. For Frost a good verse paragraph conducts itself like a good marriage, which respects the individuality of the members without allowing too much separation.

In respecting Amy's individuality, the husband is afraid he has allowed her to become too separate. She has been hardly able to form a one-line sentence. He would accommodate her apartness, just as his blank verse accommodates what is separate with the utmost intangibility of division between lines.

> Let me into your grief. I'm not so much
> Unlike other folks as your standing there
> Apart would make me out. Give me a chance.
> ("Home Burial," ll. 59–61)

He even accuses her obdurate apartness of being an affectation, a posture she indulges in: "I do think, though, you overdo it a little" (l. 62). Why shouldn't their love be able to accommodate the loss without dishonoring their son?

> What was it brought you up to think it the thing
> To take your mother-loss of a first child
> So inconsolably—in the face of love. ("Home Burial," ll. 63–65)

The grammar of his sentences, riding hesitantly across lines in search of the proper difficult completion, suggests how commitment to ampler relation might prevent the wife's apartness from becoming too willful and suicidal.

When Amy finally finds her voice, her first words to cross a line ending compose a mere syntactic fragment.

> If you had any feelings, you that dug
> with your own hand—how could you?—his little grave;
> ("Home Burial," ll. 72–73)

The interpolation of an adverbial phrase and a parenthetical question delay grammatical completion as long as possible, as if what she has seen is too horrible to repeat. Her first words to compose a whole, four-line sentence mock the husband's energetic digging of the grave. The leaping of the verb "leap" across successive lines is a leaping up of gravel she can view only from afar, with astonishment, as a profane marvel, so alien is it to her own immovable heaviness of heart.

What most preys upon the wife's mind are the words spoken by the husband at the time he dug the grave. His speech at present is an offense, because his talk about rotting birch was an offense. When plea for connection came, the husband was simply too separate from her to care. The moment she tries to connect the conversation about rotting birch with "what was in the darkened parlor" (l. 96), the words that are elided become too unnerving to voice. For the only possible connection is the unspoken thought that wood coffins do not last much longer than rotting birch. When Amy finally manages to speak in expansive sentences (ll. 97–99), holding out the promise of ampler connections, she finds such connections lacking in everyone else, especially her husband.

> The nearest friends can go
> With anyone to death, comes so far short
> They might as well not try to go at all.
> No, from the time when one is sick to death,
> One is alone, and he dies more alone.
> Friends make pretense of following to the grave,
> But before one is in it, their minds are turned
> And making the best of their way to life
> And living people, and things they understand.
> ("Home Burial," ll. 97–105)

Fourth-and-seventh syllable caesuras dramatize the falling away of friends before one is halfway to the end: "One is alone, and he dies more alone"; "But before one is in it, their minds are turned." The wife is a New England Everyman, deserted by all her friends before her pilgrimage to the grave is complete, yet plodding on defiantly to the end, overriding the invisible boundaries created by unpunctuated line endings to complete the pilgrimage on her own. The only voyage people can make with ease, crossing the lines until the break between them almost disappears, is the voyage back to "life / And living people." Suicidal suggestions in phrases like "sick to death" are carefully fenced off, but having been evoked they are too unsettling, given Amy's desire to flee the house, to be banished wholly from the mind. We hope that her wildness will not enact the wrong kind of freedom and that the outcome of her story will be neither so tragic nor decisive as the ending of "The Impulse," where what begins as a war of wills, a mere game of hide-and-seek between husband and wife, turns out to be no playful exercise: "and then she ran and hid / In the fern. / He never found her" ("The Impulse," ll. 19–21).

In Frost's gender wars, as in the civil war elegies of Whitman, Lowell, and Tate, an antiphonal style struggles to unite the parties in the strife that divides them. Like the husband and wife in "West-Running Brook," a self-divided mind continues to search for release in the expected and desired contraries that make any marriage possible. In "The Home Burial," however, even when the war of words seems to subside into a truce, violences still lurk in the empty spaces and silences that her husband, Amy thinks, cannot be tuned to: "'You—oh, you think the talk is all'" (l. 112). There seems to be no way the husband's more objective view of death can retain the seriousness of his wife's internal view, which is resolved to reform the world's way of grieving. The wife's speculations may not lead to changes in assumptions and practices. But her demand that death should mean something, that it should be of some use, is paradoxically a more tender, but also a stronger and more traditionally pragmatic attitude than her tough-minded husband's. True knowledge, for the wife, as for the pragmatist, is something we "make up" about the facts. It yields the kind of truth that the mind possesses only of its own artifacts and fictions.

Having said this, we have immediately to add, as an antiphonal voice to the argument, that Frost's husband has his own brand of pragmatism, and that he is still closer than his wife to C. S. Peirce, the co-founder of pragmatism, in his understanding that reality is not interpretation all the way down. In "Home Burial" a child is dead, and that death and his parents' powerlessness before it have all the helplessness of hitting the barrier of what is unalterably other. This is the barrier that Peirce calls "secondness," "the conception," as he says, "of being relative to, the conception of reaction with, something else" (1931–35, 6:32). Unlike "firstness," which Peirce calls the category of quality, in the sense of "suchness," facts are facts; this is why we sometimes speak of "brute" facts. And what fact could be more brute or brutal than death? Because it is given, because it simply is the case, whether anyone can understand or use the fact, death marks the limit of any pragmatic system of meaning. Though we can know secondness only indirectly, as in the death of a child or a spouse, the indirectness does nothing to diminish the impact. On the contrary, as Frost's tough-minded husband seems to recognize more clearly than his wife, death, like any form of secondness, is flat and final, immedicable, incapable of being modified by anything we do or say about it. There may be no consolation in the husband's knowledge that nothing can console him. Yet knowing the worst may bring in time its own power to heal.

Who, then, is stronger, Amy or her husband, and how can we tell? A powerful elegy like "Home Burial," which refuses to answer most of the questions we put to it, shows that our theories about tough- and tender-minded mourners, like our earlier attempts to associate good elegies with strong mourners, with internal views of death, or even with forms of lyric catharsis, sooner or later reach the limits of any explanatory power they may have. Perhaps this is why Frost's "Home Burial" is so harrowing to read. We realize that in seeking a law or rule governing death, the wife in "Home Burial," like most theorists of elegy, is seeking immunity to risk or chance, which is precisely what no one in a contingent world can have or should want.

A strong mourner like Amy's husband or Milton's swain in "Lycidas" tries to resemble a theater audience, whose emotions are felt deeply but not painfully. Amy, however, wants to *live* her life, not just be a spectator of it. A so-called tender-minded mourner, Amy may be stronger in the end than her tough-minded husband, because she knows sadness, even tragedy, can etch her more sharply. Perhaps a mourner's deep unhappiness is what makes her life serious, not just a play or a game. She knows we are all defined by what we have lost.

Because the most unbearable parts of "Home Burial" are also the subtlest and most tenderly counterpointed—the most "antiphonal," few elegies are at once so honest and so wrenching, so full of what Randall Jarrell calls "the grimness and the awfulness and the untouchable sadness of things" (1953, 68). There are no winners or losers, no strong or weak contestants in such poems. All that matters in the end, in criticism as in life, is a willingness to be vulnerable and open to risk. Of course, just as therapeutic success is no guarantee of aesthetic success, so the human attractiveness of being vulnerable and open should not disguise the fact that it is perfectly possible to share Frost's generous hospitality to experience and still write a very bad poem. Critics of elegy may find it less important to discriminate between tough- and tender-minded attitudes than between attitudes that are genuine and spurious. Socrates says that all philosophy is a meditation on death. As readers of elegy we should refuse to consolidate the present level of our ignorance and be ready, like Socrates, to ask new and better questions.

7 ✲ The Paradox of Genre: Impact and Tremor in Tennyson's Elegies

"When the commonplace 'We must all die' transforms itself suddenly into the acute consciousness 'I must die—and soon,' then death grapples us," George Eliot's narrator says in *Middlemarch*, "and his fingers are cruel" (bk. 4, chap. 42). In *The Thread of Life* Richard Wollheim makes a similar distinction between an "impact" and a "tremor." The terrible news of a friend's sudden death makes an "impact." News that I have terminal cancer, provided it is accepted and believed, induces a "tremor." As Wollheim says, "the tremor is a part of our natural sensibility, and we may think of it as a sensible index of self-concern" (1984, 237). An event that makes an impact, even when it throws an elegist offbalance, as if he had received a blow, is usually artfully staged, like the ritual of leave-taking in Tennyson's "Ulysses" or "The Passing of Arthur." By contrast, in his postscript to "Tiresias," news of Edward Fitzgerald's death catches Tennyson offguard. He continues to reel from the shock. And in *In Memoriam* Hallam's death has the same tremulous effect on Tennyson that the new astronomy has on Donne or Pascal.

Elegies generate their tremors in two main ways: by creating the tremulous ripple effect of a verbal ambiguity or two-way meaning, and by transgressing a code, as Tzetvan Todorov suggests in his essay "The Origin of Genres" (1976). Let me consider the verbal and rhythmic nuances first. To generate a tremor an elegist may use late-breaking caesuras that signal closure or the skipping of a heartbeat, as in Ben Jonson's poem on the death of his son: "Farewell, thou child of my right hand, and joy; / My sinne was too much hope of thee, lov'd boy" ("On My First Sonne," ll. 1–2). Tennyson often creates similar tremors of feeling by using two-way syntax or phrases that hover ambiguously between contrasting emphases. Is "a glory done" in *In Memoriam* (121.4) a *glory* done or a glory *done*? Even a simple echo-like repetition can send tremors of feeling down a lyric. The deathward declensions in Frost's "Nothing Gold Can Stay," for example, are so lightly insistent that they quaver with subdued feeling like the first leaves of spring. Occasionally, as in Browning's lyric, "A Toccata of Galuppi's," a controlled stage death alternates with a death that is uncontrolled and real. Browning movingly portrays the contrast between the nostalgic impact of music that commemorates the "Dear dead women" with the golden hair (l. 44) and the tremor of a "cold music" that, in foretelling the speaker's own death, "creep[s]" silently "through every nerve" (l. 33).

More generally, a tremor is induced whenever an elegy, in trying to establish itself by transgressing some norm, juxtaposes a convention and a tolerant, humane testing of that convention. One paradox of genre consists in this, that the norms of a literary kind become fully visible only when transgressed. As Todorov explains, "the fact that a work 'disobeys' its genre does not make the latter nonexistent; it is tempting to say that quite the contrary is true. And for a twofold reason. First, because transgression, in order to exist as such, requires a law that will, of course, be transgressed. One could go further: the norm becomes visible—lives—only by its transgressions. . . . But there is more. Not only does the work, for all its being an exception, necessarily presuppose a rule; but this work also, as soon as it is recognized by its exceptional status, becomes in its turn . . . a rule" (1976, 160).

Failure to deviate at all from an elegiac formula is found at its most extreme in an obituary notice. To read the words, "Hallam, Arthur, on Friday, 13 September, suddenly in Vienna, son of the historian Henry Hallam," might produce an impact. But they create none of the tremors of feeling we experience when reading *In Memoriam*. One way Tennyson's elegy produces its effect is by transgressing the convention that the traditional language and ancient symbols of a pastoral elegy like "Lycidas" should exorcise the terror of dying. Unlike Milton, Tennyson fears that the God who consigns Hallam to an early grave in *In Memoriam* is a "wild Poet," working "Without a conscience or an aim" (34.7–8). In a world "red in tooth and claw," a savage world that is still strangely evanescent, turning hills into shadows and "solid lands" into melting mist (123.7), the death of Tennyson's friend may be of the same order as the melting of an icicle. This is why the melancholy of many nineteenth-century and modern elegists seems deeper, more tremulous, than the melancholy of Milton or Donne. By exploring six more specific ways in which Tennyson's elegies transgress earlier conventions, I hope to illuminate Todorov's paradox that the norms of a genre would be hard to recognize apart from the slight tremors of subversive questioning that are continually testing these norms and loosening their hold.

The View from Here and the View from Nowhere

The Greek elegists commemorate the permanence of an objective order of nature, set against the transience of man. Tennyson beautifully adapts the convention in "Tithonus," which contrasts the perfect circular motion of Aurora, the dawn, as she renews her "beauty morn by morn" (l. 74), with the pathos inherent in the human cycle of "earth in earth" (l. 75)—a one-way trip of ashes to ashes, dust to dust. *In Memoriam* produces a seismic shock by transgressing this code: instead of being stable and enduring, nature is as much in flux as man. For John Keble the book of nature is a second Scripture, a medieval Book of Hours. For Tennyson in *In Memoriam* it is a mere book of moments, a spectacle of Heraclitean transience and flux.

When the impact of an objective, clinical view of death is substituted for the tremor of "the view from here," which always touches a phenomenological nerve, it often produces a shock effect. Such is the result of using the aloof observation of a coroner's report in the second stanza of Wordsworth's elegy, "A Slumber Did My Spirit Seal." But the impact of the view from outside—"No motion has she now, no force; / She neither hears nor sees" (ll. 5–6)—cannot quite displace the tremor of the "view from here." Shock and trauma survive in the silences of the caesural pauses and the breaks between stanzas and lines. *In Memoriam* induces a tremor when it replaces the convention of a stable objective world with a time-lapse photograph of the earth extending over billions of years (123.1–8). Instead of providing a secure resting place or platform, the external view of a world in flux is as tremulous as the internal view, "leaving reader and poet together to confront" what one critic calls "the mysterious and unwilled changefulness of experience" (Peltason, 1985, 5).

There seems to be a degree of objectivity appropriate to each act of knowing and remembrance. Thus the tremor that passes through Tennyson at the news of Hallam's death in *In Memoriam* or "Break, Break, Break" is appropriately more subjective than the impact made by "an empire's lamentation" in his funeral ode for Wellington. But how can any mourner substitute the impact of a more objective view of death without surrendering a residue of unassimilable subjectivity? Death wrenches a mourner away from his most cherished and familiar experiences at the very moment he tries to retreat protectively inside them. In section 7 of *In Memoriam*, for example, the mourner is too overcome with grief to advance beyond the tremors of his two-way syntax, poised between hope and desolation. Even when he tries to be more detached, there is a danger that a prescribed form of mourning, a "sad mechanic exercise" (5.7) based on the impact of dulled memory rather than genuine recollection, will offer the wrong kind of objectivity. The desire to stand outside one's life, to look down like Chaucer's Troilus on this "litel spot of erthe" from the eighth sphere (*Troilus and Criseyde*, V. 1809, 1815), is the viewpoint of the dead, which is as far out as the elegist can go. Without such a view, the estranged Victorian elegist may retreat too far into solipsism and the prison house of self. But pushed too fast or too far, detachment can produce blackout and indifference, or even Pascal's fear of terrifying waste spaces.

> There rolls the deep where grew the tree.
>   O earth, what changes hast thou seen!
>   There where the long street roars, hath been
> The stillness of the central sea.
>
> The hills are shadows, and they flow
>   From form to form, and nothing stands;
>   They melt like mist, the solid lands,
> Like clouds they shape themselves and go. (*In Memoriam*, 123.1–8)

Tennyson would be remembered, I think, even if he had written only these lines. Here, if anywhere, we hear what Herbert Tucker has called "the ground swell of doom" in Tennyson's verse (1988, 23). The imposition of the stern parataxis ("and they flow," "and nothing stands") on the yielding similes ("like mist," "Like clouds") establishes a momentary pathos. But the absolute parity of all the forms, of the moving and the motionless, of the gentle and remorseless, amounts to a sudden collapse in beauty and interest. The pageant seems about to end in terrifying absurdity, making the silence of Pascal's waste spaces seem by comparison like the pause between two movements of a sonata. The tremulous flow "From form to form" holds the key to this "book of Moments," as Timothy Peltason, quoting Denis Donoghue, has called *In Memoriam*: "a book in which one moment, one lyric may continue from the last or may seem to replace it absolutely" (Peltason, 1985, 4–5).

The clash between the tremors of a view from here and the annihilating impact of a view from nowhere generates a conflict between the first-person world of the liberal humanist, who is nourished like the youthful Tennyson on "the great vine of *Fable*" ("Timbuctoo," ll. 218, 240), and the spirit of "keen *Discovery*," which inhabits the third-person world of the scientist and some of his post-structuralist heirs. Instead of unifying our qualitative knowledge of the world with the exact sciences, the task of explaining the world is always in danger of reducing knowledge of ourselves and literature to terms of some prevailing ideology or method. Everything is predetermined by some chosen category that excludes most first-person knowledge from its scope. As in Marx's analysis of reification, the mourner's alienated consciousness is divorced from a world of alienated objects "it can only contemplate across" what one critic calls "a puzzling abyss" (Joseph, 1992, 121). If a third-person view leaves the view-holder out, it cannot put him back in again. And a world that excludes the dreamer who dreams his dream and holds it true is obviously not the world in which the mourner of *In Memoriam* wants to live. In Thomas Nagel's phrase, a third-person view of the world is a "view from nowhere." In laying the foundation for the conquest of Darwinian science, Lyell, Chambers, and their contemporaries had done an extraordinary thing. They had formulated a third-person system of the world that had all the disadvantages of being impersonal without any of the advantages of being stable. Removing one of the norms of the ancient Greek elegists, accidental variation had fashioned a natural order in which the scientists themselves could no longer find a meaningful place.

Forgetting and Remembering

Elegy is always "in memoriam"—an art of re-viewing and recollecting the past, as opposed to merely remembering it. Yet Tennyson also transgresses this convention by reminding us, often with a slight shock of recognition, that elegy is equally an art of forgetting. Indeed, until the mere impact of a sensory impression of the dead is effaced, until the dead are forgotten, they cannot be genuinely recalled either. Recollection is an art; and, as Kierkegaard observes, "what is recollected is not indifferent to recollection as what is remembered is indifferent to memory" (1940, 30). The mere impact of a photograph or of a setting remembered in photographic detail may distract the elegist from the act of recollection that turns the Somersby rectory or the "Dark house" in Wimpole Street into a geography of his mind. Like the composition of place in an Ignatian meditation, the scenes over which the elegist continues to brood tremulously are recollections, not mere memories. Without recollection there could be no meditation, and without meditation no discovery and growth.

Tennyson transgresses an elegiac code whenever he tries to forget rather than remember. But how is this possible? To write an elegy at all is implicitly to commemorate and recollect. One way to forget is to disguise an elegy as something else, as Tennyson does in his verse epistle to Dufferin. His son's death, as we shall see later, is precisely what Tennyson tries to elide or repress. The elegist wants to forget his son until he can assimilate the loss and better commemorate it. An alternative solution is to evoke a lost place or person as an absent presence. In section 101 of *In Memoriam* Tennyson anticipates a scene of neglect and oblivion after his family leaves Somersby and the garden boughs and flowers fall into ruin. Yet the power of the negatives, "Unwatched," "Unloved," "Uncared for" (ll. 1, 5, 9, 13), depends, in one critic's words, "on the unsaying of the very detail" they seem "to present" (Richardson, 1988, 32). "Unloved," the repeated adjectives at the head of lines insist on saying. But also "loved," and deeply so, by the elegist who discovers, with a slight tremor of elation, that no mirroring of place, however bleak, can be unhinged from the memorial of a self-conscious mind. In James Richardson's words, "there is a palimpsest, a dimness" in such lines. "No," they say, "but yes." Because "Tennyson's simplest and most profound delight in language is with its ability to say yes and no at the same time" (1988, 32), he finds he can best remember Somersby or Hallam when he seems to forget.

Merely to remember a death is not to commemorate it. An elegy recollects and re-presents an event; unlike a death or an obituary, it does more than just transcribe it. Mere memory is to authentic recollection what descriptive language is to performative language. An elegist who merely remembers what is close at hand will develop no skill in recollection. Though people can mourn together in a funeral ode, they recollect in private. Death may have changed Wellington into "Something far advanced in State" ("Ode on the Death of the Duke of Wellington," l. 275). Yet when the pun on "State" invites the elegist to imagine the change, he can think of nothing more inspiring than an apotheosis of machine-like simplicity and practical capacity: "There must be other nobler work to do / Than when he fought at Waterloo, / And Victor he must ever be" (ll. 256–58). The funeral ode is versified obituary that does nothing to alter Wellington in its act of remembering him. By contrast, a private recollection often sets free both the mourner and the person who is mourned.

Once again *In Memoriam* provides the best example of how an elegy replaces the random unfolding of a mere memory, which is an indifferent act, with the ordered sequence of a recollection, which involves imaginative effort and discovery. One critic complains that when Tennyson speaks of Hallam's "noble breast" early in the poem (11. 19), "the adjective is sentimental, not because it is sentimental to call a friend 'noble,' but because of a failure of expression. Tennyson has given no particular occasion and no analogy" (Brower, 1962, 35). Later, however, the mourner uses intimate particulars ("Sweet human hand and lips and eye," 129.6) and a number of precise oxymorons ("known and unknown; human, divine," 29.5) to evoke Hallam as a "Strange friend, past, present, and to be" (129.9). By the end of the elegy the vagueness of a mere memory has been replaced by the defining details of an authentic recollection.

A mourner may suppress a painful memory. Until it is recollected, like repressed material coming into focus under psychoanalysis, neither the memory itself nor the pain associated with it can be forgotten or assuaged. At first, only grim antipuns, by fending off the dark meanings built into them, can help Tennyson place the traumatic events far enough away to re-present and evaluate them: "I seem to fail from out my blood / And grow incorporate into thee" (2.15–16). "Fail" unlocks "ail," another form of "sick" ("Sick for thy stubborn hardihood," l. 14). Even the preposition "for" may mean "because of." To cure the sickness caused by his unhealthy longing dark secrets have to be confessed. Just as Rousseau says he writes his *Confessions* to rid himself of the guilt of falsely accusing an innocent servant girl of stealing a worthless ribbon, so Tennyson seems to write his elegy to expiate an inexplicable guilt he feels: "Behold me, for I cannot sleep, / And like a guilty thing I creep / At earliest morning to the door" (7.6–8). But what possible offense can Tennyson have committed against Hallam?

I think the very act of survival leads to guilt. Like many survivors of the holocaust, the mourner has the awesome feeling that he is not worthy of survival; he has not survived enough. It is therefore important that in the elegist's imagination the ghost who may feel pitched into a grave, like Shakespeare's Banquo, whose death is somehow undeserved, a source of guilt to the living, or even painfully unfair, should be made to sleep well. Paradoxically, the best way to forget the dead by giving them a quiet grave is first to remember them. Only a past that has been genuinely recollected can also be forgotten.

Gerhard Joseph offers a different explanation. He ingeniously suggests that "the prime source" of the mourner's elegiac "dis-ease" is the guilt he feels over "cannibalizing [Hallam] for purposes of aesthetic self-aggrandizement" (1992, 18). There may also be a third source of anxiety: in mourning the death of someone who has taken up residence in himself, Tennyson keeps running the risk of incest. Unable to marry his sister, the woman Hallam was engaged to, Tennyson ends by marrying someone with the same name. Meanwhile, he continues to identify with Hallam's bride in fantasy, assuming her part and speaking of her "widowed . . . heart" as if it were his own (85.113). Even in elegies by Hardy and Housman, the marriage of the dead man's beloved to the survivor may be a disguised act of homage or love. Leading his life backward in memory, Tennyson is also able to lead it forward again, slowly easing the conscience of the "guilty thing" who creeps outside the dark house in Wimpole Street, a victim of unlocalized malaise, like one of Nietzsche's "pale criminals," whose wavering sense of being both traitor and betrayed at once precedes and motivates his evil dreams about God and nature being at strife.

Forgetting becomes unhealthy whenever we repress what we know. Momentarily forgetting the object-specific nature of his loss—not just the death of Hallam but also the eclipse of any lodestar for faith in the burned-out universe predicted by the Second Law of Thermodynamics—the mourner in *In Memoriam* allows his free-floating melancholia to create a more generalized impact by diffusing at large over life. Tennyson may forget because he is afraid to remember a loss more personal and poignant than mere generalized grief. More wholesome than his free-floating melancholia is his hard-edged, because object-specific, mourning, which may bring slow detachment from Hallam in its wake. Forgetting must not come too soon, otherwise Hallam may seem betrayed. But release should come before the elegy is over, since life is for the living and no grief should last forever, not even in an elegy that "can go to extraordinary figural lengths to keep itself alive" (Joseph, 1992, 17).

As Antony H. Harrison reminds us in his essay on Wordsworth and Swinburne, there is also a "politics of mortality," a politics of remembering and forgetting, which bears upon the topic (1990, 177–204). In his elegies Tennyson is writing as both the Burkean conservative of "Love thou thy land" and as the transgressor of norms, as the subversive poetic equivalent of the political radical in "Locksley Hall Sixty Years After." Committed to remembering the past and conserving the impact of tradition, the elegist owes allegiance to Burke's continuum of the dead, the living, and the unborn. But as a radical he also wants to forget. T. S. Eliot is surely right about Tennyson: he was "the most instinctive rebel against the society in which he was the most perfect conformist" (1932, 337). The impulse toward coherence and stability in literature and politics, toward remembering a past they want to conserve, is deeply rooted in the consciousness of Tennyson's mourners. But faced with the unknown, they also waver between hope and fear. Having destroyed something, can death, like radicalism in politics, put something better in its place? Whatever one's politics, death the leveler is always a highly visible radical. A constant reminder of human equality, it is also the great transgressor of norms.

Kristeva's Paradox

Most elegies give the person who has died a dwelling place in nature: Lycidas is made a genius of the shore, and Adonais becomes "a portion of the loveliness / Which once he made more lovely" ("Adonais," 43.1–2). In *In Memoriam* Tennyson transgresses this convention by turning Hallam into "some diffusive power," vaguely immanent "in star and flower" (130.6–7), but already assuming the same sublime relation to all created things as the nameless God of Israel, who transcends nature and all words about Him. When describing the slow descent of "ambrosial air" into "brake and bloom / And meadow" (86.1–4), the mourner can momentarily achieve a beautiful balance between the forms of nature and their spiritual content. But the "air" has no explicit association with Hallam. Instead of allowing the well-loved Hallam to make a lovely world more lovely, Tennyson seldom introduces any middle ground between grotesque infernal signs like the yew tree and the dark house (which are all body but no soul) and sublime diffusive powers (which are all spirit but no body), continually struggling to escape the constraints of "matter-moulded forms" (95.46).

Trying to achieve the impossible and say the unsayable, Tennyson's victims of melancholia reify their words and end up saying less than they should mean. Such is the paradox Julia Kristeva formulates in her semiotic study, *Black Sun: Depression and Melancholia* (1989). According to Kristeva, all the signs and symbols in our language are made accessible by a negation of a fundamental loss—the loss of a primal object, the mother or Thing. This is what the soul had in its Palace of Art or the Lady of Shalott in her tower. Relieved of the primal object, language is for the first time possible. But what makes language possible, the detachment of words from their objects, is precisely what melancholic self-absorption tries to deny. Because melancholia results from a denial of loss, from a desire to live forever in an incubator, Kristeva calls it the negation of a negation. Such dual negation creates an infernal state of emptiness and vacancy, where sense data assert their tyranny, producing the gallows humor of "The Vision of Sin" or reified signs like the yew tree or burial ship in *In Memoriam*. After loss is acknowledged and normal language returns, the mourner may aspire to a phase of imageless vision, capable of inducing a silence of amazed possession, or to a more restrained and precise account of the limits of what language can say. The mourner may transgress verbal norms by retreating into oxymorons like the "lucid veil" (67.14), the "silent-speaking words" (95.26), or the apparent contradiction of Hallam's becoming "deeplier loved" as he is "darklier understood" (129.10). Paradoxically, however, the mourner who aspires to the ultimate integrity of silence usually ends up in an infernal state that confronts him with silence of an opposite kind: the silence of the void. Only in an intermediate region is representation of a familiar world attainable. In each of the three phases—the infernal phase of unmediated sensation, the normal stage, and the apocalyptic stage of imageless vision—different tropes and signs are used. In the first and third phases, the mourner often cultivates grotesque and sublime language, respectively, to descend both *below* and *above* what is usually sayable. Infernal ironists, the victims of melancholia, say *less* than they should mean, and prophets of paradise and apocalypse struggle to say *more*.

In an infernal state of language, physical impressions acquire a life of their own, carrying the impact of an unmediated sensation. In the "Dark house" lyric of *In Memoriam* each dismembered metonymy— the "Doors," the "heart that used to beat," the "hand that can be clasped no more"—says less than it should mean. As Dante knew, hell reifies its signs. And in evoking the so-called realism of Baudelaire's urban hell, Tennyson allows his words to harden into empty signifiers, into bodies without their souls, or into envelopes without their anticipated messages or contents.

> Dark house, by which once more I stand
>   Here in the long unlovely street,
>   Doors, where my heart was used to beat
> So quickly, waiting for a hand
>
> A hand that can be clasped no more—
>   Behold me, for I cannot sleep,
>   And like a guilty thing I creep
> At earliest morning to the door.
>
> He is not here; but far away
>   The noise of life begins again,
>   And ghastly through the drizzling rain
> On the bald street breaks the blank day. (*In Memoriam* 7)

Tennyson even makes a fetish of the sudden wrenching of grammar, using the break at the end of the fifth line to transform a bleak inventory of sense impressions into a desperate apostrophe and prayer: "Dark house, . . . / Behold me." Just as we cannot interpret the "Paralyzed force, gesture without motion" of T. S. Eliot's hollow men as we would interpret the signs that make up a figure of sloth or cupidity in Dante's *Inferno*, so we cannot interpret the creeping of Tennyson's insomniac "At earliest morning to the door" (7.8) as a gesture of guilt only, because that would give him back his status as a figure or type. The mourner makes litter of his signs. He takes us on a tour of a linguistic graveyard, of a landscape filled with the corpses of words that have lost the power to memorialize the dead because they have lost their power to signify.

Yet Eliot finely and rightly praises this lyric as "great poetry, economical of words, a universal emotion related to a particular place, and it gives me the shudder that I fail to get from anything in *Maud*" (1932, 333). Part of the poem's power, I think, comes from the mourner's ability to turn upon himself. Having used dead or infernal language to say less than he should mean, he is suddenly pulled in the opposite direction, tempted by fantasies of projection to say more than he has any right to mean. For once the "Dark house" and "Doors" are asked to "Behold" the mourner's abasement and guilt (7. 6), any attempt to read this lyric as an inventory of sense impressions is like trying to read Blake's "The Sick Rose" as botanical description. If the "Doors" seem privy to the mourner's darkest secrets, it is because they have the same power to torment as the disembodied "eyes" in "The Hollow Men." Eliot's speakers "dare not meet" these eyes, because they have projected upon the eyes more meaning than they can possibly have. Similarly, Tennyson's mourner is immobilized by the "Dark house" and "Doors," because he has first internalized them, projected upon them his fear and guilt, then tried to expel them. Like the God who makes Himself "an awful rose of dawn" in "The Vision of Sin," or who assumes the form of an avenging raven in Browning's "Caliban upon Setebos," the alien doors onto which the mourner has earlier projected his beating heart are thought to have special knowledge of their victim, even though it is knowledge they could not actually possess.

Instead of providing the mourner with authentic representations of death, projective identification may repress such knowledge of death as the mourner has. It may disguise his loss by treating nature rather than Hallam as a corpse, and by turning the world itself, rather than just the mourner, into a "hollow form with empty hands" (*In Memoriam*, 3.12). Something similar happens in *Maud*, where the quickened tempo of the speaker's pulse is imagined to be outside himself, in the wheeling movements of the dance and in the beating hooves of the brother's horses as they pound over his grave. At times even his language becomes alien and infantile. As Kristeva sums up in a striking phrase, "melancholy people are foreigners in their own maternal tongue." "The dead language they speak . . . conceals a Thing buried alive" (1989, 53), just as Maud's lover fantasizes his own live burial. Ironically, the fantasy of internalization, which makes the rise and fall of Maud's cold and luminous beauty flow and ebb with the surge of the lover's pulse, does nothing to dispel her tyranny. On the contrary, the sheer psychic force of the projection represses the lover's knowledge of her death and preserves intact all the guilt and terror it is meant to allay.

Apart from projective identification, there is another way in which Tennyson can transgress verbal norms by aspiring to say more than he could ordinarily mean. Collapsing words back into a single synonym, a single unity of energy, a melancholy speaker like the lover in *Maud* may try to recover what is not strictly possible, a "poem universe" that returns the lover to the womb and the user of language to some primal word. To be merged with Maud is to be merged with the beloved object in a reversal of the process of "desynonymizing," whereby the philosopher, according to Coleridge, establishes distinctions among words originally equivalent in meaning.

I have argued that the infernal burial ship, yew tree, and dark house in *In Memoriam* are grotesque, because they are like bodies without their soul, mere envelopes of meaning without the letter inside. Infernal in the way the landscapes in "Childe Roland" and "The Hollow Men" are infernal, they convey the impact of brute sensation. Quite different from these grotesque metonymies are sublime traces of meanings that elude definition. Like "the chord of Self, that, trembling, passed in music out of sight" in "Locksley Hall" (l. 34), they tremble out of view the moment we try to touch them. The synaesthesia in the line just quoted makes the very idea of such tremulous passing both contradictory and elusive. Though it is surely the harp string that trembles, that vibration is transferred to the music itself. The transfer is only partial, however, because the visual impression of passing out of sight applies to the ever diminishing vibrations of the harp string rather than to the soul itself, which passes, not literally out of sight, but only out of auditory range. Such is the condition of Coleridge's Utopia of a synthetic "language of nature," an undifferentiated whole like the "boundless day" of *In Memoriam* (95.64) that exists only as a remote possibility on the receding horizon of language, and which eludes most people who reach out to touch it.

In *Maud*, as the lover's chain of epithets, made more relentless by the repeated suffix—"gemlike, ghostlike, deathlike" (I.iii.95)—tries to collapse language back into one fearful synonym, Kristeva's paradox about saying less than one ought to mean by trying to say more reappears in a different form. When words flow back into a sensory whole, they become more sublime but less intelligible. And when they are separated out again into discrete units, they become more intelligible but less sublime. Composing in grammatical wholes, the lover's impressionistic syntax uses the surge of pulsing participles to transgress verbal norms. The result is something sublime but unintelligible, something that tries to mean more than it can say, something as tremulous and untranslatable as "seabeachmadness, wintrygleam, daffodil-stardeath."

Brokenness and Continuity

Most elegies invite us to read across events, to discover continuities between the first and second anniversaries of Hallam's death, for example, the first and second Christmas, the earlier and later uses of the infant crying in the dark, and so on. Even when later occurrences of the burial ship or yew tree are not meant to supersede what came before, as an antitype is thought to supersede its type in a figural reading of Scripture, we are asked to register the continuities over an interval of time. As Eric Griffiths says, the continuities between Hopkins and the sailor who is pitched to his death in *The Wreck of the Deutschland* "are the constituents of a span of timed thought, and it is the span we are asked to realize" (1989, 349).

If one norm of elegy is the search for some stabilizing continuity in the midst of discrete fragments of change, then it must be conceded, I think, that Tennyson, like many elegists, transgresses this norm as often as he observes it. The glorious ascent of Lycidas makes an impact on the reader. But because nothing in *In Memoriam* can claim comparable authority, the provisional organizations of meaning achieved within any moment of a poem Tennyson once considered calling his *Fragments of an Elegy* must expose themselves to the tremor of "disruption or disproof in the moments that follow" (Peltason, 1985, 5). Often Tennyson uses the momentary indecision created by a line break to suspend us between two kinds of brokenness, between a breakdown and a breakthrough.

> He is not here; but far away
>   The noise of life begins again, (*In Memoriam* 7.9–10)

The first line is hard to scan, because as Eric Griffiths says, "the words seem to require four even stresses or four even absences of stresses." If we pause at the line ending, and speak the line as a regular iambic tetrameter, we hear an echo of the angel's words to Mary Magdalene in the first three Gospels: "He is not *here*, but *far away*." Yet the run-on drops the line "into the blank space of the page," as Griffiths notes, "to re-emerge from it as something quite alien to hope: 'But far away / The noise of life begins again.' What revives is not the friend he misses but the beat of regular iambics and 'the noise of life,' the daily round, they represent" (1989, 127). As tremulous as the light that flickers through the drizzling rain is the mourner's evocation of "the long unlovely street" (7.2). Broken apart by strong caesural pauses, the phrase wavers between a spatial, adjectival use of "long" and a temporal, adverbial use. The street's long prospect is devoid of charm. But it is also "unlovely" in a deeper sense, since emptied now of Hallam's love. The breaking of day at the end of the lyric is equally ambivalent. Does the light sift through a sickly filter of drizzling rain only to break apart on the bald street? Or does the recollection of the tomb from which Christ is resurrected allow the day to break out of blankness? Do we experience the impact of something breaking down or the tremor of something breaking through?

There are comparable tremors of brokenness and indecision in the oracular ninety-fifth section of *In Memoriam*. When the sunken "daystar," having repaired "his drooping head" in "Lycidas," "Flames in the forehead of the morning sky" (ll. 168–69, 171), the spectacle of death and resurrection affirms a marvelous continuity. By contrast, in the corresponding sequence in *In Memoriam*, line breaks, ellipses, and two-way grammar allow oddly broken sounds to be heard like echoes, then pondered and remembered in silence.

> And strangely on the silence broke
>> The silent-speaking words, and strange
>> Was love's dumb cry defying change
> To test his worth; and strangely spoke . . . (*In Memoriam*, 95.25–28)

When an oxymoron ("silent-speaking") finds itself repeated in a second oxymoron ("love's dumb cry") everything we hear starts to be heard tremulously, two or three times, like echoes. Because echoes give the impression of having traveled great distances, they are the auditory equivalent of section 123's time-lapse photograph of the earth extending over billions of years. As Gerhard Joseph says, "sound like sight is most evocative—and melancholy—when it is experienced at a far, far remove from its original source" (1992, 97). As the reversing pattern *abba* locks the two forms of silence into a chiasmic vise ("strangely," "silence," "silent-speaking," "strange"), these echoes prove astonishingly stubborn, not at all faint or attenuated. The second use of "strange" is picked up by an adverbial version of itself at the end of the quatrain, where it rides expansively across the break between stanzas: "And strangely spoke [stanzaic break] The faith, the vigour, bold to dwell / On doubts" (*In Memoriam*, 95. 28–30). Further protracted by a timeless infinitive phrase, "bold to dwell," the "faith" and "vigour" are left poised for a moment over the empty space at the end of line 29. We expect the infinitive to be completed by a prepositional phrase beginning with "in": to dwell "in hope," perhaps, or even "in God." But because the mourner is dwelling on his doubts, hovering or brooding over them, he is using a different sense of "dwell" to evoke that very experience of wavering or trembling shared by readers who are trying to decide how Tennyson will cross the slight break between lines and complete his run-on.

Even the meaning of the noun "change" is unexpectedly allowed to change. When Tennyson speaks of "love's dumb cry defying change / To test his worth" (95.27–28), is love defying change in order to test its own worth, as we originally assume? Or is love challenging change to do the testing? Is change the adversary that love must defy, or is change the secret ally, the agent that conducts the testing and so proves love's worth? The momentary uncertainty about the grammar, which is made more uncertain by the brief hovering over the line break, imparts an elegiac tremor to the lines. So does Tennyson's revival of the verb "fluctuate" 's odd transitive meaning of "making tremulous by throwing into wavelike motion": "And fluctuate all the still perfume" (95.56). The mourner uses as well as mentions the idea of a tremor by allowing "fluctuate" to fluctuate for an instant between its normal intransitive and its much stranger transitive meaning.

The New Criticism, or old formalism, in which many students of the 1950s and 1960s were trained, looked for order and coherence in Tennyson. Post-structuralism sees discontinuities, disorders, breaks. Many critics would now agree that the sheer length and repetitiveness of *In Memoriam* refuse to fulfill the generic promise of a pastoral elegy, which isolates and contains the mourner's grieving. Even after Hallam's culminating communication with Tennyson in the garden, the action of the elegy is still in urgent progress. A drama continues even after the story should formally conclude. In controlling grief, the elegist also transgresses norms by trying *not* to make the reader feel that art is totally coherent and controlled. The comfortable framework of art confines the reader to a knowable universe. But death is an unmanageable, mind-expanding event. A wholly controlled elegy makes at most an impact on a mourner and a reader. But an elegiac tremor is induced whenever Tennyson chooses to break down boundaries and create a sense that his elegy, like his life, is simultaneously continuous and broken. Hallam's poetry of mere reflection is to his poetry of sensation in his 1831 review of Tennyson's poems what the *impact* of bad news that we continue to remove from us and contemplate at some distance is to the *tremor* of a more immediate concern, a brokenness we experience like the taste of self-knowledge, and which is often accompanied by profound inner change.

Concision and Indefinition

Because individual lyrics of *In Memoriam* have all the lapidary concision of epitaphs, they seem to meet one of classical elegy's most important norms: they achieve a maximum cathartic effect with a minimum of material. Even after finishing a short elegiac monologue like "Ulysses" or "Tithonus," we feel we are at the end of a tragic drama, so concentrated and cathartic is the experience. But the more of *In Memoriam* we read, the more we realize that it also violates this norm. The long elegy seems endlessly to end, and so never ends at all, except by a kind of optional stop rule that says, "now we shall have an epithalamium that writes 'finis' to our story." The mourner seems afraid to reach the end. Perhaps like Gibbon's melancholy prospect of taking "everlasting leave of an old and agreeable companion" (1869, 3:816), the prospect of ending *In Memoriam* threatens to end the seventeen-year afterlife that Hallam has enjoyed during Tennyson's composition of the poem. Or the elegist may use his *morae*, his delays and digressions, to defer closure, because like Browning's Guido he is afraid that he has not really said one word out of the whole world of words he had to say. By being indefinite as well as concise, secret and reserved as well as confessional, the mourner creates the impression that his real story is never told.

In his elegy for Sir John Simeon, "In the Garden at Swainston," Tennyson uses vague and indefinite language to induce a tremor of stupor and confusion.

> Nightingales sang in his woods:
>   The Master was far away:
> Nightingales warbled and sang
>   Of a passion that lasts but a day;
>   Still in the house in his coffin the Prince of courtesy lay.
>
> Two dead men have I known
>   In courtesy like to thee:
> Two dead men have I loved
>   With a love that ever will be:
>   Three dead men have I loved and thou art last of the three.
> ("In the Garden at Swainston," ll. 6–15)

Though the tremor of open vowels sounds as resonant as the nightingales' "high requiem," the celebratory impulse is held in check by a stupefying numbness. If the mourner has literally loved the dead Simeon as he has loved two other "dead men" "With a love that will ever be" (ll. 13–14), why does he continue to say "Two dead men" instead of "Three"? Is he too numbed by pain or too entranced by the nightingales' warbling to remember what he has said? Though the stupor or numbness comes from the removal, not merely of Simeon, but also of any clear indication of what tone is to be elicited from the words, "the vagueness is where Tennyson is most precise." As James Richardson finely says, "we should not, in the large gestures of his language, lose sight of his essential emotional accuracy" (1988, 90).

In the final line of the elegy the mourner corrects his mistake, but not without registering another ambiguity. "Three dead men have I loved and thou art last of the three" (l. 15). Does the elegist mean simply that Simeon is the most recent of his friends to die? Or does he mean, more devastatingly, that with Simeon's death his capacity to love has died, too? Tennyson drops no hint as to which meaning we should choose. The strangeness of the elegy is made to depend on a reader's registering both possibilities at once. Does the elegy conclude with bare obituary plainness? Or, for a chilling instant, as the last of the mourner's friends (not just the most recent but possibly the only remaining one) is swept up into the dismal fellowship of the dead, does the elegy imply that the mourner will have no more friends to write elegies for? The odd blend of concise diction and indefinite meaning confirms Richardson's judgment: "Tennyson is a poet of deep inarticulateness, but he is an *emotional* intelligence of the highest order" (1988, 90).

To provide the comfort of a limit, an elegy like "Crossing the Bar" uses highly repetitive patterns and concise images. But to prevent the elegist from forcing conviction or falsifying belief, Tennyson allows the poem to tremble on the brink of silence and indefinition. Pulled opposite ways at once, Tennyson hovers between "one clear call" (l. 2) and a tide "Too full for sound" (l. 6), between the limiting "bourne of Time and Place" (l. 13) and a "deep" that is "boundless" (l. 7). On the printed page we can actually see the phrase "the boundless deep" beginning to swell out and engulf the elegist's own contracting words. In the two central stanzas, the expansive pentameters in the first and third lines shrink dramatically to a mere trimeter in the second lines—"Too full for sound and foam," "And after that the dark!" (ll. 6, 10)—and then to a drastically truncated dimeter in the fourth lines—"Turns again home," "When I embark" (ll. 8, 12).

> But such a tide as moving seems asleep,
>   Too full for sound and foam,
> When that which drew from out the boundless deep
>   Turns again home.
>
> Twilight and evening bell,
>   And after that the dark!
> And may there be no sadness of farewell,
>   When I embark; ("Crossing the Bar," ll. 5–12)

As fluctuation is made visible on the page as an ebb and flow of long and short lines, the merely potential assertiveness has an aura of surmise and mere longing about it that, far from binding Tennyson to the farther shore, makes the whole voyage tenuous.

Elegiac composition has a double aspect. When print domesticates the strange, making irregular states of mind more patterned and regular, it can subdue distress and moderate pain. But a cadenced voice may seem suddenly strange or unfamiliar when the blank space that encroaches on a truncated line helps a reader visualize the elegist's own fear of being engulfed. When printed as one of *In Memoriam*'s short tetrameter quatrains, which appears to the eye to be as plain and concise as an epitaph, a harmonious Tennysonian sound pattern often looks oddly bare and unadorned. What we see is estranged from what we imagine being heard. And what we strain to hear may be out of reach: it is like a voice without an auditor, or a ghost trying to make contact with a living reader.

In Memoriam also presents a conflict between the impact made by precise moral judgments and the tremor cast by indefinite romantic fantasies and spells. Hallam the magician continues to exercise power from his glimmering tablet in the church or from the strange phosphorescent glow that envelops the garden. Though a vivid perceptual memory, centered on such gestures as the mourner's outstretched hand and beating heart, reminds us of Hallam's power to charm and seduce, the essence of such charm is that it is indefinite: it cannot be explained. Indeed, the mourner's reserve is a source of marvelous energy and tension. All the passion seems to lie in that restraint. Because the sin against the holy ghost is to write without revealing oneself, without risking being mocked as the widow of some drowned seaman, Tennyson often invites us to read against the visible grain of his tense, reserved stanzas.

Timothy Peltason reminds us that *In Memoriam*, "taken too often as the comfortably conventional expression of conventionally comfortable feelings" (1985, 3), is in fact an extravagant and idiosyncratic poem. Divided on many issues, Christopher Ricks and Harold Bloom are united in "their thoroughgoing attacks upon the tradition of 'homosexual construction' as over against Alan Sinfield's 'materialist' affirmation of man-to-man desire in *In Memoriam*" (Joseph, 1992, 236–37). Bloom and Ricks may be right. I certainly sympathize with their opposition to current ways of dissolving the elegy's specifically literary features in psychological contexts. But there is also, I think, an energy and suppressed erotic power in *In Memoriam* that seems to be held, by repression, in an excitable state of readiness. The mourner's desire to touch Hallam's hand, to invest it with the same seductive power as Dickens invests Steerforth's arm for David, coexists with an equally strong desire to deny, defer, or silence such satisfaction. Since *In Memoriam* is an elegy of diverse and diffused erotic expression, there is a danger that gay studies of Tennyson will demystify this power, dispelling the magic by emptying the poem of its tense, excitable energy in precisely the way that the elegy's own extraordinary reticence refuses to do. If there is a homosexual content in the elegy, and Hallam the mentor holds the same place in Tennyson's intellectual life as Socrates holds within the life of the Greeks, it must be said that, even in confessing how he and Hallam used to "thread" Socratic dreams (89.36), the mourner resourcefully protects his secret.

Despite Hallam's gifts of grace as a reader of Tuscan poetry and his skill as a "master-bowman" in oratory and debate (87.21–40), the enchantments of love are too mysterious to be fully grasped or confessed. As a vigilant spectator, however, who is morally critical of seduction, Tennyson finds that what excites his pulse and intoxicates his blood while waiting to clasp Hallam's hand in the "Dark house" elegy has to be chastened at the end of *In Memoriam* by the morally definite, less private gesture of his ritually giving away the bride's hand to the groom.

> O happy hour, behold the bride
>   With him to whom her hand I gave.
> (*In Memoriam*, "Epilogue," 69–70)

The extramoral danger in Hallam's love is implicit in the ease with which the gesture of the outstretched hand modulates into the stretching forth of the lame hands of faith in a world of hollow form and empty hands (3.12; 55.17). An outstretched hand that does not retain its capacity to move beyond specific desires, which the hunger of imagination always finds wanting, may be hard to tell apart from the sinister, death-like stretching forth of science's arms, like the tentacles of an octopus, to charm "Her secret from the latest moon" (21.20). Such is the interplay of seductive charm and moral definition in the elegy that, even as indefinite romantic gestures are made precise and social, the energy of the mourner's erotic fantasy is allowed to move toward a just and generous vision of what a more inclusive married love might be like.

The fluctuation between concision and indefinition in Tennyson's elegies corresponds to the distinction Donald S. Hair draws between "heart-affluence" and "discursive talk" (1991, especially 130–34). The latter is the language of propositions and judgments; "heart-affluence" is the more nuanced and supple language of imagination and feeling. The language of judgment is arbitrary; it is the Lockean view. The language of indefinition is Lucretian; it is language as cry, prayer, petition, language that charts the unknown and in some ways repairs the rift between the two modes of discourse. The distinction between a Lucretian and a Lockean use of words has interesting affinities with J. L. Austin's contrast between performative and constative speech. Like performative discourse, a probing, tentative language of indefinition and confession is not to be believed so much as tested. There is little in *In Memoriam* that could be called ordinary reasoning, but the same could be said of Pascal's *Pensées* or even Wittgenstein's *Philosophical Investigations*. In all three works the aphorisms and conceits penetrate past assessment to become part of the sensibility from which assessment proceeds. Though the confessional language runs risks of inconsistency and personal confusion, in asking for more than intellectual refutation or agreement it also invites the commitment of "real assent," a term I borrow from J. H. Newman.

Staged versus Real Deaths

The traditional language and ancient symbols of pastoral elegy compose a kind of liturgy, releasing emotion even while controlling it. But sometimes an elegist lacks the leisure to compose his feelings. Caught offguard by the tremor induced by a "real" death, Tennyson transgresses the norm that requires the elegist to stage his grief ritually. As Browning's Bishop Blougram tells Gigadibs, real deaths induce a tremor partly because they take us by surprise. We are no readier for them than the actor who played death on stage only to be touched by "Death himself" when he retired to the dressing room.

> It's like those eerie stories nurses tell,
> Of how some actor on a stage played Death,
> With pasteboard crown, sham orb and tinselled dart,
> And called himself the monarch of the world;
> Then, going in the tire-room afterward,
> Because the play was done, to shift himself,
> Got touched upon the sleeve familiarly,
> The moment he had shut the closet door,
> By Death himself. ("Bishop Blougram's Apology," ll. 66–74)

In "The Vanity of Human Wishes" Dr. Johnson takes "the monarch's" part, the view from outside, surveying humanity from China to Peru. He finds at the end, however, that until he makes the personal application and allows the spectacle to touch him individually, his survey, for all its majesty, is mere "sham orb and tinselled dart." Unlike the play-acting, which is designed to make an impact on an audience, the familiar touch upon the sleeve imparts a tremor of self-concern.

A theater is a place for viewing, and the impact of a staged death appeals mainly to the eye. Its "pasteboard crown, sham orb and tinselled dart" are meant to dazzle from a distance. By contrast, a real or off-stage death induces a tremor by appealing to a more intimate and immediate sense, the sense of touch. A real death touches us upon the sleeve familiarly, and it takes place just when we think the play is over, when the closet door is shut and no one can see what is happening.

Some deaths in Victorian literature are too self-consciously staged to seem fully real. Even in Tennyson's most staged elegies, however, the pathos is usually under stricter control than the perfectly genuine but indulgent pathos in George Eliot's *Amos Barton* or Dickens' *Old Curiosity Shop*. In Tennyson's "Ulysses," for example, the voyage into death, though highly ritualized, is not nearly so soothing as the death of Dickens' Paul Dombey or Little Nell. Ulysses' valedictory rites allow us to feel to the full the impact of impending doom. But that feeling is controlled by the heroic mounting of obstacles, which is reinforced by the steady crossing of the breaks at the end of lines. Even the tone and syntax of Ulysses' coda send opposite messages. Read in one way, the final phrases drift down, one by one, with as steady and decisive a conclusion as any poem can have. But from its beginning, the heroic coda has also been possessed by the magic of repose, by a tremulous hypnotic rhythm that enchants and beguiles the speaker. Earlier in the poem Ulysses creates an illusion of infinite regress by making the margins gleam, fade, and then retreat from view. The shimmering, mobile words—"Gleams," "fades," and "move"—impart a tremor of vertigo and add an unsettling evanescence to the solid arch through which an "untravelled world" is seen racing away from Ulysses at alarming speed.

The elegiac tremors that pass through "Ulysses" and "Demeter and Persephone" are not to be found in the ritually composed stage deaths of "The Passing of Arthur" and "The Lady of Shalott." Persephone's descent to the underworld is painful and real, but Arthur's death is not. It is more like Desdemona's death in *Othello*, which, though the soul of pathos, is a mere piece of theater. In "The Lady of Shalott" there is no true death to rouse us to our senses, but merely a swan song. Like Ophelia, the Lady seems hardly to die at all, but merely fades away. One of Tennyson's best recent commentators, who comprehensively surveys modern criticism of "The Lady of Shalott," reminds us how parabolic and inhuman the Lady really is. Gerhard Joseph covers the whole spectrum of possibilities, from New Critical readings to Hillis Miller's post-structuralist association of the Lady with Penelope, Arachne, and Ariadne (1992, 117). The criticism ranges from Isobel Armstrong's feminist association of the Lady with the enforced passivity of women to Geoffrey Hartman's punning observation that in death the Lady of Shalott becomes a mere "floating signifier" (108). Whether choosing a Marxist or a deconstructionist vessel, Joseph keeps using the poem to document the "contemporary shift from authored 'work' to a 'text' floating freely down to Camelot" (118). It is difficult to believe fully in the death of someone who can mean so many different things to different readers. By contrast, there is nothing parabolic about Fitzgerald's death in the postscript to "Tiresias" and Lionel's death in the verse epistle to Dufferin. Both deaths are painfully literal, and catch us offguard. Surprised and moved by the suddenness of these deaths, we do believe in them.

Whereas a pastoral elegy will try to rally at the end for an expected consolation, Tennyson in his elegiac postscript to the monologue "Tiresias" transgresses this norm by contemplating with a tremor his own imminent death and by wondering, aloud, "What life, so maimed by night, were worth / Our living out?" ("To Edward Fitzgerald," ll. 79–80, 86). Tiresias's vision of being "gathered to [his] rest" and "mingl[ing] with the famous kings of old" ends on an upbeat note ("Tiresias," ll. 162–63). For its highly contrived impact the elegiac postscript to Fitzgerald substitutes the tremor of feeling with which a reader contemplates his own death. By speaking, not simply of his own futile march toward the grave, but of "*Our* living out" (l. 80) and "*our* poor . . . dawn*" (l. 77, my emphasis), Tennyson has made Fitzgerald's death our own.

Though Tennyson's anxieties are partly controlled by the conversational ease and urbanity of a verse epistle, his voice quavers with feeling. Tremors are audible in the repetition, three times, of the dread word "night": "past, in sleep, away / By night, into the deeper night! / The deeper night?" ("To Edward Fitzgerald," ll. 74–76). The rest of the elegy consists of grammatical fragments, with no syntactical completion until the closing optative. In the bleak memory of "so many dead, / And him the last" (ll. 82–83), Tennyson's elegy seems to be going to pieces, breaking up for a final time. These effects are achievements of art, of course. But because they conspire with real and painful experiences that take place outside of art, they leave the impression that the elegist's art has been compromised, interfered with, in some sense marred. Because Tennyson has not had time to reassemble his sense of self, we seem to eavesdrop on his stupor and confusion. Without a chance to put in place any of the elaborate defense mechanisms that associate the dead King Arthur with dignity and purity, Tennyson finds he cannot cheer himself up or allow himself to be eloquent.

A staged death like Arthur's or the Lady of Shalott's makes a strong rhetorical impact. The silent, almost unnoticed passing of Tennyson's son Lionel in the verse epistle to Dufferin induces a strong shock or tremor. As in the lines to Fitzgerald, death intrudes from outside the epistolary convention; it seems harshly at odds with the social convention of writing a letter of thanks to the dead son's hosts in India. One poetic genre has been rudely pushed aside by the uncivil intrusion of another. Indeed the second genre—the elegy—makes the conventions of the first genre void, because it seems to remove all grounds for being thankful. Yeats speaks of the "discourtesy of death" ("In Memory of Major Robert Gregory," l. 48). And there is something discourteous about death's intrusion in this poem. Like an uninvited guest, it blunders into a graceful verse epistle, a father's letter of thanks to his son's hosts, where it has no right to be. And yet this unspeakable breach of courtesy is beautifully repaired by Tennyson's own decorum, which gives Lionel's words about the Dufferins' unspeakable kindness to him a heartbreaking turn.

> But ere he left your fatal shore,
>   And lay on that funereal boat,
>   Dying, 'Unspeakable,' he wrote
> 'Their kindness,' and he wrote no more;
> ("To the Marquis of Dufferin and Ava," ll. 33–36)

Like his dying son, Tennyson refuses a banal logic of articulating gratitude in favor of a truer and more poignant equivocation: "and he wrote no more." That last clause introduces an elegiac tremor: its indirection and brevity make the death shocking, turning the brevity of a letter into a brevity that is final.

Tennyson, like his son, falters in his capacity to find words. The second-syllable caesura after "Dying" seems to stop the letter writer in his tracks, almost bringing the poem to a halt. Even the wrenching of word order in the phrase quoted from the son's letter, which is broken apart by the inserted clause "he wrote," seems to break down and sunder Lionel's life. The elegist's voice breaks down, too, as it stops to ponder after the early-breaking caesuras—"Dying," " 'Their kindness' "—the enigma of premature endings. The wildness that his lines acquire in touching on the "Unspeakable" loss generates a tremor of emotion that momentarily shatters the urbane tone. Though we are stunned by what Emerson calls "the one wild line out of a private heart," Tennyson barely touches the subject in passing, so painful is the wound. Forcing himself to imagine his son's coffin fall and flash in the Red Sea, Tennyson suffuses the lines with what Randall Jarrell calls "the grimness and awfulness and untouchable sadness of things" (1953, 68).

Elegies like Tennyson's epistle to Dufferin and Wordsworth's "A Slumber Did My Spirit Seal" confine the dead person to a watery grave or a literal down-to-earth world in which, in contrast to the staged deaths of Arthur or the Lady of Shalott, it is impossible not to believe. Even in "Tithonus" a comparable down-to-earthness keeps coming through the high-flown sentiments, as the literalness of becoming a mere sod or piece of "earth in earth" combines naturally with the ennobling love of the goddess. Some elegies operate in apparent ignorance of the classical conventions. Tennyson's son and Wordsworth's Lucy have not only failed to live through death, like Lycidas, by the aid of the pastoral convention that turns the person mourned into a "genius of the shore." They seem not to be aware of taking part in a rite of passage at all. Oblivious to the "touch of earthly years," both before and after her death, Lucy seems too elemental a force to credit, even by implication, the ritual commemoration that is taking place around her. Her death is as unpretentious as her spontaneous being as an elemental creature, almost a nature spirit, not quite human, but not wholly natural either. Like Lucy's sudden removal, Lionel's death strikes the mourner dumb. But there is no suggestion that the forces that operate in nature have contrived that this is so. It just happens, like the unforeseeable event that creates a break between the two quatrains of "A Slumber Did My Spirit Seal," even though there seems at first to be no discernible change in either subject matter or tone. So, too, in Tennyson's verse epistle, the change death brings seems at first so minimal—"and he wrote no more" (l. 36)—that we are in danger of missing it. It is the unawareness of Lionel or Lucy, the total unconsciousness of being tragic or pathetic, that makes each death painful.

Some elegies make audible the pauses of voyagers who have arrived, then turned again home to mingle like Tiresias "with the famous kings of old" ("Tiresias," l. 163). In walking to a "right death," like the heroes of the mystics, Tennyson's seer, Tiresias, makes an impact on the reader by throwing light on Heraclitus' dark saying: "Mortals and immortals alive in their death, dead in each other's life" (1987, 104). Other elegies are more tremulous. Despite a piercing clarity and economy, they leave a trace of embarrassment and strain. In a cheerless, dark, and possibly meaningless world, anything Tennyson can say about his son's death has an air of irrelevance and inadequacy, of awkward silence, which is quite at odds with the urbane self-possession of the letter writer, for whom embarrassment is half a sin. Our response to the magic and repose of Arthur's passing out to sea is totally at odds with the shock of seeing Lionel pass down into it. We do not believe in Arthur's stage-tragedy death, and so we have leisure to grieve over it. But we are shocked by Lionel's death because, as Tennyson imagines the burial at sea, allowing the unnameable form inside the coffin to pass forever from the mind's eye, the horror of that distant event seems unspeakably real. Nothing can mute its shock, because nothing has quite prepared us for it. Caesural breaks make audible the tremors of pain, the losses that cannot be ritually absorbed and somehow made less desolating.

The Power of Genre: A Pragmatic Criticism

Any study of elegy is a study of genre; and generic criticism is a traditional enemy of the literary text. To correct the tendency of a generic critic to search for axioms and norms, a rhetorical critic shows how elegies are as distinctive as a tremor of grief, or as a shock wave of pain, and are never wholly explicable in general terms alone. To talk about the tremor induced by Tennyson's verse epistle to Dufferin is to talk about the way it transgresses an elegiac norm. Its grief is most acute when most hidden, and its power to heal most apparent when consolation is renounced altogether and the elegiac germ of the poem is disguised as something else: as a letter of thanks to a friend. A close reader of elegy will make us aware of the difference between a theory of the genre and Tennyson's idiosyncratic conduct of a given poem. Alert to the tremors of feeling created by line breaks and caesural pauses, a rhetorical critic will seek the most suggestive misfit between prescribed rules and what Helen Vendler has called "the imp of the perverse, the Muse of the unpredictable next line" (1988, 25).

A second advantage of rhetorical criticism is that it is pragmatic: it helps readers make better or more convincing arguments. As pragmatists we seek in a theory of genre the least willful distortion of what we experience as we read. It is the explicit incompleteness of any explanatory theory of elegy that "creates the seeming completion or fullness" of a poem like *In Memoriam* that we are trying to explain. The theory's incompletion "makes the literary text seem to elude us, to contain more than we can know" (Rosmarin, 1985, 44). For this reason it may even be useful at a certain stage of criticism to treat each elegy sui generis, since drawing attention to family resemblances may blunt the strangeness of an elegy. And strangeness is like death: it keeps us in touch with elusiveness and mystery. No one has any specialized knowledge of death; in this area there are only the ideologies that inhibit freedom and limit hope.

Like the distinction between strong and weak mourners, which crosses historical boundaries and is justified not just historically or theoretically but also pragmatically, the distinction made in this chapter between an impact and a tremor is to be used as a tool of critical explanation. It engenders power, not by what it enables a magician or seer, a Christ-Orpheus, to do inside a pastoral elegy like "Lycidas," but by what it enables an enterprising reader to do. The alternative to such flexible pragmatic criticism is to assume, like Dr. Johnson, that a poem's uniqueness lies only in its typicality: "Lycidas" is merely an example of its genre, "a pastoral, easy, vulgar, and therefore disgusting" (1906, 1:112)—a pronouncement that inhibits critical inquiry and that displays what one commentator has called a peculiarly "classical form of stupidity" (Sparshott, 1970, 332).

The impacts and tremors I have been tracing in Tennyson's elegies also describe the process of a genre's breakdown and renewal. When an elegiac convention, instead of making its anticipated impact, generates a tremor of unbelief or critical questioning, it may lead a poet to write more idiosyncratically and honestly. Instead of trying to emulate Milton or Shelley, Tennyson may discover that "*In Memoriam* is also a poem about making do, about submitting to the flow of moments, to the uncertainties that succeed every certainty" (Peltason, 1985, 46). If the first shock of unbelief is followed by an aftershock of recognition, by a discovery that "There lives more faith in honest doubt" (*In Memoriam*, 96.11) than in a merely pro forma affirmation of belief, the poet may discover a new way of writing elegy. With time, any initial shock effect will probably wear off, and the subversive questioning of a new kind of mourner, of someone like the wife in Frost's "Home Burial," may be needed to generate new tremors of dissatisfaction and grievance. Such serial shocks and aftershocks even describe the genesis of chapters in this book. Dissatisfied with traditional accounts of elegy, which too often assume that all mourners aspire to the condition of the pastoral elegist, I wanted to show how norms live and become visible by transgressing other norms. Judged by the criteria of pastoral elegy, there is too much Tennyson in *In Memoriam* and too little Hallam. But because no one would ever make the same criticism of Augustine's *Confessions* or Newman's *Apologia*, I began to suspect that we may be requiring such an elegy to meet the wrong norms. When I found that lyric anxiety and even a touch of confessional egotism cannot be assimilated without residue into the tragic catharsis prescribed by pastoral elegy, I also discovered that this same stubborn residue can be made into the nucleus or germ of a second genre: confessional elegy. And when I found again that a core of silence and a brokenness at the heart of eloquence cannot be reconciled with confessional elegy's huge trajectories of grief, thrown like an arch across long spans of time, I discovered that two of the defining norms of Romantic and modern elegy, respectively, were at last coming into clearer focus for me.

8 ❧ Elegy and History: Testing the Conventions

Literary historians tend to claim either too little knowledge of the past or too much. If they claim too little, they may still write useful factual chronicles, but what they narrate will not contribute to our critical knowledge. Conversely, if literary historians claim too much critical knowledge, they tend to produce innovative interpretations of the past that are unhistorical. Though minor remedies have been proposed for both disorders, I want to examine in Tzetvan Todorov's influential essay, "The Origin of Genres," the more radical claim that both historical and critical knowledge is available to students who make a study of genres the cornerstone of their research. "Genre," he claims, "is the point of intersection of general poetics and literary history; in this sense, it is a privileged object, which is enough to make it the principal subject of literary studies" (1976, 164).

After considering some practical obstacles to implementing Todorov's proposals in a study of elegy, I suggest a remedy: it seems to me that the most authoritative critical histories have already been written. These histories, which are waiting for scholars and critics to decipher, are encoded in the elegies' own testing of conventions. We can trace the outlines of a critical history of elegy in the poets' critical reception of dead predecessors and in their strong creative response to their heritage. Whether the responses that a critical history of elegy chronicles are combative acts or acts of homage, they will be genuinely subversive or vivid enough to make us remember the people and traditions they commemorate, the deaths to which they bear witness. For a poet like Geoffrey Hill, who finds it barbarous that elegiac language should exult in itself, even when commemorating a death camp, the pastoral elegy's power to heal and console may be deeply insulting. If a purgation of the holocaust, even by the best elegists, commits its own atrocities, the modern testing of conventions must be strenuous enough to establish a distrust of elegy itself and a defeat of its own traditional powers.

Two Approaches to Literary History: Positivist and Critical

Many New Historicists demand *less* knowledge of the past than a critical historian should be willing to settle for. To assume, for example, that Kenneth Allott's footnotes to "Thyrsis" in his scholarly edition of Arnold's poems would furnish materials for a critical history of elegy is to assume with the neo-positivists that history is a mere chronicle of time- and place-specific facts. I do not deny that readers of Arnold's "Thyrsis" should be familiar with Arnold's incomparable correspondence with Clough, which is rivaled only by Keats's letters. They should also consult Victorian histories of Oxford. Perhaps it is even useful to know that "Sibylla" was keeper of the Cross Keys Inn in South Hinksey. Far more important, however, is the education we receive when we try to read "Thyrsis" within the traditions and conventions of pastoral elegy, going back as far as Theocritus and Bion. To do so is to see how the various conventions appearing in the elegy function with respect to each other and the tradition from which they were drawn, and why certain conventions that appeared suitable to Milton and Shelley are abandoned or modified by Arnold. As one commentator says, "this is a daunting task to assume for even one poem, and is generally avoided (in favor of moral summary) except by the most acute, learned, and hardworking critics, whose pages pose these perpetual questions, and at least attempt some answers" (Vendler, 1988, 50). Because it is important to consider how conventions in an elegy are transmitted, tested, and modified, it is possible, as David Perkins says, to insist "too strongly on the particularity, the definiteness of each moment of the past and of each poem. . . . These must be time- and place-characteristic" if they are to "be the subject of a historical generalization and enter into literary history" (1992, 23).

Since Fredric Jameson posited his influential theory of a "political unconscious," it has been fashionable to claim that all poetry is directly or indirectly political. But when writers wish to address political affairs directly, they usually turn from poetry to prose. And even an elegy that has been shaped directly by political events, Yeats's "Easter 1916," represents less a particular historical moment than an aesthetic of martyrdom and the divided sensibility of a self-critical patriot. If we look hard enough for four-leaf clovers there is a good chance of finding some. I find it difficult to see, however, how a reader can be conscious of influences that are by definition outside consciousness. And because political readings of elegies are likely to fulfill any theory of a political unconscious that informs them, many commentators with political agendas eventually find themselves in the same embarrassing dilemma as Browning's narrator in *The Ring and the Book*.

The narrator of that vast sprawling poem, a kind of newspaper epic, finds he must tell a twice-told tale by interpreting historical documents that are already organized through the testimony of its witnesses as one version of the poem's authenticating model. I am referring to the influential hermeneutical model advocated by Schleiermacher and by Barthold Niebuhr, the author of *The History of Rome*, according to which an interpreter "feels" his way into the sensibility of a historical agent or commentator. The interpreter who peers into the mirror of history finds that he is trying to recover in the past a reflection of his own act of peering into mirrors. Because the empathy and impersonation of a dramatic monologue are the very categories Browning, like Niebuhr, uses to explain history, he discovers in the court records of the Roman murder case a version of his own art of writing monologues. The whole enterprise turns out to be a huge *petitio principii* in disguise. Such is the specularity risked by political readings.

If the critical histories of some New Historicists require knowledge that seems too political, too local and place-specific, to be genuinely critical, some post-structuralist histories assume the validity of critical models that are too obviously a reflex of the historians' own mentality and biases to be genuinely historical. E. Warwick Slinn, for example, wants to assimilate the Victorian poets to a nondualist model of objective idealism he finds in Hegel; he appears to have a "saving" faith in this model. But like recent attempts to pass off Hegel's *Phenomenology of Spirit* as sociology and to pretend that Hegel was an atheist whose talk about "the true theodicy" of history was simply a ruse to deceive his Prussian employers, Slinn's attempt to excise teleology, to claim that there is "no staircase" and no ascent (1991, 21) in Hegel, is unhistorical. This is not a Hegel whom the Victorian Neo-Hegelian philosopher Edward Caird, the scholar Benjamin Jowett, who consistently Hegelianizes Plato in his magisterial edition of Plato's *Dialogues*, or even Tennyson or Browning, would have recognized. Indeed there is strong historical evidence that, though Tennyson owned a translation of Hegel's *Lectures on the Philosophy of History*, he was, like Berkeley and the metaphysician J. F. Ferrier (whose works he read), a subjective, not an objective, idealist. Whatever reality may be, Tennyson finds he cannot detach it from a perceiver. Without us and our marvelous consciousness, even the universe would not exist. So Tennyson dreams his dream and holds it true, lest without him on the scene the whole affair should veer off into random disorder.

Tennyson's idealism strikes me as deficient in humility, and seems implicitly to deny that there can be more things in heaven and earth than are dreamt of in his philosophy. But are historians who are conscious of deep falsehoods and expendable fictions in the history of ideas free to substitute their own saving principles? Can they use Hegel to dismantle teleology and dispel fictions of self-presence, just because they feel a therapeutic need to perform these operations? When a high priest of culture like Slinn scents heresy in the Victorians, instead of trying to exorcise or ignore it, is he not constrained to honor what is still refractory in the past? The sovereignty of the dreamer may be a fiction for Tennyson, as it clearly is for Slinn and for those post-structuralist theorists to whom Slinn tries to assimilate Hegel. It seems important to add, however, that Tennyson has his own "saving" faith in this fiction. To dream one's dream and hold it true (*In Memoriam*, 123.10) combines high joking with inner seriousness. But it is not an expendable joke. Tennyson would argue that no deeper truth has been found, either because it does not exist or because no one has been profound enough to find it.

Even when a critic like Slinn seems to read the Victorians unhistorically, then, it must be conceded that there is precedent for his procedures among the Victorians themselves. As Frank Turner has shown in *The Greek Heritage of Victorian Britain* (1981), the discovery by George Grote and the Utilitarians of a logical, Utilitarian Socrates challenges the more conservative, and apparently more historical, portrait drawn by the Liberal Anglicans R. D. Hampden and Connop Thirlwall. Because it is just as surprising to claim Socrates as a precursor of Bentham as it is to see Hegel as a German Derrida, Slinn appears to be doing to Hegel what Grote in his *History of Greece* does to Socrates. In praising Socrates as the greatest of the sophists, the inventor of a new analytic method, Grote turns Socrates into a Greek Utilitarian, a precursor of himself. It is usually possible to find historical justification for even the most unhistorical readings. By "justification" I mean not simply historical precedent but also something important in the spirit of a past culture—the new intellectualism of Socrates, for example, or Hegel's ambiguous status as "the last philosopher of the book and the first thinker of writing" (Derrida, 1974, 26)—which only a surprising (but possibly just) interpretation of Socrates as a Utilitarian or of Hegel as a deconstructionist enables George Grote, Jacques Derrida, or Slinn to recover.

It is easier to supplement the deficiencies of a positivist theory of history than to correct the excesses of a post-structuralist theory like Slinn's. In the first case we have merely to add to a chronicle of facts a testing of conventions that are general enough to qualify as proper objects of literary knowledge. But Slinn raises a more complex question. Is it ever possible to reconcile the scholar's "historical" faith in a past that exists objectively with the critic's "saving" faith in an idea about that past that transforms our understanding?

In his brilliant critique of scientific historiography, *Presuppositions of Critical History* (1874), F. H. Bradley defends the "saving faith" of literary historians like Slinn. But even in showing why histories of any kind are always about the historians, Bradley makes it clear that a price must be paid for their necessary subjectivity and biases. For all historians are also priests of Nemi, condemned to be slain by their successors. Even when a theorist of reception like Hans Robert Jauss tries to reconstruct a past horizon of expectations, he has to stand within his own horizon. A literary history that is always about the historian has to be rewritten in each generation. Some would say that the political agendas of recent interpreters have accelerated the rate, and a new history is now required every five or ten years. Though such considerations have led David Perkins to conclude that literary history is both necessary and impossible (1992, 17, 175–86), it is useful to recall that the only faithful account of the past would be the past itself, and that would not be history. Only the most naive theorists have presumed to present a naked Clio.

Todorov on Genres: Speech Acts and Literary History

Both historical and logical constraints limit the interpretations that a critical historian of elegies is free to make. Let me first consider the logical constraints. Denis Donoghue has argued that some theories are mutually incompatible. He accuses Hillis Miller of illogically combining speech act theory with deconstruction, which "doesn't allow," he thinks, "for any stable ground on which a speaker may perform an authentic speech act" (1993, 46). I am not convinced that Miller's notion of a groundless performative, which seems to me one of the paradoxes involved in any genuine act of faith, is the "narcissistic delusion" Donoghue thinks it is (49). But even if we disallow the claim that deconstruction revokes the power to initiate meaning, which speech act theories assume, Donoghue's principle that some theories are logically contradictory may still be valid.

There is a logical constraint, surely, to any free choice of a theory that, if consistently embraced, eliminates the possibility of future free choice or volition. J. L. Austin's theory of performative utterance presupposes free will: until David's words of power have been willed into being in Browning's "Saul," nothing occurs. If David were compelled to believe, would the substitution of coercive for persuasive speech be compatible with faith? And if Browning were not allowed to assent freely to a belief in immortality in *La Saisiaz*, would he truly want it? Might immortality not seem more a punishment than a reward, as it clearly seems to Tennyson's Tithonus? Michel Foucault's disturbing prediction that humanity as a category will disappear, erased "like a face drawn in sand at the edge of the sea" (1973, 387), makes the opposite assumption. But Foucault is involved in the same contradiction as Browning's Johannes Agricola, who chooses to embrace a theological doctrine that abolishes all future choice. He resembles Tennyson's lotos-eaters, who, having decided to renounce all volition, resolve to will for a final time: "O rest ye, brother mariners, we *will* not wander more" ("The Lotos-Eaters," l. 173, my emphasis). How free is a free man to sell himself into slavery? As a humanist who freely chooses a controversial theory that the evidence alone does not require, how free is Foucault to abolish his own humanity?

The most effective control on a critical historian's freedom to interpret has still to be considered: it is history's power to set us free from the idols of our present cave by conducting a kind of civilizing conversation with the past that "runs a course of lucky events," as Frost says (1968, 18), tracing the path of our bewilderment as it goes. History's ability to put us into an "untimely" relation with the present (to use Nietzsche's phrase) helps explain, I think, the great attractiveness of Tzetvan Todorov's theory of genres, which allows us to read our own experiences back into the discursive origins of elegies without disregarding differences between Milton's and Donne's beliefs and our own.

Todorov distinguishes between two approaches to genre: the order of literary history and the path of critical discovery. Arguing that "all genres result from speech acts," he uses literary history to explain "why all speech acts do not produce literary genres" (1976, 163–64). His answer is that a society chooses and codifies only those speech acts that coincide most closely with its dominant values or beliefs. Since genre "is not in itself either a purely discursive or a purely historical fact" (165), Todorov argues that critical questions about the origin of genres can never be separated from historical questions about why different societies have come to codify selected forms of speech.

A purely critical approach to literary knowledge would begin with the observed genres, and try to work back to their "discursive germs." A purely historical approach would follow the opposite path. Moving from the simple to the complex, it would show how "genre is the historically attested codification of discursive properties" (164). The influence of dominant codes and beliefs should help literary historians explain why the pastoral elegy, for example, is easier to write during the Renaissance and nineteenth century than during the modern period. At the same time, because the pastoral elegy originates in a speech act with which every reader can still identify, Todorov's theory also helps explain how this genre can keep alive even an archaic past by making part of the reader's present consciousness a mourner's intimate address to the dead person: a convention more moving, I think, than any other in elegy, which I want to discuss in a moment.

In Greek the etymological link between the genre we call elegy and its discursive origin is explicit in the ancient name for flute, "a name that," as Peter Sacks points out, "survives in the Armenian word," *elegn*, for the instrument Gluck's Orpheus uses to pipe Eurydice out of hell. Another Greek phrase, *ai ai legoi*, linking the elegy to Apollo's "cry of grief over Hyacinth" (Sacks, 1985, 331), suggests that when we try to isolate the discursive germ of all elegies, the difference between the speech act and the genre it produces is sometimes only minimal. Lamenting is a primitive speech act or cry; and the lament is a genre (which in an Anglo-Saxon elegy like "The Wife's Lament" may be literary, though often it is not).

Usually, however, the discursive origin of a genre, being more complicated, is harder to discern. Only a linguist could begin to formulate all the transformations that turn acts of invocation and ritual naming into an intricate pastoral elegy like "Lycidas." Peter Sacks has written well about the elegiac "custom of repeating the name of the dead," whose function was originally "to raise the spirit of the dead man from the grave" (1985, 25). At the discursive base of the genre is the classical elegist's quasi-magical power to turn bleak descriptive naming into performative speech. His ritual decree, "For *Lycidas* your sorrow is not dead" (l. 166), reverses the flat descriptive force of "*Lycidas* is dead, dead ere his prime" (l. 8). And the climax of the elegy hovers between a prophecy and a baptism, in which Lycidas acquires a felicitous new epithet.

> Hence forth thou are the Genius of the shore,
> In thy large recompense, and shalt be good
> To all that wander in that perilous flood. ("Lycidas," ll. 183–85)

If Lycidas is a true "Genius of the shore," he will behave in a predictably beneficent way. The conferring on Lycidas of a new office and function is a rite of exhortation and decree in disguise.

Elegies that are the product of medieval faith, particularly those belonging to an Augustinian confessional tradition, use history and typology to codify a very different form of utterance. Like Christ's proclamation in Revelation 1.8—"I am Alpha and Omega, the beginning and the ending"—speech acts whose ends are contained in their beginning are the discursive origins of elegies like the medieval *Pearl* or Donne's *Second Anniversary*, which end where they begin, though on a higher plane of knowledge. At the end of *The Second Anniversary*, Donne plays John the Baptist to the dead Elizabeth's Christ-like proclamations. But that act is implicit at the start, where Donne heralds the nothingness of life after Elizabeth Drury's death. Like having an experience of recurrence in advance, there is a sense that the end's presence in the beginning precedes the elegist's discovery of it. As in any poetry of types, there are also traces in confessional elegies of Plato's doctrine of anamnesis. Elizabeth Drury provides a pattern of virtue that reminds the mourner of a prior heavenly existence. Since "discovery" of that pattern is really a kind of "remembering," every step forward is like a step backward, as if the mourner were being reminded of something he already knew.

A classical elegy like "Lycidas" transcends death by performative decree. Confessional elegies like *Pearl* and *The Second Anniversary* transcend it by tautology: because Alpha is also Omega, the beginning is really the ending in disguise. By contrast, many Romantic and modern elegies codify, not the triumphal ritual decrees of "Lycidas," but the caesural breaks or dashes that keep testing the conventions of pastoral and confessional elegies against a mourner's grievous reticence, including his reluctance to put his deepest thoughts into words. These elegists use silence and absence to keep alive, without comprehending and so dispelling, the negativity they inherit. Though the seminal speech act in *In Memoriam* and several elegies by Hardy and Whitman is the vocative of intimate address, there is no indication that the person addressed hears the mourner or consents to serve as a guardian to all who wander in a perilous world. Even in "Thyrsis," the pastoral elegist can say with Milton's swain, "I speak and you hear me, therefore we are." But Tennyson and Hardy must say to the persons they mourn, "I speak and you do not hear me or reply, therefore I can know you only as the silent-speaking word that flows into the breach made by caesural pauses, parentheses, or breaks between lines." Because blank spaces and apostrophes give shape to the negativity that forms the unwritten base of such speech acts, even unsayable meanings may be intimated by Hopkins' ellipses in *The Wreck of the Deutschland*, for example, or by his dashes and caesuras, which are the very site of fracture or breakup, where God can be found.

Is Historical and Critical Knowledge of Elegies Possible?

Though the true generic history of the elegy remains to be written, Todorov would argue that both historical and critical knowledge of the genre is still in theory possible. In practice, however, it is often difficult to see how one convention is being tested, modified, and used against another. Readers may not have enough critical knowledge to understand a genre's language or enough knowledge of philosophy, theology, or general culture to see how its history is what one critic calls "a perpetual struggling dialogue between generations, temperaments, wills, and perceptions, all couched in a fraternity of shared and contested language" (Vendler, 1988, 56).

The problems are particularly acute in elegies, where the paradoxes and aporias of death—those moments of doubt or self-deliberation that prompt Shakespeare's Claudio to say, "Ay, but to die, and go we know not where" (*Measure for Measure*, 3.i.118)—mark the limits of both a critic's and a mourner's understanding. If we redefine deconstruction as a "philosophy of the limit," as Drucilla Cornell recommends (1992, ix), then a deconstructive reading of elegies may help us understand the limits constraining every reader. We want elegies to fit our desires, but we require our beliefs about death to fit the fact that death does not literally exist for the elegist; only his mourning exists. What we mourn in an elegy is never simply the other but the limits of our own understanding and a loss in ourselves. This leads Jacques Derrida to conclude in his essay on "Mnemosyne" (1986, 34, 38) that true mourning is both necessary and impossible. The mourner's very inability to commemorate more than a trace of the dead person allows him to be faithful to the mysterious otherness of that person, who can be known only as a present absence. For many modern elegists there can be no thanatology or science of death, because death is a loss to a void beyond understanding. It is "a leveler," as Northrop Frye says, "not because everybody dies, but because nobody understands what death means" (1982, 230).

Because of this built-in limit, all knowledge of elegies is *docta ignorantia*, a learned ignorance of things elegists and mourners can never hope to know. When we study death at two removes—in elegies that are themselves a meditation on death—some measure of historical and critical knowledge seems possible. But even here we meet a more pressing and practical constraint: the two forms of knowledge often exist in inverse ratio. The more historical context a scholar provides, the less opportunity to be critically reflective, and vice versa. In David Perkins' striking phrase, "historical contextualism tends to suppress critical intelligence" (1992, 128). Though every good elegy asks us to "pause for critical responsiveness," a constructed historical narrative of elegy requires "coherence and momentum" (46). It is impossible—or at least very difficult—to meet both requirements simultaneously.

Even to meet them successively a student of the genre has to perform a difficult balancing act. For half their time the ideal teachers and students will hide behind the historical scholarship of their subject and for the other half they will impose their own critical ideas and theories, or those of their contemporaries, in an attempt to show how elegies of the past exhibit things in which others are interested. Theories are necessary to familiarize what is strange, and historical scholarship is necessary to rebuild the dead elegists and present their thoughts as the *Pearl* poet, Milton, or Tennyson would have done if they were addressing space travelers from a different world and time. Though the cornucopia of theories and arguments from which critics can choose is in principle limitless, in practice only a few of these theories will have much cultural impact. If critics are not interested today in feminism, allusion, or the political unconscious, who will listen to them? If they are still beguiled by speech act theory or the aporias of deconstruction, some will say they have never grown up.

Studies of elegy today are in need of bridge builders, critics and scholars who can function in the two contexts in which ideas about a genre are most effectively communicated. Despite the protests of some scholars, who may feel their hour has come and gone, critics and theorists have to identify what is still alive in the past. And despite the opposition of some theorists, historical scholarship is still necessary to recover the intrinsic quality of that past. The Victorians seem to have recognized the paradox of this double context. In his essay *On the Interpretation of Scripture* (1860), for example, Benjamin Jowett is surely right to demand of the interpreter painstaking historical study and research. And yet D. F. Strauss, with his disquieting insights in *The Life of Jesus* about the freedom of poets and critics to impose a vocabulary of their own choosing, is right, too. There is no way most interpreters can affirm Jowett's doctrine of the decidability of meaning without at the same time affirming Strauss's liberating countertruth that the dead are dead, whereas new interpreters are alive and owe something to themselves. In practice, however, critics today, as then, are doubly constrained. Only a few theories about gender wars in elegies or about changing axioms of knowing are likely to make much of a flutter today in the academic dovecotes, even though contrasts between weak and strong mourners or between impact and tremor in elegies seem to probe more deeply into the nature of the genre. Even if a scholar is prepared to be a bridge builder, many departments and journals have declared only one of the two contexts—historical and critical—to be central. Unfortunately, any declared center is usually a still center, and the revival of interest in historical studies shows that what seems marginal today may move to center stage tomorrow.

Discourse about literature has its own complexity. But it is not the complexity of a deductive system like logic or mathematics. Because it has more in common with poetry, the discourse I advocate sets primary store upon aesthetics. Instead of placing elegies within the sphere of politics or philosophy, I prefer to consider the independent aesthetic power each elegy possesses. Opposing the fixities of ideology, the aesthetic critic will not allow the learned and sometimes ungainly theorist to block the irreducible simplicities that touch the mind and enter the heart, as Wordsworth says, "like revelations of the moment" (1974, 2:83). But because the undulations of mind in an elegy, its nuances and tremors, have to be preserved as one of the glories of the genre, an aesthetic critic may also have to curb a desire for easy apprehension by encouraging habits of persistent scrutiny and meditation.

No valuable truth about life-and-death matters has ever been expressed in a single phrase or formula; only an idolatry of words would allow us to think it could be. Though there is a largeness of spirit in most great elegies that comes from an exact sense of what the right ends of love and living are, to see at all in such poems is to see, like St. Paul, "through a glass darkly" (1 Corinthians 13.12). The truest interpretation of *In Memoriam* and *The Mystery of the Charity of Charles Péguy* is often the most difficult interpretation, the one embracing as many precise and imprecise, as many spoken and unspoken, meanings as possible.

Accuracy and formal precision of the kind required by a study of ideology and theory are usually achieved at a price. Released from the complications of a poem's formal density, such accuracy and precision seldom speak precisely about our subtlest experiences in reading elegies. As *In Memoriam* makes clear, language is often vague, and meaningfully so. My complaint about many literary theorists is, not that they have been imprecise, but that they "have been precise in the wrong places, which," as Francis Sparshott once remarked of the analytic philosophers, "has prevented them from being precise in the right places" (1958, 7).

The kind of certainty to be sought and prized in discourse about literature must try to preserve the imprecisions and uncertainties of literature itself. For these are the "soft spots," the sensitive places in any body of knowledge, and the best way to protect and understand them is to be as precise as possible about our unsettling confrontations with elegies that are most exact by being inexact, looking several ways at once. A totally precise language (like symbolic logic) has no specific subject matter; and it is hard to see how a totally inclusive subject (God) can be made intelligible in words that have any claim to be precise.

Elegy and History: Testing the Conventions

In an age when theory deflects attention from aesthetic and experience-based responses to the work of art, I want to defend a claim about literature that is now out of fashion. I want to reaffirm the view that the most important aesthetic decision an elegist can make is to identify, not with consolations that are conventionally available to the mourner, but with the uncertainties of a puzzled and questioning reader, looking perhaps for the first time into the eyes of death or grappling with other limitations. An impulse to question and test conventions is often represented inside an elegy by the practice in "Lycidas" of interrogating things that are hard to understand, including a God who allows bad people to prosper and good people to die before their promise is fulfilled.

By canvassing readers and critics, we should be able to gauge the aesthetic response to elegies of at least some of our contemporaries. But when we move back into earlier historical periods, we lack detailed accounts of reading experiences from which a history of reception could be written. This deficiency is remedied, however, and a history of response becomes possible, when we recognize that the best histories of reception have already been written. They are inscribed for attentive readers to discover and decode in the master texts of every genre.

Theocritus is read today partly because Milton admired and imitated him. And we read Milton partly because the story of his critical reception is also a story of strong imaginative response, encoded in texts by Wordsworth, Keats, and Arnold, who achieved something original and new themselves. The canon formations that count most do not take place in college curriculum meetings, in publishers' offices, or in scholarly manifestos. Because the evolving canon of elegies is ultimately the creation, not of critics but of other elegists, we need a functional history of the genre that can show why the testing of conventions is not an arid formal exercise but a life-and-death issue. As a struggling dialogue between wills and temperaments, this testing poses new crises for understanding and new shocks to values and beliefs from one generation to the next.

A functional history of elegy tries to explain how conventions are tested and modified: How does the inclusion of a new convention, A, require the exclusion of alternative conventions, B and C? When *In Memoriam*, for example, culminates in a Wordsworthian assimilation of the dead man's voice to the rolling air (130.1), we are expected to see how the allusions to "Tintern Abbey" eliminate the possibility of an important Miltonic convention. Tennyson had hoped to talk with the dead Hallam as familiarly as Milton's swain addresses Lycidas. Now in the running waters and the rolling air, in the rising and the setting sun, he encounters something that is at once more sublime and less personal than he anticipated.

> Thy voice is on the rolling air;
> I hear thee where the waters run;

> Thou standest in the rising sun,
> And in the setting thou art fair.
>
> What art thou then? I cannot guess;
>> But though I seem in star and flower
>> To feel thee some diffusive power,
> I do not therefore love thee less: (*In Memoriam*, 130.1–8)

The very presence of a diffusive voice hints at what is missing in the elegy.

A proper critical history of the genre must also explain why conventions of the Augustinian confession appeal to Tennyson at the time they do, and how these conventions exclude the more concentrated cathartic power of a pastoral elegy like "Adonais" or Thyrsis." Such a critical history will also be the work of an aesthetic critic who is keenly aware that Tennyson's choice of frugal tetrameter quatrains deliberately excludes the ampler, more sonorous music of Shelley's and Arnold's elegies.

Hallam *was*—that is the way of endless grief and mourning. Hallam *is*—that would be a comfort, if only Tennyson knew how to clarify his vision of Hallam by rending the veil, passing "Beyond the utmost bound of human thought" ("Ulysses," l. 32). The elegist has *negative* faith that Hallam is more than dust upon the wind. But lacking Milton's confident faith in polysemous meanings, Tennyson is still impelled to test conventions: How can he say that Hallam, like Lycidas, is simultaneously a Christian saint, a pagan genius, an absence, and a corpse? Milton can boast that Lycidas is both an absence to him and an angel. But Tennyson knows that Hallam would be the first to smile at the idea he is an angel or a saint. Donne can invoke Elizabeth Drury as a saint, because he believes that saintliness is one of her attributes. But Tennyson, sensing that sanctity is not an attribute but something created by his own love, challenges even this convention. Hallam has sanctity because Tennyson still loves him and uses his friend to look "behind the veil" in a final push past the mysterium tremendum.

Though the best readers judge the elegist, not by the truth of what he says, but by the way he says it, they also keep testing traditions through their tolerant and humane appeal from the conventions of elegy, which are a proper subject of critical histories, to something too elusive and personal to be represented fully in the language of these histories. I am referring to the individuality of each reader's response. Sooner or later every reader of elegies asks two questions: Is the bedrock of doubt the total nothingness of death? Or is death, not the opposite of life after all, but only the last of our new beginnings? Like Plato, who refused to expound his deepest thoughts in writing, because he felt they would be valueless out of context, elegists acknowledge the value of disciplined responses to death that are too personal to qualify as arguments but too tenacious to dismiss as mere proclivities or whims.

We are all condemned to misrepresent past attitudes to death by reading our own beliefs into them. But by testing the conventions, great elegists, like good readers, can act simultaneously as historians and critics. As critics, they learn to test and renew the conventions bequeathed to them and made lucky by the Muse's favor. And as conservers of tradition, they are also proud to turn as they pass, like the "gentle Muse" in "Lycidas," acknowledging their obligation to dead predecessors.

> So may some gentle Muse
> With lucky words favour my destin'd Urn,
> And as he passes turn,
> And bid fair peace be to my sable shrowd. ("Lycidas," ll. 19–22)

Each act of turning links the generations, partly removing death's trace by charging future poets to do for our contemporaries what Milton's shepherd-poet does for his friend. As each elegist, looking toward the future, makes valedictory pronouncements about his own "destin'd Urn," he also invites us to experience with him the effort of imagination and the challenge for sympathy required by every profound encounter with the past.

Bibliographical Essay

The best general cultural and historical studies of death from medieval to modern times are two works of radiant scholarship by Philippe Ariès: *The Hour of Our Death*, translated by Helen Weaver (New York: Knopf, 1981), and *Western Attitudes to Death: From the Middle Ages to the Present*, translated by Patricia M. Ranum (Baltimore: Johns Hopkins University Press, 1974). Ariès contrasts the "tame" death of medieval and Renaissance culture with the "wild" or "untamed" death of the Romantics and the "dehumanized" death of our own century. Though not specifically devoted to elegies, invaluable supplements to Ariès' study are found in the histories of epistemological and cultural change charted by Michel Foucault in *Les Mots et Les Choses*, translated into English as *The Order of Things; An Archaeology of the Human Sciences* (New York: Vintage, 1973), and by C. S. Lewis in *The Discarded Image: An Introduction to Medieval and Renaissance Literature* (Cambridge: Cambridge University Press, 1964). Lewis's interest in world models and their influence on the mind alerts us to the danger of describing the change of models from "Lycidas" to "Thyrsis" or from *Pearl* to *In Memoriam* as "a simple progress from error to truth" (222). Foucault's account of the "four similitudes" that "up to the end of the sixteenth century . . . played a constructive role in the knowledge of Western culture" (17) accurately describes the function of resemblance in English pastoral elegy. His later theory of classification sheds light on the axioms of knowing presupposed by the exhaustive anatomies and taxonomies of Donne, Johnson, and the Augustan elegists. The explanation of how "knowledge and thought" withdraw "from representation" at the end of the eighteenth century clarifies the influence of Kant's critiques and the ascendancy of new models of knowing in Romantic elegy (242). Foucault's theory of how language displaces representation as the new object of knowledge in late nineteenth-century literature helps explain the genesis of purist trends in elegy. Most radical is Foucault's idea that humanity itself is a recent invention, and that man, "like a face drawn in sand at the edge of the sea" (387), is in danger of being "erased." This disturbing, prophetic strain in Foucault's thought is confirmed, in part, by modern elegies on war and the holocaust. Foucault should be read in conjunction with two other major works of sobering insight: José Ortega Y Gasset's *The Dehumanization of Art and Other Essays in Art, Culture, and Literature* (Princeton: Princeton University Press, 1968) and George Steiner's *Language and Silence: Essays on Language, Literature, and the Inhuman* (New York: Atheneum, 1967).

The anxiety of the Romantic and post-Romantic elegist is made more acute by a faith that sublimity resides in the mind's power over a universe of death. The topic is examined with eloquent dexterity and precision by Harold Bloom in his chapter on "Enlightenment and Romanticism" in *Ruin the Sacred Truths: Poetry and Belief from the Bible to the Present* (Cambridge: Harvard University Press, 1987). On the implications for elegy of Victorian speculations about the four last things of Christian eschatology—death, judgment, heaven, and hell—readers will wish to consult Michael Wheeler's *Death and the Future Life in Victorian Literature and Theology* (Cambridge: Cambridge University Press, 1990). Its analysis of Victorian sermons, tracts, biographies, and anthologies of sacred poems for mourners is splendidly inclusive. It also establishes an important theological and cultural context for its interpretation of two Victorian elegies, *In Memoriam* and *The Wreck of the Deutschland*, and Newman's eschatological masterpiece, *The Dream of Gerontius*.

Important for an understanding of the recurrent confessional features of English elegy, which unite such diverse testaments as the medieval *Pearl* and *In Memoriam*, is John Freccero's *Dante: The Poetics of Conversion* (Cambridge: Harvard University Press, 1986). Freccero's impressive learning is matched by his sensibility as a critic. Especially valuable to students of elegy is Freccero's analysis of the Augustinian theology of conversion and the logic of autobiographical narrative, especially on pp. 263–71. My own earlier monograph, *The Lucid Veil: Poetic Truth in the Victorian Age* (London: Athlone, 1987), explores the changing axioms of knowing in many nineteenth-century elegies, including Ferrier's doctrine of the inconceivability of death, the origins of agnostic elegy in the skeptical development of Kant's critical philosophy, and the ascendancy of nonrepresentational axioms important to any understanding of "purist" elegy.

The Elegy as an Evolving Genre

Central to any study of Romantic and post-Romantic elegy is the principle of generic veiling. The most thorough treatment of the topic in the nineteenth century is John Keble's *Oxford Lectures on Poetry (1832–41)*, translated by E. K. Francis (Oxford: Clarendon Press, 1912), 2 vols. Keble argues that all epic dramatic genres are displacements of the poet's lyric impulse, which, like Virgil's, is often elegiac in origin. Displacement plays an equally important role in Northrop Frye's theory of genres in *Anatomy of Criticism: Four Essays* (Princeton: Princeton University Press, 1957) and in Geoffrey Hartman's study of how a lyric like Wordsworth's "The Solitary Reaper" is "generically a veiling of its [elegiac] source" (*Wordsworth's Poetry 1787–1814* [New Haven: Yale University Press, 1964], 18). Hartman shows how Wordsworth's speakers "encounter a mysterious and supervening thought of death," often when they least expect it (20). He is clearly out of sympathy, however, with what he calls elsewhere "Frye's sophisticated armature of categories" and with "all emphasis on forms and genres in conservative criticism, which tends to be—let us admit it—Aristotelian" (*Criticism in the Wilderness: The Study of Literature Today* [New Haven: Yale University Press, 1980], 184). In *Wordsworth's Poetry* Hartman argues that elegy in the Romantic period comes to refer "more to states of mind expressed by it than to formal genres" (11). For an authoritative analysis of this new and freer approach to elegy readers should consult F.E.L. Priestley's chapters on "Style and Genre" and "The Creation of New Genres" in *Language and Structure in Tennyson's Poetry* (London: André Deutsch, 1973). Priestley recognizes that "the questions raised by grief and the kind of answers that can be offered are not permanently valid from age to age." For the nineteenth century elegist "the questions and answers are . . . more complex, the answers more hesitant and speculative" (122).

Individual Studies of Elegy

Among recent studies of elegy, one of the most far-ranging and distinguished is Peter M. Sacks's *The English Elegy: Studies in the Genre from Spenser to Yeats* (Baltimore: Johns Hopkins University Press, 1985). Combining a workable psychological interpretation of the genre with sensitive readings of individual elegies, the book also includes excellent bibliographies. The concentration on individual elegies, however, gives Sacks little opportunity to analyze the range of elegiac experimentation in poets like Tennyson and Yeats, although the chapter on Hardy does include a representative sample of elegies from *Poems of 1912–13*. In considering the part played by elegiac conventions in the "task of mourning," Sacks tends to make psychological value a criterion of aesthetic value, and tacitly assumes that the best elegies are the performances of what I call "strong mourners." But weak mourners may dominate so direct and poignant an expression of a husband's grief as Henry King's "The Exequy." And strong mourners turn up in defective elegies like Browning's "Prospice," where the bumptious husband seems to bounce out of his moral gymnasium into the silence of eternity.

Other wide-ranging and humane studies of elegy include Abbie Findlay Potts, *The Elegiac Mode: Poetic Form in Wordsworth and Other Elegists* (Ithaca: Cornell University Press, 1967), Donald Mell, *A Poetics of Augustan Elegy* (Amsterdam: Mouton, 1974), Ellen Lambert, *Placing Sorrow: A Study of the Pastoral Elegy from Theocritus to Milton* (Chapel Hill: University of North Carolina Press, 1976), Eric Smith, *By Mourning Tongues: Studies in the English Elegy* (Ipswich: Boydell Press, 1977), and—especially to be commended—Ruth Wallerstein, *The Laureate Hearse*, part 1 of *Studies in Seventeenth Century Poetics* (Madison: University of Wisconsin Press, 1950) and Jahan Ramazani, *Yeats and the Poetry of Death: Elegy, Self-Elegy, and the Sublime* (New Haven: Yale University Press, 1990).

The most elegiac and Virgilian English poet is Tennyson. Whether it is ebbing away in grief in the verse epistle to Dufferin or mounting to subdued elation in "Tithonus" and "To Virgil," we may say of Tennyson's poetry what Walter Pater says of Marius the Epicurean's life: it is essentially elegiac, a *"meditatio mortis"* (1970, chap. 28, 277). No one has written with more authority and insight about this quality in Tennyson than Herbert F. Tucker in his recent study, *Tennyson and the Doom of Romanticism* (Cambridge: Harvard University Press, 1988). Admirably inclusive in its treatment of Romantic allusion, and informative about current theoretical issues, Tucker's book speaks memorably about the "ground-swell of doom" and fatality in Tennyson's verse (23).

Few studies of elegy are more illuminating in their learned intuitions about style, prosody, or critical theory than four recent books on Tennyson. For a sympathetic and energetically imaginative treatment of Tennyson's poetic practice and knowledge of language theory, readers should consult Donald S. Hair's wide-ranging study, *Tennyson's Language* (Toronto: University of Toronto Press, 1991). Arguing that "the fragment" is "the essential form" of *In Memoriam*, Hair shows how "this form is bound up with the language theories that lie behind the poem" (89). Addressing problems of structure and belief and the "deep mystery of [Tennyson's] spiritual regeneration" (7) in his monograph, *Reading "In Memoriam"* (Princeton: Princeton University Press, 1985), Timothy Peltason offers a subtle and conceptually powerful reading of Tennyson's elegy. More circumscribed, though just as rewarding to read, are the first five chapters of James Richardson's book, *Vanishing Lives: Style and Self in Tennyson, D. G. Rossetti, Swinburne, and Yeats* (Charlottesville: University Press of Virginia, 1988). Richardson argues convincingly that Tennyson "is primarily an elegist of the *self*, and what he renders more fully than any other poet is the sense of life as transparent, ghostlike, dissolving, ungraspable, nearly unrememberable (4). Using close stylistic and metrical analysis, Richardson gracefully discharges his self-set task of "explaining how poetry works and why it matters" (x).

More theoretical and equally illuminating is Gerhard Joseph's *Tennyson and the Text* (Cambridge: Cambridge University Press, 1992), which hovers between two critical positions. Half the time Joseph the Arnoldian posits "an historical Tennyson knowable more or less as he [and his works] . . . 'really' were" (6), and half the time he offers a "more self-imputing Paterian 'Tennyson,'" a poet who is "perpetually weaving, woven, and rewoven by post-Saussurean words of the ever fluctuating reader" (6). Joseph is especially good on the recessional quality of Tennyson's echoes, which are well described as "the auditory equivalent of the visual time-exposure of 'picture'" (97). Even at his most confessional, when recounting enthusiasm as a sophomore for the beauty of an elegiac passage in "Morte d'Arthur," Joseph manages to combine warm appreciation with theoretical understanding and critical good sense.

A bibliography of all the good writing on English elegies would fill a book larger than the present one. Since any selection is arbitrary, I have cited only essays or chapters of books that have opened new depths and excitements for me. Two exacting critics of elegiac language, who find poetry in the most minimal elements of prosody and grammar, are Christopher Ricks and Helen Vendler. Ricks's *The Force of Poetry* (New York: Oxford University Press, 1987) contains a masterful study of elegiac absences and endings in the poems of Philip Larkin (274–84). Of equal grace and distinction are Helen Vendler's analyses of "the high stoic elegies of Stevens' plain sense of things" (313–14) in *On Extended Wings: Wallace Stevens' Longer Poems* (Cambridge: Harvard University Press, 1969), especially chaps. 9–11. She is particularly deft at tagging what she elsewhere calls "the imp of the perverse, the Muse of the unpredictable next line" ("Feminism and Literature," *The New York Review of Books*, May 31, 1990, 25). In an earlier essay, "Reading Walt Whitman," Vendler uses the critic's most important tools— comparison and analysis—to show how "Whitman's idea of an American elegy is one that promises the dead no afterlife, one that celebrates its rite far from those of the churches, and one that ends . . . in the Hades of the mind—'There in the fragrant pines and cedars dusk and dim.'" Vendler argues that by abandoning the convention of addressing the dead, which she finds "more moving than any other in elegy," Whitman in "Lilacs" risks "everything in the service of the true" (*The Music of What Happens: Poems, Poets, Critics* [Cambridge: Harvard University Press, 1988], 141, 145).

As memorable today as when it was first written is Rosamond

Tuve's commentary on the "obscure and almost primitive power" of "Lycidas" in her *Images and Themes in Five Poems by Milton* (Cambridge: Harvard University Press, 1957), 73–111. Also exemplary in its demanding freshness of personal encounter is J. Hillis Miller's analysis of the trope *prosopopoeia* in Hardy's elegies on Emma in *The Linguistic Moment* (Princeton: Princeton University Press, 1987). Other original readings of Hardy's elegies can be found in John Hollander's *Melodious Guile* (New Haven: Yale University Press, 1988), 143–47, and in three exceptionally able essays published in the journal *Victorian Poetry*: Robert Langbaum, "The Issue of Hardy's Poetry," *VP* 30, no. 2 (1992): 151–63; David Gewanter, " 'Undervoicings of Loss' in Hardy's Elegies to His Wife," *VP* 29, no. 5 (1991): 193–207; and Melanie Sexton, "Phantoms of His Own Figuring: The Movement toward Recovery in Hardy's 'Poems of 1912–13,' " *VP* 29, no. 5 (1991): 209–26.

Two other critical approaches to elegy deserve mention. In *Victorian Poets and Romantic Poems: Intertextuality and Ideology* (Charlottesville: University Press of Virginia, 1990), Antony H. Harrison, a recent practitioner of the New Historicism, offers a challenging account of how Swinburne's elegies subvert Wordsworth's defense of immortality in his celebrated ode. Unlike some theorists who forfeit the chance of being proved right by avoiding the risk of being proved wrong, Harrison uses both poetry and its intellectual context as a laboratory in which theories can be tested.

Less capable of being identified with a single school, Lawrence Lipking's innovative study, *The Life of the Poet: Beginning and Ending Poetic Careers* (Chicago: University of Chicago Press, 1981), examines the form of elegiac tribute that Mallarmé calls *tombeau*, a genre that can define a dead poet's "legacy more elegantly and practically," Lipking believes, "than any other" (138). Arguing that such "elegies are the heart of literary history," Lipking analyzes two other critical points in the poet's career: "the moment of initiation or breakthrough" and the "moment of summing up" (ix). It seems to me that, not just *tombeau*, but all three moments in Lipking's scheme can be adapted to the study of elegy. Because an elegiac monologue like Tennyson's "Ulysses" is also the discovery by a poetic aspirant of his own genius, it also marks a moment of early breakthrough in the career of a great elegiac poet. Elegiac retrospects like Tennyson's "Merlin and the Gleam" and Yeats's "The Circus Animals' Desertion," which are full of references to each poet's earlier work, are clearly examples of *harmonium*, or the moment of summing up; while "Crossing the Bar" and "Under Ben Bulben" are valedictions or *tombeaux*, moments of "passage, when the legacy or soul of the poet's work is transmitted to the next generation" (ix).

Psychological and Philosophical Approaches to Elegy

In the voluminous psychological literature on death, the essay most applicable to elegies is Sigmund Freud's "Mourning and Melancholia," published in 1917. According to Freud, the melancholy that may temporarily immobilize even a strong mourner is allowed to deepen in a weak mourner into the fixated grief of the melancholiac, the mourner who unconsciously mourns some loss in the self. Like my analysis of melancholia in Tennyson's elegies, any study of "weak mourning" in elegies will concentrate on the psychic mechanisms of "projective identification" and "introjection" identified by Freud and later refined by Melanie Klein. In an elegiac monologue like "Tithonus," however, the melancholia Tennyson dramatizes seems less the result of the mourner's introjection of a lost object, both loved and hated, as in *Maud*, than the result of his attempt to find in beauty and sublimation some counterpoise to his loss. Such indeed is the explanation of melancholia that Freud offers in "On Transience" (1915–16), a slightly earlier, less familiar essay than "Mourning and Melancholia."

Of all Freud's interpreters, none has exercised a greater influence on literary critics than Jacques Lacan. And of Lacanian interpreters, none has more perceptive comments to offer on the language of mourning and melancholia than Julia Kristeva in *Black Sun: Depression and Melancholia*, translated by Leon S. Roudiez (New York: Columbia University Press, 1989). Normally, speakers are at home in their mother tongue. But in melancholy people, speech becomes alien and estranged. Kristeva is especially astute in identifying and analyzing models of retardation in melancholic language. "Speech delivery is slow, silences are long and frequent, rhythms slacken, intonations become monotonous, and the very syntactic structures . . . are often characterized by nonrecoverable elisions" (34). Like George Steiner, Kristeva also has an acute sense of the crises precipitated for thought and speech by the atrocities of modern war. "Are we still in the presence of nothing," she ponders, "when confronting the gas chambers, the atomic bomb, or the gulag?" (223).

A highly evolved feminist criticism is now well established, and ought to be welcomed as a new and valuable form of intellectual life. Kristeva's feminist revisions of Freud and Lacan raise the possibility of a distinctively feminist reading of elegies. As Peter Sacks has shown, Amy Clampitt's elegy, "A Procession at Candlemas," challenges elegiac conventions that allow male figures of authority to monopolize "a role once shared by female counterparts" (1985, 321). We can see a comparable struggle in progress in Frost's "Home Burial," which culminates in the woman's resolve to reform the world's way of mourning. For feminist interpretations of elegies by Christina Rossetti, readers may wish to consult Dolores Rosenblum, *Christina Rossetti: The Poetry of Endurance* (Carbondale: Southern Illinois University Press, 1986), a volume in the feminist criticism series. Though Rossetti poses a special problem, because in a lyric like "Listening" she seems to long for the domestic servitude that makes most feminist critics wince, the struggle between the sexes can profitably be read as a struggle for power and mastery, whose language and concepts seem less in danger of violating the supple aims of imaginative literature than thematic labels like women's writing, black writing, gay writing, and so on. Eva Kosofsky Sedgwick's important contribution to contemporary gay theory, *Epistemology of the Closet* (Berkeley: University of California Press, 1990), is only marginally concerned with elegies. But it offers intriguing insights that future students of the subject might wish to pursue. "A very specific association of gay male sexuality with tragic early death is recent," Sedgwick suggests, but "the underpinnings have long been in place. One might look, for instance, to Achilles and Patroclos, to Virgilian shepherds, to elegiac poetry by Milton, Tennyson, Whitman, and Housman, as well as to the Necrology of Vito Russo's *Celluloid Closet*" (144).

Apart from Kristeva, who shows how victims of melancholia are estranged from their own mother tongue, critics have paid little attention to the genius of estrangement in elegies. The best work on language and estrangement has been done by critics not specifically concerned with elegies: by Stephen Booth in his work on tragedy, by Eric Griffiths on the estranging medium of the printed word, and by Denis Donoghue on mystery. Students of elegy interested in adapting the methods of these critics should consult Stephen Booth's *An Essay on Shakespeare's Sonnets* (New Haven: Yale University Press, 1969) and *King Lear, Macbeth, Indefinition, and Tragedy* (New Haven: Yale University Press, 1983); Eric Griffith's *The Printed Voice of Victorian Poetry* (Oxford: Clarendon Press, 1989); and Denis Donoghue's "T. S. Eliot's *Quartets*: A New Reading (1965)," in *T.S. Eliot: Four Quartets: A Casebook*, edited by Bernard Bergonzi (London: Macmillan, 1969), 212–36.

Most students of elegy try to be faithful, if not to the letter, then at least to the spirit, of the historical scholarship, the methods of rhetorical and critical analysis, the structuralist or post-structuralist forms of theorizing, in which they have been trained. But elegies also raise life-and-death issues: any in-depth study of the genre encroaches on theories of knowledge and thanatology, on theology and metaphysics, and cannot be confined to literary criticism alone. Without being deflected from attention to the elegies themselves, students of the form will want to draw on the scholarship and insights of Ernest Becker's *The Denial of Death* (London: Collier Macmillan, 1973), which features the thought of two philosophers and theologians, Kierkegaard and Otto Rank. Siding with Rank against Freud, Becker argues that neurosis is "the miscarriage of clumsy lies about reality" (178), and concludes that "what we call a creative gift is merely the social license to be obsessed" (186). Like Becker, Miguel de Unamuno contends that the discovery of death "causes nations, as it does men, to enter upon spiritual puberty, the awareness of the tragic sense of life" (*The Tragic Sense of Life in Men and Nations*, translated by Anthony Kerrigan [Princeton: Princeton University Press, 1972], 69). Invaluable for its scrupulous dissection of the phenomenon of grief—its symptoms, embarrassments, and pain—is C. S. Lewis's monograph, *A Grief Observed* (London: Faber and Faber, 1961). Important analyses of death and grieving as rites of passage are found in Elisabeth Kübler-Ross's classical study, *On Death and Dying* (New York: Macmillan, 1969), and in two works by Victor Turner, *The Ritual Process: Structure and Anti-Structure* and *Image and Pilgrimage in Christian Culture: Anthropological Perspectives*, published in 1969 and 1978, respectively.

Several contemporary philosophers, all schooled in the analytic tradition but all venturing far beyond the confines of that school, have contributed to an understanding of the subject. Of special interest is Richard Wollheim's explanation of why death is a misfortune, even though its alternative, eternal life, would be a misfortune, too. Students of elegy will want to consult the brilliant concluding chapter of Wollheim's book *The Thread of Life* (Cambridge: Harvard University Press, 1984), "Cutting the Thread: Death, Madness, and the Loss of Friendship," 257–83. Equally masterful is Thomas Nagel's essay on death at the end of *The View from Nowhere* (New York: Oxford University Press, 1986), which explains why "the objective standpoint simply cannot accommodate at its full subjective value the fact that everyone, oneself included, inevitably dies" (230). Robert Nozick's absorbing essays on "Death," "Traces," and "The Unlimited" in the final section of his book *Philosophical Explanations* (Cambridge: Harvard University Press, 1981), 579–85, 600–10, clarify the dilemma confronting every elegist who refuses to force belief and falsify assent. "We must not confuse what we desire with what is the case," warns Nozick. The "act of maintaining the most rigorous intellectual standards, uninfluenced by our hopes and aspirations, exhibits stern integrity in the face of temptation." But "the question is: does this scrupulous act have any *meaning*?" (609–10).

Though Northrop Frye, unlike the writers considered in the last paragraph, is not a philosopher, the end of his book *The Great Code:*

The Bible and Literature (Toronto: Academic Press, 1982) takes up where Nozick leaves off. Frye suggests that elegies confront "the total nothingness of death" with a different question: "What speaks to us across death? . . . what comes after? or what lies beyond? These are metaphors from time and space respectively: language still clutches to its accustomed metaphors, even when they seem clearly not to apply. . . . After all the centuries of sacramental processing, this whole subject seems to be as much up for grabs as it ever was" (230–31). It is now clear from a notebook at the Pratt Library, Victoria College, University of Toronto, that Frye once planned to write a novel on the subject.

Two recent commentators, Martha Nussbaum and Jacques Derrida, formulate paradoxes about death that extend analyses attempted in this study. In *Love's Knowledge* (New York: Oxford University Press, 1990), a book of interdisciplinary essays on philosophy and literature, Nussbaum clarifies the paradox that, though death is a misfortune, so is its opposite. As she explains, "one is to hate and fear the thought of . . . death, to try to prevent it by any means one can—and yet to know that a mortal life is the only life in which the people one loves could actually be. This tension, which is close to being a contradiction, seems to be a part of the best human life" (381). A related paradox, that true mourning is both necessary and impossible, is developed by Jacques Derrida in his essay on "Mnemosyne" in *Mémoires for Paul de Man*, edited by Avital Ronell and Eduardo Cadava (New York: Columbia University Press, 1986). For a lucid gloss on this paradox, see Drucilla Cornell, "The Call to Mourning," in *The Philosophy of the Limit* (New York: Routledge, 1992), 72–75.

Bibliography

Works Cited in Text

Abrams, M. H. 1965. "Structure and Style in the Greater Romantic Lyric." In *From Sensibility to Romanticism*. Edited by F. W. Hilles and Harold Bloom. New York: Oxford University Press.

———. 1971. *Natural Supernaturalism: Tradition and Revolution in Romantic Literature*. New York: Norton.

Adams, Henry. 1909. "The Rule of Phase Applied to History." In *The Degradation of the Democratic Dogma*. New York: Macmillan.

Ariès, Philippe. 1974. *Western Attitudes to Death: From the Middle Ages to the Present*. Translated by Patricia M. Ranum. Baltimore: Johns Hopkins University Press.

———. 1981. *The Hour of Our Death*. Translated by Helen Weaver. New York: Knopf.

Arnold, Matthew. 1960–77. *The Complete Prose Works of Matthew Arnold*. Edited by R. H. Super. 11 vols. Ann Arbor: University of Michigan Press.

Austin, J. L. 1962. *How to Do Things with Words*. Cambridge: Harvard University Press.

Bate, Walter Jackson, ed. 1952. *Criticism: The Major Texts*. New York: Harcourt, Brace.

Bayley, John. 1981. *Shakespeare and Tragedy*. London: Routledge and Kegan Paul.

Becker, Ernest. 1973. *The Denial of Death*. London: Collier Macmillan.

Berger, Harry. 1966. "Biography as Interpretation: Interpretation as Biography." *College English* 28: 113–25.

Berlin, Isaiah. 1976. *Vico and Herder: Two Studies in the History of Ideas*. New York: Viking Press.

Bloom, Harold. 1987. *Ruin the Sacred Truths: Poetry and Belief from the Bible to the Present*. Cambridge: Harvard University Press.

Booth, Stephen. 1969. *An Essay on Shakespeare's Sonnets*. New Haven: Yale University Press.

———. 1983. *King Lear, Macbeth, Indefinition, and Tragedy*. New Haven: Yale University Press.

Bradley, F. H. 1876. *Ethical Studies*. Oxford: Clarendon Press. Reprinted 1970.

———. 1883. *The Principles of Logic*. London: Kegan Paul, Trench.

———. 1893. *Appearance and Reality: A Metaphysical Essay*. Oxford: Clarendon Press.

————. 1930. *Aphorisms*. Oxford: Clarendon Press.

Brower, Reuben A. 1954. "Yeats." *Major British Writers*. New York: Harcourt, Brace.

————. 1962. *The Fields of Light*. New York: Oxford University Press.

Bruns, Gerald L. 1974. *Modern Poetry and the Idea of Language: A Critical and Historical Study*. New Haven: Yale University Press.

Bryant, Mark. 1984. *Riddles Ancient and Modern*. New York: Peter Bedrick.

Burke, Kenneth. 1962. *A Grammar of Motives and a Rhetoric of Motives*. New York: Meridian.

Bush, Douglas. 1963. *Mythology and the Renaissance Tradition in English Poetry*. New York: Norton.

————. 1971. *Matthew Arnold: A Survey of His Poetry and Prose*. New York: Macmillan.

Coleridge, S. T. 1906. *Biographia Literaria*. Edited by George Watson. London: J. M. Dent.

Colie, Rosalie. 1966. *Paradoxia Epidemica*. Princeton: Princeton University Press.

Cornell, Drucilla. 1992. *The Philosophy of the Limit*. New York: Routledge.

Culler, A. Dwight. 1977. *The Poetry of Tennyson*. New Haven: Yale University Press.

Derrida, Jacques. 1974. *Of Grammatology*. Translated by G. C. Spivak: Baltimore: Johns Hopkins University Press.

————. 1986. *Mémoires: for Paul de Man*. Edited by Avital Ronell and Eduardo Cadava. New York: Columbia University Press.

Donoghue, Denis. 1965. "T. S. Eliot's *Quartets*: A New Reading," in *T. S. Eliot: Four Quartets: A Casebook*. Edited by Bernard Bergonzi. London: Macmillan (1969).

————. 1993. "Bewitched, Bothered, and Bewildered." *New York Review of Books*, March 25, 46–53.

Eliot, George. 1967. *Middlemarch: A Study of Provincial Life*. London: Oxford University Press.

————. 1973. *Scenes of Clerical Life*. Harmondsworth: Penguin.

Eliot, T. S. 1916. Harvard University doctoral thesis. *Experience and Knowledge in the Philosophy of F. H. Bradley*. London: Faber and Faber (1964).

————. 1932. *Selected Essays*. London: Faber and Faber.

Escher, M. C. 1983. *M. C. Escher: 29 Master Prints*. New York: Harry N. Abrams.

Ferrier, J. F. 1842. "Berkeley and Idealism." *Blackwood's Edinburgh Magazine* 51: 812–30.

————. 1854. *The Institutes of Metaphysics: Theory of Knowing and Being*. Edinburgh: Blackwood.

Feuerbach, Ludwig. 1957. *The Essence of Christianity*. Translated by George Eliot. New York: Harper and Row. Originally published 1841.

Flaubert, Gustave. 1919. *Gustave Flaubert, Correspondance, troisième série, 1854–69*. Paris: E. Fasquelle. Translated from *The Letters of Gustave Flaubert 1857–1880*. Edited and translated by Francis Steegmuller. Cambridge, Mass.: Harvard University Press. Vol. 2 (1982), 20.

Foucault, Michel. 1973. *The Order of Things: An Archaeology of the Human Sciences*. New York: Vintage.

———. 1988. *Madness and Civilization: A History of Insanity in the Age of Reason*. Translated by Richard Howard. New York: Vintage.

Freccero, John. 1986. *Dante: The Poetics of Conversion*. Cambridge: Harvard University Press.

Freud, Sigmund. 1917. "Mourning and Melancholia." In *A General Selection from the Works of Sigmund Freud*. Edited by John Rickman. New York: Liveright (1957).

Frost, Robert. 1968. *Selected Prose of Robert Frost*. Edited by H. Cox and E. C. Lathem. New York: Collier Books.

Frye, Northrop. 1957. *Anatomy of Criticism: Four Essays*. Princeton: Princeton University Press.

———. 1968. *A Study of English Romanticism*. Chicago: University of Chicago Press.

———. 1971. *The Critical Path: An Essay on the Social Context of Literary Criticism*. Bloomington: Indiana University Press.

———. 1982. *The Great Code: The Bible and Literature*. Toronto: Academic Press.

Gardner, Helen. 1978. *The Composition of Four Quartets*. New York: Oxford University Press.

Gardner, Martin. 1983. *The Whys of a Philosophical Scrivener*. New York: Quill.

Gewanter, David. 1991. "'Undervoicings of Loss' in Hardy's Elegies to His Wife." *Victorian Poetry* 29: 193–207.

Gibbon, Edward. 1869. *The History of the Decline and Fall of the Roman Empire*. 3 vols. London: Alex. Murray and Son.

Greimas, A. J. 1989. "The Veridiction Contract." *New Literary History* 20: 651–60.

Griffiths, Eric. 1989. *The Printed Voice of Victorian Poetry*. Oxford: Clarendon Press.

Hair, Donald S. 1991. *Tennyson's Language*. Toronto: University of Toronto Press.

Hallam, Arthur. 1943. "Theodicaea Novissima." Reprinted in *The Writings of Arthur Hallam*. Edited by T. H. Vail Motter. London: Oxford University Press.

Hamilton, Sir William. 1829. "Review of M. Cousin's *Course on Philosophy*." *Edinburgh Review* 50: 196–221.

Hardy, Emma. 1979. *Some Recollections*. Edited by Robert Gittings and Evelyn Hardy. Oxford: Clarendon Press.

Hare, Julius and Agustus. 1838. *Guesses at Truth, by Two Brothers*. London: Taylor and Walton.

Harrison, Antony H. 1990. *Victorian Poets and Romantic Poems: Intertextuality and Ideology*. Charlottesville: University Press of Virginia.

Hartman, Geoffrey. 1964. *Wordsworth's Poetry 1787–1814*. New Haven: Yale University Press.

———. 1980. *Criticism in the Wilderness: The Study of Literature Today*. New Haven: Yale University Press.

Hegel, G.W.F. 1857. *Lectures on the Philosophy of History*. Translated from 3d German ed. by J. Sibree. London: H. G. Bohn.

———. 1967. *The Phenomenology of Mind*. Translated by J. B. Baillie. New York: Harper Torchbooks.

Heraclitus. 1987. *Fragments*, in *Early Greek Philosophy*. Edited by Jonathan Barnes. London: Penguin.

Hill, Geoffrey. 1984. *The Lords of Limit: Essays on Literature and Ideas*. London: André Deutsch.

Hirsch, E. D. 1967. *Validity in Interpretation*. New Haven: Yale University Press.

Hollander, John. 1975. *Vision and Resonance: Two Senses of Poetic Form*. New York: Oxford University Press.

———. 1988. *Melodious Guile*. New Haven: Yale University Press.

Hopkins, G. M. 1938. *Further Letters of G. M. Hopkins*. Edited by C. C. Abbott. London: Oxford University Press.

Houghton Library MSS.

Emily Dickinson, Autograph File, TL. to Louisa Norcross.

———. 4 Autographs, A. L. to T. W. Higginson, 1879–82.

Robert Frost, 15 letters to Amy Lowell, bMS. Lowell 19 (459).

Robert Lowell on Robert Frost, bMS. Am. 1905 (2812).

Wallace Stevens *Two or Three Ideas*, fmS. Am. 1333.5 (1), later published in *Opus Posthumous*.

Jakobson, Roman. 1956. "Two Aspects of Language and Two Types of Linguistic Disturbances." In *Fundamentals of Language*. Edited by Roman Jakobson and Morris Halle. The Hague: Mouton.

James, William. 1897. Ingersoll Lecture.

———. 1909. "On A Certain Blindness in Human Beings." In *Talks to Teachers on Psychology: And to Students on Some of Life's Ideals*. New York: Henry Holt.

———. 1911. *Pragmatism: A New Name for Some Old Ways of Thinking*. London: Longmans, Green.

Jarrell, Randall. 1953. *Poetry and the Age*. New York: Knopf.

Jauss, Hans Robert. 1982. *Toward an Aesthetic of Reception*. Translated by Timothy Bahti. Minneapolis: University of Minnesota Press.

Johnson, Samuel. 1906. *Lives of the English Poets*. 2 vols. London: Oxford University Press.

Joseph, Gerhard. 1992. *Tennyson and the Text*. Cambridge: Cambridge University Press.

Kant, Immanuel. 1881. *Critique of Pure Reason*. Translated by Max Müller. 2 vols. London: Macmillan.

———. 1914. *Critique of Judgement*. Translated by J. H. Bernard. London: Macmillan.

———. 1923. *Critique of Practical Reason*. Translated by T. K. Abbott. London: Longmans, Green.

Keble, John. 1912. *Oxford Lectures on Poetry (1832–1841)*. Translated by E. K. Francis. 2 vols. Oxford: Clarendon Press.

Kermode, Frank. 1966. *The Sense of an Ending: Studies in the Theory of Fiction*. London: Oxford University Press.

Kierkegaard, Søren. 1940. *Stages on Life's Way*. Translated by David F. Svenson and Walter Lowrie. Princeton: Princeton University Press.

Kolb, Jack. 1981. *The Letters of Arthur Henry Hallam*. Columbus: Ohio State University Press.

Kristeva, Julia. 1982. *Powers of Horror: An Essay on Abjection*. Translated by Leon S. Roudiez. New York: Columbia University Press.

———. 1986. *The Kristeva Reader*. Translated by Toril Mol. New York: Columbia University Press.

———. 1989. *Black Sun: Depression and Melancholia*. Translated by Leon S. Roudiez. New York: Columbia University Press.

Kübler-Ross, Elisabeth. 1969. *On Death and Dying*. New York: Macmillan.

Lambert, Ellen. 1976. *Placing Sorrow: A Study of the Pastoral Elegy from Theocritus to Milton*. Chapel Hill: University of North Carolina Press.

Lang, C. Y., and Edgar F. Shannon, Jr., eds. 1981, 1987. *The Letters of Alfred Lord Tennyson*. 2 vols. to date. Cambridge: Belknap Press of Harvard University Press.

Langbaum, Robert. 1992. "The Issue of Hardy's Poetry." *Victorian Poetry* 30, no. 2: 151–63.

Larkin, Philip. 1983. *Required Reading: Miscellaneous Pieces 1955–1982*. London: Faber and Faber.

Lewis, C. S. 1961. *A Grief Observed*. London: Faber and Faber.

———. 1964. *The Discarded Image: An Introduction to Medieval and Renaissance Literature*. Cambridge: Cambridge University Press.

Lipking, Lawrence. 1981. *The Life of the Poet: Beginning and Ending Poetic Careers*. Chicago: University of Chicago Press.

Locke, John. 1924. *An Essay Concerning Human Understanding*. Edited by A. S. Pringle-Pattison. Oxford: Clarendon Press. Originally published 1690.

McGann, Jerome J. 1985. "Introduction: A Point of Reference." In *Historical Studies and Literary Criticism*. Edited by Jerome J. McGann. Madison: University of Wisconsin Press.

McKay, K. M. 1988. *Many Glancing Colours: An Essay in Reading Tennyson*. Toronto: University of Toronto Press.

Mansel, H. L. 1867. *The Limits of Religious Thought Examined in Eight Lectures*. London: J. Murray.

Maritain, Jacques. 1930. *Art and Scholasticism, with Other Essays*. New York: C. Scribner's Sons.

Martz, Louis. 1962. "John Donne in Meditation: The Anniversaries." In *Seventeenth-Century English Poetry: Modern Essays in Criticism*. Edited by William R. Keast. New York: Oxford University Press. From *The Poetry of Meditation: A Study in English Religious Literature of the Seventeenth Century*. New Haven: Yale University Press (1954).

Mandelbaum, Maurice. 1971. *History, Man, and Reason: A Study in Nineteenth-Century Thought*. Baltimore: Johns Hopkins University Press.

Mell, Donald. 1974. *A Poetics of Augustan Elegy.* Amsterdam: Mouton.

Mill, John Stuart. 1974. *System of Logic: Ratiocinative and Inductive.* Edited by J. M. Robson and R. F. McRae. *Collected Works of John Stuart Mill.* Vols. 7–8. Toronto: University of Toronto Press; London: Routledge and Kegan Paul.

Miller, Cristanne. 1987. *Emily Dickinson: A Poet's Grammar.* Cambridge: Harvard University Press.

Miller, J. Hillis. 1985. *The Linguistic Moment.* Princeton: Princeton University Press.

More, Paul Elmore. 1961. "How to Read *Lycidas.*" In *Milton's "Lycidas": The Tradition and the Poem.* Edited by C. A. Patrides. New York: Holt, Rinehart and Winston.

Nagel, Thomas. 1986. *The View from Nowhere.* New York: Oxford University Press.

Newman, J. H. 1887. *Sermons Preached before the University of Oxford Between 1826 and 1843.* London: Rivingtons.

———. 1968. *Apologia Pro Vita Sua.* Edited by David J. De Laura. New York: Norton. Originally published 1864.

Nietzsche, Friedrich. 1968. *Twilight of the Idols and the Anti-Christ.* Translated by R. J. Hollingdale. Middlesex: Penguin. Originally published 1889 and 1895.

Nozick, Robert. 1981. *Philosophical Explanations.* Cambridge: Harvard University Press.

Nussbaum, Martha. 1990. *Love's Knowledge: Essays on Philosophy and Literature.* New York: Oxford University Press.

Ortega Y Gasset, José. 1968. *The Dehumanization of Art and Other Essays on Art, Culture, and Literature.* Princeton: Princeton University Press. Originally published 1948.

Pater, Walter. 1970. *Marius the Epicurean.* Edited by Harold Bloom. New York: Signet.

Peirce, Charles Saunders. 1931–35. *Collected Papers of Charles Saunders Peirce.* Edited by Charles Hartshorne and Paul Weiss. 8 vols. Cambridge: Harvard University Press.

Peltason, Timothy. 1985. *Reading "In Memoriam."* Princeton: Princeton University Press.

Perkins, David. 1992. *Is Literary History Possible?* Baltimore: Johns Hopkins University Press.

Perl, Jeffrey M. 1989. *Skepticism and Modern Enmity: Before and after T. S. Eliot.* Baltimore: Johns Hopkins University Press.

Poirier, Richard. 1977. *Robert Frost: The Work of Knowing.* New York: Oxford University Press.

———. 1987. *The Renewal of Literature: Emersonian Reflections.* New York: Random House.

Poundstone, William. 1988. *Labyrinths of Reason: Paradox, Puzzles, and the Frailty of Knowledge.* New York: Anchor Press, Doubleday.

Potts, Abbie Findlay. 1967. *The Elegiac Mode: Poetic Form in Wordsworth and Other Elegists*. Ithaca: Cornell University Press.

Priestley, F.E.L. 1973. *Language and Structure in Tennyson's Poetry*. London: André Deutsch.

Prince, F. T. 1954. *The Italian Element in Milton's Verse*. Oxford: Oxford University Press.

Ramazani, Jahan. 1990. *Yeats and the Poetry of Death: Elegy, Self-Elegy, and the Sublime*. New Haven: Yale University Press.

Redfern, Walter. 1984. *Puns*. Oxford: Basil Blackwell.

Richards, I. A. 1924. "Poetry and Belief." In *Principles of Literary Criticism*. New York: Harcourt, Brace.

Richardson, James. 1988. *Vanishing Lives: Style and Self in Tennyson, D. G. Rossetti, Swinburne, and Yeats*. Charlottesville: University Press of Virginia.

Ricks, Christopher. 1972. *Tennyson*. New York: Macmillan.

———. 1987. *The Force of Poetry*. New York: Oxford University Press.

Rorty, Richard. 1982. *Consequences of Pragmatism: Essays, 1972–1980*. Minneapolis: University of Minnesota Press.

Rosenblum, Dolores. 1986. *Christina Rossetti: The Poetry of Endurance*. Carbondale: Southern Illinois University Press.

Rosmarin, Adena. 1985. *The Power of Genre*. Minneapolis: University of Minnesota Press.

Royce, Josiah. 1910. *The World and the Individual*. 2 vols. New York: Macmillan.

Sacks, Peter M. 1985. *The English Elegy: Studies in the Genre from Spenser to Yeats*. Baltimore: Johns Hopkins University Press.

Santayana, George. 1927–40. *The Realm of Being*. New York: C. Scribner's Sons.

———. 1955. *Scepticism and Animal Faith: Introduction to a System of Philosophy*. n.p.: Dover. Originally published 1923.

Sartre, Jean-Paul. 1964. *Les Mots*. Translated by Bernard Frechtman. Greenwich, Conn.: Fawcett.

Schneider, Elisabeth. 1968. *The Dragon in the Gate: Studies in the Poetry of G. M. Hopkins*. Berkeley: University of California Press.

Sedgwick, Eva Kosofsky. 1990. *Epistemology of the Closet*. Berkeley: University of California Press.

Sexton, Melanie. 1991. "Phantoms of His Own Figuring: The Movement toward Recovery in Hardy's 'Poems of 1912–1913.'" *Victorian Poetry* 29: 209–26.

Shelley, P. B. 1815. "On A Future State." Reprinted in *The Selected Poetry and Prose of Percy Bysshe Shelley*. Edited by Carlos Baker. New York: Modern Library (1951).

Slinn, E. Warwick. 1991. *The Discourse of Self in Victorian Poetry*. Charlottesville: University Press of Virginia.

Smith, Eric. 1977. *By Mourning Tongues: Studies in English Elegy*. Ipswich: Boydell Press.

Sparshott, Francis. 1958. *An Enquiry into Goodness*. Chicago: University of Chicago Press.

———. 1970. "Notes on the Articulation of Time." *New Literary History* 1: 311–34.

———. 1982. *The Theory of the Arts*. Princeton: Princeton University Press.

Spencer, Herbert. 1880. "The Unknowable." *First Principles*. 4th ed. New York: D. Appleton.

Steiner, George. 1967. *Language and Silence: Essays on Language, Literature, and the Inhuman*. New York: Atheneum.

Strauss, David Friedrich. 1845. *The Life of Jesus, Critically Examined*. Translated by George Eliot. 3 vols. London: Chapman.

Thomas, Lewis. 1990. *Et Cetera, Et Cetera: Notes of a Word-Watcher*. Boston: Little, Brown.

———. 1992. *The Fragile Species*. New York: Scribner's.

Thompson, Lawrance, and R. H. Winnick. 1971. *Robert Frost: The Years of Triumph*. New York: Holt, Rinehart and Winston.

Todorov, Tzetvan. 1976. "The Origin of Genres." *New Literary History* 8: 159–70.

Traubel, Horace. 1906. *With Walt Whitman in Camden*. London: Gay and Bird.

Tucker, Herbert F., Jr. 1988. *Tennyson and the Doom or Romanticism*. Cambridge: Harvard University Press.

Turner, Frank. 1981. *The Greek Heritage of Victorian Britain*. New Haven: Yale University Press.

Turner, Victor. 1969. *The Ritual Process: Structure and Anti-Structure*. London: Routledge and Kegan Paul.

———. 1978. *Image and Pilgrimage in Christian Culture: Anthropological Perspectives*. New York: Columbia University Press.

Tuve, Rosemond. 1957. "Theme, Pattern, and Imagery in *Lycidas*." In *Milton's "Lycidas": The Tradition and the Poem*. Edited by C. A. Patrides. New York: Holt, Rinehart and Winston. From *Images and Themes in Five Poems by Milton*. Cambridge: Harvard University Press.

Unamuno, Miguel de. 1972. *The Tragic Sense of Life in Men and Nations*. Translated by Anthony Kerrigan. Princeton: Princeton University Press.

Vaihinger, Hans. 1924. *The Philosophy of "As If."* Translated by C. K. Ogden. New York: Harcourt.

Vendler, Helen. 1969. *On Extended Wings: Wallace Stevens' Longer Poems*. Cambridge: Harvard University Press.

———. 1975. *The Poetry of George Herbert*. Cambridge: Harvard University Press.

———. 1988. *The Music of What Happens: Poems, Poets, Critics*. Cambridge: Harvard University Press.

Walcott, Derek. 1989. "The Master of the Ordinary." Review of *Philip Larkin: Collected Poems, New York Review of Books*, June 1, 37–40.

Wallerstein, Ruth. 1950. *The Laureate Hearse*. Part 1 of *Studies in Seventeenth Century Poetics*. Madison: University of Wisconsin Press.

Wheeler, Michael. 1990. *Death and the Future Life in Victorian Literature and Theology*. Cambridge: Cambridge University Press.

Wittgenstein, Ludwig. 1961. *Tractatus Logico-Philosophicus*. Translated by D. F. Pears and B. F. McGuiness. London: Routledge and Kegan Paul.

————. 1972. *Philosophical Investigations*. Translated by G.E.M. Anscombe. Oxford: Basil Blackwell.

Wollheim, Richard. 1984. *The Thread of Life*. Cambridge: Harvard University Press.

Woodring, Carl R. ed. 1961. *Prose of the Romantic Period*. Boston: Houghton Mifflin.

Wordsworth, William. 1974. *Essays upon Epitaphs: The Prose Works of William Wordsworth*. Edited by W.J.B. Owen and Jane Worthington Smyser. Vol. 2. Oxford: Clarendon Press.

Wright, T. R. 1988. *Theology and Literature*. Oxford: Basil Blackwell.

Poetry Editions Used

Ammons, A. R. 1981. *A Coast of Trees*. New York: Norton.

Arnold, Matthew. 1965. *The Poems of Matthew Arnold*. Edited by Kenneth Allott. London: Longmans, Green.

Auden, W. H. 1976. *W. H. Auden: Collected Poems*. Edited by Edward Mendelson. New York: Random House.

Browning, Robert. 1981. *Robert Browning: The Poems*. Edited by John Pettigrew and Thomas J. Collins. 2 vols. New York: Penguin.

Chaucer, Geoffrey. 1963. *The Complete Poetical Works of Geoffrey Chaucer*. Edited by Walter W. Skeat. 2d ed. Oxford: Clarendon Press.

Clampitt, Amy. 1983. *The Kingfisher*. New York: Knopf.

————. 1985. *What the Light Was Like*. New York: Knopf.

Clare, John. 1984. *The Oxford Authors: John Clare*. Edited by Eric Robinson and David Powell. Oxford: Oxford University Press.

Dickinson, Emily. 1955. *The Poems of Emily Dickinson*. Edited by Thomas H. Johnson. 3 vols. Cambridge: Belknap Press of Harvard University.

Eliot, T. S. 1936. *T. S. Eliot: Collected Poems 1909–1935*. New York: Harcourt, Brace.

————. 1943. *Four Quartets*. New York: Harcourt, Brace.

Frost, Robert. 1969. *The Poetry of Robert Frost*. Edited by Edward Connery Lathem. New York: Holt, Rinehart and Winston.

Gray, Thomas. 1937. *Works*. Edited by A. L. Poole and Leonard Whibley. Oxford: Clarendon Press.

Hardy, Thomas. 1937. *The Complete Poetical Works of Thomas Hardy*. Edited by Samuel Hynes. 2 vols. Oxford: Clarendon Press.

Hill, Geoffrey. 1983. *The Mystery of the Charity of Charles Péguy*. André Deutsch.

Hopkins, G. M. 1967. *Poems*. Edited by W. H. Gardner and N. H. Mackenzie. 4th ed. London: Oxford University Press.

Johnson, Samuel. 1941. *The Poems of Samuel Johnson*. Edited by David Nichol Smith and Edward L. McAdam. Oxford: Clarendon Press.

Jonson, Ben. 1963. *The Complete Poetry of Ben Jonson*. Edited by William B. Hunter, Jr. New York: Norton.

Keats, John. 1978. *The Poems of John Keats*. Edited by Jack Stillinger. Cambridge: Belknap Press of Harvard University.

King, Henry. 1657. *Poems, Elegies, Paradoxes, and Sonnets*. Reprinted by G. Saintsbury, *Caroline Poets*. Vol. 3. Oxford: Clarendon Press (1921).

Larkin, Philip. 1989. *Collected Poems*. New York: Farrar, Strauss and Giroux.

Lowell, Robert. 1960. *For the Union Dead*. New York: Farrar, Strauss and Giroux.

Pearl. 1953. Edited by E. V. Gordon. London: Oxford University Press.

Pound, Ezra. 1957. *Selected Poems of Ezra Pound*. New York: New Directions.

Rossetti, Christina. 1979–90. *The Complete Poems of Christina Rossetti*. Edited by Rebecca W. Crump. 3 vols. Baton Rouge: Louisiana State University Press.

Shelley, P. B. 1905. *The Complete Poetical Works of Percy Bysshe Shelley*. Edited by Thomas Hutchinson. London: Oxford University Press.

Stevens, Wallace. 1954. *The Collected Poems of Wallace Stevens*. New York: Knopf.

Swinburne, A. C. 1925–27. *The Complete Works of Algernon Charles Swinburne*. Bonchurch edition. Edited by Edmund Gosse and Thomas James Wise. 20 vols. London: Heinemann.

Tate, Allen. 1977. *Allen Tate: The Collected Poems 1919–1976*. New York: Charles Scribner's Sons.

Tennyson, Alfred. 1987. *The Poems of Tennyson*. Edited by Christopher Ricks. 2d ed. 3 vols. London: Longmans, Green.

Whitman, Walt. 1959. *Complete Poetry and Selected Prose*. Edited by J. E. Miller. Boston: Houghton Mifflin.

Wordsworth, William. 1940–49. *The Poetical Works of William Wordsworth*. Edited by Ernest de Selincourt and Helen Darbishire. 5 vols. Oxford: Clarendon Press.

Yeats, W. B. 1960. *The Collected Poems of W. B. Yeats*. New York: Macmillan.

Index

Numerals in italic type indicate the locations of the main discussions.

Carlyle, Thomas, 88, 141
Chambers, Robert, 214
Chaucer, Geoffrey: *The Book of the Duchess*, 107–8, 111; *Troilus and Criseyde*, 213
Christ, Jesus, 10, 55, 70, 242
Clampitt, Amy, 138, 194; "The Dakota," *138–40*, 143; "A Procession at Candlemas," *195–96*, 257; "What the Light Was Like," 138, *140–43*, 144
Clare, John, "Love and Memory," *185–86*
Cleveland, John, 43
Clough, Arthur Hugh, 12, 20, 28–29, 30–31, 34, 36–37, 39–42, 45–48, 237
Coleridge, J. D., 38
Coleridge, Samuel Taylor, 51, 89, 185, 220–21; *Aids to Reflection*, 40
Cornell, Drucilla, 244, 260
Cousin, Victor, 40
Crashaw, Richard, "Hymn to Saint Teresa," 188
Culler, A. Dwight, 35, 39

Dante Alighieri, 51, 54, 60, 69–70, 219
Darwin, Charles, 59, 79, 81–82, 214
Death: as assault, 181; compared to flight or descent of birds, *194–96, 198–99*; declensions toward, 88, 98; dehumanized, 251; discourtesy of, 129–30, 132, 149, 231; idea vs. phenomenon of, 87, *186–94*; inconceivability of, 5, 86–88, 252; mystery of, 44; objective and internal views of, 208–9, *212–14*, 229; paradoxes and aporias of, 244; as question, 142; self-reflexive forms and, 165; self-replicating power of, 168; staged vs. real, 195, 211, *229–33*; tamed, 186, 196, 251; untamed, 251; in Victorian fiction, 229–30
Deconstruction, 143, 230, 239–40, 245
De Quincey, Thomas, 83
Derrida, Jacques, 121, 239, 244, 260
Descartes, René, 66, 74
Dickens, Charles, 227, 229, 230
Dickinson, Emily, 81, 106, *118–23*, 124, 144–45; autograph letters, *121*; lyric 37, *122–23*; lyric 272, *119–20*; lyric 303, *121–22*; lyric 465, 122; lyric 712, 120; lyric 1129, 120; lyric 1382, 126
Dobson, Matthew, 114
Doing-by-saying. *See* Performative utterances
Donne, John, 66, 80, 103, 123, 186–87, 189, 210–11, 241, 251; *Anniversaries*, 5, 50–51, 58–59, 68, 77, 248; *First Anniversary*, *55–56*, *57–58*, 193; *Second Anniversary*, *56–59*, 77, 242–43; "A Funerall Elegie," 58; "Goodfriday, 1613. Riding Westward," *1–2*, 9; "Hymne to God my God," *187–88*, 190; "A Nocturnall upon S. Lucies Day," *185–86*; "A Valediction Forbidding Mourning," 55
Donoghue, Denis, 213, 240, 258
Dostoyevsky, Fyodor, 6
Drury, Elizabeth, 55, 58–59, 243, 248
Dryden, John, 186, 189; "Absalom and Achitophel," 149; "To the Pious Memory of . . . Mrs. Anne Killigrew," 170, 187, *188–89*

Elegists: Greek, 212, 214; making of, *50–55*
Elegy(ies); Anglo-Saxon, 242; Augustan, 251; ballad as, 103, 131, 134; breakdown and breakthrough in, 5, 54–55, 95, 105, 120, 138, *147–79*, 181, 222, 243; Civil War, *161–69*, 208; classical (pastoral), 9, *12–49*, 51, 56, 59, 68, 77, 100, 103–5, 147, 170, 211, 224, 229, 230–31, 234–36, 241–43, 248–51; definition of, 122; elegiac verse epistle, *231–33*, 234; elegy for, 43; estrangement and, 258; history and, 236–49; impact (versus tremor) in, 180, 186–88, 190, *210–35*, 245; medieval, 5, 52–55, 104, 242; modern, 78, 105, *147–79*, 235, 243; one-way departures of, 152; politics and, 217; pragmatism and, 199, 201–4, 208, 233–34; purist (Symbolist), 99, *100–102*, 251–52; of reserve, 105–6; riddles in, 107–11; Romantic, 8, *103–118*, 143–45, 147, 170, 186, 235, 243, 251–52; Romantic vs. classical, *104*; Romantic vs. Victorian, 33–43; stupor in, 225, 231; subtext of, *126–33*, 145
Eliot, George: *Middlemarch*, 154–55, 210; *Scenes of Clerical Life*, 6, 229
Eliot, T. S., 4; "Burnt Norton," 68–70; "The Dry Salvages," 70–71; "East Coker," 51, 68, 70; essay on *In Memoriam*, 4, 217, 219; essay on Philip Massinger, 110; *Four Quartets*, 66–71, 77–78; "The Hollow Men," 178, 219–21; "Little Gidding," 5, 67, 69, 162, 170, 177; *Murder in the Cathedral*, *155–57*, 172

Emerson, Ralph Waldo, 232
Empson, W. H., 167
Epicurus, 5
Epistemes (axioms of knowing), 105–6, 251–52
Epistemology, 79–102; Berkeley and, 79–82, 85, 87, 105; epistemological paradox, 201; Ferrier and, 80, 82–83, 86, 105; impossible modes of knowing and, 87; Kant and, 79–81, 83; Romantic, 105
Epitaphs, 62, 82, 84–85, 153, 172, 224, 226; in Pope, 189; in Wordsworth, *113–15*
Escher, M. C., 96
Eulogy, 36, 116, 177
Explanation versus proof, 71–72, 74–77

Faith: absurdity of, 7; biblical, 76; contradictory nature of, 2; Eliot on, 4; and doubt as "counter-terms," 169; free assent of, 5, *71–77*, 78; "historical," 240; Lutheran notion of, 74; paradoxes of, 240; Pelagian, 20, 33; "saving," 7, 76, *239–40*; vs. skepticism, 4, 75–76, 166
Feminist theories, 181, *195–96*, 217–21, 245, *257–58*, gender wars, 199 209, 245; sexual politics, 200, 201, *203–9*
Ferrier, J. F., 5, 80, 82–83, 86–87, 105, 238, 252
Feuerbach, Ludwig, 81
Flaubert, Gustave, 143
Foucault, Michel, 7, 79–82, 92–93, 98–101, 105, 241, 251; on four similitudes, *47–48*, 56, 59, 105, 241, 251
Frames: of decrees, 18; of definitions, 17; in "Lycidas," 16; stepping in and out of, 83; as structures of consciousness, 87–88; of time, *145*; within a frame, 83, *156*
Freccero, John, 252
Freud, Sigmund, 50, 61, 181, 257, 259. *See also* Psychology
Frost, Robert, 97; "Birches," 140; "Education by Poetry," 201; "The Figure a Poem Makes," 241; "Home Burial," *144*, 180, *199–200*, *203–9*, 235, 257; "The Home Stretch," 154, *200–201*; "The Impulse," 208; "Nothing Gold Can Stay," *210–11*; Stevens on, 93; "West-Running Brook," 7, 195, 199, *201–3*

Frye, Northrop, x, 12, 55, 59, 88; *Anatomy of Criticism*, 253; *The Great Code*, *259–60*

Genre: anatomy as, 55–56, 58, 80, *190–94*, 251; ballad, 131, 134; barriers of, 155; boundary poem, 140; breakdown and renewal of, 234; commingling of marriage and funeral rites as, 154; confession as, 58, *59–61*, 77–78, 191, 248, 252; dramatic monologue vs. confessional elegy, 54; elegiac monologue, 224; elegiac sonnets, *124–26*; epithalamium, 224; exegesis vs. fiction, 46; experimentation with, 68; funeral ode, 212, 215; haiku, 97; imitation of Juvenal as, *190–91*; lyric of reserve, 111; lyric sequence, 68; newspaper epic, 238; obituary notice, 211; paradox of, 211; philosophic treatise, 68; Pindaric ode, *181–83*; power of, *233–35*; satire, 190; theory of, 77–78, 233–36, *241–43*, *252–53*; transformation of elegy into apocalypse, *155–61*; transgressing codes or norms of, 190, *210–11*, 212, 214, 217, 222, 224, 229, 231, *233–35*; under siege, *33–43*, 49; veiling of, 117, 214; verse epistle, 65, 190; versified obituary, 215. *See also* Elegy
Gewanter, David, 256
Gibbon, Edward, 224
Glanvill, Joseph, 35–36, 40, *45–49*, 58
Gnosticism, 42
Grammar: absolute constructions of, 198; active, 15, 175; apodosis, 75, 83; auxiliary verb of volition, 86; cognates, 94, 117, 168; contraction of, 74, 122, *137–38*, 167; copula, 25–26, 160; deictics, 133; genitives, subjective and objective, 94–96, 117–18, 131, 168; God as noun vs. God as verb, 8–9, 43; historic present tense, 170; holophrase, 178, 221; hortatory verbs, 27, 42, 137, 242; hyphenated compounds, *177–78*; imperatives, 27–28, 100; imperatives in disguise, 13; injunctions, 27, 193, 201; interplay of definite and indefinite articles, 158; interplay of singular and plural forms, 97, 115; intransitive questing, 12, 43; Keats as noun vs. Keats as verb, 42; modal verbs, 144; multiple meanings, 137, 186, 246; optatives, 27, 43, 76, 231; use of parenthesis, 29, 85, 121, 170, 185, 243;

Paradox (*continued*)
180–209; and study of elegy, 245; of tough- and tender-minded mourners, 199, 208–9; of verbal power, 4, 13–20, 46, 48, 170; of veridiction, 147
Pascal, Blaise, 186, 210, 213, 228
Pater, Walter, 104, 161, 255
Patmore, Coventry, 106; "Departure," 111, 112, 145
Pearl, 5, 52–55, 66, 68, 77, 100, 242–43, 245, 251–52; alliterative verse in, 53
Peirce, Charles Saunders, 208
Peltason, Timothy, 4, 61, 212–13, 222, 227, 234–35, 254
Performative utterances ("doing-by-saying," speech acts), 4, 13–20, 23, 27–34, 46, 48–49, 147, 176, 215, 228, 240–43
Perkins, David, 107, 237, 240, 244
Perl, Jeffrey, 4
Pico della Mirandola, Count Giovanni, 11
Pindar, 100
Plato, 79, 248–49; *Dialogues*, 238
Platonic: epistemology, 79; Idea, 35; light, 46–47, mist, 39; pattern, 58; theory of *anamnesis*, 55, 243
Platonism, 34, 42. *See also* Cambridge Platonism
Platonized love, 65
Poirier, Richard, 98
Politics: agendas of literary historians and, 240; elegy and, 217, 245; unconscious and, 237–38; 245
Pope, Alexander, 10, 186, 188–90; "Elegy to the Memory of an Unfortunate Lady," 189, 190; "Epistle to Dr. Arbuthnot," 85; *An Essay on Man*, 56
Pound, Ezra, 99–100
Poundstone, William, 2
Priestley, F.E.L., 253
Prince, F. T., 21
Prosody: alexandrines, 19, 35, 174; alliterative verse in *Pearl*, 53; assonance, 32, 91, 114, 130, 174; breaking a word between lines, 181; chiasmus of sound, 22; "common measure", 121; consonance, 174; contracting and expanding lines, 182–83, 226; crossing boundary between cantos, 174; crossing boundary between stanzas, 27–31, 63, 83, 98, 159–60, 172, 174, 176, 195, 223; couplets, closing, 128; —, fluent use of, 171, 173; —, framed, 97; —, heroic, 173, 193; —, tetrameter, 126; dactyls, 25, 84; dimeter, 226; end-stopped lines,

31, 109, 138, 163; hemistich, 22, 25; hexameter, 129; hypermetric lines, 35, 84; hyphens in printed poetry, 30, 32, 134, 177, 181; iambs, 25; long quantities, 25; metrical contraction, 128, 154, 183, 226; metrical pulse, 27, 204; monosyllables, 17, 35; parities of rhythm, 113–14; Petrarchan sonnet, 36, 39; Pindaric ode, 36, 39; polyphony, 126, 129, 131; refrain containing own antiphon, 155; rhymes (*see* Rhymes); run-ons (enjambment), 26–33, 42, 97, 112, 121, 126, 130, 160, 163, 181–82, 193, 198, 204–7, 223, 230; Shakespearean sonnet, 36; pauses at line breaks, 73, 109, 113, 135, 137, 207; space between stanzas, 135; Spenserian stanza, 19, 35, 39; spondees, 109, 156, 183; sound at odds with sense, 126–33, 128, 225; successive stresses, 24, 126, 130; tercets, 94, 159, 195; *terza rimas*, 54; tetrameter quatrains, 62, 66, 226, 248; tetrameters, 108, 129; three-stress line, 39; trochees, 25; two-syllable line, 197
Pseudo-Dionysius, 56
Psychology: *déjà vu*, 39, 86; introjection, 65, 257; projective identification, 64–65, 184, 220–21, 257; psychoanalysis, 61, 170, 216; psychological value as criterion of aesthetic value, 180–209, 253. *See also* Freud, Sigmund; Klein, Melanie; Kristeva, Julia
Puns, 2, 5–6, 53, 55, 64, 99, 110, 116, 130, 161–65, 175, 178, 182, 187–88, 191–92, 215, 230; anti-, 64, 149, 162, 164, 202–3, 216; by discovery, 182; lethal, 171

Ramazani, Jahan, 254
Rank, Otto, 259
Recollecting versus remembering, 212–13, 214–17
Renan, Ernest, 173–74
Rhetoric: anagram, 174, 179; anaphora, 22, 26–27, 140, 193; antithetical, 169; aphorism, 57, 93, 152, 171, 195, 228; aphoristic fragments, 40; aporias, 244–45; apostrophe, 28, 84, 137, 166, 243; chiasmus, 15, 22, 57, 140–42, 171, 192–93, 223; cliché, renovation of, 110, 172, 191–93; dashes, 114, 121; disjunction, 103, 133–38; framing noun between two adjectives, 130, 160; hendiadys, 90; hyperbaton, 29–30, 113,

Rhetoric (*continued*)
137, 159, 168, 232; hyperbole, 135; ineffability topos, 5; kenning-like word
pairs, 74–75; literal and figurative
meanings, 187–88; lodging word inside
longer word, 216; lodging word inside
sound pattern, 161; metaphor, 10–14,
35, 59, 173, 175; metaphors of situation, 175, 178–79; metaphysical conceit, 56; metonymy, 219; *morae*, 225;
oracles, 57; oxymoron, 2, 72, 105, 107,
154, 159–60, 164, 172–73, 215, 223;
parataxis, 62, 73, 178, 195, 213; *per
aenigmate*, 53; polysyndeton, 25; puns
(*see* Puns); revival of a word's forgotten
etymology, 137, 161; rhetorical criticism, 234; rhetorical question, 84, 189;
rhetorical turn, 1, 21, 173, 191–92;
simile, 20, 64, 161; synaesthesia, 221;
tautology, 51, 96, 160, 243; tmesis, 51,
53, 140; verbal tennis, 53–54; word
links, 54. *See also* Style
Rhymes: alternating, 22; arch of, 136;
bridging 22; broken, 169; concatenating, 52, 54; convergence and dispersion
of, 21–24; deathlike, 136–37, 171;
dyslectic, 136; feminine, 132; enclosing
and included, 48; heroic couplets in,
22–23; imperfect (near-rhymes), 21, 90,
121, 130, 136, 171–74; rhetoric of, 21;
within sound pattern, 131–32; sundered, 32; symmetrical, 22; transformation of *171–79*
Richards, I. A., 81
Richardson, James, 61, 148, 215, 225,
254–55
Ricks, Christopher, 3, 24, 133, 155, 165,
169, 172, 227, 255
Riddles, 2, 53, 107–12, 145
Rilke, Rainer Maria, 186
Rimbaud, Arthur, 177
Rosenblum, Dolores, 258
Rosmarin, Adena, 77, 234
Rossetti, Christina, 118–19, 122, 144–45;
"After Death," *124–25*; feminist inter-
pretations of, 257–58; "Praying Always,"
122, *123–24*; "Remember," *125–26*
Rossetti, Dante Gabriel, 81
Rousseau, Jean-Jacques, 216
Russell, Bertrand, 100
Russo, Vito, 258

Sacks, Peter M., 50–51, 181, 183, 242,
253, 257

Santayana, George, 93, 95, 97, 100, 174
Sartre, Jean-Paul, 157
Saussure, Ferdinand de, 121
Schleiermacher, Friedrich, 238
Schneider, Elisabeth, 178
Sedgwick, Eva Kosofsky, 258
Self-divided minds, *148–55*, 170, 178,
208
Self-reflexive language and knowledge,
18, 36, 57–58, 72, 80, 156, 162, *165–
69*, 195; in Stevens, *93–98*
Sellwood, Emily, 61, 106, 216
Semiotics, 115, 216–22, 121, 218–21
Sexton, Melanie, 256
Shakespeare, William, 69, 186; *Hamlet*,
24, 51, 230; *Henry V*, 113; *King Lear*,
200; *Macbeth*, 116, 213; *Measure for
Measure*, 126–27, 244; *Othello*, 230;
Shakespearean sonnet, 36; sonnets 73
and 129, *187*; *The Tempest*, 192;
Twelfth Night, 133
Shelley, Percy Bysshe, 9, 226, 228;
"Adonais," 11–12, *18–19*, *20–21*,
24–26, 31, *33–45*, 46, 48, 77, 81, 87,
104, 217, 248; "A Defense of Poetry,"
11; "Hymn of Apollo," 80; "On a Future State," 40; *Prometheus Unbound*,
40, 45
Sidney, Philip, 10
Silence: Christ's, 134, 144; of emptiness,
130, 112–18, 133–34, 138–43, 218,
243; in Hardy, *131*; integrity of, 133,
218; of mourners, *118–26*; and negativity, 243; of plenitude, 112–14, *117–18*,
138–43, 218; of reserve, 108, 112,
115–16, 118, 145; "silent-speaking"
words, 66, 105–6, 109, 218, 223, 243;
speaking through, 103–46; Steiner on,
22; unspoken meanings, 126–32, 207;
in Wordsworth, *112–18*
Simeon, John, 225–26
Sinfield, Alan, 227
Slinn, E. Warwick, 238–40
Smith, Anne Egerton, 74, 76
Smith, Eric, 254
Socrates, 2, 5, 209, 227, 239; Socratic
dialectic, 73
Sparshott, Francis, 234, 246
Speech acts. *See* Performative utterances
Spencer, Herbert, 132
Spenser, Edmund: "Daphnaïda," 107; *The
Shepheardes Calender*, 14–15. *See also*
Prosody, Spenserian stanza
Steiner, George, 22, 92–93, 252

Victorian culture, three phases of, 33–43
Virgil, 11, 20, 253–54, 258

Wagner, Richard, 194
Walcott, Derek, 154
Wallerstein, Ruth, 254
Wheeler, Michael, 252
Whitehead, Alfred North, 100
Whitman, Walt, 199, 208, 243, 255, 258;
  "When Lilacs Last in the Dooryard
  Bloom'd," 165–69, 255
Wit (versus judgment), 10, 77, 159
Wittgenstein, Ludwig, 106–7; *Philosophical Investigations*, 228
Wollheim, Richard, 5, 9, 210, 259
Woolf, Virginia, 194
Wordsworth, Dorothy, 86
Wordsworth, William, 8, 37, 79, 84, 104–6, 138, 173, 189, 217, 246, 247; "Elegiac Stanzas," 20, *117–18*; *Essays upon Epitaphs*, *113–15*; *The Excursion*, *113–14*; "It Is a Beauteous Evening," 113; Lucy poems, 103, 116, 132, 145; "Michael," 112, "Ode: Intimations of Immortality," 8, 42, 79–80, 89–92, 112, 256; *The Prelude*, 176; *The*

Recluse, 104; "She Dwelt among the Untrodden Ways," 112, 116; "Simon Lee, The Old Huntsman," 117; " A Slumber Did My Spirit Seal," 66, *108–10*, 212, 232–33; "The Solitary Reaper," 113; "Surprised by Joy," 28, *111–12*, *117*; "Tintern Abbey," 80, 86, 89, 247; "The Two April Mornings," *115–17*, *145*; "We Are Seven," 5, 87
Wright, David, 114
Wright, T. R., 1–2

Yeats, William Butler, 7–8, 69, 162, 253;
  "The Arrow," *150*; "The Circus Animals' Desertion," 154, 256; "Easter 1916," *100–101*, 152, 173, 237; "The Fisherman," 100; "The Folly of Being Comforted," *150–51*; "In Memory of Major Robert Gregory," 8, *148–50*, 231; "Lapis Lazuli," 176; "The Second Coming," 154; "The Tower," 153; "Two Songs from a Play," *151–52*; "Under Ben Bulben," 152, 256

Zen koan, 2

Library of Congress Cataloging-in-Publication Data

Shaw, W. David (William David)
   Elegy and paradox : testing the conventions / W. David Shaw.
      p.   cm.
   Includes bibliographical references and index.
   ISBN 0-8018-4836-9 (acid-free paper)
   1. Elegiac poetry, English—History and criticism. 2. Death in
literature. 3. Paradox.   I. Title.
PR508.E5S5   1994
821.009'354—dc20   93-50617